REGULATION and PUBLIC INTERESTS

REGULATION and PUBLIC INTERESTS

The Possibility of Good Regulatory Government

Steven P. Croley

PRINCETON UNIVERSITY PRESS

PRINCETON AND OXFORD

Library of Congress Cataloging-in-Publication Data
Croley, Steven P., 1965–
Regulation and public interests : the possibility of good
regulatory government / Steven P. Croley.
p. cm.
Includes bibliographical references and index.
ISBN 978-0-691-13085-9 (cloth : alk. paper) —
ISBN 978-0-691-13464-2 (pbk. : alk. paper)
1. Trade regulation. 2. Administrative law—Economic aspects. 3. Social choice. I. Title.
K3840.C76 2007
352.801—dc22   2007018559

British Library Cataloging-in-Publication Data is available

This book has been composed in Sabon

Printed on acid-free paper. ∞

press.princeton.edu

Printed in the United States of America

1   3   5   7   9   10   8   6   4   2

To my parents,

HAROLD AND MARTHA CROLEY

○

Contents

Acknowledgments

THIS BOOK REPRESENTS many influences, known and unknown. Among the former, I have benefited from many conversations about its subject matter with my colleagues at the University of Michigan Law School, as well as with my administrative law colleagues around the country, too numerous to name. Three in particular deserve special mention, however, for their sustained interest in my project, especially during its formative stages—Bob Cooter, Rick Hills, and Kyle Logue. I also benefited from many comments on portions of this book from workshop participants at the law schools at the University of California at Berkeley, the University of Chicago, Florida State University, Georgetown Law Center, Harvard University, the University of Michigan, Northwestern University, the University of Southern California, and Vanderbilt University. I am indebted as well to Don Herzog, for his careful and incisive reading of the penultimate version of the entire manuscript. Jackie Julien and Nancy Paul provided flawless secretarial assistance, for which I am also very grateful. Chuck Myers and Richard Isomaki at Princeton University Press provided careful and wise editorial help, from which I benefited greatly too. Finally, I am grateful for the training and encouragement I received when I first began to grapple with this subject matter years ago as a law student and graduate student, especially but not only from Susan Rose-Ackerman and R. Douglas Arnold. A heartfelt thanks to all of you. Thanks also go to the University of Michigan Cook Research Fund, for partial funding of this research.

REGULATION and PUBLIC INTERESTS

Introduction

An Uneasy Commitment to Regulatory Government

IN THE UNITED STATES TODAY, mainstream attitudes toward the modern regulatory state are well captured by the joke Woody Allen tells about overhearing a lunch room conversation between two complaining inhabitants of a retirement home:

"The food here is so terrible."
"Yeah, and always such small portions."

On the one hand, the regulatory state—"big government," "the bureaucracy," "Washington"—is a target of endless criticism. Social commentators, politicians, and academicians routinely rail against the regulatory system. Calls to "downsize" government, reduce "regulatory red tape," and promote "free enterprise" are perennial, as certain as death and taxes.

In part, this phenomenon owes to the rhetoric of politics, and also to the politics of rhetoric. Aspiring politicians promote themselves by running against big government, while established politicians emphasize their experience in navigating an overextended bureaucracy on behalf of their constituents. Not since the 1960s have either Republicans or Democrats run on a platform that defends big government, much less advocates for increased reliance on regulatory government as a solution to social problems. Thus the last Democrats to occupy the White House, for example, trumpeted their extensive efforts to "reinvent" government by relying more on market-based incentives and less on command and control. Government regulation is something to be tamed, managed, not promoted.

Similarly, academicians are rewarded professionally for debunking political institutions. By long-standing tradition, members of the academy have undertaken to show what is wrong with social and political institutions, to identify their weaknesses and paradoxes, not to celebrate what is right with them, and for good reason. So Ph.D. dissertations on Congress, the executive branch, or particular regulatory agencies far more often expose the imperfections of those institutions than they highlight their successes, while legal-academic analysis of Supreme Court jurisprudence explains what the Court got wrong, or else right but for the wrong reasons. "All is well" makes for boring academic work. No doubt these dynamics are reinforcing: Critical academic commentary provides scholarly support and theoretical justification for such deregulatory initiatives as the Council on Competitiveness in the 1980s and the Contract with America and Reinventing Government efforts in the 1990s, just as such politicians' deregulatory initiatives provide scholars critical of regulatory government with a sympathetic and influential audience.

At the same time, however, calls for regulatory reform are in part simply constitutive of the larger march of social progress. Finding ways to deliver more goods and services with smaller expenditures of human and economic resources, including the resources of government itself, is part of the human endeavor. Who could object to reducing truly unnecessary bureaucratic red tape, or finding new ways to exploit market-like incentives where those incentives produce results superior to traditional government regulation? In this light, reform is properly always in fashion.

But again these are partial explanations. For one thing, the question remains why politicians' calls for regulatory reform always sell, and why, for example, reforming big government is in the United States (but much less so in Germany, Japan, or Sweden) such an important marker of social progress. Part of the answer, too, is that criticism of regulatory government also reflects a long-standing skepticism towards centralized government that, although accentuated in recent decades, has colonial roots. Since the Founding, the legal-political culture of the United States has been characterized by an enduring wariness towards centralized regulatory power, and concomitant commitments instead to free enterprise, autonomy, and localism. Moreover, important periods of political reform—for instance the Progressive movement, and the environmental revolution—saw changes precipitated by grassroots movements, initiatives from the "ground up" rather than the "top down." Even then, centralized regulatory government was as often viewed as part of the problem—too cozy with business trusts, too friendly to polluters—as it was part of the solution.

And this skepticism toward regulatory government is self-fulfilling. Chronicles of regulatory failures are eventually seen as the norm, to be expected. In turn, the refrain that regulatory government is doomed to fail becomes internalized after repetition. Citizens and commentators come to expect less, and therefore demand less, from regulatory government. Meanwhile, confidence in regulatory institutions comes to be viewed as idealistic. Similarly, proposals to reform rather than abandon regulatory government also come to be seen as panglossian, hopelessly uninformed.

2

Paradoxically, however, this skepticism toward regulatory government may be outweighed by Americans' apparent commitment to and strong reliance upon centralized regulatory institutions, like Woody Allen's convalescent home diner who wants more food though it is terrible. After all, regulation is ubiquitous. The work-product of the regulatory state—regulations issued by seemingly innumerable federal regulatory agencies—governs every aspect of modern life. Literally: Working, transacting, traveling, communicating, indeed eating, drinking, and breathing, are all activities governed by federal agencies.

Of course, this ironic reliance on centralized regulatory institutions too has early roots, extending back to the establishment of a national government in place of a federation after the American Revolution. And since the Civil War's establishment of the primacy of centralized government, Americans have repeatedly turned to federal regulatory government in times of crisis to address the country's most stubborn problems—from the banking crises and business corruption of the early twentieth century, though the Great Depression, stock market crisis, and labor unrest of the 1930s and 1940s, through the environmental crisis and civil rights revolutions of the 1960s and 1970s, to the threat of terrorism and the creation of the huge new Department of Homeland Security at the beginning of the twenty-first century, to name a few. Thus the evolution of the regulatory state has not been gradual, but rather reflects accelerated growth in response to periods of crisis and national trauma. In this light, regulation seems not only ubiquitous but inevitable.

Thus exists a serious and curious disconnect between the familiar politico-rhetorical treatments as well as academic presentations of regulatory government, on the one hand, and regulatory reality—which reflects heavy reliance upon and even faith in regulatory government—on the other. The modern United States of America is thoroughly committed to regulatory government in actual practice, and yet rhetorically and ideologically that commitment seems awkward, if not hypocritical.

The pages that follow seek to ease part of this tension. Specifically, this book argues that the most influential tradition of scholarly analyses critical of the regulatory state has been oversold. More specifically, it argues that a body of related critical analyses of the regulatory state, "public choice theory," rests on a seriously incomplete and undertheorized understanding of regulatory government, and furthermore that its empirical predictions are not supported by careful consideration of the evidence about how regulatory agencies operate or what they do. This book then offers an alternative, though in some ways complementary, vision of regulatory government that emphasizes the legal-procedural mechanisms by

3

which administrative bodies actually regulate. It shows how those mechanisms can be—and on important recent occasions have been—employed to produce regulatory outcomes that promote public interests, that is to say, outcomes that vindicate an uneasy faith in regulatory government.

The central thesis advanced here is that the cynical view of regulation shows far too little attention to the actual processes through which administrative agencies regulate, and that such inattention is largely responsible for the dominant, jaundiced view of regulation. Once the administrative regulatory state is unpacked—once it is considered in the light of its procedural complexities—grim conclusions about the inability of regulatory institutions to advance the general welfare give way to more optimistic assessments. Citizens' and politicians' regular reliance on regulatory government now appears less ironic, for if regulatory institutions prove capable of addressing important social problems, then it is little wonder that Americans have created administrative agencies in response to those problems. The effort here, then, is both critical and constructive. It seeks to show what is wrong with the public choice account of regulation, and in particular to highlight what is missing from that account, but at the same time to take certain insights from the public choice theory and to show how those insights can support a much more benign view of the regulatory state.

To anticipate the main theme, the ingredients of a complete understanding of regulation that are missing from the public choice account are largely legal-institutional. That is to say, they concern the legal vehicles— such as the Administrative Procedure Act—through which regulatory agencies translate legislative requirements and commands into particularized regulatory decisions. Most critics of regulatory government skip over, or downplay, administrative law. At the same time, most academic lawyers who focus on administrative law skip over, or downplay, claims about the functions and disappointments of regulation. This book seeks to merge the methodological and conceptual sophistication of the economists and political scientists who focus on regulation, on the one hand, with the attention to the complexities of legal-procedural rules and legal institutions shown by academic lawyers, on the other.

The argument is organized into four parts. Part 1, "The Cynical View of Regulatory Government, and Its Alternatives," parses the dominant and jaundiced view of regulatory government. Chapter 1 poses the question whether regulation may at times advance public interests, and considers methodological approaches to answering that question. Chapters 2 and 3 scrutinize the public choice theory of regulation by focusing on

4

its specific claims and on the strengths of its theoretical and empirical underpinnings, concluding that the account rests on shaky ground. Chapter 4 identifies weaknesses in the most ambitious challenges to the public choice theory, and then introduces an alternative account developed and tested throughout the rest of the book.

Part 2, "The Administrative Regulatory State," switches course. It first considers the institutional and legal complexities of administrative government. Chapter 5 provides a tour of the legal-procedural mechanisms by which regulatory agencies produce authoritative regulatory decisions. Chapter 6 presents basic descriptive data showing the extent to which modern government really is administrative government. Informed by chapters 5 and 6, chapters 7 and 8 develop further the administrative-process approach to regulation introduced in chapter 4.

Part 3, "Public Interested Regulation," moves from forest to trees. Chapters 9 through 12 present several examples of major regulatory initiatives that advanced social welfare, detailing the decisionmaking procedures the relevant agencies employed and the institutional context in which they regulated. With those case studies in mind, part 4, "Public Choice and Administrative Process," completes the analysis. It evaluates further the competing pictures of regulatory government presented in parts 1 and 2 in the light of the evidence presented in part 3. Chapters 13 and 14 show how the examples of part 3 undermine the public choice account of regulation, while they provide empirical support for the alternative account of regulation presented here. Finally, chapter 15 considers several important objections to the conclusions of part 4.

To be clear from the start, the thesis of this book is not that regulatory government works well all or even most of the time. It aims neither to foster complacency towards regulatory reform nor to apologize for the regulatory status quo. The more modest ambition of this effort, rather, is to show that cynical but commonplace accounts of the regulatory state have enjoyed an influence that far exceeds their conceptual rigor and empirical support: Regulatory failure is not inevitable. Under certain conditions—conditions that are plausible given the real-world legal-institutional environment in which federal administrative agencies operate—regulatory outcomes can and sometimes do advance broad social interests and increase social welfare. While caution towards regulatory government is to some extent surely healthy, at the same time reliance upon regulatory institutions as the least-worst solution to pressing social problems in an ever-complex world is not misplaced.

PART I

THE CYNICAL VIEW OF
REGULATORY GOVERNMENT,
AND ITS ALTERNATIVES

Chapter One

The Basic Project

CRITIQUES OF REGULATORY GOVERNMENT are as old as government regulation itself. And by now, confidence in public regulatory institutions—in the modern administrative state—is widely dismissed as idealistic. No doubt this is true partly as a result of the power of familiar critiques. Often, regulatory bodies certainly do appear to cater to the powerful, the well-funded, and especially the organized. As will be detailed shortly, this general dynamic is widely taken to be a consequence of the basic "rules" of modern politics, and not without justification. The combination of elected legislators who require economic resources to maintain their positions, on the one hand, and regulatory agencies that enjoy considerable regulatory power but depend on the legislature for political and budgetary resources, on the other, provides a recipe for a regulatory state that works to advantage well-organized yet narrowly focused political interest groups—"special interests"—at least according to conventional wisdom. Such groups exchange economic and political resources for what are essentially regulatory rents. Regulatory institutions deliver those rents as parties to an illicit exchange, an outcome as regrettable as it is thought to be common.

But sometimes they don't. At times, regulatory institutions instead appear to advance broad, diffuse interests in ways that increase social welfare. At times they do so even to the detriment of more powerful, concentrated interests. If that is right, the question becomes, how is it possible? More specifically: Under what set of conditions can regulatory bodies, federal administrative agencies in particular, deliver broad-based benefits—"public interest" or, better, "public interest*ed*" rather than "special interest" regulation? What channels of agency authority—that is, which decision-making procedures—are insulated from the usual consequences of interest-group politics? And *why* do they at times seem to deliver broad-based benefits even over the strong opposition of well-organized and well-funded interests? Perhaps more urgently, why would the narrow interests thwarted by those channels tolerate decision-making environments that allow agencies to deliver broad-based benefits at their expense? Or is there little they can do about it?

On the other hand, is the notion that regulatory institutions at times truly advance broad interests and enhance social welfare simply mistaken? Are even apparent examples of public-interested regulations, upon closer scrutiny, merely camouflaged instances of special-interest control proving just how sound the critique of regulatory government is? Alternatively, are public-interested policies instead merely proverbial exceptions that prove the rule—a few rare, insignificant examples in a sea of special-interest regulation? If the regulatory state occasionally generates results that advance social welfare, are those occasions really frequent enough and significant enough to call into question the conclusions of the public choice account of regulation? If not, calls to jettison the regulatory state seem well placed after all. If so, however, more modest calls for regulatory reform short of deregulation may follow instead.

These questions will animate the entire analysis that follows. The epistemological issue asks how one goes about answering them. Doing so requires, first, some initial definitions. If the cynical view of regulatory government holds that regulation produces special interest regulation, testing that proposition requires a definition of special interest regulation and, by implication, a definition of regulation that is not special interest regulation. Doing so also requires some means by which such regulation, and its alternative, are identified.

For present purposes, "special interest" regulation denotes regulation that delivers regulatory rents to the greater detriment of society. A little more specifically, special interest regulation denotes regulatory decisions that deliver profits to interest groups that exceed the efficient, competitive return to the members of such groups. In addition, such rents, delivered in the form of implicit subsidies, barriers to entry, and so on, undermine social welfare because the losses associated with those supercompetitive returns harm the rest of society—the group members' competitors or citizen-consumers generally—by an amount greater than the benefits accruing to the special interest group. Put differently, special interest regulation is regulation an omnipotent and benign regulator would never produce.

"Public interested" regulation, then, denotes the alternative: regulation that improves social welfare. It is not the result of regulatory decisions intended to improve the interests of a select few at the greater expense of the many. Public-interested regulation delivers no rents or, if it does, the gains to those who benefit from the regulatory decision outweigh any losses to the rest of society. Public-interest regulation is therefore beneficial on net; in economic terms, it is Kaldor-Hicks efficient. An omnipotent and benign regulator would produce only public-interested regulation. (Alternative, and complementary, conceptions of public interest regulation will be considered in chapter 13.)

Preliminary definitions aside, evaluating the public choice account of regulation also requires specification of that account's logic, according to which regulatory institutions produce regulations that reduce social welfare. If the public choice account is a model, in other words, then it is a model that embodies specific claims about how and why regulatory institutions do what they do. Assessing the strength of the model accordingly requires analysis of those claims.

Without belaboring the subject, quick attention to the methods by which the public choice account—indeed by which any theory of regulation—is properly assessed will help to frame what is next to come. One evaluative approach scrutinizes a theory's logical and conceptual rigor: A strong theory is coherent. Its premises are mutually compatible. And its conclusions follow from its premises. A strong theory is also complete. The scope of its premises and conclusions encompass the empirical phenomena it purports to explain. Finally, a strong theory is refutable. It generates predictions that can be falsified, at least in principle. It does not slip into modifying, corrective assumptions whenever confronted with information inconsistent with its predictions. A strong theory is therefore conceptually stable. Accordingly, one way of evaluating a theory of regulation assesses its conceptual stability.

An alternative method of evaluation focuses less on a theory's internal analytical strength and more on whether its premises and assumptions are plausible given what is otherwise known about human and organizational behavior. Whatever the logical relationships among a theory's premises and conclusions, this methods asks whether the theory's premises resonate with empirical observations of the real world—in particular, of the regulatory institutions it contemplates. A strong theory employs established understandings of the way real people behave and real organizations operate. A strong theory does not challenge common understandings of behavior that, for independent reasons, themselves enjoy considerable empirical support. Put simply, this method considers a theory's realism. At best, an unrealistic theory may yield reliable predictions; it cannot provide illuminating explanations.

Yet another approach focuses on the reliability of a theory's predictions, asking whether actual regulatory outcomes are those which the theory predicts. Strong theories predict well. Tenable theories encounter outcomes that are not predicted by them, but at least are not inconsistent with them. Weak theories encounter outcomes that unambiguously contradict their expectations.

Finally, a related method of evaluating the public choice theory asks whether the rules and procedures through which actual regulatory decisions are made comport with the theory's expectations. Here the evaluation considers whether existing procedural decisionmaking rules seem well suited for generating the types of substantive regulatory outcomes a theory predicts, whether, in other words, regulatory process rules themselves are the kinds of decisionmaking mechanisms that the theory would expect, given its assumptions about the forces operating on regulatory decisionmaking and given the types of substantive regulatory outcomes the theory predicts. One subquestion here asks whether agencies' decisionmaking procedures seem likely to encourage participation in regulatory decisionmaking by those whom the theory contemplates will most affect the shape of regulatory outcomes, and similarly whether those processes seem well tailored to generate or conceal whatever type of information the theory contemplates regulatory decisionmakers require or lack. Likewise, this process-oriented inquiry considers whether regulatory decisionmakers themselves possess sufficient authority for producing the regulatory outcomes that the theory envisions they produce.

To be sure, these evaluative criteria overlap, differing in part according to emphasis. Assessing a theory's predictive power, for example, obviously requires some assessment of its conceptual power: A theory's predictions can be tested only insofar as its conceptual apparatus generates coherent, identifiable predictions in the first place. For another example, the procedural approach overlaps with the methods that assess a theory's realism and predictive power: Asking whether existing regulatory decisionmaking procedures square with a theory's process expectations *is* to ask about its realism, and, similarly, asking whether those expectations find real-world support is an alternative way of measuring the theory's predictive power, albeit along procedural rather than substantive lines.

But while these assessment devices overlap to some extent, they nevertheless provide distinct vantage points from which to evaluate different theories of regulation. Moreover, some of these methods are much easier to employ than others. For example, measuring the effects of substantive regulatory outcomes can be difficult. As many students of regulation have observed, it is often hard to determine just what the full consequences of a given regulatory decision *are*—to know just who benefits (and by how much) and who bears its costs. Insofar as such effects are difficult to measure, it is difficult to assess a theory's predictive power solely by comparing its expectations against substantive policy outcomes. Where one gets only a hazy picture of regulatory outcomes, more evaluative weight must be borne by other methodologies. Even so, ideally all of these methods should be brought to bear on any theory, as far as practicable, and accordingly what follows employs all of them.

But not all at once. The following chapter first lays the groundwork for close scrutiny of the conceptual and, later, the empirical power of the public choice theory of regulation. It does so by articulating that account's main claims.

Chapter Two

The Cynical View of Regulation

JUST WHAT IS THE CYNICAL view of regulation a cynical view of? It is, in short, a view of the legal work-product of the administrative state. It is not, for example, principally a theory of legislation, even though (as will be seen below) students of regulation focus unduly on legislators and legislative incentives. For as observed above, the innumerable activities of everyday life are deeply affected by the legal work-product of federal administrative agencies, the "fourth branch" of government. From the food and water citizens ingest to the air they breathe, every aspect of modern life is thoroughly shaped by the decisions of regulatory agencies. Such agencies, which by legal definition include all authorities of the United States excluding the Congress, the courts, and the governments of the territories or possessions of the United States and of the District of Columbia,[1] promulgate regulations prescribing, proscribing, and conditioning the behavior of individuals, groups, and firms. Federal regulatory agencies are commonly charged with generating and enforcing regulatory policy governing areas such as communications, consumer safety, energy, environmental protection, industrial relations, securities, transportation, and workplace safety, to name just a few. Their decisions dwarf those of the other three branches, certainly by volume and arguably by importance as well. Simply put, modern government *is* administrative government.

The size and sheer power of the administrative state immediately raise questions about its efficacy as well as its political legitimacy. If modern government is administrative government, the question becomes, for good or ill? One standard justification for the administrative state holds that administrative regulation is justified to correct market failures. By this account, regulation is justified because it corrects for concentrated market power, imperfect information, externalities, undelineated property rights, collective-action problems, and high transaction costs. Further, agencies do so by filling the "gaps" in legislation that, because of scarcity of congressional time, information, or political capital, is inevitably vague and open-ended. Better, the fact that agencies, though themselves not electorally accountable, are the surrogates of accountable legislators (and an elected president) justifies administrative regulation politically as well as economically; agencies correct market failures as agents of the citizenry, once removed.[2]

Yet the mere presence of market failures and the scarcity of congressional resources hardly justify agency authority. A pressing question remains whether agencies can fill statutory gaps to address market failures effectively. One view critical of administrative regulation holds that agencies are at best inefficient and at worst counterproductive. Thus phrases like "bureaucratic red tape," "regulatory overhead," and the need to "streamline the bureaucracy" and "reinvent government" are commonplace in popular political discourse. A far more critical view finds the standard rationale for administrative regulation perverse. On this view, agencies serve not to correct but rather exactly to exacerbate market failures by delivering illicit regulatory favors to those who already enjoy excessive market power.

This cynical view of regulation sees it as the consequence of unfortunate political dynamics, the result of a regime that enables certain groups to demand or elicit from agencies regulations that advance their interests to the greater detriment of others. This view might be right. But it raises questions about the exact mechanisms by which such regrettable results are produced. That basic story runs as follows.

A General Statement of the Public Choice Account

Elected politicians prefer to remain in office. They are able to remain in office only so long as they continue to win the electoral favor of their constituencies. Winning that support requires substantial political resources, in particular, votes and money to attract votes during political campaigns. Because very few politicians can finance their own political causes independently, they seek to attract resources from supporters and potential supporters.

Enter organized interest groups. Interest groups possess the very resources politicians require for their political survival. Sometimes such groups are large and well disciplined such that their membership can deliver a significant number of votes to a political candidate. Much more often, interest groups do not themselves contribute significant numbers of votes directly to politicians, but instead contribute financial support to political campaigns, which turn money into votes through campaign advertising and the like. Either way, the important point is that interest groups can supply invaluable resources to those politicians who secure their support.[3]

Naturally, interest groups have their own goals as well; they exist not simply to meet elected politicians' needs. Rather, they seek to advance particular policies that further the interests of their members and, similarly, to defeat or dismantle policies that retard their members' interests. Politicians, as policymakers and policy-breakers, are well positioned to advance interest groups' goals. They can do so by providing the very policies that an organized interest group seeks or by defeating one that it opposes, powers they exercise in exchange for the group's support. Each side gains: Politicians receive the political resources necessary for their continued political survival, and interest groups enjoy the benefits of the policies they favor.

Although this exchange relationship between elected politicians and organized interest groups constitutes the linchpin of most critiques of regulatory government,[4] it tells only half of the story, or rather two-thirds of it. Administrative agencies figure into the exchange equation as well, given that they implement legislative directives by filling in the innumerable gaps in virtually all legislation. As already observed, Congress commonly delegates to administrative agencies the power to make countless regulatory decisions. Agencies in turn exercise that delegated power by creating, defining, and enforcing the legal rules that govern much of modern society. Thus, "regulation" is best understood as the work product of agencies; "regulatory decisionmaking" almost always (though implicitly) references the *administrative* implementation of very general legislative directives, as the discussion in chapters 5 and 6 will demonstrate in detail.

The implication here is crucial: Because regulation infrequently takes the form of highly specified legislation, interest groups seeking to advance their regulatory policy goals require much more than a friendly legislator or legislature. They also require a willing bureaucrat or agency. This means either that interest groups must successfully press their concerns directly before administrative agencies, or that legislators must be able to control agencies well enough to deliver the policies that interest group constituencies seek, or both. If agencies are not responsive to interest group goals, and if legislators cannot influence agencies enough to implement the regulatory policies sought by their interest group supporters, then all of the votes and campaign contributions in the world (resources of no use to agencies themselves) will not generate the regulatory outcome an interest group seeks.

Fortunately for groups demanding favorable regulation, as well as for legislators seeking to earn electoral-political support from appreciative interest groups, Congress has at its disposal a set of carrots and sticks with which to influence agency behavior. That influence extends ultimately from Congress's fundamental power of legislation, including the power to repeal legislation, and its corollary power to spend, or refuse to spend, money. From an agency's point of view, the possible consequences of these powers are straightforward. Congress can increase or decrease an agency's budget, depending in part on Congress's assessment of the agency's performance. Similarly, Congress can expand or contract the scope of an agency's authority by amending or, in the extreme, by repealing the agency's enabling act or other important pieces of legislation that give the agency its power. Agencies unresponsive to congressional cues about what regulation should look like may thus see their regulatory jurisdiction curtailed. Finally, though cumbersome, Congress can also by legislation undo any agency decision, giving Congress one form of veto power over agencies. Conversely to all of these possibilities, Congress can provide cooperative agencies with more generous funding, greater statutory authority, legislative blessing of agency decisions, and so on.

Of course, exercising these powers requires Congress keep abreast of what an agency does; punishment and reward presuppose information about which of them is warranted. Here too, Congress has several mechanisms in its repertoire.[5] For example, it can order studies and reports of agency action. Congress can also hold oversight hearings to evaluate specific action or proposed action. In addition, Congress can and does monitor agencies through congressional offices, informal staff contacts, and agency liaisons. And if all of that is not enough, Congress can also rely on information from interest groups themselves, who have their own strong incentives to keep abreast of agency behavior.

Now for the punch line: These various methods of congressional control allow legislators to satisfy interest groups' regulatory demands by prompting agencies, the ground-level regulators, to make the regulatory decisions interest groups seek, if agencies are disinclined to do so on their own. Obtaining favorable budgetary and statutory treatment from legislators motivates agencies to supply desired regulatory treatment.[6] Interest groups are happy to provide electoral resources to legislators who can inspire desired regulatory treatment by agencies. Legislators, in order to secure needed electoral resources, are motivated to ensure that agencies supply the regulation that their interest group supporters seek. Hence the "iron triangle"[7] or, less darkly, the "issue network"[8] relationship among groups, legislators, and administrative agencies that typically character-izes the public choice account of regulation. According to this account, agencies become "captured" by the very parties whose behavior the agen-cies are supposed to shape; perversely, control runs in the direction *from* interest group *to* agency, opposite from what might be hoped for or sup-posed by a public-interest model of regulation.[9]

But it's a free country. Nothing about the dynamics so far described indicates what is normatively undesirable about the legislator-agency-in-terest group triad. Indeed, the image of legislators who are sensitive to the preferences of their constituencies, of interest groups that mobilize to advance lawful goals and to participate in open elections, and of legisla-tors who control (unelected) agencies that they themselves have (after all) created is hardly an undemocratic one. The question thus becomes what makes this account of regulation so troubling.

The trouble is twofold. First, interest group competition for the loyal-ties of elected legislators is lopsided. That is, certain types of interest groups dominate the electoral system because they are unusually effective at mobilizing.[10] This is true because small groups are better situated, rela-tive to groups with many members, to overcome the collective-action problems that generally impede group mobilization.[11] Similarly, groups whose individual members have a large absolute stake in the matter are also better able to mobilize; from their members' points of view, more depends on their successful mobilization. Often these two characteris-tics—few members and large stakes—coincide, which makes mobilization easier still. The flip side is that groups whose members are numerous, and groups whose members have a small individual stake in a given matter, will tend not to organize, which is to say that they will not exist in a group structure at all.

Interest-group participation in regulatory politics is further skewed, the story continues, given that regulatory decisions often would generate dif-fuse benefits but impose concentrated costs—consider most workplace safety or environmental regulation, for example—or provide concen-trated benefits while imposing diffuse costs—as is true for regulation that restricts market entry. Either way, parties on one side of a regulatory pro-gram will be spread much more thinly than those on the other. That distri-bution translates into pitting mobilized groups against unorganized inter-ests, with the predictable result that regulators will feel pressure from, and will respond to, only one side of the regulatory interests at stake. Far from the balanced interest group competition contemplated by pluralist theories of politics, which the public choice account explicitly rejects, interest group activity in this light essentially means that the organized few accomplish their regulatory aims over the unorganized many.

That's not the worst of it. More disturbing, self-serving interest groups are able to advance their policy goals even where their gains are outweighed by greater losses borne by the unorganized.[12] Precisely because the many are no competition for the few, there are numerous occasions for those able to mobilize to achieve regulatory successes that harm the unorganized substantially.[13] Although the losses to any individual among the unorganized may be imperceptible, their total magnitude may far outweigh the gains enjoyed by members of the mobilized special interest group. And even where those losses are perceptible to the regulatory losers, by hypothesis there is little they can do about it.

The consequences of lopsided interest group influences on regulatory policy, in other words, are not merely distributional. Instead, powerful and narrowly interested groups often realize their policy preferences to the much greater expense of those who, unorganized or poorly organized, are unable to advance their competing regulatory preferences very far. That regulatory policies generate net social losses is what gives the public theory its pejorative ring. Interest group rents are detrimental to society as a whole. They undermine social welfare.

The public choice theory of regulation thus analogizes regulatory decisionmaking to market decisionmaking,[14] treating legislative, regulatory, and electoral institutions as an economy in which citizens, legislators, agencies, and interest groups exchange regulatory "goods," which are "demanded" and "supplied" according to the same basic principles governing the demand and supply of ordinary economic goods.[15] Such regulatory goods include, for example, regulations that affect control over entry into a market and accessibility to the substitutes and complements of certain goods.[16] These regulatory outcomes are demanded by those who stand to gain from them. A producer of a given good, for example, would enjoy great economic benefit from regulations that made substitute goods more expensive and complement goods cheaper.[17] As the sole supplier of regulation, only the state can supply demanded regulatory goods, which legislators, through agencies, are willing to do in exchange for the political support they need to stay in office. Regulatory trades take place, then, because they further the (private) economic interests of those on the demand side and the (private) political interests of those on the supply side. The resources necessary to meet suppliers' political needs constitute the "price" of regulatory goods.

But then the outcome of these forces of supply and demand is, as always, a function of the constraints under which the participants in the regulatory marketplace operate. And therein lies the difficulty, for while the public choice theory analogizes regulatory behavior to market behavior, it also implies that the analogy ultimately breaks down. The regulatory state operates *like* a market, but not nearly as well. Due to interest group power, the market for regulation is far from competitive.

To be more precise, there are three crucial differences between regulatory decisions and competitive market decisions. First, regulatory decisions are "all-or-nothing" propositions. Whereas in the economic marketplace citizens can decide, for a famous example, to patronize airlines or rail lines or neither, according to their individual preferences, the state's regulatory decision about whether to provide favorable regulation to the airlines or else to the railroads affects all citizens, whether they fly, ride the rails, or do neither.[18] And once the state makes a decision about which package of regulatory goods to supply, individual citizens and taxpayers have no opportunity to "exit" the regulatory market.

Second, regulatory decisions are more lasting than marketplace decisions. Whereas a citizen could elect to fly one week, and then ride a train the next week, the decision to provide a federal regulatory subsidy to the airlines or to the railroads will not be frequently reexamined once made. Finally, regulatory decisions are collective decisions, and as such must be made simultaneously. Whereas citizens can make market choices one at a time, they can express their regulatory preferences only in crude bundles during elections.

Because regulatory decisions are, relative to market decisions, global, infrequent, and simultaneous, regulatory outcomes are undisciplined: Individual citizens have little or no occasion for registering their particular regulatory interests, including their interests against regulatory policies that bring them no benefits. As George Stigler, principal architect of the public choice theory, explains:

> The condition of simultaneity imposes a major burden upon the political decision process. It makes voting on specific issues prohibitively expensive: it is a significant cost even to engage in the transaction of buying a plane ticket when I wish to travel; it would be stupendously expensive to me to engage in the physically similar transaction of voting . . . whenever a number of my fellow citizens desired to register their views on railroads versus airplanes. To cope with the condition of simultaneity, the voters must employ represen-

tatives with wide discretion and must eschew direct expressions of marginal changes in preferences.[19]

Citizen participation in regulatory decisionmaking is thus both very rare—taking place only as often as elections for political representatives—and very crude—voters vote for political candidates with very little information about those candidates' positions on regulatory issues, and must moreover vote for a mixed package of such policies at once.[20] For ordinary citizens, the costs of registering or even of formulating regulatory preferences far exceed the benefits.

Not so for organized interest groups. For them, the benefits of pursuing favorable regulatory outcomes are often worth the costs. This is true given the concentrated distribution of those benefits among interest groups' members. Given that the benefits of regulatory goods are higher for organized groups than for individual voters, the former enjoy much more influence in regulatory decisionmaking relative to the latter.

The price of favorable regulation for interest groups is not always cheap, however. For one thing, overcoming what Stigler calls "the procedural safeguards required of public processes"[21] is not costless. Regulation-seeking interest groups face the costs of communicating with politicians and participating in regulatory decisionmaking, including the costs of consultants, lawyers, and lobbyists. Second, such groups incur the costs of earning the support of legislators, which is to say, the costs of providing legislators with political benefits—votes and financial resources. This second cost implies another: Regulation-seeking groups must also pay the costs of "regulatory competition." That is, they must outbid competitor groups, which means that they have to not only supply legislators with resources that translate to political benefits, but with more of such resources than competing groups. Thus, no given interest group will enjoy all of the regulatory goods it desires; scarcity constrains any group's regulatory purchasing power.

Even so, the regulatory market works on the whole to the advantage of organized groups with narrow interests. Interest groups with the most at stake in a particular regulatory decision, who spend the most to buy that decision, typically see their demands for regulation met by legislators who acquiesce in order to enjoy continued electoral success and the benefits that holding office brings. In the process, ordinary citizens lose, though they rarely perceive their loss in any particular case. Nor is the end result purely distributional. The regulatory goods that organized groups obtain often come at a high social cost; concentrated group gains usually "fall far short of the damage to the rest of the community."[22] Again, as regulatory goods are sold to groups representing concentrated interests, the few gain, and the many lose by more.

The public choice theory's account of regulation carries with it a reform agenda: The view that the fundamental differences between regulatory and market decisionmaking explain the problem with regulation strongly suggests that market outcomes are preferable to regulatory outcomes. Indeed, public choice theorists often argue for increased reliance on markets as an alternative to government regulation. Limiting regulators' power, and thus their ability to advance the interests of small groups at the greater expense of general interests, would enhance social welfare. Market outcomes, however imperfect, are better than the regulatory products of an intractable regulatory regime.

And the regime is indeed intractable, according to public choice theory, which does not contemplate that the right combination of reforms might improve regulatory decisionmaking. In fact, the theory distinguishes itself from prior work on regulation in part through its greater realism concerning that very question. Whereas earlier scholars prescribed various budget- and personnel-oriented reforms of the regulatory system, public choice theorists argue that such reforms hopelessly underestimate the problem.[23] The regulatory system advances concentrated interests not accidentally or incidentally, but rather by its very structure and design.[24] Thus, regulatory "reform" means for the public choice theory not institutional reform of the regulatory system, but its abandonment. The news is that bad.

EMPIRICAL EXPECTATIONS OF THE PUBLIC CHOICE THEORY

If the public choice story is correct, it should be able to explain or predict regulatory phenomena. And indeed, the account carries with it several predictions. These extend to the substantive regulatory decisions made by administrative agencies, but also, if more subtly, to the specific legal-procedural mechanisms through which agencies regulate.

Substantive Predictions: Policy

The theory's substantive predictions are straightforward, almost tautological. First, the theory predicts that regulatory outcomes favor the interests of organized interests well situated to press their regulatory demands.

In other words, the theory predicts that, looking to actual regulatory decisions, the interests of organized groups prevail over larger but more diffuse interests. To the extent the consequences of regulatory decisions are measurable, one should be able to identify real regulatory rents. And indeed public choice theorists sometimes point to empirical studies corroborating these predictions (as will be seen later).

The theory also makes negative predictions. That is, regulatory policy outcomes that deliver broad benefits to unorganized citizens at the expense of organized interest groups would run contrary to the theory's clear expectations. Of course, regulatory consequences are sometimes unintended, and so the rare regulatory outcome that unexpectedly hurt organized interests and benefited citizens generally may not prove much. But certainly the theory predicts that where mobilized interests commit their energies to influencing regulatory outcomes, they are able to do so and do not lose out to broad, public interests. Thus Stigler writes:

> It is of course true that the theory would be contradicted if, for a given regulatory policy, we found the group with larger benefits and lower costs of political action being dominated by another group with lesser benefits and higher cost of political action. Temporary accidents aside, such cases simply will not arise: our extensive experience with the general theory in economics gives us the confidence this is so.[25]

There it is. The theory predicts both that organized interests for whom the regulatory stakes are highest will win, and that they will not lose.

Procedural Predictions: Decisionmaking

The theory's predictions extend to more than regulatory substance, however. Because the public choice theory holds that regulation provides regulatory rents to well-organized groups with fairly narrow interests, an examination of regulatory decisionmaking processes would be expected to reveal procedural mechanisms facilitating influence on decisionmakers by such groups. That is, because the public choice theory holds that regulatory decisions further narrow interests *by design*, an examination of decisionmaking processes should reveal procedures devised precisely to identify and create regulatory rents: Administrative processes should afford well-organized parties easy access to regulators, and opportunities for informing administrators about the regulatory goods they demand. By the same token, those processes should facilitate agencies' provision of regulatory goods to influential groups.

Concomitantly, one would expect to find barriers to participation by those whose interests are sacrificed through regulatory rent-seeking. In fact, given that the public choice theory holds that general interests are advanced, if ever, only through "temporary accidents," it further suggests that administrative procedures will not encourage widespread participation even in the rare event that a given decision advances broad interests. Regulatory decisions advancing broad interests (due to unintended consequences) should, like any other, be the product of decisionmaking processes designed to facilitate rent seeking.

The theory also suggests the regulatory procedures would allow agencies to provide regulatory goods without generating easily accessible information about the adverse consequences of the policies they adopt. Regulatory rents should not be provided, in other words, through processes that showcase their existence. Instead, information generated through regulatory decisionmaking procedures should camouflage how decisions will advance the interests of those influencing administrators. And that information should tend to flow only between those demanding and those supplying regulatory rents.[26]

In addition, the public choice theory suggests that regulatory decisionmakers are subject to little or no critical outside scrutiny. That is, to the extent agency decisionmaking is subject to oversight by other governmental institutions, those institutions will not interfere with agency-provided regulatory rents. For example, Congress may well oversee agency decisionmaking, but it does so only to ensure that agencies satisfy the demands of politically powerful groups. The same would hold true for the executive branch; White House oversight should reinforce agency supply of favorable regulation to politically powerful groups. And as for the judiciary, it should show considerable deference to agency decisions, perhaps ensuring that agencies are legally authorized to undertake challenged actions, but not otherwise closely analyzing the substance of what an agency has done in a way that severely impedes the supply of regulatory goods to favored groups. In short, insofar as agencies aim to supply regulatory goods to rent-seeking interest groups, external oversight should not interfere; and insofar as agencies are slow to satisfy the demands of special interest groups, oversight should encourage them to do so.

Finally, patterns of actual participation in regulatory decisionmaking processes should not reveal a multiplicity of participating interests. That is, the public choice theory would not predict the presence of numerous participants with incompatible goals in the development of particular regulatory decisions. Rather, one should find relatively few parties participating in any given decision. And those participants should include, at least as a general rule, only the relevant agency decisionmaker together with representatives of the group seeking the regulatory good.

To summarize, the public choice theory predicts that ground-level regulatory decisionmaking processes are accessible primarily to well-organized groups seeking regulatory rents, that those processes generate information primarily about those groups' regulatory demands and how they can be met, that regulatory decisionmakers operate in an environment free from oversight that interferes with agency supply of regulatory goods, and finally that only a few parties typically participate in the development of a regulatory policy. These predictions will be tested in chapter 13. First, the next chapter considers whether the theory bears close conceptual scrutiny.

Chapter Three

Is Regulatory Capture Inevitable?

W HILE NOT ALL STUDENTS of regulation see socially beneficial regulation as an unlikely proposition, the bleak picture presented in chapter 2 has proven enormously influential. This account holds sway over much scholarly discourse about public law institutions generally, and regulatory bodies in particular. Even those who approach regulation indirectly—from the perspective of other legal fields or even other disciplines—often seem osmotically influenced by the public choice theory's conclusions. Thus, for example, contributors to such diverse fields as tax and constitutional law regularly invoke the public choice picture in the course of analyzing or explaining particular regulatory phenomena. While few academicians explicitly endorse the strong version of the theory articulated by Stigler, scholars routinely reference—virtually always in a short-handed way—"public choice theory" as an *abbreviation* for analysis of how or why narrow regulatory interests routinely prevail over others. In short, the theory has enjoyed considerable staying power and, though usually invoked casually as a placeholder for genuine analysis, it accounts for much academic skepticism toward public-law regulation. This understates it.

This is to say nothing of the theory's influence on more popular conceptions of regulatory government. The general regulatory capture story also informs much generalist political commentary on the performance of the regulatory state. Here too, commentators reference "interest groups" or "capture" in passing (whereas most scholarly discourse typically references "public choice reasons," but the difference is essentially one of terminology) as a terse explanation of particular regulatory phenomena. Here too again, invocation of the theory serves as a shorthand or placeholder for more complete analysis, analysis considered unnecessary because the theory is assumed to be strong and its conclusions familiar.

ESSENTIAL PREMISES OF THE PUBLIC CHOICE ACCOUNT

But turn up the microscope. While compelling on one level of generality and appealing in its parsimoniousness, on close analysis the public choice account shows its holes and thin spots. Seeing them clearly requires more detailed consideration of the account's essential claims. After all, there is no such thing as a "public choice *reason*," notwithstanding that common turn of phrase. There is, rather, a public choice *theory* embodied by public choice *claims*, whether conceptual or empirical. Viewed more closely, the theory contains several crucial premises.

1. First, interest groups seek regulatory decisions that advance the selfish interests of their members. That is, interest groups do not commonly organize to pursue regulatory policies that advance broad, social interests. Rather, they participate in regulatory politics to benefit their members, no matter the social-welfare implications of those policies. For convenience, call this premise of the argument the *interest group motivation claim*.

2. Second, small, narrowly focused interests groups, whose members individually have much at stake, are unusually well able to overcome the collective action problem that generally impedes mobilization by groups representing diffuse interests, resulting in a strong bias in the demand for regulation in favor of narrow interests. In other words, the interest-group competition over regulatory policy is lopsided. This premise constitutes the theory's *collective action claim*.

3. Third, legislators seek to trade favorable regulatory treatment for needed political resources from the interest groups best able to provide them, a goal born of legislators' desire to maintain their positions in office. Call this the *legislator motivation claim*.

4. Fourth, legislative control over administrative agencies is strong enough to allow legislators to deliver the regulatory treatment interest groups seek from agencies. That is, agencies do not enjoy substantial autonomy from legislators, but rather conform to legislative preferences concerning regulatory outcomes. This proposition constitutes the theory's *legislative dominance claim*. Or:

5. As an alternative to legislator motivation and legislative dominance, agencies for their own independent reasons provide interest groups with favorable regulatory treatment, rather than advance social welfare or otherwise pursue their own conceptions of the public interest. In this case, it matters little whether the legislature controls agencies, as agencies on their own initiative provide favorable regulatory decisions to organized interest groups. Call this proposition the *agency favoritism claim*.

Each step is important. The coupling of the interest group motivation claim and the collective action claim is what raises concerns about interest group activity in the first place: Interest groups are out for only their own good, and only narrowly focused groups whose members have a lot at stake will be able to mobilize to press their agenda. The collective action claim in particular is important to the theory because it establishes the type of interest groups that make the most effective demands upon legislators and administrators. If, instead, many equally powerful groups were able to mobilize to compete for legislative or administrative attention, then the results of regulatory politics might be more pluralistic and socially desirable. To the extent that legislators hear from many types of interest groups with different and opposing regulatory preferences, the implications of a legislator's reelection-minded calculus become more complicated: The legislator may be pushed and pulled in different directions, sometimes deciding that satisfying the regulatory preferences of broad-based groups is politically advantageous. By a similar token, if only a few groups were able to mobilize, but did so to advocate general interests rather than only their members' interests, one would not worry so much about the consequences of interest group influence. Because interest group activity is instead both selfish and lopsided, legislators have more to gain from being solicitous of certain interests, and necessarily less solicitous of more general interests.

The legislator motivation claim is similarly important, though not quite indispensable, to the public choice theory's vision. Were legislators by and large immune to interest groups' regulatory preferences, it might not matter much how lopsided interest-group activity was. Because legislators *are* motivated to satisfy those preferences in order to preserve their own positions, however, lopsided interest group pressure translates into lopsided regulatory consideration.

Finally, the legislative dominance claim is necessary to the extent that agencies do not for their own reasons seek to satisfy the regulatory preferences of special interests groups. Were legislators unable to control agencies enough to generate the regulatory outcomes favored by their interest-group constituencies, legislator motivation would matter little. The problem, according to the theory, is that legislators can prompt agencies to provide the regulatory benefits that powerful yet narrowly interested groups seek. The theory concludes, accordingly, that agencies responding to legislative signals provide those benefits, thereby perfecting the exchange between legislators and rent-seeking interest groups.

That leaves the agency favoritism claim. Agency favoritism means that even where legislators are not motivated or able to enlist agencies to provide favorable regulation to narrow interests, agencies will do so all the same. If for whatever reason agencies on their own render decisions bene-fiting such groups, then for this additional reason regulatory outcomes will undermine social welfare. Here again, the picture is discouraging, for agencies deliver favorable regulatory treatment to undeserving interest groups who, given the interest group motivation claim and the collective action claim, most demand it.

In sum, the public choice account contemplates that its claims about interest group motivation and collective action are true, and that either its legislative motivation and legislative dominance claims also are true, or if not then its agency favoritism claim is true: Interest groups pursuing their selfish interests are the important unit of analysis. Interest-group competition is uneven. Legislators seek to provide regulatory decisions favoring their most politically powerful groups, and legislators can con-trol or at least influence administrative agencies to do so, or else adminis-trators provide favorable regulatory treatment to influential interest groups even in the absence of legislative control.

Focusing on these core premises of the public choice theory, the ques-tion becomes whether they can bear the weight of critical analysis, which in turn raises questions about their origin. Where do they come from—what are the theoretical bases for the theory's hallmark claims? Public choice theorists have not simply invented these premises. Instead, they have some theoretical justification; they borrow from certain intellectual traditions, and they derive from certain background conceptual under-standings. As a result, however, they prove to be only as strong as those traditions and understandings.

So back up. To understand fully the strengths and weaknesses of the theory's key claims, it is necessary to consider their foundation. That foundation employs ideas surrounding the logic of collective action, dele-gation, and principal-agent relationships. That is, the public choice theo-ry's essential claims borrow heavily from the logic of collective action, as well as from observations about the costs of delegation, as follows.

THE THEORETICAL UNDERPINNINGS OF THE PUBLIC CHOICE THEORY'S CORE CLAIMS

The (Il)logic of Collective Action

Consider this. If citizens themselves could overcome the market failures to which much regulation purportedly responds, there would be little need for a regulatory state. Given the obstacles to concerted action, however, they cannot: Citizens cannot build highways, inspect food and drugs, protect the environment, ensure the safety of nuclear plants or the airlines, allocate the airwaves, provide domestic security, or provide other public goods. To do such things would require vast amounts of coordination and cooperation, assuming unrealistically that citizens could afford to give such problems sustained attention in the face of life's many competing demands. And even if some citizens decided to contribute toward some public good—whether out of a sense of public spirit or because those citizens happened to value the public good more than others—still others could enjoy the benefits of that good without pitching in. Thus, for reasons famously articulated by Mancur Olson,[1] and subsequently refined by many others,[2] the production of public goods will tend to be too low. Indeed, the logic of collective action implies that, under certain circumstances, the bigger the "public" in question, the farther below the desirable level will the supply of public goods be. Because that logic and its consequences are central to the public choice theory of regulation, attention to its nuances, sometimes overlooked by casual consumers of the logic, is necessary. So indulge a short and crucial review.

Olson's classic work emphasized the danger of anthropomorphizing groups. A *group*—defined simply as "a number of individuals with a common interest"[3]—will not always make the investment in some *group good* (or "collective good" or "public good")—defined as any benefit or good accruing to all of the group's membership[4]—that an individual would make, were a single individual faced with the same decision facing the group. This is true because a rational member of a group, upon considering whether to contribute time, money, and other resources to gain something that benefits the group collectively—that provides a public good to the group's membership—may refuse to do so even where all group members agree that they all would be better off if everyone participated. The single individual will refuse to participate insofar as the costs of participation would exceed the benefits. The costs of participation may exceed the benefits because the individual alone would bear those costs, whereas the benefits from participation equal the marginal contribution the individual would make to the collective good, divided by the number of group members. The costs are private bads; the benefits, public goods. Thus, the individual member will realize that not contributing avoids all the individual costs, but forgoes virtually none of the benefits (only the individual's share of the group benefits that participation would have produced). The individual will therefore have an incentive not to participate. If all other potential members reason similarly, the group good in question will be underproduced.[5]

Extending this basic insight, Olson generated two general conclusions. First, many groups will produce *no* collective goods. Specifically, a "homogenous" group—homogenous in the sense that its members all have the same willingness to contribute toward the group good—in which it is worth no single member's cost of investing in a collective benefit, and therefore is worth no member's investment (since the group is homogenous), will produce no collective good, notwithstanding any potential group gains from doing so. Olson calls such groups, which have no organizational structure, "latent groups."[6]

Second, no group will produce the *optimal* level of a collective good. That is, even where a group is nonhomogenous such that one (or more) of its member's own private benefits from a collective good justifies *that* member's investment in the good—Olson calls such a group a "privileged group"[7]—eventually that member's marginal costs of providing the group good will exceed that member's own marginal gains, by which point that member will stop making the investment. Put differently, at some point the unusual member(s) will stop producing what amount to beneficial externalities for other group members, even though there would be additional net benefits from further investments in the group good.

Olson further argued that the larger a given group, the greater the suboptimality of the group good,[8] adding that numerically large groups will tend not to produce any group goods at all, while small groups will tend to provide a positive, but suboptimal, amount of group goods.[9] Finally, he argued that in order to generate the provision of a group good for a numerically large latent group, that group's members must be subject to coercive sanctions for failing to contribute to group efforts, or else they must be selectively induced to contribute by being rewarded with private benefits in exchange for their contributions.[10] These solutions are not necessary for privileged groups, which by definition have at least one member already providing some amount of the group good on its own. Nor are they always necessary for Olson's third and final category of groups, "intermediate groups," which are latent groups whose membership is sufficiently small that group members might bargain their way to the provision of a collective good through coordinated agreement.[11]

Unfortunately, Olson's argument does not always carefully distinguish its empirical claims from its analytical claims, notwithstanding that his conclusions are in fact contingent on several conditions, an observation often overlooked by casual consumers of the argument and especially by those who reference it loosely to ground public-choice conclusions about regulation. For example, Olson's conclusion that group goods will not be supplied at optimal levels even in privileged groups depends on the nature of the group good in question, specifically, whether the good is a "continuous good" or instead a "step" good.[12] Where a collective good comes in bundles of a fixed quantity—a step good—one group member just might invest in one or more bundles providing the optimal level of the good for the entire group.[13] For another example, Olson's claim that the larger the group, the smaller each member's incentive to contribute[14] is actually false for public goods characterized by jointness—that is, goods the enjoyment of which by one member of the group does not reduce another member's enjoyment.[15] In fact, as others have shown, where the group good in question is joint, Olson's claim that the provision of that good will be inversely proportional to the size of the group gets the relationship between group size and the quantity of the group good provided exactly backwards.[16]

More fundamentally (and less technically), Olson's solution for mobilizing latent groups—sanctions or selective inducements—as well as his observation that intermediate groups might provide group goods through bargaining among their members, both assume away the very problem he identifies. This is true because selective inducements and bargaining processes are *themselves* group goods. Mobilizing a latent group requires somebody willing to administer a sanction or supply an inducement. But to do either of these is to supply a group good: Punishing noncontributors or enticing would-be noncontributors benefits the relevant group as a whole. Thus, the very same logic according to which individual group members have no incentive to provide a group good holds that these solutions either will not be provided, or will be provided in suboptimal amounts. The same is true for intermediate-group bargaining: The bargaining process itself is a group good, and members thus have an incentive not to participate.[17] The logic of collective action, taken to its conclusion, thus actually predicts that intermediate as well as latent groups will lack organizational form—will provide *no* public goods.

Such serious problems do not escape Olson's notice altogether. For example, recognizing that his logic predicts that latent groups will have no organization form, while such a conclusion seems at odds with observable facts, he writes:

> Though many groups with common interests, like the consumers, the
> white-collar workers, and the migrant agricultural workers, are not

organized, other large groups, the union laborers, the farmers, and the doctors have at least some degree of organization. The fact that . . . [some] large groups have been organized would seem to contradict the theory of "latent groups" offered in this study.[18]

The question is even more compelling than Olson suggests, however. Today, each of the groups he lists (more or less correctly in 1965 when he wrote) as lacking developed organization structure—consumers, white-collar workers, agricultural workers—in fact now have it. However that may be, Olson argued that the organizational overrepresentation of smaller, business-oriented interests, relative to the interests of large minority groups, consumers, and veterans, for example, vindicated his "logic."[19] In particular, he argued that business organizations tend to be composed of a very small number of firms, and that such overrepresentation thus demonstrates the organizational advantages that privileged and intermediate groups enjoy over latent groups.[20]

Seeking to account for the organization and lobbying activities of even large groups as well, Olson furthermore argued that the existence of large lobbying organizations owes to their ability to provide organization members with private goods or services—selective inducements—in exchange for which they provide resources that support collective political activities. Lobbying, according to this account, is a "by-product" of the provision of private goods to group members—hence Olson's " 'by-product' theory of large pressure groups":[21]

> The lobby is then a by-product of whatever function this organization performs that enables it to have a captive membership. . . . Only an organization that also sold private or noncollective products, or provided social or recreational benefits to individual members, would have a source of these positive inducements.[22]

This response is incomplete, however, for while it explains why individual members of large organizations might contribute to a collective good, it still fails to explain who would transform those contributions into the collective good. In other words, the by-product theory does not explain who is at the "other end" of the organization actually supplying the group good by monitoring contributions and administering sanctions to members who fail to contribute.[23] Again, the logic of collective action, taken by itself, implies that there would be no provider of those collective goods either. A member of a privileged group might provide a group good, including monitoring and sanctioning activities, because the private benefits of doing so outweigh the costs, but this possibility cannot rescue latent or intermediate groups without collapsing the distinctions among them.

Yet as noted, examples even of large lobbying groups are easy to find, notwithstanding that smaller such groups do seem to outnumber larger groups as a matter of empirical fact.[24] Moreover, many small groups— including, for example, business-oriented political interest groups with relatively few members—have organizational structure; their activities consist of more than simply the provision of a group good by unusual members. Thus does the *logic* of collective action give way to the *puzzle* of collective action: Large and small *organizations* coordinating the supply of group goods do exist. Indeed, today they seem fairly common. What accounts for their existence? What is the missing mechanism that accounts for interest-group politics?

Catalysts for Collective Action

Russell Hardin, for one especially influential example, sheds light on this issue. Hardin argues that, in addition to selective material benefits, individuals might contribute to a collective good in return for the solidaristic benefits such participation may generate, or in response to moral or other noninstrumental motivations,[25] as Olson himself anticipated.[26] These incentives might similarly motivate the initial mobilization of a group as well as the monitoring and sanctioning activities necessary to sustain the group organization.

Individual members of a group may be motivated to contribute to a group good in response to moral considerations in at least two ways. First, a member may contribute to the group good not because that good itself has moral significance, but for the simple reason that moral considerations counsel in favor of contributing one's fair share. Even where a member may be able to get away with free riding on the contributions of others, doing so may violate important principles, such as that of "doing one's part." As Hardin notes, such a norm does not necessarily avoid the collective-action problem altogether, for individual observance of the norm of doing one's part likely depends on the belief that many others are doing their part as well.[27] More fundamentally, fairness norms can mitigate the problem of collective action only insofar as there exists some very prominent conception of what it means to do one's fair share. To the extent that "fairness" does not distinguish among many different, and incompatible, fair-contribution rules, members of a group who seek to conform to notions of fairness must overcome the collective-action problem of agreeing upon a particular conception of fairness. These obstacles notwithstanding, the moral ramifications of not cooperating may well mitigate collective-action problems in some circumstances.

Second, moral motivations may prompt contribution to a collective good because the good itself has moral significance. Moral considerations of this sort may account in part for the existence of political organizations oriented toward the "public interest." According to Hardin, alluding to Olson: "Contemporary labor union political activities may be a by-product; the Sierra Club's generally are not. Nor can one sensibly construct rational arguments for individual contributions to Sierra Club political activities, at least not rational in the sense of narrowly self-interested."[28] Instead, members contribute to advance their vision of the good; that others may or may not contribute is mostly beside the point. Moral considerations may very well motivate the provision of collective goods by organizational leaders as well; group leaders also may take initiative out of a sense of moral commitment to the group's goals.

Alternatively, the benefits of participation itself may motivate contribution to a group good. Whether or not a group member attaches moral significance to the act of contributing, that member may benefit from the very activity of making a contribution. For one thing, making a contribution may bring with it the benefits associated with a sense of solidarity— a private good quite apart from the individual contributor's private share of the group good in question. Although such benefits would presumably be very small if the collective effort were plainly futile, those benefits do not necessarily depend on widespread contribution to the group good (indeed, up to a point they may increase as group participation falls). On the other hand, in certain circumstances such benefits might merge with the welcome sense that one is participating in a significant and successful collective undertaking. One possible consequence of this latter possibility is that a certain, critical amount of collective action may have a "tipping" effect: Once it becomes clear that history is being made, for example, individuals may be eager to participate in its making.

Finally, groups may be organized by political entrepreneurs, who receive a different sort of private benefit from the act of providing a group good. According to Hardin: "Political entrepreneurs are people who, for their own career reasons, find it in their private interest to work to provide collective benefits to relevant groups."[29] Hardin further argues that political entrepreneurs might be founders and figureheads of political interest groups or, instead, candidates for elective office. Such candidates might realize that latent group members may vote for candidates who seek to provide them with group goods.[30] In fact, to the extent that political entrepreneurs are sensitive to the implications of the logic of collective action, they may be especially responsive to some groups' interests, out of a belief that "a little [group] activity implies a lot of [voter] sympathy."[31] This possibility might be of substantial empirical significance, for political decisions by their very nature have a certain multiplier quality: If a group can provide enough collective resources to attract the attention of a well-placed political entrepreneur, that entrepreneur could promote policies that have practical consequences of a size much larger than the size of the resources needed to attract the entrepreneur's attention originally—an observation to be pursued in more detail below.

Thus, several possibilities—moral motivations, solidarity, political entrepreneurship—may serve as catalysts to the mobilization of latent interests. These same catalysts may also spark the bargaining processes necessary to mobilize intermediate groups. Such catalysts may operate with special force during times of actual or perceived "crisis," when group members are increasingly motivated to pursue collective interests. (Consider the heightened activism associated with the civil rights, consumer, and environmental movements.) All of these possibilities contemplate, however, that the organization of latent and intermediate interests takes place outside of the strict logic of collective action. As Hardin and others have rightly argued, that logic can account for the perpetuation of groups with certain special characteristics, but the origin of public-good-providing groups cannot be derived from it.[32]

Delegation and Its Consequences

Whatever the catalyst, one very important way citizens respond to the predicament implied by the logic of collective action is by delegating regulatory authority to political representatives who supply public goods. Though the act of delegating is itself a public good requiring coordination, delegation is otherwise the only feasible alternative to providing collective goods directly and on a sustained basis, one to which citizens resort especially when an issue becomes highly salient. Because there are far fewer legislators than citizens, coordination and cooperation among them are relatively easier, and moreover legislators are paid to think about regulatory matters on a regular basis. Unfortunately, however, legislators too face their own set of collective action problems, for among other things regulatory policies usually bring group benefits to legislators. And like individual citizens, individual legislators have their own private values and goals—reelection not the least. While these may sometimes motivate individual legislators to take the initiative on regulatory issues, often they do not. After all, a legislator has only finite resources with which to pursue many, sometimes conflicting, goals. Thus, like individual members of the public, individual members of the legislature have inadequate incentives to make the optimal investments in regulatory decisionmaking, though they make some.

Given some catalyst, such as political entrepreneurship, and especially when an issue generates heightened attention, legislators, like citizens, respond to their collective-action problems by delegating authority over many regulatory matters. Because legislators themselves cannot build highways, inspect food and drugs, protect the environment, ensure the safety of nuclear plants or the airlines, or allocate the airwaves—though of course they pass general statutes concerning such matters—legislators instead delegate regulatory authority to administrators, that is, to administrative agencies. Whereas legislators are paid to think about general regulatory problems on a recurrent basis, regulators are paid to think about specific regulatory problems every day. Thus, individual regulators have greater individual incentives to develop sound regulatory policy, as their professional rewards are tied to successful regulatory decisions more closely than are legislators'. To be very sure, administrators too have individual values and goals that diverge from their group values and goals, and they too face their own set of collective-action problems. They respond by delegating authority to subagencies, composed of even smaller numbers of individuals with even narrower goals. And so on. Thus do layers of collective-action problems give rise to layered delegations of power, where delegation is a collective good made possible by some catalytic force (or else provided by some atypical member of a heterogeneous group).

But delegation has its costs, serious costs, a consequence of the discrepancy between what the delegators—the principals in a principal-agent relationship—want and what the delegatees—their agents—actually deliver. Once citizens delegate lawmaking authority to legislators, for example, it is difficult for the citizenry to know whether legislators exercise that authority to further the citizenry's collective interests. Ideally, of course, legislators would protect their principals' interests in the very same way that the principals themselves would. But citizens cannot follow their legislators around to make sure they do so, and thus principal-agent "slack" allows legislators to "shirk"—to sacrifice their constituencies' collective interests for their own private goals and interests. To generalize the point: Because agents to whom principals delegate power have incentives to shirk wherever their own interests diverge from the interests of those they represent, and because agents are seldom perfectly loyal to their principals, principal-agent relationships are not costless. Instead, they suffer from more or less slack—more or less room for agents to pursue their own interests to the detriment of their principals' common interests.

Naturally, delegator-principals can guard against slack by monitoring their delegatee-agents. Citizens can develop techniques for monitoring their legislators to try to minimize principal-agent slack and thereby help ensure that regulation really reflects the citizenry's values and preferences. One way they can do so is by forming "watchdog" interest groups that monitor legislators and administrators. Monitoring is costly, however, and principals will make monitoring investments only up to the point where the marginal costs of doing so equal the marginal benefits. Moreover, because monitoring is itself a public good, the problem of collective action plagues any attempt to monitor. Besides, the monitors will require monitoring themselves, to ensure that interest-group leaders (typically political entrepreneurs) remain faithful to *their* agents. As a result, citizens can never be sure, or can only be so sure, that their legislative representatives are really advancing their interests—the main teaching of the principal-agent model.

The bottom line is that citizens' delegation of regulatory decisionmaking power to legislative representatives creates principal-agent slack with dire consequences.[33] Because most citizens are largely uninformed about most regulatory decisions, and because they moreover lack incentives to become well enough informed to reward legislators who do not shirk, legislators do not—cannot—protect the broad regulatory interests of their constituencies. Meanwhile, organized interest groups—industry groups, occupational groups, and trade associations—who *are* informed because they have an especially high demand for regulatory goods, do monitor legislators, punishing those who fail to provide such goods and rewarding those who provide favorable regulation.[34] Thus interest groups capitalize on the opportunities created by principal-agent slack in order to obtain regulatory decisions that advantage them. So the story goes.

THE CONCEPTUAL CRITIQUE

Close attention to the logic of collective action, delegation, and principal-agent slack makes the public choice theory's core claims clearer. It also reveals the theory's weaknesses. Laid bare, each of the theory's essential propositions proves contestable or doubtful. Here's why.

THE INTEREST GROUP MOTIVATION CLAIM

First, the claim that interest groups seek to advance only the interests of their members overstates matters, in at least two ways. For one, many interest groups, even those representing well-financed, business-oriented interests, often at least purport to represent general interests. That is, they claim that the regulatory policies they support would benefit society generally, by boosting American competitiveness, benefiting consumers, promoting new technologies, and so on. Interest groups making such claims may be wrong about them, and they may often make them disingenuously, but at least part of the time even groups organized to promote a specific trade or industry appear to favor regulatory policies that plausibly do advance broad interests. It is often the case, for example, that competing business-oriented interest groups seeking diametrically opposed regulatory decisions both argue that their preferred regulatory outcome would most benefit society as a whole. (The controversy in recent years surrounding bank deregulation, which pitted banks against insurance companies and investment companies, as discussed in chapter 12, provides just one case in point.) Opposing groups cannot both be right that the outcome they favor would most benefit society in general, but then neither can both be wrong about that. As regulators will act or fail to act in a way that most promotes one side's interests or the other's, regulators who deliver what one side wants may in fact advance broad public interests. Moreover, wherever an interest group can credibly claim that the regulation it favors will advance social interests, such claims seem likely to increase that group's chance of success—by providing regulators with political cover, by giving regulators a means to resolve close cases, and so on.

More important, many organized interest groups appear primarily to promote interests extending beyond those of their own membership.[35] In fact, the very purpose of environmental groups, consumer groups, and other "public interest" groups is to promote the broad-based interests of large segments of society, not the selfish interests of their members. Nor do such groups claim to represent public interests incidentally to their own members' interests, unlike some special interest groups. Here again, such groups' claims about whether the regulation they favor truly advances broad societal interests are certainly open to dispute,[36] but the point remains that the existence of these groups jeopardizes—requires at least some modification of—the public choice theory's interest group motivation claim. It seems empirically false that interest groups inevitably pursue only the interests of their members.

THE COLLECTIVE ACTION CLAIM

The existence of seemingly broad-based interest groups calls into question not only the theory's interest group motivation claim, but also its collective action claim. Again, the theory holds that ordinary citizens lack incentives to pursue their regulatory interests, given the relative costs and benefits of doing so. The benefits are low, the costs high. In Stigler's words, for example:

> What is the consumer's recourse if he is being exploited by a federal marketing order which either neglects his interest or, as is the case at present in the United States, positively arms and protects a cartel in exploiting this consumer? His sole defense is to organize a political campaign to change or eliminate that marketing scheme. For the individual consumer this is a bleak prospect. The costs—in time, effort, and money—to change legislation are large; the reward to any one consumer from joining a consumer lobby is negligible.[37]

Collective-action barriers constitute the individual voter's obstacle to organizing to further her regulatory interests; the individual consumer's "rewards" from her own contribution would be "negligible." Making a financial contribution to a campaign organized to change a marketing scheme, much less organizing such a campaign, would not be worth the costs. According to Stigler: "If a family were to devote such a sum as [ten to twenty dollars per year] to stirring up opposition to the marketing order . . . it would be a wretched option: the family would receive negligible benefits from its own activity."[38] The benefits to all consumers of a single family's contribution would be small; the benefits to that family would be nil. Thus, for reasons deeply rooted in the logic of collective action, most citizens lack any real incentive to try to influence regulatory outcomes.[39] For this reason, the ordinary citizen cannot compete with special interest organizations.

As seen, the public choice account not only emphasizes the collective-action barriers facing the ordinary citizens, it also posits that regulation-demanding interest groups can overcome *their* collective-action problems. But if some groups, especially occupational groups, trade associations, and other special interests, can overcome collective-action problems, why cannot other groups—in particular those representing the interest of the average citizen—do so as well? If some kind of extrarational catalyst is necessary to trigger solutions to the collective-action problem, why suppose that economic or business-oriented interests are *more* likely to exhibit such behavior than other types of groups?[40] Indeed, if ideological, moral, and solidaristic motivations provide catalysts for overcoming the logic of collective action, it seems plausible that ideologically oriented interests would, relative to economically oriented interests, be more likely to mobilize in the first place. To that extent, the "logic" of collective action might predict more interest-group activity by ideologically committed groups than by groups with the narrow economic interests of their members in mind.

In *Free Riders and Collective Action*, an addendum to *The Economic Theory of Regulation*, Stigler confronts the problem of how to square the implications of the logic of collective action with the observable existence of many organized interest groups, which as seen above haunted Olson as well:

> The free rider proposition asserts that in a wide range of situations, individuals will fail to participate in collectively profitable activities in the absence of coercion or individually appropriable inducements. The proposition does not specify the circumstances favorable to collective action, and hence does not explain why there are innumerable operating and presumably not wholly ineffective collective bodies— literally thousands of trade associations, for example.[41]

The public choice theory provides two such explanations for the observation that numerous, seemingly effective—according to the theory regrettably effective—interest groups exist. According to the first, there is power in small numbers. This "small number solution"[42] holds that a group member will be more inclined to participate toward a group good the smaller the group in question, for two reasons.[43] First, the smaller the group, the greater the chance the good's provision will depend on each member's participation. Second, the smaller the group, the more an individual member's participation will affect, in Stigler's words, "the scale of operation of the collective action."[44]

But this small-numbers solution is no more satisfying than Olson's "special interest" explanation, which it essentially recapitulates.[45] First of all, it is not true that the probability of collective action depends more strongly on each member's participation for small groups; that relationship certainly does not hold as a matter of logic. Instead, the small-numbers argument implicitly contemplates a step good with the particular characteristic that it springs into being, in some discrete quantity, only once a (unspecified) critical number of group members contribute to the good. But the relationship between the probability of collective action, on one hand, and the number of potential contributors, on the other, depends on the nature of the group good in question.[46] This qualification is not a technical one: The activities of political interest groups—lobbying, participation in regulatory decisionmaking, providing political resources to friendly legislators—all seem best characterized as continuous goods, not step goods. Indeed, Stigler's own survey of organized trade associations reveals a wide range of groups with varying budgets, staff sizes, and number of members, suggesting that organized interest groups' activities constitute continuous goods, in which case it is not clear why members of even small groups would contribute to a collective political enterprise.[47]

Moreover, even focusing for a moment on step goods, there is no reason to believe that, as Stigler argues, "the probability of collective action depends more strongly"[48] on the contribution of each member of a small group, as compared to a large group. Some collective endeavors may require the participation of many members before the joint effort ever gets off the ground; others may not. Once again, Stigler's argument holds only for very specific though unspecified types of collective goods. Conceptually, there is no necessary connection between group size and the influence the marginal member's contribution has on the probability that the good will be produced.

The connection between small group size and the "scale" of the group good produced is similarly spurious. In the first place, the scale of the collective good is not something individual group members care about, any more than they care about the fraction of the total group good that their own participation generates (a fraction that is larger for small groups simply because the denominator is smaller). Thus, considerations of scale will not prompt contribution to a group good for any group, large or small. Again, a group member contemplating contributing to a collective good will ask only whether the (absolute) returns on that contribution, to her, justify the (absolute) costs.

In addition, while sometimes those benefits may justify the costs—for "privileged" groups they do by definition—whether they do has no connection whatsoever to group size.[49] No matter the size of the group in question, a member's contribution will benefit all members at a cost borne only by that member. For that reason, the member will not participate at all, or participate at some suboptimal level. This holds for small groups no less than for large. As a matter of theory, small groups are not more likely to be privileged.[50]

Moreover, focusing on small organized groups creates some tension with the public choice theory's argument that group size is positively correlated with a group's ability to secure regulatory goods. According to that argument, an interest group's political resources increase with its size, since larger groups are able to deliver more votes to legislators. To be sure, votes are not the only resource a group may have; money also determines a group's political power. But money after all is used to secure votes, and the importance of votes thus constitutes one central determinant of group power, as public choice theorists recognize.[51] And, to the extent that vote-conscious legislators understand that, for large groups, a little organization may imply a whole lot of sympathy—that is, a lot of potential votes—then larger groups for a second reason should have greater influence than small groups have.[52] From this point of view, a public choice theorist should anticipate that larger, not smaller, groups would have considerable political power.

The public choice theory's second solution to interest-group collective-action problems holds that asymmetry among group members can lead some members to provide regulatory goods only for themselves—"the asymmetry solution."[53] That is, members who undertake most of the collective endeavor might advance their own interests, which may diverge from the interests of other group members. For example, if some firms do not contribute to a collective effort to influence regulation, but instead choose to free ride on the efforts of other firms in the same industry, they risk finding that that free ride goes, in Stigler's words, "to a destination they do not favor."[54]

But this "solution" simply assumes the collective action problem away. To say interest group members have asymmetrical interests—where "asymmetrical" refers not to the quantity of a good different group members demand but rather to which specific good they demand—is just to say that they are not really in the same group after all. Although members may have some overlapping interests, they also have individualized interests. To the extent their interests are individualized, they face no collective-action problem. To the extent their interests are overlapping, they face one, which raises the question of how they overcome it. If members with common interests can unproblematically organize around *those* interests, maybe the pluralist view of interest groups politics that the public choice account explicitly sought to replace has more merit than recognized. At any rate, it is no solution to the collective-action problem to say that some groups mobilize because some of their members have regulatory interests that compete with other group members. That solution answers the collective-action problem by assuming it away.

On close scrutiny, then, the public choice theory's reliance on the collective-action problem introduces considerable conceptual indeterminacy into the theory.[55] Whether larger or smaller groups will enjoy a competitive advantage in the market for regulation (as well as how larger and how smaller such advantaged groups must be) is just not clear in the abstract. In addition, the theory analogizes the pursuit of favorable regulation to private cartelization, but the analogy's yields are limited first because the theory of cartelization itself is not well developed, and second because the public choice theory is not very precise about how the political process affects what would-be regulatory cartelists are able to gain from the political system or even why they would resort to regulation rather than private cartelization.[56]

As a result, the biggest difficulty for the theory concerns the exact mechanism by which even narrow interest groups mobilize. That is, the very same logic that concludes that large groups will tend not to organize, because each individual member reasons that it is not in her individual interest to contribute toward the collective enterprise, should predict the same for any group, no matter its size. If a group is not privileged, then, none of its members will expect to receive benefits from contributions to the group enterprise that compensate for a member's private costs. Taken to its conclusion, the logic of collective action really implies that groups as such, as opposed to individual group members whose behavior happens to provide a beneficial externality for other members, are not as central to understanding political behavior as is commonly supposed.

Of course there are answers. As already seen, group members may mobilize for reasons having to do with their own sense of fairness, for political or ideological reasons, and to show solidarity, for example. In addition, some groups are founded and maintained through the efforts of political entrepreneurs. But again, these catalysts seem especially applicable to broad-based interest groups, and less powerful as explanations for the activities of narrow, rent-seeking groups. In any event, the answers Olson and following him Stigler offer to explain why some interest groups mobilize and others do not are not compelling. Taken on its own terms, then, the public choice theory's essential collective action claim is, at best, fuzzy.

THE LEGISLATOR MOTIVATION CLAIM

Assume that conceptual indeterminacy away: Assume for the sake of argument that legislators are pressured exclusively by narrow, industry- or trade-oriented business interest groups, because they alone are able to mobilize, and furthermore that those interest groups pursue only rent-seeking regulatory policies that would further their membership's interests at society's expense. The next question becomes whether the public choice theory's separate claim about legislative motivations, according to which legislators respond to interest group pressures in exchange for needed political resources, is itself compelling. One problem with the theory's legislator motivation claim is that it seems to imply that reelection-minded legislators inevitably satisfy interest group demands. That is, the theory contemplates that legislators are *always* very worried about the next election—that fear of electoral defeat consistently renders legislators ever willing to meet the highest bidder's regulatory demands. This vision is problematic for several reasons.

First, even legislators for whom reelection is the single most important, overriding goal need not always supply interest groups with the regulatory policies they prefer. For one thing, not all legislators are electorally vulnerable.[57] Legislators from "safe" districts, even those who would never jeopardize their reelection prospects, have no strong incentive to satisfy all interest groups' regulatory demands, since the benefits of doing so would not, for them, be substantial. Whether a reelection-minded legislator would determine that satisfying a given group's regulatory demands was necessary would depend on how close the legislator was to some comfortable reelection threshold, as well as on considerations about whether supporting or failing to support some interest group's cause would likely move the legislator above or below that reelection threshold.[58]

Second, even assuming that legislators are always worried about job security, it is not clear exactly what kind of legislative behavior that worry generates. Knowing how a given legislator would respond to uncertainty about the next election requires complicated information about factors such as the legislator's baseline electoral prospects, her degree of risk aversion (what level of error will the legislator tolerate once the expected result of the next election is a victory?), the duration of her time horizon, her ability to answer objections from groups whose regulatory demands were not met, and so on. Simply knowing that a legislator seeks security of office does not, without more, imply anything specific about how that legislator will behave, and how that legislator will satisfy the regulatory preferences of competing interest groups in particular.

What is more, while the public choice theory's portrayal of legislative incentives usually seems to contemplate some electorally vulnerable member of the House of Representatives, the story becomes much more complicated remembering the Senate's contribution to regulatory policy.[59] To be sure, senators too need to be reelected, but longer terms and the real possibility of conflicts between the two chambers on matters of regulatory policy make the public choice theory's legislative motivation claim much more intricate than it first appears.

More fundamentally, though, the premise that legislators trade regulatory goods for electoral resources also inexplicably assumes away other goals that a legislator may have. While it seems reasonable to assume that legislators seek to retain their positions in office, it seems implausible to assume that job security constitutes legislators' *single* goal—that legislators seek office solely to maintain it. If legislators only voted in accordance with the dictates of a (complicated) electoral calculus, one would question why they sought office in the first place. Pecuniary advancement could not explain it, for legislators are not paid very much, and although the public choice theory posits that legislators seek to hold office in part for the pecuniary advantages they will reap in the future as former office holders, there are more direct—that is, more rational—routes to financial success. Nor could the pursuit of power explain why legislators would always supply regulation to the groups who demanded it most, for power implies some realm of discretion. No accepted conception of power is consistent with legislative behavior that is mechanical.[60]

Legislator ideology, in other words, complicates matters further. Assuming, then, that reelection is one very important goal for any given legislator, but one that may be traded off against other important goals, the question becomes how much weight reelection gets relative to other goals. In fact, there is evidence that legislators serve different roles over the course of their legislative careers—as ombudspersons, policy experts, senior statespersons—not all of which are consistent with meeting interest groups' regulatory preferences, and during which legislators have more or less room to advance their own ideological commitments.

But once other goals are attributed to legislators, knowing how they will respond to groups demanding favorable regulation now requires information about how competing goals might be balanced against reelection. And once a legislator is reasonably certain about winning the next election, she would then presumably focus on other goals. Nor is this multidimensional vision of legislative motivation unrealistic. For one thing, empirically legislators' jobs typically are secure. As a rule, legislative turnover is in fact low,[61] and a number of legislative districts are widely considered safe, giving legislators latitude to pursue ideological goals. In addition, as an empirical matter ideology is for many legislative decisions a better predictor of legislative behavior than the reelection calculus,[62] a finding reinforcing and reinforced by the observation that many legislators need not worry so much about the next election.[63]

Finally, it is not clear that a nonideological legislator focused only or mostly on winning the next election would necessarily promote the interests of special interest groups anyway. The reelection calculus may be more complicated. It is plausible, for example, that legislators' reelection goals at times inspire careful attention to the preferences of broad-based groups, whose views may matter to a large number of voters, and less attention to the preferences of narrow groups whose campaign contributions may or may not yield large numbers of votes.[64] A reelection-minded legislator might reasonably surmise that broad-based interest groups represent more voters even if they can deliver fewer campaign contributions. To that extent, even the vulnerable legislator will not be motivated to deliver regulatory rents only to narrow interest groups.

THE LEGISLATIVE DOMINANCE CLAIM

But this speaks only to the complexities of legislative motivation. To the extent that administrators, too, are motivated by ideological commitments, the theory is threatened again. Administrators motivated by ideological considerations or their own sense of what constitutes the public good, rather than exclusively by calculations of how their decisions will affect their budgets and scope of authority, may not be easily susceptible to legislative control. Furthermore, administrators may be as attentive to the regulatory preferences of broad-based interest groups as they are to narrow groups. Here again, then, the link between interest group preferences and regulatory policy outcomes becomes more attenuated.

Administrator motivation is not all that raises questions about the legislature's ability to control regulatory agencies. Although the legislative dominance claim implies that Congress can prompt agencies to deliver the regulation sought by legislative constituencies, it is unclear whether administrative decisionmaking procedures really facilitate congressional control of regulatory agencies more than they liberate agencies from the legislature, a question to be explored in more detail shortly.[65] To anticipate that discussion to come, it is at least as likely that regulatory decisionmaking processes insulate agencies from legislative influence. To the extent that is so, the legislature cannot easily employ agencies to deliver regulatory rents.

There are additional complicating factors. For one, agencies are not influenced by Congress alone. Rather, they must answer to a president and to the courts. Nor is it clear that institutions like judicial review facilitate agency delivery of regulatory rents, as many others have pointed out.[66] Although judicial review can be seen as furthering congressional influence of agencies (by holding agencies faithful to the language of regulatory statutes), judicial review also makes it difficult for agencies to cater to the regulatory preferences of one group without due consideration of facts or arguments that may support the regulatory preferences of an opposing group. To the extent that judicial review promotes regulatory evenhandedness by agencies, another issue to be explored below, Congress's ability to direct agencies to satisfy interest group preferences becomes more precarious.

Anticipating the objection that legislators cannot monitor administrators costlessly and that, consequently, administrators might pursue their own agenda, the public choice theory responds that administrators must heed legislators' wishes to ensure their own survival.[67] But that response largely assumes away the principal-agent problem between legislators and agencies, an assumption reminiscent of the dated "transmission belt" model of administrative decisionmaking, according to which agencies reliably convert legislative directives. Originally, the transmission belt model was associated with early public interest theories of regulation: Legislators passed statutes advancing the public interest, and administrators smoothly implemented those statutes without compromising public-interest legislative goals. While the public choice theory assigns exactly the opposite motivation to legislators, it inexplicably retains much of the transmission-belt premise that agencies neatly follow legislative cues.[68] Yet the matter warrants deeper investigation. For example, as Richard Posner rightly points out, legislative supervision is costly, and its cost rises sharply with an increase in legislative productivity.[69]

Indeed, whether legislators or agencies dominate the relationship between them is a matter of debate.[70] It could well be that principal-agent slack makes it possible for administrators to pursue general-interest regulation, especially given that almost all administrators are insulated from electoral political pressures. In the abstract, it is just not clear whether administrators, as distinct from legislators, seek regulatory policies demanded by special interest groups. In predicting regulatory outcomes, in other words, much may depend on administrators', not only on legislators', motivations.

THE AGENCY FAVORITISM CLAIM

This suggests a way out: Even if the legislature has too little control over agencies to ensure that agencies deliver regulation favorable to important legislative constituencies, agencies might be motivated to do so anyway. That is, agencies may advance the regulatory interests of special interest groups not because legislators force them to do so, but for independent reasons. Thus the agency favoritism claim rescues the public choice account even if the legislative dominance claim (and the legislation motivation claim) is (are) false. If agencies aim to provide regulatory decisions that special interest groups seek, then there may be little at stake in the legislative dominance debate. Of course, if the public choice theory's interest group motivation claim and collective action claim were also false, it would be remarkable if regulatory agencies *nevertheless* catered to the regulatory preferences of special interest groups. Presumably, agencies might do so only in response to lopsided pressures from overrepresented special interests, not in a pluralistic world where many interest groups seek to advance social welfare. Thus, this alternative, agency-favoritism strand of the public choice theory still largely depends on the theory's other essential claims, just not its legislative dominance claim.

While public choice theorists usually emphasize the relationship between the legislature and regulatory agencies—a relationship that constitutes the fulcrum of the public choice theory—in fact public choice theorists sometimes point to alternative reasons why agencies are inclined to advance the regulatory interests of rent-seeking groups. So, for example, replace the "iron triangle" with the "revolving door": Administrators cater to special interests not because they are locked in an exchange relationship with legislators but rather to advance their own interests, such as favorable future employment prospects with regulated interests.

The question becomes, then, why administrators would consistently have their own reasons for satisfying the regulatory demands of special interests, in the absence of legislative pressure to do so. Public choice theorists who emphasize this premise (a minority) point to two sets of considerations, one motivational and one structural. Unfortunately, however, neither seems especially powerful. While this issue is taken up in detail later in chapter 5, a couple of brief notes are in order in the meantime.

On the motivational side, it seems unlikely that agency decisionmakers would satisfy the regulatory preferences of special interest groups for self-interested reasons. First, this possibility seems at odds with common understandings of what motivates many administrators in the first place, which is some philosophical commitment to an agency's regulatory mission. Second, while some administrators may perform their jobs in part for the employment experience their jobs give them, it seems unlikely that administrators would make decisions hoping to improve their future employment prospects, for it is not clear what incentives an industry group, for example, would have to hire former administrators who had made decisions favorable to the industry, and moreover such groups might prefer the experience and disposition of former regulators whose decisions were most aggressive against them.

The structural premise is different: Although agency personnel are not motivated to engage in regulatory favoritism, for structural-institutional reasons their decisions nevertheless tend to be biased in favor of special interests. In particular, agency decisionmakers rely heavily on data to make many of their decisions. To the extent that regulated special interests supply much of the data on which agencies rely, it is possible that agencies will come to depend upon biased data. Information biases may then translate to regulatory biases, not because agencies intend to produce biased regulatory decisions, but rather because they cannot help it; they are "informationally captured."

But here too the argument requires indulgent speculation. For one thing, many of the specific decisionmaking procedures agencies commonly employ—like rulemaking and adjudication under the provisions of the Administrative Procedure Act[71]—are designed to foster the neutral production, dissemination, and exchange of information, as commentators and courts have often observed. Similarly, many of the decisionmaking methodologies agencies employ—such as peer review and cost-benefit analysis—are designed exactly to avoid informational biases in their decisionmaking. So while it is not impossible that agencies are (nevertheless sometimes) "captured" by the information supplied by self-interested groups, it seems unlikely that information biases explain a great deal of regulation. It might be surprising indeed to find that even though legislators cannot induce agencies to provide preferential regulatory treatment to favored interests, and even though agencies are not inclined to do so for their own reasons, nevertheless administrative decisionmakers for structural reasons just cannot avoid providing regulatory rents.

The argument of this long chapter leads here: None of the public choice theory's core claims is irresistible. To the contrary, the theory is vulnerable to the extent that interest groups advocate regulatory policies that benefit more than their own members; that broad-based interest groups representing diffuse interests compete with more narrow groups for legislative favor; that legislators are not motivated solely by electoral considerations and therefore do not seek only to satisfy interest groups' regulatory preferences; and that legislators cannot control regulatory agencies and agencies do not for independent reasons advance the regulatory preferences of special interest groups. Because interest groups represent more than their own members' interests, and legislators have mixed motivations, and legislative control over agencies is finite, and agencies do not inevitably provide whatever regulatory benefits special interests demand, one can credibly question whether the theory of regulation dominant today much advances the understanding of regulation. The public choice theory's familiar and influential conclusions notwithstanding, it could well be that regulation often promotes public interests, even if it also sometimes promotes special interests too. All things considered, then, the regulatory state's merits might well outweigh its demerits.

This conclusion sounds rather sanguine, no doubt. As will be seen, however, the argument is not that the administrative state regulates in a happy manner that always ensures due consideration of broad-based interests, much less that self-serving interest groups are uninfluential participants in regulatory decisionmaking. The point is more subtle and modest: The public choice theory's parsimoniousness masks several complications that attenuate the theory. Once those complications are revealed, the theory's usefulness ultimately turns on a number of empirical questions about which the theory itself provides scarce guidance. Once groups advocating broad-based interests enter the picture in competition with special interest groups, for example, one must consider whether and how often they succeed in their regulatory goals. Similarly, once legislative motivation encompasses not only reelection goals but also ideology, new questions arise concerning the trade-offs legislators are willing to make between electoral success and fidelity to principle. Finally and most importantly for present purposes, once legislative influence over administrative decisionmakers is understood to depend on issues such as administrators' own motivations, the extent to which administrative decisionmaking processes discipline rather than liberate administrators, and whether presidential control and judicial review reinforce rather than undermine legislative control, the public choice theory's power is properly seen as resting on doubtful premises about such matters. In the end, the theory might nevertheless explain or predict regulatory outcomes successfully, but only if its dubious premises hold.

And even setting aside its theoretical weaknesses, the public choice account's deregulatory policy reforms do not follow from its own framework. They come, rather, as a non sequitur: Regulatory decisionmaking fails because it does not look enough like market decisionmaking, and therefore greater reliance on the unregulated market would improve social welfare. This policy prescription raises the question, however, whether changes in regulatory decisionmaking procedures might lead to more desirable regulatory outcomes. Some public choice theorists assert that changes in regulatory decisionmaking are not possible, but have not fully explained why that is so. Yet some of the specific problems with regulatory decisionmaking that the theory highlights seem surmountable, at least in principle. If legislators really must satisfy interest-group demands for desirable regulation in order to remain in office, reforms in the area of campaign finance, for just one example, might go far to alleviate the problems that lead public choice theorists to call for deregulation. Without providing at least some rationale for setting aside alternative responses to the problems the public choice theory emphasizes, the theory has not gone very far to make its case, unless, perhaps, the empirical evidence the public choice theory marshals on it behalf proves overwhelming notwithstanding the theory's conceptual difficulties, a possibility to be considered in part 4.

The point here can be put another way. If there are conceptual cracks in the theory such that it is unclear whether administrative decisionmaking will inevitably advance the regulatory preferences of rent-seeking interest groups, then the theory's deregulatory policy prescriptions do not follow. In this case, the regulatory world becomes more complicated, and policymakers now confront the messy task of determining when regulatory decisionmaking may yield more desirable regulatory policies and when it may not, and trying to promote more occasions for the former over the latter. If, on the other hand, the public choice theory *is* powerfully predictive, then its reform proposals do follow, given its conclusion that interest group rent-seeking is inevitable. In this light, from the standpoint of would-be deregulators, a strong version of the public choice theory must hold. If, as just argued, the theory is highly questionable, then all deregulatory reform bets are off.

Chapter Four

Alternative Visions of Regulatory Government

COUNTERPUNCHING IS EASY. Providing a robust alternative to the public choice theory is not. Indeed, even the most thoughtful critics of the public choice theory have offered no viable theory comparable in sophistication or scope. To date, there is no thoroughgoing alternative theoretical framework for understanding, much less predicting, regulatory outcomes.

INCOMPLETE ALTERNATIVES TO THE PUBLIC CHOICE THEORY

The Neopluralist Challenge

One interesting challenge is posed by Gary Becker, who aims to vindicate the pluralist theory which the public choice account explicitly seeks to replace.[1] Like advocates of the public choice theory, Becker assumes that organized interest groups compete with one another to obtain favorable regulation. In his model, however, a given group will calculate how many resources it should spend in pursuit of that good, given the value of the political good to its members and the countervailing efforts of other groups. Furthermore, regulatory outcomes are not all-or-nothing propositions, as often suggested in the public choice theory, but rather reflect the zero-sum equilibrium of countervailing group forces: A "winning" group will gain only up to the point where an opposing group will exert enough resistance to limit the winner's gains. The implication of Becker's model is that only the most efficient groups—that is, those that demand political benefits the most as measured by their ability to invest in them—will be able to acquire them, and only insofar as it is worth no other group's cost to resist. As William Mitchell and Michael Munger summarize:

> Becker has offered an imaginative approach that challenges previous work and apparently heralds a return to the views of Bentley, Truman, and Latham. Becker's . . . contribution is to use tools eschewed by conventional interest group theorists in political science to turn the discipline back toward reconsidering what orthodox pluralists have been saying all along.[2]

Because groups will make investments to influence regulatory decisionmakers whenever the return on those investments would justify their costs, outcomes will reflect all groups' demands for favorable treatment.[3] Efficient policies—those demanded most—will thus tend to win out over inefficient ones.

While few share Becker's optimistic view of interest-group competition or his conception of outcome efficiency, many join him in resisting the public choice theory's conclusions about regulatory government. In fact, many legal scholars seem to subscribe at least in part to this neopluralist alternative. In partial contrast to Becker, however, these legal scholars are ambivalent towards the consequences of interest-group behavior, on the grounds that interest-group competition can and often does produce undesirable results. But in stark contrast to the public choice theory, the neopluralists are unprepared to conclude that regulatory government inevitably leads to the domination of the undetecting many by the organized few. Their main descriptive claim holds instead that interest-group competition is *sufficiently* pluralistic, especially given the presence of many public interest groups apparently representing broad interests, to undermine the public choice theory's claims and predictions. On this view, regulatory decisionmaking is more varied than the public choice theory would suggest. While some interest groups may very well enjoy excessive influence, regulatory outcomes are not invariably undesirable.

Sensitive to the threat of regulatory rent-seeking, but unwilling to endorse public choice theory's deregulatory program, these scholars further argue that well-aimed reforms of regulatory decisionmaking processes could successfully curb excessive interest-group influence. Some call, for example, for new methods of statutory interpretation that seek to protect underrepresented interests or that force explicit deliberation and disclosure of statutory goals by legislatures, thereby making rent seeking more difficult.[4] Others call for more standing rights to interest groups representing underrepresented interests in court.[5] Such proposals aim to level the interest-group playing field, giving regulatory pluralism a better chance.

But while neopluralism resists the public choice claim that interest group influence on regulatory decisionmakers works to benefit the organized few at the expense of the undetecting many, it provides little justification for that resistance. It does not explain, for example, how interest groups, particularly those seemingly representing general interests—consumer groups, environmental groups, and the like—emerge. Whereas the public choice theory's treatment of the collective-action problem is problematic, the neopluralist challenge provides no treatment at all. It neither squarely confronts the problem of collective action, nor explains how interest groups overcome that problem, nor explains why it is unimportant.

This omission is significant given the neopluralist premise that interest group competition is more pluralistic than the public choice theory acknowledges. Jack Beermann, for one example, expresses a view characteristic of legal scholars who resist the public choice theory's message:

> In our own political system, we see the average person's interests represented through organizations such as consumer advocacy groups, although public choice would argue that only a narrow band of consumer interests are likely to be represented. Still casual observation indicates that there is relatively widespread participation in interest groups representing the interests of great numbers of people.[6]

Edward Rubin, for another example, puts the point more directly:

> Using free-rider effects to explain interest groups behavior presents both empirical and theoretical difficulties. Empirically, the last two decades have seen the rise of several major public interest lobbies that have effortlessly borne innumerable free riders with them in their rise to power. Indeed, many of these lobbies invoke the presence of free riders as a raison d'etre, as a call to participation from their fare-paying members. The consumer movement champions the rights of the impoverished, the uninformed, and the disaffected; the environmental movement declares itself the protector of future generations; and the anti-abortion movement defends the rights of the unborn. The success of such "public interest" groups and their free-riding constituencies defies the predictions of public choice's interest-group theory.[7]

Others make similar claims.[8]

But this argument concludes that the problem of collective action must not be very important only by assuming it away. This is true because the claim that the existence of general-interest interest groups defies the public choice theory's predictions must assume that those who purport to represent broad interests indeed do so fairly well: Consumer and environmental groups undermine the public choice theory's predictions only if they constitute examples of successfully organized and efficacious diffuse interests. The question becomes, then, whether consumers and environmentalists have mobilized into organized groups to advance their collective interests. The next question becomes whether such groups can overcome principal-agent slack sufficiently to ensure that group leaders truly advance the regulatory preferences of their memberships. If those groups purporting to represent ordinary consumers' and voters' interests in fact do not—if for example their activities advance only the narrow interests of a few politically entrepreneurial activists—then again such groups' existence proves little.

Moreover, assuming that public interest group leaders pursue regulatory policy goals that really advance the interests of whose whom they purport to represent, still the mere existence of such groups does not undermine the public choice theory or the logic of collective action on which it rests. For that logic purports to show that on the whole small groups fare better than large groups. Public choice theory need not deny the possibility that, in certain circumstances, large groups may emerge. In particular, where the benefits of collective action are very large—as they may be in certain regulatory contexts—they might justify participation even by large numbers.

In addition, the view that the existence of groups representing seemingly broad interests undermines the public choice theory may overlook the theory's bigger picture. A few small public interest groups in a regulatory regime overpopulated by rent seekers does not allay worries about the systematic effects of interest-group influence on regulatory outcomes. Any neopluralist confidence in interest-group competition is well placed only insofar as broad-based interest groups' influence is significant relative to other groups'.[9] Thus, those who point to public interest groups to call into question public choice theory must further show that those groups have some meaningful influence in regulatory decisionmaking, relative to competing interests.

In the meantime, it is not yet clear why one should share the neopluralists' commitment to regulation at all. That is, the neopluralist account provides little reason for believing that the public choice theory's deregulatory reforms are misguided. And while that account comes with its own reforms that would help correct for interest-group imbalances, it provides little reason to be confident that those reforms would sufficiently compensate for uneven interest-group influence.

Nor does available empirical evidence provide strong support for the neopluralist view. Just for example, William Browne's study of interest-group competition following the consumer and environmental movements finds that an increase in the number of interest groups does not automatically translate to greater interest-group *competition*.[10] Distinguishing between interest-group activity in "general policy domains" from interest-group activity on "particular policy issues," Browne finds that while more groups are active in recent years in certain policy domains, there is little interest-group competition on specific policy issues within them. Instead, individual groups tend to create and occupy narrow policy-issue niches in which they face no competition from other groups. By developing policy niches, individual groups enjoy dominance on the specific issues in which they have developed expertise. To be sure, groups may initially compete over the occupation of a policy niche, which provides some support for the neopluralist vision, but the point remains that an increase in the number of interest groups active in the regulatory arena does not translate neatly into more interest-group competition.

Thus, the neopluralist challenge appears neither stronger nor more developed than the public choice theory it rejects. While it correctly points out that the presence of broad-based interest groups gives one pause about some of the public choice theory's expectations, the account has little to say about how groups purportedly representing ordinary citizens emerge, whether they are truly representative, and especially whether interest group competition is pluralistic enough to contain rent-seeking by special interest groups. If the neopluralist commitment to regulation is well placed, it is so for reasons that have yet to be supplied.

The Public Interest Challenge

The public interest account of regulation provides another challenge to the public choice theory. Whereas the public choice theory contemplates that legislators seek above all else to secure their own positions, the public interest view instead postulates that legislators also have other-regarding goals. That is, at times they seek to advance the general interests of the citizenry at large—the public interest[11]—not their own selfish, electoral interests. Sometimes, legislators and the citizenry agree on what furthers general interests. Other times, legislators believe that they, but not the citizenry, truly understand what furthers general interests. In such a case, their other-regarding goals can lead them to act in a "Burkean" manner— doing what is "best" for the misguided citizenry rather than what the citizenry might prefer.[12] Either way, legislators are motivated at times to advance general interests.

Principal-agent slack figures importantly in the public interest account. Much like the public choice theory, it contemplates that legislators can exploit slack to pursue their own self-interested goals. Where slack is high, they will not be rewarded by the citizenry for pursuing general-interest policies that the citizenry would favor. And, worse, they stand to lose political support by favoring such policies where special interests oppose them.

Slack thus makes possible regulatory favoritism: The citizenry's obstacles to monitoring afford opportunities for legislators to pursue narrow-interested policies to the detriment of the citizenry's general interests.[13]

But the public interest theory contemplates further that legislators have a choice. They can exploit slack by favoring special interests, in return for which special interests provide political support. This possibility resonates strongly with the public choice theory, and indeed public-interest theorists acknowledge that special-interest regulation may be a familiar regulatory outcome. Alternatively, however, legislators can behave in a Burkean fashion and pursue what they deem to be in the citizenry's interest notwithstanding the political costs imposed by special interests that such a strategy entails. The citizenry may well not agree with the regulators' vision of desirable regulatory policy, but where slack is high any such disagreement does not matter. What does matter is that the legislator acting as a Burkean forgoes the political support that championing special interests would have brought, and potentially suffers the costs of opposition by implicated special interests (who might try to bring to the citizenry's attention Burkean decisions that the citizenry would not support). A legislator might pursue general interests nevertheless, though for other-regarding reasons.

Where slack is low, on the other hand, legislators have every incentive to pursue general interests, according to the public interest theory. Legislators may do so out of benevolence, because for other-regarding reasons they want to effectuate those regulatory policies the citizenry wants. Or they may do it for selfish reasons, simply to reap the political benefits that public support brings with it. Either way, legislators will support general-interest regulation when under the public's eye. In fact, one benefit of supporting general-interest regulation today is that doing so may increase a legislator's future opportunities for supporting politically beneficial special-interest regulation. As Michael Levine and Jennifer Forrence (the public interest account's most sophisticated spokespersons) explain:

> If a regulator . . . can invest time, effort, and resources in being on the general-interest side of issues that become very "hot," she can generate more general support. . . . Such efforts can have dual benefits: not only can they . . . engender widespread political support for general-interest positions, but they can also be used by regulators to signal trustworthiness on those issues for which it will continue to be too costly for the general polity to monitor the regulator. . . . In

so doing, she will hope both to get support on the issue in question and to reinforce the notion that her unobserved behavior is equally in step with the preferences of the polity.[14]

As a result, some regulatory issues, in particular those of which the citizenry is especially cognizant, are resolved in a way that advances general interests.

Thus the bite of the public interest view, which holds that Burkean and especially general-interest regulation sometimes best describes regulatory outcomes. The public interest theory further predicts that "if there are regulatory issues that are on the public agenda, outcomes on those issues will *more frequently than not be characterized as general interest*"[15]—the theory's "most important prediction"[16] and one that most distinguishes it from the public choice account. Moreover, the theory is testable—whether its predictions concerning slack and general-interest regulatory policies conform to empirical reality is susceptible to measurement—though public-interest theorists themselves have not gone very far to test those predictions. The theory identifies several slack-reducing forces—incumbent self-publicity, political rivalry, general-interest groups, public-policy scholars, and the news media—and predicts that when these forces reduce principal-agent slack by putting regulatory issues on the public agenda, general-interest regulatory policies will usually result.[17]

The empirical evidence enlisted in support of the theory is rather modest, however. Proponents of the public interest view mention deregulation of the airlines as the main example lending empirical support to their theory.[18] In 1978, Congress passed the Airline Deregulation Act,[19] which required the termination of regulation of market entry and rates by 1983, and the dissolution of the Civil Aeronautics Board (CAB) by 1985. It did so furthermore at the initiation of the CAB itself, with the support both of CAB administrators—including two CAB chairs, John Robson and Alfred Kahn—and of much of the commission's staff.[20] Such events are difficult to explain according to the public choice theory, which is exactly what the public interest account challenges. As Levine writes:

> Imposition of airline deregulation over the opposition of the industry and the aviation bar is flatly inconsistent with the Stigler hypothesis and the capture hypothesis. It is possible to explain in terms of the lawyer-dominance hypothesis, the Peltzman hypothesis, and the Posner taxation hypothesis only if the actors and claimants preferred to play in one spectacular, but short-lived, "Gotterdammerung." . . .

Eliminating rate regulation on the upside as well as the downside is difficult to reconcile with the Peltzman modification of the Stigler theory, since it leaves the agency in no position to continue to alternate in bestowing benefits on the industry and user groups. Entry control was eliminated without any clear knowledge on anyone's part as to which firms would benefit and which would be harmed.[21]

To this, defenders of the public interest account add deregulatory initiatives in areas such as trucking, telecommunications, and securities, in further support of their view.[22] In 1976–79, the ICC deregulated the trucking industry, making entry into the interstate trucking easier and increasing the size of deregulated zones surrounding terminals and commercial areas. In the late 1970s and early 1980s, the FCC undertook deregulation of the communications equipment business and cable television. The SEC deregulated brokerage commissions during the same period. Congress passed deregulatory statutes in each of these areas, but in doing so Congress followed more than it led agency initiatives. At any rate, these examples too are taken to lend support to the public interest account of regulation on the grounds that "[n]one of these events is predicted or explained very well by [other] theories of regulation."[23]

Public-interest theorists furthermore argue that all of these initiatives were the product of a low-slack regulatory atmosphere. Hearings on airline deregulation before the Senate Subcommittee on Administrative Practice and Procedure, for example, "began a process that resulted in intense media coverage of the issue from 1976–78."[24] And by virtually all accounts, deregulation of the airlines, like deregulation in the other areas, eventually enjoyed general support; existing regulation in these areas was widely considered to have benefited either no one at all or else only the airlines themselves. General-interest outcomes generated in low-slack regulatory climates thus provide some empirical support for the public interest challenge.

But assuming that all of these initiatives were indeed undertaken in a climate of low regulatory slack—that ordinary citizens were really cognizant of these regulatory issues—the examples hardly vindicate the public interest account. This is true because the regulatory decisions identified are all instances of dismantled regulatory programs. The public interest theory thus turns out to be a theory of *de*regulation. And deregulation in the above areas was widely considered to be in the public interest precisely because regulation in those areas proved undesirable. All things considered, then, those regulatory initiatives—first regulation then deregulation—left the public back where it started, minus the resources spent initially regulating and then deregulating. The public interest theory of regulation thus suffers some embarrassment in the absence of examples of successful *affirmative* regulation.

After all, one could argue consistently with the public interest theory's claims, that regulation *never* serves general interests, though regulators themselves sometimes do make regulatory decisions that further popular general interests. This argument accepts the public choice theory's conclusions, adding one twist: Under ordinary circumstances, which for collective-action reasons are conditions of high principal-agent slack, lawmakers will confer regulatory benefits on politically supportive special interest groups. At times, however, where the news media, policy analysts, or political adversaries have made salient the adverse general consequences of those decisions, politicians will deregulate, again to advance their own survival.

According to this variation, it is much easier to raise public awareness about failed regulatory programs than it is to raise public awareness about needed but nonexistent or underdeveloped regulatory programs. Consequently, regulatory policies that advance narrow interests at the greater expense of general interests might from time to time be dismantled as a result of the efforts of the slack-reducing forces that public-interest theorists identify—news media, watchdog interest groups, "Golden Fleece Awards," and so on—but the public is seldom mobilized on behalf of affirmative efforts to regulate. And if it is, the publicity necessary to ensure that established regulatory programs are not captured by special interests is unlikely (for reasons the public interest theory itself identifies) to last very long. In this light, occasional deregulatory initiatives are not inconsistent with the public choice prediction that regulation benefits special interests at the greater expense of general interests. The public interest account therefore does not go very far to displace the public choice theory, its intended target.

The Civic Republican Challenge

The neopluralist and public interest accounts resist public choice theory's wholesale indictment of the regulatory state by making what are ultimately modest modifications within the same conceptual terrain: The former emphasizes the plausibility of interest-group competition, while the latter attributes to legislators occasional public-interested goals. The "civic republican" challenge, in contrast, begins from altogether different

61

footings, offering a fundamentally different vision of the regulatory state according to which regulatory outcomes are best understood as the product of collective deliberation about regulatory goals and values.[25] On this account, regulatory outcomes are not reducible to the underlying private interests and preferences of those who participate in regulatory decisionmaking processes.

For starters, the civic republican view rejects the public-choice, neopluralist, and public-interest premise that regulatory decisionmaking involves simply preference aggregation. It holds instead that regulatory decisionmaking can, should, and to some extent does involve the identification of shared regulatory values—of what those with a stake in a given regulatory decision eventually come to prefer.[26] Accordingly, collective judgments about regulatory priorities and policies are identified following a process of dialogue and deliberation among interested parties, during the course of which those parties settle upon a decision roughly constituting a consensus about the appropriate course of regulatory action, given all concerns.

Although the civic republican account offers a description of regulation challenging that of public choice theory and its competitors,[27] the account is vague with respect to exactly who participates in regulatory decisionmaking and what their behavioral motivations are. Concerning the former, the idea seems to be that, in addition to government decisionmakers, many parties whose interests are implicated by a given regulatory issue participate in that issue's resolution. A little more specifically, parties with partly formed commitments to different regulatory outcomes emerge in response to particular regulatory issues to pursue their visions of good regulatory government by participating in decisionmaking processes.

The civic republican account attributes two related behavioral characteristics to such participants in regulatory decisionmaking. First, because it contemplates that interested parties' preferences are endogenous to the regulatory decisionmaking process itself, it imagines that participants approach decisionmaking open-mindedly, without uncompromising commitments to any particular outcome. Indeed, this postulate most distinguishes the civic republican theory from its rivals: The theory holds that the preferences of those participating in regulatory decisionmaking ultimately crystallize during the decisionmaking process. Regulatory preferences are shaped by the very process of deliberation over the possibilities.

Second, the theory contemplates that decisionmaking participants exhibit public spiritedness far beyond that exhibited by the public interest account's Burkean legislator. That is, even private parties seek to advance not only their own, self-regarding interests, but the broader interests of the entire political community. Regulatory decisionmakers' goals emerge during the decisionmaking process not simply because parties only fully recognize their own private interests through deliberation, but because it is during the decisionmaking process that parties come to understand what other parties' concerns, goals, and values are, and how those concerns, goals, and values can be accommodated with their own.

For their part, regulators themselves act as mediators among private parties. They solicit the participation of many outside parties whose interests are implicated by the regulatory decision at hand, and then encourage, monitor, participate in, and interpret the results of the deliberation that takes place among them. In this way, regulators translate the collective judgments reached by those participating in the deliberative process into concrete regulatory decisions. Regulators might have their own views about the merits of regulatory alternatives, but those views, too, become part of the deliberative discussion. The civic republican account does not envision, in other words, that regulators as a group pursue interests independent of, and at the expense of, the goals of the other participants. Instead, regulators are themselves a crucial part of the deliberative process,[28] aiding the discovery of regulatory policies most compatible with collective judgments about shared regulatory commitments.

The result of regulator-sponsored deliberation is regulatory outcomes representing a compromise by participating deliberators, an equilibrium among participants. But in contrast to the interest-group equilibrium among competitors with preformed interests contemplated by other theories, the civic republican theory envisions a *deliberative* equilibrium reflecting ex post collective judgments about desirable regulatory outcomes.

While the civic republican theory is unclear, even by the low standards of its competitors, about exactly who participates in regulatory decisionmaking and about exactly what their motivations are, it is at times more specific than its rivals concerning the political-institutional environment that produces deliberative regulatory decisions. In particular, the theory holds that agency-sponsored deliberative judgments about desirable regulatory outcomes can be, and to some extent are, born of the administrative processes governing agency decisionmaking. Mark Seidenfield puts the claim most boldly, arguing that "administrative agencies' place in government [and] their internal structure . . . encourages deliberative decisionmaking aimed at furthering public rather than private values."[29] In a similar vein, Cass Sunstein and Robert Reich argue that certain aspects of administrative law and regulators' position in government encourage other-regarding deliberation about values implicated by particular regulatory decisions.[30] Sunstein furthermore identifies the Office of Management and Budget as one particular locus of a more deliberative approach to regulatory decisionmaking,[31] while Steven Kelman identifies regulatory negotiations overseen by agencies under the Negotiated Rulemaking Act and agency use of regulatory advisory bodies, as deliberation-promoting features of the regulatory decisionmaking regime.[32] These features make deliberative regulatory outcomes possible.

While sharing others' concerns with the excesses of interest-group influence, civic republicans seek neither to abandon regulatory government—as some public choice theorists do—nor simply to reshape regulators' incentives—as some public interest theorists do—but rather to dilute self-regarding interest-group influence by fostering the widespread public participation in policymaking that pluralism never delivered. As Kelman puts it: "The basic change is to promote the development of forums in both the legislative and administrative processes where representatives of different points of view can meet together in face-to-face discussions with each other on an ongoing basis."[33] Identifying White House decisionmaking and administrative rulemaking as specific fora suitable for greater reliance on consensus-oriented decisionmaking techniques, Kelman emphasizes the importance of broad participation, including the participation of "representatives of less concentrated concerns," as an antidote to concerns that deliberative policymaking may exclude some perspectives and values.[34] Similarly, Reich, along with Gerald Frug, calls for reshaping regulatory institutions in a way that promotes more widespread participation in regulatory decisionmaking, specifically greater reliance by agencies on expanded public hearings, citizen groups, and ad hoc task forces composed of government and public personnel, as well as on public input at agency regional and local offices.[35]

By seeking to expand the avenues for deliberative regulatory decisionmaking, the civic republican account aims to respond head-on to the public-choice indictment of regulatory government.[36] Unlike the pluralist and public interest accounts, however, the civic republican view seeks to do more than improve regulatory decisionmakers' incentives. Instead, proponents of the civic republican view would both increase the number of parties participating in regulatory policymaking and encourage dialogue among them.[37] By prescribing redesigned regulatory decisionmaking processes that facilitate broad participation and regulatory give-and-take, they seek to minimize the self-interested pursuit of regulatory rents by special interests.

Regrettably, however, the civic republican vision provides no account of how parties emerge to engage in regulatory deliberation. The theory simply assumes the presence of public-spirited deliberators, as if collective action were unproblematic. Nor does the theory explain why such parties emerge—explain, that is, what motivates them. It is not sufficient simply to say that participants in regulatory decisionmaking are other-regarding, for one still wonders why their other-regarding motivations manifest themselves in regulatory decisionmaking in particular. Other-regarding behavior may take many forms. Moreover, the theory does not contemplate that public-spirited participants in regulatory decisionmaking are wholly other-regarding—thoroughly selfless. Rather, it contemplates that parties consider the interests and preferences of others, as well as their own, such that their own selfish interests do not trump all other considerations. But these self- and other-regarding motivations require further specification before one can generate behavioral predictions based upon them. When is a party advocating only selfish interests, and when is that party responsive to others' interests, and how is that difference identified?

Even assuming that many relevant interests manage to emerge in response to a pending regulatory policy decision, and assuming that they consider others' and not only their own interests, the civic republican theory seems to assume further that so long as other-regarding parties occupy a chair at the regulatory table, regulatory outcomes will reflect the values, interests, and perspectives of those engaged. But there is no reason to believe that deliberation alone is sufficient to generate desirable regulatory outcomes, for even decisions that are the product of broad consensus may be undesirable on the merits given the nature of the deliberative process. For example, some parties may speak more convincingly about how their position constitutes the most sensible compromise; others may speak unconvincingly. Thus, even after-the-fact unanimity is no assurance that all relevant interests and perspectives are well reflected in a given regulatory outcome, any more than the fact that all interests are organized implies in a pluralist model that regulatory outcomes must reflect all organized interests evenly. Just as some organized groups may possess greater economic resources with which to pursue their regulatory interests, so too some deliberators may enjoy greater deliberative skills with which, even in good faith, to skew the deliberative decisionmaking outcomes.

This leads to yet another difficulty: The theory seems to allow little room for irreconcilable differences among participants in regulatory decisionmaking. What happens, in other words, when decisionmakers reach an impasse? Here again, merely positing other-regarding motivations is insufficient. Participants in regulatory decisionmaking might disagree about what constitutes desirable regulatory policy, even taking others' interests and concerns to heart. Do other-regarding decisionmakers inevitably find their way to one among alternative plausible regulatory outcomes, and if so how?

These gaps do not exhaust the conceptual weaknesses of the civic republican theory, but they suffice to show that whether the theory captures something important about regulatory decisionmaking would be difficult to know simply by looking at actual regulatory policies. Because the theory is not specific enough about what the results of regulatory deliberation look like, evidence supporting the theory and evidence calling it into question are hard to distinguish.

That leads to the question of its empirical strength. Like the public interest account, the civic republican view claims evidentiary support from regulatory phenomena that the public choice account seems incapable of explaining. For example, Kelman argues that "a self-interested account" cannot possibly explain all existing regulation:

> What about the growth of health, safety, and environmental regulation during the late 1960s and early 1970s? These programs were adopted against the wishes of well-organized producers. They were intended for the benefit of poorly organized consumers and environmentalists. (Much of the organization of environmentalists into interest groups *followed* environmental legislation, rather than preceded it.)[38]

And further, mentioning the very same regulatory policies on which proponents of the public interest theory rely:

> In the late 1970s, the greatest victories for industry deregulation were won in exactly those industries, such as trucking and airlines, where well-organized producers benefitted from regulation and the consumers who would benefit from deregulation were largely unorganized. By contrast, little occurred in areas such as environmental policy where well-organized producers supported deregulation. In other words, the pattern of deregulation was exactly the *opposite* of that predicted by the self-interested model.[39]

Rather than identify concrete examples of regulatory outcomes generated through deliberation and advancing a civic republican conception of desirable regulatory policy, the theory argues that evidence offered by a rival theory does not support that other theory, implying that there must be some other explanation.

But while some other theory besides the public choice theory indeed seems necessary to explain why concentrated interests (e.g., airlines) that opposed deregulation were deregulated while concentrated interests (e.g., polluters) that favored deregulation were not—where both outcomes advanced general interests—it is not at all clear that the civic republican theory fills that gap. It does so if and only if those policies were demonstrably the product of other-regarding deliberation. Indeed, the fact that the civic republican view draws on some of the same phenomena as does the public interest theory may be a greater problem for the civic republican view, for the theory provides no reason to conclude that those policies really were the result of other-regarding deliberation rather than the consequence of self-interested legislative decisionmaking under conditions of low slack.

Apart from identifying evidence at odds with the public choice theory, the civic republican account at times points to environmental regulation for concrete examples of deliberative, other-regarding regulatory decisionmaking. Thus, for example, Reich and (separately) Frug identify an instance when the administrator of the Environmental Protection Agency, William Ruckelshaus, decided to convene citizens of the area surrounding Tacoma, Washington, to deliberate with the agency over the "ample margin of safety" that the EPA should establish to protect citizens from inorganic arsenic produced when Tacoma's American Smelting and Refining Company (Asarco), an important employer in the area, smelted ore into copper.[40] As Reich explains, the series of public meetings provided a forum in which environmental groups, local citizens groups, and Asarco employees could deliberate in a sympathetic, other-regarding fashion over the employment-safety trade-off most appropriate for their community. The Asarco case thus illustrates, according to Reich, the possibility of enhanced "public deliberation and social learning"[41] about regulatory outcomes.

Unfortunately for the civic republican view, however, it yields little evidence of deliberative regulatory decisionmaking. First, the examples the theory identifies constitute rather weak evidence. For instance, Reich's and Frug's Asarco illustration, whatever else it shows, highlights the unwelcome response that the agency's efforts generated from citizens and from the press, who believed that the agency was unjustifiably delegating to them difficult decisions involving technical matters.[42] In one light, then, the example teaches that even when agency personnel strive to foster deliberation among those whose interests are implicated by a particular decision, they may not be able to find willing deliberators, much less lead them to a solution all will embrace. Moreover, as Reich explains, the Asarco plant closed down because of falling copper prices before any decision about the appropriate regulatory course of action concerning the plant's emissions had been made.[43] Thus, the illustration provides no evidence for believing that deliberation can produce desirable regulatory outcomes: The Asarco meetings produced no decision at all.

Second, examples of cooperation between regulated entities and public interest groups—whose participation in regulatory decisionmaking the civic republican account clearly encourages—producing undesirable regulatory outcomes in the environmental area are not difficult to find. Bruce Ackerman and William Hassler's famous study of the "unholy alliance" between environmental groups and producers of "dirty" coal provides a case in point.[44] And while studies like Ackerman and Hassler's might not be given great evidentiary weight insofar as they focus on legislative rather than agency decisionmaking, other studies of environmental decisionmaking where decisionmakers employed precisely the administrative techniques endorsed by the civic republican theory similarly call into question the plausibility of discovering shared regulatory values through public-spirited deliberation.[45]

Thus, while many might agree that other-regarding deliberation over regulatory alternatives would be desirable if only possible, the civic republican theory provides little reason to believe that its hopes for regulatory deliberation by other-regarding parties are realistic.

INTEGRATING THE ADMINISTRATIVE PROCESS

So: Neither the public choice theory nor its alternatives provide very satisfying accounts of their subject matter. Such an unsatisfying state of affairs justifies further inquiry. Something is missing.

Given that the administrative process constitutes part of any theory of regulation—because Congress effectuates little regulatory policy without relying heavily on administrative agencies to do the heavy lifting—it is puzzling why leading theories of regulation (with the very partial exception of the civic republican theory) seek to explain and predict regulatory outcomes without closer attention to the specific processes by which those outcomes are generated, or in other words why regulatory decisions are widely taken to be a function primarily of legislative incentives.[46] What follows seeks to establish the centrality of the administrative process to any theory of regulation. Because the administrative process constitutes the legal-institutional channel through which virtually all ground-level regulatory decisions are developed and implemented, fully understanding how regulation works will require far more attention than existing theories have given to the actual administrative procedures through which particular regulatory policies take shape. Moreover, focusing on the administrative process reveals that procedural reforms of the regulatory state's decisionmaking apparatus may very well go far to answer criticisms about the inevitability of regulatory failure. In particular, public choice claims that regulatory decisionmaking inevitably benefits the few at the great expense of the many seem unpersuasive following closer study of *how* agencies regulate.

To be sure, the legal rules governing agency decisionmaking and the legal-procedural environment in which agencies operate may, in the name of parsimony, be assumed away. But that economizing assumption must then be scrutinized to determine what it buys and what it sacrifices. After all, in the name of parsimony one could also develop a theory of regulation that elided legislators' incentives and focused instead only upon administrative-process rules. Though perhaps counterintuitive, it is perfectly possible that the legal rules governing agency decisionmaking affect the content of agencies' final decisions as much as the directives agencies receive from Congress do.[47] Because the very processes through which regulatory decisionmakers act affect the decisions they make, focusing only on decisionmakers' incentives, motives, and goals without consideration of how they are shaped, reinforced, and altered by the decisionmaking procedures will yield incomplete understandings of regulatory outcomes. Moreover, given that legislators do not themselves directly regulate, students of regulation who draw conclusions about regulation based on legislators' motivation are likely to miss an important part of the picture.

Granted, the administrative process is not the only thing elided from many theories of regulation. For one thing, treating Congress as a monolithic actor, as the above accounts also do, abstracts from the distinct influences the two houses of Congress have on regulatory outputs. Add to that the consequences of legislative committee structure and legislative rules of procedure. That still leaves out the preferences of legislators' constituents and the relationship between those preferences and legislators' behavior, and, in turn, the determinants of constituent preferences. Similarly, "the administrative process" can itself be disaggregated. Its dimensions include not only the legal rules according to which administrative decisions are made—administrative law—but also the informal norms that affect regulatory decisions—administrative behavior—and also the effects of agency oversight by Congress, the president, and courts, not to mention the consequences of agencies' organizational structure and culture. All of these have consequences for the substance of regulatory outcomes.

A *comprehensive* theory of regulation would thus entail several elemental theories, each incorporating only a part of the chain of causation leading up to particular regulatory decisions. Such a theory would attempt to explain how constituents' demands (theories of interest formation) influence legislators' behavior (theories of legislative behavior), which, subject to legislative organization (theories of legislative structure) and the rules governing legislative procedures (theories of legislative process), influence administrators' behavior (theories of public administration), which, subject to bureaucratic organizational structures (theories of bureaucratic organization) and the rules governing administrative decisionmaking (theories of administrative law), influence initial regulatory outcomes, which are subject to oversight by each of the three branches (theories of administrative law).

Way too much. On the other hand, the danger of omitting any determinant of regulatory outcomes may, or may not, be considerable. Consider an example. Suppose that agency personnel are typically public-spirited; whatever their quirks and imperfections, they intend by and large to develop regulations that serve broad, general interests—their own conceptions of "the public good." Suppose further that legislators typically are not public-spirited—they aim to further the narrow interests of their powerful electoral supporters, even where those interests conflict with general interests. Finally, assume that legislators cannot effectively monitor agencies to whom they have delegated substantial regulatory power and, as a result, that legislators' preferences are not reflected very well in regulatory policies. Under these plausible assumptions, any theory of regulation that elided administrative process on the assumption that regulatory outcomes can be well explained as a function of *legislators'* narrow-interested preferences would account for regulatory outputs very poorly. It just could be that the goals of agency personnel are crucial determinants of regulatory policies. Are they, or are they not? If so, what are those goals? Such questions can be assumed away, but not without possible compromise of the power of any theory that does so.

Indulge another example, which highlights agencies' decisionmaking processes. Suppose again that legislators generally seek to further the narrow interests of their powerful supporters, but now that they can monitor agency personnel effectively to ensure that agencies, no matter what the goals of their personnel may be, do largely what legislators want them to do. Suppose also, however, that agencies' decisionmaking processes provide a broad range of interested parties meaningful opportunities to examine regulatory proposals, and that parties with objections to proposed regulatory decisions can publicize those objections—to the press, the public, legislators' political adversaries, and others—making it very difficult for agencies to cater without detection to the narrow interests of powerful groups and creating a source of potential embarrassment to legislators who direct agencies to do so. Under these different but again plausible assumptions, any theory that incorporated both legislators' and administrators' motivations but elided agencies' decisionmaking processes would miss the mark. It just could be that those decisionmaking processes are crucial determinants of regulatory outcomes. Do agencies' decisionmaking processes in fact give parties representing broad interests access to regulatory proposals, or do they not? If they do, to what extent? With what consequences? Wherever agencies' decisionmaking processes affect regulatory outcomes, any theory of regulation that abstracted from those processes is vulnerable.

This is not to argue, however, that students of regulation should focus on everything that affects regulatory outcomes all at once. Any theory of regulation that incorporated every dimension of the regulatory process would be unwieldy, to say the least. Indeed, each of these several determinants of regulatory outcomes is the subject of considerable literatures. As a result, models that incorporate more than one aspect of the regulatory process must, for strong practical reasons, simplify. Moreover, while omissions run the risk of missing the most important determinants of regulatory outcomes, the yield from incorporating certain aspects of the regulatory process might be modest. It is entirely possible that regulatory outcomes are largely explicable with reference only to a particular aspect of the regulatory regime, such as legislators' motivations, as if it were determinative. Presumably, it is with just this observation in mind that most students of regulation have focused on legislative directives, highlighting legislators' electoral incentives, while a few have explored the effects of legislative process and committee structure,[48] the consequences of bureaucratic structure,[49] and the relevance of public administration.[50]

The administrative process itself, meanwhile, has yet to be fully integrated into a theory of regulation, notwithstanding that ground-level regulatory decisions are made through particular administrative procedures. Although considerable scholarly attention has been spent on regulatory government and the consequences of regulatory decisionmaking, the administrative process remains scarcely connected to prevailing accounts of regulation. The remainder of this book will undertake that project. To get from here to there, begin with the following sketch of regulation that highlights administrative procedure.

INTRODUCING THE ADMINISTRATIVE PROCESS THEORY OF REGULATION

As recounted in chapters 2 and 3, the public choice theory holds that regulatory decisionmaking provides occasions for Congress to deliver regulatory rents to narrow interests. One could argue, however, in the opposite vein. According to this contrary view, agency authority exercised through administrative procedure creates opportunities to advance general-interest regulation. From this perspective, delegation of lawmaking authority to regulatory agencies impedes rather than promotes interest-group capture. So whereas the public choice theory laments the growth of the regulatory state on the grounds that it provides expanded opportunities for regulatory rent-seeking, this "administrative process theory" of regulation sees administrative growth as a welcome shift of regulatory responsibility away from legislators and towards decisionmakers who are better situated to pursue general interests and thus advance social welfare. Given the nature of administrative decisionmaking, particularly in contrast to legislative decisionmaking, administrators motivated by commitments to public interests can do what similarly motivated legislators may find difficult to do themselves (a result that, incidentally, legislators might not mind so much).

This picture contemplates first that administrative regulators are in fact motivated to advance what they believe to be in the public interest, at least on important occasions. The administrative process theory contemplates also that administrative regulators have the ability to do so. That ability stems from the particular processes according to which agencies regulate, that is, the decisionmaking procedures prescribed by the Administrative Procedure Act and other procedural statutes which limit legislative influence on regulatory agencies. Administrative regulators motivated to advance broad-based interests are further empowered to do so given their institutional position vis-à-vis the president and the courts. That is, administrative agencies' relationships to the executive and judicial branches further compromises Congress's ability to control agencies and therefore allows administrators to advance regulatory policies they believe are most desirable.

In addition, the administrative process theory posits that interest groups that may often dominate legislative politics and thus legislative decisionmaking do not enjoy the same degree of influence in the administrative arena. This is true because the specific ways in which agencies regulate render the political resources so valuable in the legislative sphere less valuable in the administrative sphere. At the same time, agency decisionmaking relies on types of information available to a wide range of interest groups. Furthermore, agency decisionmaking reflects administrators' assessments of the reliability of information about the costs and benefits of alternative regulatory outcomes, information generated in part through administrative decisionmaking processes. Finally, the theory concludes that, given the above, administrative regulation may very well serve broad-based interests far more often than the public choice theory and therefore conventional wisdom suggest.

Now, one can assume most anything. If this more sanguine account of the regulatory state is to have any explanatory bite—if it is more than a theoretical possibility—several conditions must really hold. To be more specific, and for purposes of vivid contrast with the public choice theory, the administrative process theory entails the following core claims:

1. First, the behavior of administrative regulators often reflects commitment to some conception of the public interest. That is, administrators are motivated by more than concerns about matters such as the impact of their decisions on their budgets or on the scope of their authority, and in particular they are often motivated by concerns for general, public-oriented interests. This premise constitutes the theory's *administrator motivation claim*.

2. Second, the legal process rules prescribing the mechanics of regulatory decisionmaking by agencies—administrative decisionmaking processes—promote agency autonomy from Congress more than they advance legislative control. In other words, administrative process rules through which agencies regulate provide agencies with opportunities to regulate in ways that may well not reflect congressional preferences. Call this the *agency autonomy claim*.

3. Relatedly, extralegislative influences on agency decisionmaking, specifically presidential oversight and judicial review, further promote agency autonomy more than they advance legislative control. In particular, executive oversight and judicial review enhance agency autonomy

from legislators and interest groups who seek regulation that favors narrow interests. This step constitutes the theory's *institutional environment claim*.

4. Fourth, administrative decisionmaking processes to some degree level the field of interest-group competition by providing less powerful interests with the means to compete with more powerful interests. More specifically, the legal-procedural ways in which agencies regulate attenuate the advantages that more powerful interest groups enjoy over less powerful interest groups in the legislative arena. Put differently, as a result of the differences between legislative decisionmaking and administrative decisionmaking, the political resources most valuable in electoral politics are not so valuable in regulatory politics. This premise is the theory's *administrative neutrality claim*.

5. Finally, administrative decisionmaking processes also allow agencies to identify socially desirable regulatory outcomes. That is, administrative process rules generate information that reveals the costs and benefits of alternative regulatory outcomes and thereby allow agencies under the right circumstances to choose socially beneficial regulation. This step constitutes the theory's *social welfare claim*.

Each premise here matters. First, the theory requires that administrators seek to advance more than the regulatory goals of powerful interest groups. Such motivation is not enough, if administrators lack the political or legal wherewithal to advance more general interests, but it is necessary. To the extent administrators themselves seek to cater only to interest group preferences, out of expectations of favorable future employment opportunities, for example, then administrative regulation would not reflect public interest motivations, no matter how unable legislators and interest groups were to influence agencies to deliver regulatory rents. Thus the administrator motivation claim.

In addition, administrative decisionmakers must truly enjoy some substantial degree of legal and political decisionmaking autonomy as well. That is, they must occupy some legal and political terrain within which their regulatory decisions are controlling. Because legally powerless administrators can do nothing to advance general interests, no matter how motivated to do so they may be, the agency autonomy claim is necessary too. Agency autonomy means especially that legislative control over agencies is limited. Socially beneficial regulation is possible only if agencies are not controlled by legislators who force agencies to advance the narrow interests of politically powerful interest groups.

Similarly, agencies must have sufficient autonomy to exercise their legal authority with some measure of independence from other authoritative bodies as well. Hence the institutional environment claim. If agencies must answer to the executive and judicial branches of government in ways that merely enforce congressional control, then again regulation that deviates from congressional preferences would be unlikely. Because the administrative process theory views executive oversight and judicial review as institutions which enhance agency autonomy from both Congress and interest groups, it preserves the possibility of public-interested regulation.

Speaking of interest groups, the possibility of socially beneficial regulation requires more than legally autonomous agencies. In addition, agencies must have autonomy from the interests they regulate as well. For such interests seek to influence administrators not only through legislative intermediaries but directly as well. The theory's administrative neutrality claim rejects the notion that whatever imbalances characterize interest-group competition in the legislative arena reappear in the administrative setting. For example, if agencies' decisionmaking processes render administrators wholly dependent on factual information supplied from certain types of interest groups and not others, then regulatory outcomes would be skewed in favor of the interests that controlled the flow of information. Because the procedures through which agencies identify and evaluate regulatory alternatives provide opportunities for a wide variety of interests to supply administrators with facts and arguments, and similarly to question the facts and arguments provided by competing interests or generated by agencies themselves, regulatory decisionmaking procedures provide significant protection against informational capture. Put differently, the theory's administrative neutrality claim preserves the possibility of decisionmaking evenhandedness on the part of regulatory agencies notwithstanding that interest groups on one side of a particular regulatory issue may outnumber or outspend others.

That is not quite all. The administrative process theory's social welfare claim holds that agency decisionmaking processes also allow agencies to consider the social costs and benefits of alternative regulatory outcomes. That is, agencies are not merely bombarded with opposing facts from competing interest groups and forced to choose among them or compromise down the middle. Rather, agencies are equipped to assess information about regulatory ends and means, and in particular to do so with informational independence from those interests with the biggest stake in regulatory outcomes. Otherwise, even administrators who seek to promote public interests and who have the legal autonomy to do so will be unable to identify socially desirable regulatory outcomes. In short, agencies require not only autonomy and authority but also the resources to gather, evaluate, and make use of complex scientific and economic information.

The contrast between this general picture and that provided by the public choice theory could not be more clear: Whereas the public choice theory emphasizes legislative control of agencies against a backdrop of lopsided interest-group competition, the administrative process theory instead sees substantial agency autonomy from legislators. Whereas the public choice theory posits that legislators are motivated to provide regulatory benefits to narrow constituencies, the administrative process theory instead posits that administrators seek to advance their conceptions of the public interest. Whereas the public choice theory contemplates that agencies show regulatory favoritism towards rent-seeking interest groups, the administrative process theory contemplates rather that regulatory decisionmaking rules partially compensate for unequal interest-group power. And so on.

To be crystal clear, the administrative process theory does not contemplate that regulatory outcomes inevitably advance social welfare or always reflect a considered balance of competing regulatory goals and political interests. For reasons identified below, the theory also allows for regulatory favoritism and regulatory failure, in particular when the conditions for public-interested regulation do not hold. Thus some regulatory outcomes may be compatible with both the public choice theory and the administrative process theory. The key is that some are not.

Part 4 will assess the relative strengths of the two theories in light of several case studies of major regulatory initiatives. First, however, part 2 will vindicate the administrative process theory's emphasis on agencies' decisionmaking procedures, agencies' autonomy, and agencies' institutional positions relative to the other branches of government.

PART II

THE ADMINISTRATIVE REGULATORY STATE

Introduction to Part 2

So this much we know: The public choice theory contemplates that agencies advance the interests of politically powerful interest groups because such groups' organizational advantages allow them to exert influence on legislators and because legislators in turn are able to influence regulatory agencies to the extent agencies themselves are not susceptible to group biases. Proponents of the public choice theory imply without extended investigation that agency decisionmaking procedures facilitate regulatory rent-seeking. The administrative process theory, in contrast, posits that fuller consideration of the procedures through which agencies regulate provides better understanding of regulatory outcomes, and furthermore that those procedures can lead to regulatory outcomes that advance rather than undermine social welfare.

What we don't know yet is the extent to which agencies possess regulatory autonomy, as the administrative process theory contemplates, or the extent to which they are instead controlled by Congress and interest groups, as the public choice account holds. Because regulatory outcomes will depend in part on the legal process rules according to which agencies make decisions, as well as on agencies' broader decisionmaking environment, examination of regulatory decisionmaking processes and of how those processes promote agency autonomy, on the one hand, and how amenable they are to congressional and interest-group influence, on the other, is therefore necessary. This chapter and the three that follow turn to that task.

Chapter Five

Opening the Black Box: Regulatory Decisionmaking in Legal Context

The APA and Administrative Procedure

Agencies regulate. But exactly what forms does agency regulation take? Technically speaking, agencies do not produce "regulations," but rather "rules" and "orders." "Rules" are the result of agency rulemaking processes; "orders," of agency adjudication processes. Rules, orders, and the processes that generate them are defined and prescribed by the Administrative Procedure Act of 1946 (APA), codified in Title 5 of the U.S. Code. The APA thus serves as agencies' decisionmaking template, applicable wherever Congress has not otherwise provided, and supplemented at times by other procedural statutes, presidential orders, and agencies' own procedural decisions.

The APA does not itself authorize agencies to regulate. That authority comes from specific statutes creating agencies and conferring regulatory jurisdiction upon them. But with few exceptions extending mainly to nonregulatory agencies, whenever Congress delegates regulatory authority to agencies, they must carry out that authority through administrative processes outlined in the APA. Understanding whether and how agency decisionmaking likely facilitates regulatory rent-seeking or instead promotes social welfare thus requires considerable familiarity with the different species of agency decisionmaking processes prescribed by the APA and related legal authorities, with special attention to the legal-formal opportunities for participation and influence that those decisionmaking processes afford.

Substantive Rulemaking

Rulemaking constitutes the most important type of agency decisionmaking, and substantive rules are the most important type of agency rules. According to section 553 of the APA,[1] one of the act's core provisions, agencies authorized by statute to issue substantive "rules"—defined by the APA as "agency statement[s] of general or particular applicability and future effect designed to implement . . . or prescribe law or policy"[2]—without first providing a hearing on a record can do so by following three main steps. First, the agency must, through publication in the *Federal Register* (the comprehensive daily bulletin of the regulatory state published by the Office of the Federal Register as required by statute since 1935) provide notice that it is contemplating the adoption of some proposed rule together with the text of that rule or a summary of its substance. In bureaucratic parlance, this step is the agency's "NPR," notice of proposed rulemaking. In practice, this step often follows informal contacts by any party encouraging or discouraging the agency from initiating a rule, and agencies sometimes provide "advance notice of proposed rulemakings" (ANPRs) to alert potentially interested parties of a forthcoming proposed rule.

Second, the agency must then allow any interested party an opportunity to comment on the agency's proposed rule, including the opportunity to provide data relevant to the substance of the rule and to propose alternative language. Third, after receiving any such responses, and generating whatever additional information the agency deems necessary, the agency must promulgate along with its final rule, at least thirty days before the rule is to take effect, a "concise general statement" explaining why, in light of both the agency's own information and the comments it received, the rule took the final form it did. The agency publishes the final rule in the *Federal Register* near the time the rule becomes final, and the rule is then codified in the *Code of Federal Regulations*.

Thus do agencies engage in "ordinary" or "informal" or "notice and comment" or "section 553" rulemaking. While these three steps outline the substantive rulemaking process, that process often takes several successive rounds of notice and comment, and sometimes dozens or even hundreds. First, agencies often provide more than one opportunity for comment on a proposed rule. The APA prescribes minimum requirements; agencies at their discretion may provide more. In addition, where an agency's factual basis for a proposed rule has changed in the time since the rule was first proposed, the agency must provide additional opportunity to comment on its new reasoning for its proposed rule. In any event, the rulemaking process can be time consuming, and can involve participation of many parties.

While notice and comment are the core ingredients of the rulemaking process, in certain circumstances agencies can skip or postpone the notice and comment stages of substantive rulemaking. First, section 553 allows agencies for "good cause" to forgo notice and comment temporarily when the public health requires more immediate action. In such a case, the agency issues an "interim final" rule, binding immediately but then subject to notice and comment within thirty days of its issuance. Agencies may also issue "interim rules" before conducting notice and comment. Interim rules are issued as placeholders when an agency's rule has been invalidated judicially but where the reviewing court has allowed the agency to cure its rule's defects. Interim rules remain in place only so long as it takes the agency to undertake notice and comment for a revised rule consistent with the judicial decision invalidating the original rule. Finally, agencies sometimes issue "direct-final" rules, which are rules of a narrow and technical nature, often revising or correcting an earlier rule, in response to which they agency anticipates no objection and therefore expects notice and comment to be pointless. Direct-final rules become binding unless any party objects to the agency skipping the notice-and-comment process. Interim-final rules, interim rules, and direct-final rules thus constitute procedural exceptions to the ordinary notice-and-comment process.

Ordinary rulemaking is distinguished first from "formal" rulemaking. The words "hearing" and "record" (more precisely, their legal equivalents[3]) in a statute empowering an agency to make rules trigger the formal rulemaking process, governed by sections 556 and 557 of the APA.[4] That is, in the *formal* rulemaking mode—which is required only for limited categories of agency decisions such as utility rate setting and decisions dealing with food additives, for example—an agency must conduct a hearing during which parties provide testimony, and present evidence taken on a record, and may cross-examine adverse witnesses.[5] Where the rulemaking agency determines that no party will be prejudiced, formal rulemaking can be conducted instead through the mail.[6] In that event, formal rulemaking partially resembles informal rulemaking. Even here, however, submitted evidence is recorded, and all of the other requirements of formal rulemaking still apply.

Important aspects of agencies' rulemaking processes do not always appear on the face of the APA. First, some of the specific requirements of rulemaking have been articulated by federal courts upon interpreting the act's core provisions. For example, courts have held that a rulemaking agency's "notice" under section 553 must give potentially interested parties a fair opportunity to respond with comments by explaining the general factual or other bases on which the agency's proposed rule rests.[7] Agencies must explain not only what they intend to do but why. Courts have also held that 553's requirement of a "concise general statement" explaining a rule's final form cannot be so concise or general that courts cannot effectively review an agency's final rule; agencies can withhold their rulemaking rationale neither from interested parties nor from courts.[8] In similar other ways has the rulemaking process been specified through judicial interpretation of the APA.

No less importantly, the other two branches of government have supplemented agencies' rulemaking obligations under the APA by legislation and executive order. Sometimes these supplemental requirements are directed to particular agencies, as in the case of the Toxic Substances Control Act,[9] which requires the EPA to develop rules governing the testing of substances based on considerations of costs and a range of specified health risks. Other statutes supplementing the APA's rulemaking requirements apply to all agencies, such as the National Environmental Policy Act (NEPA),[10] the Paperwork Reduction Act,[11] and the Regulatory Flexibility Act.[12] These acts require rulemakers to assess the environmental impact of certain rules, develop information on the paperwork burden that will accompany rules, and reduce the burden of rules on small entities, respectively. In addition to such legislation, presidential executive orders also have supplemented agencies' rulemaking obligations, most importantly by requiring agencies to conduct cost-benefit analyses of their "major" rules and to obtain White House approval for such rules. These executive-branch requirements must also be taken into account in any effort to understand how agencies make rules.

While notice-and-comment and formal rulemaking are the two main rulemaking processes outlined in the original APA, other types of rulemaking warrant explanation too, in the interest of understanding the full range of agency decisionmaking processes. For example, the Negotiated Rulemaking Act of 1990 (NRA),[13] codified as part of the APA, creates another subspecies of rulemaking by authorizing agencies to organize and conduct negotiations among parties interested in the formulation of a particular rule—a "negotiated rulemaking." The NRA essentially codified and routinized a practice agencies had sometimes previously employed seeking to form a consensus among interested parties prior to commencing notice-and-comment rulemaking. Negotiated rulemaking was encouraged by the Clinton administration, as exemplified for instance by the president's memorandum of March 4, 1995, addressed to agency heads formally instructing all agencies to "convene groups consisting of front line regulators and the people affected by their regulations" for "conversation [that] should take place around the country—at our cleanup sites, our factories, our ports."[14]

In a negotiated rulemaking, an agency convenes a committee composed of representatives of parties whose interests are implicated by the rule the agency is considering developing. Then, the assembled committee members, along with the agency and with the help of a facilitator, negotiate in an attempt to devise a proposed rule that all find acceptable. Ordinary notice-and-comment processes begin after the participants in the negotiated rulemaking have come to a consensus about the form the proposed rule should take (or once it is clear they will not reach a consensus). But, at least according to negotiated rulemaking's proponents, who seek to bring the virtues of alternative dispute resolution to administrative decisionmaking, ordinary notice-and-comment proceeds more quickly and with less conflict on the heels of a successful negotiation.[15] Because interested parties have helped to draft the rule in the first place, notice and comment will then proceed smoothly. In any case, the NRA officially authorizes negotiated rulemaking and imposes certain transparency requirements on agencies that elect to use the process, though agencies conduct negotiated rulemakings at their discretion, and empirically this celebrated process has not been used with great frequency.

"Hybrid rulemaking" constitutes yet a fourth species of rulemaking—"hybrid" because this mode is more formal than ordinary rulemaking but less so than formal rulemaking. Like negotiated rulemaking, hybrid rulemaking takes place in part outside of, though consistent with, section 553 of the APA. Unlike negotiated rulemaking, however, hybrid rulemaking statutes apply selectively to particular agencies; Congress has prescribed hybrid rulemaking for certain agencies for developing certain kinds of rules. Typically, hybrid rulemaking requires those agencies to conduct public hearings in the course of developing a rule, though hybrid hearings are not subject to the other procedural stringencies of formal rulemaking.

Ordinary rulemaking, formal rulemaking, negotiated rulemaking, and hybrid rulemaking thus each refer to rules corresponding to a specific process prescribed by the APA or, in the case of hybrid rulemaking, by other congressional act. All of these processes lead to the generation of a substantive rule prescribing, permitting, or proscribing certain conduct on the part of private individuals and firms. For most agencies, notice-and-comment rulemaking constitutes the most common form of regulatory decisionmaking; negotiated rulemaking, formal rulemaking, and hybrid rulemaking are far less common. The notice-and-comment rulemaking process has been variously celebrated as an indispensable tool of modern government, and criticized as ossified and unwieldy.[16] However viewed, it is a central feature of regulatory decisionmaking. Important examples will be studied in some detail in chapter 9.

Formal Adjudication

Orders, the product of agency adjudication processes, constitute the other main genus of agency decisionmaking processes. Whereas rulemaking resembles decisionmaking by a legislative committee, formal adjudication resembles decisionmaking by a court. The formal adjudication process is conducted according to APA sections 554, 556, and 557,[17] which require among other things a separation of powers between an agency's executive-prosecutorial arm and its judicial arm.[18] That is, in stark contrast to the informal rulemaking process, the formal adjudication process requires the agency to wear two very different hats, for the agency is at once a quasi-judicial, neutral decisionmaker and one of the parties to the "case."

The formal agency adjudication process is overseen by administrative law judges (ALJs), quasi-judicial civil servants who serve as an agency's semi-independent judiciary. ALJs preside over adjudicatory hearings and accept testimony and other evidence into a formal record and make decisions or recommend decisions following the adjudication process. Parties to an adjudication, including the agency itself, are usually represented by counsel, who treat the presiding ALJ with deference. As in other quasi-judicial settings, testimony is subject to cross-examination and rebuttal. In stark contrast to rulemaking, ex parte communications with the agency, as represented by the ALJ, are not permitted. The formal adjudication processes culminates with a decision—an order—by the ALJ. If a party (including the agency itself) is unsatisfied with the ALJ's decision, that party may appeal the order. Different agencies have different appellate processes, but commonly several layers of administrative appeal are possible, typically beginning with an appeal to an agency's review board, perhaps composed of a panel of ALJs. For executive-branch agencies, appeals may go all the way up to the agency's high "court," the relevant cabinet secretary. Thereafter, parties might seek judicial review by a federal court, as prescribed by the agency's organic statute, the APA, or Title 28 of the U.S. Code.

Adjudication's resemblance to familiar judicial proceedings does not mean that the agency's ultimate decision does not have broad policy ramifications, however. To the contrary, orders sometimes have far-reaching, prospective effects on entire industries or sectors of the economy. Although technically orders are addressed to the participants in the adjudication, they often apply prospectively to similarly situated parties not part of the immediate adjudication process. Formal orders have precedential significance, in other words. Formal adjudication is also binding on the agency that employs the process, in that an agency's orders in similar future cases cannot without explanation contradict previous orders. In other words, adjudicatory decisions constitute some agencies' common law, so to speak. Agencies' formal orders are typically promulgated in bound volumes resembling legal case reporters.

Like rulemaking, then, adjudication is an important procedural tool for carrying out an agency's regulatory mission. Some agencies, such as the Federal Trade Commission and the National Labor Relations Board, rely on formal adjudication heavily. Even some agencies that regulate primarily through rulemaking, such as the Environmental Protection Agency, also conduct adjudications for certain types of decisions, such as mining claims.

The formal adjudication process is triggered whenever Congress has by statute authorized an agency to make regulatory decisions that do not meet the APA's definition of a "rule"—the APA defines "order" as any decision that is not a "rule"—*and* where Congress has required the agency's issuance of an order to follow a "hearing" that takes place on the "record." In other words, just as "hearing" and "record" trigger formal rulemaking in the rulemaking context, those words or their equivalent trigger formal adjudication wherever an agency is authorized to make decisions that are not rules. Just as agencies do not elect the formal rulemaking process, they similarly do not elect to employ the formal adjudication process but are instead required to do so by statute. In contrast to formal rulemaking, however, formal adjudication is more common. The process is commonly required, for example, when agencies award, allocate, or revoke entitlements such as permits and licenses.

Informal Agency Action

Agency decisionmaking at the opposite end of the formality spectrum from formal adjudication is called, oxymoronically, "informal adjudication," the processes according to which agencies produce "informal orders." Informal orders constitute a residual category of agency decisions: Again, the APA defines an order as any agency decision not a rule.[19] Furthermore, because the formal adjudication processes prescribed by APA sections 554, 555, and 556 are by their terms triggered only when a statute an agency is charged to administer requires adjudication to conduct a hearing on the record,[20] some orders are not made in the course of a hearing made on the record. Such decisions are informal orders, for which the APA prescribes no specific processes whatsoever.

Many important agency decisions take the form of an informal order, once famously called "the life blood of the administrative process."[21] Examples include decisions to award grants, conduct inspections, set policy goals, and spur economic development.[22] Informal orders are made by front-line administrators and cabinet-level officials alike. Because the APA prescribes no specific process for generating an informal order, an agency can employ whatever process it considers appropriate, including no process at all.

Some informal orders resemble formal orders in the sense that they are directed to a specific party concerning a particular issue. For those, agencies often provide some kind of quasi-adjudicatory process, though one that lacks the procedurally robust characteristics of formal adjudication under the APA. Other informal agency decisions do not concern a particular party and follow no kind of quasi-adjudication process at all. These orders constitute the remainder of all agency decisions and, by volume, vastly outnumber all formal agency actions—that is, actions following specific procedures. They include agency "policy statements," "directives," "guidelines," "manuals," "advisory letters," and sundry types of variously labeled decisions, none governed by APA procedures. Policy statements in particular have often been relied upon by agencies, sometimes unsuccessfully when challenged in court, to articulate and enforce substantive obligations of regulated parties. Still other informal agency determinations also provide opportunities for agencies to make significant regulatory decisions. For example, a determination by the secretary of transportation that state and local officials had met federal statutory requirements to preserve public lands whenever "feasible" as a condition of their eligibility for federal highway funding, a determination at issue in one of the most well known administrative law cases, *Citizens to Preserve Overton Park v. Volpe*,[23] constitutes an informal order. Recently, agencies have increasingly issued informal decisions under the name of "guidances" instructing agency personnel concerning the implementation of regulatory decisions.

Agencies also make rules exempt from APA-prescribed processes. In particular, section 553 exempts from its notice-and-comment process all procedural, interpretive, and housekeeping rules.[24] Procedural rules are those that specify how an agency conducts its affairs, including how the agency will make other types of decisions, how parties can communicate with the agency, and so on. Interpretive rules indicate how an agency interprets a provision of a statute or regulation. Unfortunately, the APA defines neither, and courts have struggled to distinguish especially interpretive rules from substantive rules, emphasizing that interpretive rules bind the agencies issuing them but not necessarily private parties. Because agencies can issue interpretive and procedural rules without going through the notice-and-comment process, the distinction between them and substantive rules is important. In any case, from the point of view of administrative process, procedural and interpretive rules are indistinguishable from informal orders, as neither requires any APA procedure.

Last but not least, agencies regulate informally through litigation as well. More specifically, agencies enforce their regulatory decisions by litigation, that is, by bringing suit against noncomplying parties, most often through the Department of Justice. An agency's litigating posture reveals much about how a given rule or order will work in practice, and what conduct the agency intended its decision to affect. An agency's litigation posture, including especially its decisions whether to litigate in the first place, also reveals much about the agency's commitment to its prior decisions and the priorities the agency attaches to its prior decisions. For similar reasons, agencies' settlement positions reveal a great deal about the same. To be sure, public interest groups and public interest law firms play a substantial role in regulatory enforcement through litigation. Even so, agency decisions are enforced mainly through agency litigation in which the government seeks injunctions, fines, or other sanctions against noncomplying parties. In that light, litigation is an important part of any agency's regulatory decisionmaking apparatus.

AGENCY CHOICE OF PROCEDURE

Agencies possess considerable authority concerning how their decisionmaking processes are carried out. This is true for several reasons. As just explained, agencies are bound by no procedural requirements for innumerable informal agency actions. In addition, because the APA does not clearly distinguish among substantive, interpretive, and procedural rules, and because those distinctions are sometimes difficult to draw in practice, agencies enjoy considerable leeway in classifying rules as one type or another. Similarly, because the line between rules, on the one hand, and directives, statements of policies, or other such agency pronouncements is not always clear, again agencies can sometimes plausibly characterize their actions in more than one way.

More important though, wherever APA procedures plainly govern, agencies themselves specify exactly how those processes will unfold. For example, agencies determine the particular form that a substantive rulemaking will take—when comments will be due, to whom they should be directed, what issues they should address, and how many rounds of notice and comment there will be. Such determinations fall within agencies' discretionary decisionmaking powers, as contemplated explicitly by section 553 itself.[25] So even when an agency may not employ whatever decisionmaking procedure it deems appropriate, it can still fashion its decisionmaking procedures in specific ways the agency deems appropriate.[26] It is therefore well established, for instance, that a reviewing court cannot invalidate agency action on the sole grounds that, from the court's point of view, the agency did not provide proper or sufficient process—a basic principle of administrative law.[27] Given their effect on subsequent decisions, agency decisions about procedure are especially significant.

That being said, at times other statutes do require more procedure than what the APA prescribes, and several such statutes warrant mention in this connection given their broad scope and effects on agency decisionmaking. First, the National Environmental Policy Act (NEPA)[28] requires all agencies to analyze the environmental implications of major regulatory initiatives by providing an environmental impact statement of proposed action. NEPA environmental impact statements are publicly available and become part of an agency's decisionmaking record. Second, the Freedom of Information Act (FOIA)[29] requires agencies to provide requesting parties any information pertaining to agency records not falling within an exempted category of information (such as information pertaining to trade secrets and national defense). The FOIA also if less famously requires agencies to publish their rules of procedure, contact information through which the public may obtain information or make requests for agency decisions, statements of general policy, and interpretations of law adopted by an agency. (Still other statutes, including the Federal Records Act and the Presidential Records Act, require agencies to maintain all of their records.)[30] Similarly, the Open Meetings Act ("Sunshine Act")[31] requires all multimember agencies, which include most independent agencies, to hold open, publicized meetings, except in one of a number of exempted circumstances roughly similar to those of the FOIA.[32]

Finally, agencies often develop regulatory policy alternatives with the help of federal advisory committees, chartered by the General Services Administration pursuant to the Federal Advisory Committee Act (FACA).[33] Such committees are established to provide agencies with advice or recommendations concerning some particular regulatory problem or issue. They assist agencies on a wide range of regulatory issues, on topics as narrow as the health of a certain fish populations and as complex as national AIDS policy. By many accounts, federal advisory committees play a significant role in agency decisionmaking and the development of regulatory policy, particularly but not only at the earliest stages of regulatory decisionmaking.[34]

Passed to allow agencies to benefit from private expertise while guarding against undue influence by private advisors, the FACA conditions the establishment of an advisory committee on a determination that doing so would be in the public interest. The act also requires that advisory committee membership be "fairly balanced," respecting the points of view of committee members, and that the need for a committee once established be periodically reconsidered. It furthermore subjects all committee deliberations to various openness requirements: FACA committee meetings are publicized in advance and open to the public, meeting minutes are maintained, and the information on which a committee relies to base advice or recommendations to an agency must be made publicly available as well.[35] Agencies, at their option, often rely on federal advisory committees for recommendations concerning whether they should issue or revise a rule. They are infrequently required to do so, though sometimes Congress mandates the establishment of a federal advisory committee for particular regulatory issues. But whenever an agency chooses to solicit advice or recommendations from a group of parties outside of government, they must conform to the procedural requirements of the FACA.[36]

The NEPA, FOIA, Sunshine Act, and FACA are commonly perceived as narrow, technical statutes of concern mainly to legal specialists. Yet their effects are far from inconsequential. These acts constrain—but also enable—agencies in several underappreciated ways. Their combined effect also provides considerable openness of agency deliberations. Their requirements thus qualify rather than alter the conclusion that agencies enjoy significant latitude with respect to choice of administrative procedure: These good-government statutes help to ensure that, however agencies choose to proceed, agency deliberations and rationales are not inscrutable. Moreover, as illustrated later, these good-government statutes empower agencies by limiting private parties' ability to exercise undetected influence over them.

ADMINISTRATOR MOTIVATION

That leads to the next observation. Recognizing that agencies enjoy substantial discretion with respect to their choice of decisionmaking procedures and to how their decisionmaking processes are carried out, it becomes clear that regulatory outcomes depend crucially on administrators' motivations as well. For example, nothing prevents a rulemaking agency from making informal, ex parte contacts with any party at any point prior to, or for that matter following, its notice of a proposed rulemaking. Indeed, ex parte communication is extremely common in agency rulemaking, and agency communications with those affected or potentially affected by a rule usually precede rather than follow the agency's NPR. Thus, an agency motivated to advance the cause of powerful interest groups could easily do so by defining the parameters of a rulemaking or even drafting the proposed rule in a way that advantages some groups, before the rulemaking ever becomes public. Thus, much turns on administrators' motivation. Agencies might be motivated to structure their pre-notice rulemaking process in a way that favors powerful interest groups, but then again they might not. Understanding regulatory decisionmaking thus requires consideration not only of administrators' choice of procedure, but of their motives and goals as well.

But administrators' motives determine regulatory motives for reasons far beyond administrators' ability to shape procedure. Choice of procedure aside, administrators are well positioned—indeed, they are best positioned—to affect the substance of regulatory outcomes. If agency personnel are sympathetic to the interests of regulated parties and believe that more stringent regulation would be undesirable, they can regulate less stringently, less often, with less enforcement, and so on. If on the other hand, agency personnel believe that more stringent regulation would be desirable because, for example, that would advance the general welfare, they can regulate more stringently, more often, and with greater enforcement efforts. In short, individual administrators enjoy considerable latitude to pull or push regulation as they see fit, according to their own conceptions of the public interest or, if they are not motivated by public-interested concerns, according to whatever evaluative criteria they bring to a given regulatory decision. However Congress may seek to constrain agencies, delegation of regulatory authority inevitably carries with it considerable authority, discretion, and ambiguity. Each of these provides room for administrators to pursue their own regulatory objectives.

The public choice theory's vision of administrator motivations holds that administrators use their authority and discretion in order to preserve or expand their own power, which is to say their statutory authority and budgetary resources. That is, the theory holds that legislators are able to control administrative decisionmakers only because administrators respond to expectations of reward and punishment from legislators. Were administrators not responsive to legislative reward and punishment, it would matter little how well Congress could monitor agency decisionmakers; successful monitoring is a necessary but insufficient condition of legislative dominance. Just as the public choice theory identifies political preservation as legislators' paramount motivation, so too it views political preservation as administrators' paramount motivation. Political survival for administrators means avoiding not electoral defeat but budgetary weakness or regulatory irrelevance. To avoid these, administrators ultimately heed legislative demands.

But just as legislators are undoubtedly motivated by more than securing interest- group favor, however heavily that particular motivation may weigh in the mind of any given legislator in any given instance, so too agencies must be motivated by more than preserving their budgets and authority, however heavily those motivations may weigh against others. After all, administrators are not drafted into public service; they choose it. Nor are they seduced by irresistible salaries. In light of these simple observations, it seems plausible that administrators self-select into an employment pool consisting of individuals who share some ideological commitment to a given agency's mission or, more generally, who believe that regulation can ameliorate difficult social and economic problems. Put differently, those whose career paths take them to public service seem likely to be those most committed to serving the public, a conclusion that finds empirical support.[37]

Granted, some regulatory policymakers may choose to work for an agency temporarily for career reasons, to enhance their future job prospects at a law firm or lobbying firm, for example, as public choice theorists sometimes point out.[38] But by hypothesis they leave. Over time, then, those who remain with an agency and climb its ranks are those who tend to believe in its mission and who reap personal satisfaction from a sense that their public service truly serves the public. Those who spend much of their careers working for an agency probably do so out of commitment to the environment, consumer safety, or fair competition, for example. Indeed, it seems quite possible that, whatever one's original motivation for spending part of a career working for an agency, over time the agency's culture fosters a belief in the legitimacy of its regulatory mission and some confidence in its efficacy, a possibility that also finds some empirical support.[39] Those for whom such feeling does not develop will be among those most likely to leave. So, again, one might expect administrators to exhibit some genuine commitment to their agency's stated purpose.

Some administrators, in particular regulatory policymakers at the highest administrative levels, secure their jobs as a reward for their loyalty to a political party or presidential candidate. For them, a long-standing commitment to a particular agency's mission therefore cannot explain their employment. But for them, the claim that ideology is likely to be an important motivator seems especially strong. After all, those rewarded by political appointment tend to be those whose prior political loyalty demonstrates some kind of philosophical commitment to a party's or candidate's platform; political principles seem especially likely to inform their understanding of their own roles and missions. In that light, such persons seem least likely to be motivated entirely by concerns about their agency's budget or authority. Such persons also seem least likely to be motivated by considerations about past or future employment,[40] as their prospects in that latter regard are likely very bright in any event. Thus, there are reasons to believe that the regulatory decisions of high-level appointees, as well as of long-term agency professionals, are motivated in part by ideology.

All of this is to say simply that regulatory decisionmakers at the agency level—which is to say those actually making most regulatory decisions—surely make decisions in part according to ideological commitments, political principles, conceptions of the common good, and complicated combinations of the above. This is not to say that the public choice theory's legislative dominance claim is necessarily false, but rather that the claim is a strong one: If Congress ultimately controls agencies to the extent that the public choice theory requires, it must do so by swamping whatever ideological commitments motivate agency personnel in the first place. Here again, available empirical evidence on the subject suggests that budget controls—most often emphasized by the legislative dominance school—are not sufficient for the task. For example, a study of senior-level administrators investigating the effect that budget concerns and future private sector employment prospects have on agency personnel concludes that such motivators do not result in agency bias favoring business-oriented interest groups,[41] and a study of the relationship between agencies' growth and the size of agency salaries finds no positive relationship.[42]

In fact, it seems especially unlikely that many regulators would make decisions hoping to improve their future employment prospects, notwithstanding the familiar "revolving door" image, according to which administrators rotate in and out of government service and employment with regulated interests, and which reinforces the public choice theory. This powerful but empirically underexamined metaphor supports the public choice theory through its suggestion that agencies and those they regulate regularly swap personnel, helping to ensure that regulated entities enjoy favorable regulatory treatment.

But it is not clear what incentive an interest group would have to hire former administrators who made decisions favorable to that group when in public service. Because the industry would have already gotten what it wanted, hiring a formerly favorable administrator would not do the group any good. Nor would any uncommunicated "deal" between a regulator and the industry be enforceable, informally much less legally, once the administrator left public service. And the idea that an interest group would hire a former administrator who had made favorable regulatory decisions simply as a signaling device to present administrators who may be looking for a job later seems far-fetched.

More likely, the future employment prospects of administrative regulators depend entirely on the regulators' experiences with regulatory issues, not on particular decisions that were friendly to an interest group or groups. If anything, regulated interests might seek to hire those administrators who were most aggressive against them. These are the administrators whom the industry may most want to co-opt, whose minds it most wants to tap, or whose efforts it most wants to enlist. To that extent, future employment opportunities would make administrators less friendly towards groups who might hire them later, a result opposite from what the revolving door metaphor implies.

Moreover, ethical rules promulgated and enforced by the Office of Government Ethics prohibit former administrators from working on behalf of regulated industries whom they regulated while in government service. Specifically, ethical restrictions forbid former administrators, for five years after they leave government service, from representing parties whom they regulated, and furthermore require disclosure of possible conflicts of interest. These restrictions are enforced through significant professional sanctions and the possibility of criminal liability.[43]

If anything, then, government service may thus more closely resemble a lobster trap than a revolving door: Once inside the regulatory state, administrators cannot quickly and easily leave government service to pursue the narrow interests of those interests they once regulated, if they are motivated to do so at all given whatever ideological commitments that led them or kept them in government service in the first place. In this light, it is not surprising that, political appointees aside, administrators often have long tenures within government, a phenomenon that casts still further doubt on the revolving door.

In sum, it seems unlikely that regulatory outcomes can be well understood or predicted without some consideration of the goals and intentions of the administrators who convert congressional directives into regulatory particulars. While administrators inevitably must consider the jurisdictional and budgetary consequences of their decisions, and therefore cannot afford to ignore congressional preferences and cues, at the same time administrators' motivations are implausibly reducible to such considerations. Much more likely, administrators are motivated in part by their commitments to what they regard to be socially beneficial regulation. Their decisions to enter government service, and to remain there, suggest as much. Moreover, illicit bargains between regulatees seeking regulatory favors and regulators seeking desirable future employment prospects seem unlikely. Besides, legal restrictions limit the ability of former regulators to trade on their experience. For all of these reasons, then, administrators' motivations are better treated as an independent variable on which regulatory outcomes partly depend.

AGENCIES' DECISIONMAKING ENVIRONMENT

There is more. Agencies do not regulate in a legal-procedural vacuum. Rather, their decisionmaking processes are subject to the influences not only of Congress, but also of the president and the courts. That fact raises the question whether agencies' institutional position in the larger administrative state enhances or undermines their regulatory autonomy, and in particular whether the other branches of government reinforce congressional control or instead allow agencies to advance whatever regulatory goals they are otherwise motivated to pursue.

Executive Oversight

Though created, empowered, and funded by Congress, agencies answer to the president too. While agencies' institutional position relative to the president is more complicated than the formal-constitutional model of a government composed of only three branches suggests, still, agencies are in many ways accountable to the White House. This is certainly true of executive branch agencies, whose heads serve at the pleasure of the president.

In recent administrations, the president has exercised his constitutional power over the executive branch to assert increased control over agencies.[44] Several important executive orders have centralized agency decisionmaking, both by directing executive agencies to submit their major rules to the White House for review and by articulating principles to guide regulatory decisionmakers.[45] Recent vice presidents also have assumed a much greater role in regulatory policymaking and agency decisionmaking specifically, through the establishment of the Regulatory Analysis Review Group, the Task Force on Regulatory Relief, the Competitiveness Council, and the National Performance Review of the Carter, Reagan, Bush, and Clinton administrations, respectively.

Today, White House review of major agency rulemaking is conducted by the Office of Management and Budget's Office of Information and Regulatory Affairs (OIRA), whose head administrator is a presidential appointee confirmed by the Senate. OIRA staff perform reviews of agency rules to ensure they comply with cost-benefit principles established by the president in Executive Order 12866, as well as to ensure their compatibility with the administration's regulatory goals and priorities more generally. As a result of OIRA's central role in the rulemaking process, agencies are often in close contact with the White House during the development of important regulatory policy initiatives. Agency decisionmakers are not answerable to the White House only as an abstract constitutional matter, in other words, but in a concrete, day-to-day way as well—a relationship that complicates any simple model of congressional control.

And whereas the president lacks the ability to veto selective pieces of legislation, he enjoys a "line-item veto," so to speak, of agencies' regulatory initiatives. That is, the White House can support or refuse to support particular parts of an agency's proposed regulatory decision, allowing for greater micromanagement of agency decisions relative to the president's influence over the final form of legislation. Put differently, some limitations on the president's ability to influence Congress do not apply to the White House's ability to control regulatory agencies.

Not to conflate the issues here, whether presidential oversight attenuates legislative dominance, and whether such oversight promotes agency independence raise separate questions. The White House may undermine legislative control, but seek to use agencies to deliver regulatory goods to favored presidential constituencies instead of favored congressional constituencies.[46] For obvious geographical reasons, those two constituencies are not neatly overlapping. Because the president's district composes the entire country, reelection-minded administrations will have to reconcile competing interests spread out across the country, while remaining especially solicitous of interests in electorally important states. In short, the "electoral connection" between interest groups and the presidency, though in theory as potentially important as that between groups and legislators, is much longer and more twisted. Thus, arguments about the close relationship between interest groups and legislators do not easily translate.

More importantly, given a very different electoral dynamic, presidents have fewer incentives to be solicitous of the demands of narrow interest groups than does the proverbial House member, whose next, difficult election is always just around the corner. For one thing, presidents may be more responsive to, and yet have much greater capacities to shape, public opinion as compared with individual legislators.[47] Presidents can also better afford to advance general interests over the objections of powerful interest groups than can individual legislators, as issues like free trade, for one example, illustrate. Thus, presidential control over agencies is not simply interest-group control channeled through the White House.

To the extent agency decisionmakers are influenced by the president and not only by Congress, then, presidential influence may well empower agencies to advance diffuse interests, legislative pressures to the contrary notwithstanding. Indeed, a president so inclined can shield agencies from congressional and interest-group politics by throwing his political support behind an agency whose conduct has attracted legislative and interest-group critics, even while a president sympathetic to interest-group disaffection with an agency decision can initiate a change of regulatory course or at least hang the agency out to dry.

Not that executive control of agencies is unbounded. Just as congressional control of agencies is limited, so too is presidential control. Over independent agencies especially, whose highest administrators do not serve at the president's pleasure and whose multimember heads are bipartisan, presidential control is finite. But even over executive-branch agencies, the president's appointees occupy only the highest layers. In addition, like Congress, the president ultimately must delegate substantial authority to executive agencies, and the White House cannot monitor every exercise of delegated authority.

The president has considerable authority over agency organization and regulatory enforcement, no doubt. And the president's role in the budget process gives him a central place in agency agenda-setting. Even so, like Congress's, the president's powers to control agencies are considerable but blunt. As a result, the president does not have final word over most agencies' day-to-day regulatory decisions. What is more, exercising presidential control requires the expenditure of presidential political capital, which is also limited. Finally, only so many regulatory decisions can command the White House's sustained attention, and presidential control usually requires sustained attention. For all of these reasons, executive oversight of agencies does not mean White House dominance, though it does attenuate simple claims about congressional dominance given that agencies answer to another branch of government.

Judicial Review

That leaves the least dangerous branch. Unlike Congress and the White House, the judiciary performs no continuous oversight of the regulatory state. Instead, judicial review of agency decisions happens on the occasion of a lawsuit brought by some party dissatisfied with an agency's decision. In short, judicial review of agencies is ad hoc.

On the other hand, agency decisionmaking inevitably takes place in the shadow of judicial review. This is true first because, prospectively, agency personnel cannot be sure whether any given decision will result in a judicial challenge, and thus must take the possibility into consideration from the start. In fact, that understates the point: For controversial regulatory decisions presenting high stakes, agency personnel *can* be sure their decisions will lead to a challenge in court. Court challenges for important regulatory decisions are routine, and commonly the agency is sued simultaneously by those on both sides of a regulatory issue. Where much is at stake, disappointed parties almost inevitably have an incentive to litigate. For less controversial, lower-stakes decisions, an agency still cannot be sure in advance that a given decision will *not* be challenged in court.

Agency decisionmaking takes place under judicial supervision for a second reason as well. Agencies must conform their decisions to past judicial decisions. That is, agencies are in general bound by what courts have required of them in past similar cases. And where specific agency decisions have been remanded by a reviewing court, the agency is of course bound by the court's judgment concerning the particular regulatory decision. In short, judicial review imposes retrospective constraints on agencies as well. Given the frequency of judicial challenges to major agency action and the considerable case law governing agency action across every regulatory domain, agencies seldom regulate free from judicial purview. Their regulatory decisions instead reflect consideration of authoritative judicial statements about the scope and limits of agency powers.

On one level, judicial review promotes congressional control of agencies by ensuring that agency decisions are faithful to the text of legislation agencies implement. An agency that strays from the will of Congress as expressed in that legislation is likely to see its decision invalidated by a reviewing court as outside the boundaries of the agency's statutory authority. In this rough sense anyway, judicial review serves as a proxy for congressional monitoring.

But then statutory parameters are very broad. While courts periodically invalidate agency action as inconsistent with congressional will as expressed by statute, agencies more commonly lose in court, when they do, for reasons such as the inadequacy of the agency's factual record or lack of consideration of alternative regulatory outcomes. The real question, then, is whether judicial review makes it easier or harder for agencies acting within the broad parameters of their statutory authority to advance what they deem to be their proper regulatory mission, even under contrary pressures from interest groups or Congress.

There are several reasons to conclude that judicial review enables agencies to pursue the regulatory goals they deem appropriate. For one, judicial review promotes a certain political neutrality in agency decisionmaking, by requiring such things as consideration of all relevant facts, advance notice of the facts upon which an agency intends to rely, openness with respect to access to the relevant agency decisionmakers, and so on. By vindicating principles embodied in the APA and thereby helping to ensure that agency decisions to some extent reflect all implicated interests, judicial review deters illicit delivery of regulatory rents. In addition, reviewing courts subject agency decisions, unlike legislative decisions, to standards set forth in the APA that discourage agencies from rendering arbitrary, inexplicable, or unreasonable decisions.[48] Although courts show considerable deference towards the merits of agency decisions, still judicial standards of review make it difficult for agencies to ignore relevant consequences of their decisions,[49] to change course abruptly in response to political pressures where the underlying facts do not so warrant,[50] or to undervalue certain interests in order to advance others.[51] Both the "procedural" and "substantive" facets of judicial review, in other words, impede easy agency delivery of regulatory rents.

Moreover, while none of these observations alters the fact that courts will hold agencies to the requirements of their authorizing legislation, thereby securing some legislative control over agencies, it is also true that agency legislation often espouses general-interest regulatory principles. That is, it is not every day that Congress passes legislation that unambiguously grants socially undesirable benefits to favored interest groups. The political consequences of blatant favoritism can be too costly. Legislative favoritism, where present, is thus often disguised, requiring complicit agencies to implement legislation susceptible to general-interest interpretation in some other way. Because courts show considerable deference to agencies in the context of statutory interpretation too, however, again judicial review can enable agencies to vindicate broad-based interests by interpreting legislation in ways most consonant with public interests. In fact, administrative law scholars have long called on courts to insist that agencies interpret legislation in such a way, where possible, believing judicial review to be an institution particularly suitable for combating special-interest regulation.[52]

Thus does the institution of judicial review figure prominently in regulatory decisionmaking. Issues concerning congressional control, presidential oversight, interest-group influence, and participation in regulatory decisionmaking cannot be well understood without considering also the influence federal courts have on agencies. That influence has consequences both on how agencies regulate, procedurally, and on the substance of regulatory outcomes. Judicial review can be abstracted away by any theory of regulation—as can agencies' decisionmaking processes, agency administrators' motivations, and executive oversight—but at the expense of theoretical texture and explanatory yield.

Yet once these several features of regulatory government are incorporated into a fuller account of regulation, the importance of legislative control fades. Congressional influence now becomes one aspect of regulatory decisionmaking, to be understood in relation to others. Agencies themselves now are crucial and partially independent determinants of regulatory outcomes. And judicial review, like executive oversight, can at times fortify agencies against congressional and interest-group domination.

Chapter Six

Regulatory Government as Administrative Government

THE PRECEDING CHAPTER'S TOUR of administrative procedure and its sketch of the relationships between agencies and the other branches of government highlight the mechanics and institutional environment of agency decisionmaking. In contrast to reductive models of regulation according to which agencies simply do Congress's bidding and answer special interest groups' demands, a more complex picture of agency action begins to emerge. What remains to be demonstrated, however, is the sheer scope of administrative regulation. How often do agencies—as opposed to Congress—regulate, and in which of the above procedural ways, and with what regulatory significance? That agencies possess substantial regulatory power is a truism. But just how true is the truism? This chapter delivers on the claims made in chapters 2 and 3 that most of regulation is administrative regulation and that theories of regulation which abstract away the administrative process therefore leave out most of what they seek to explain.

RULEMAKING

Take rulemaking. The rulemaking process constitutes regulatory agencies' most powerful tool. But how often do they in fact employ the process? The question is easier to pose than to answer. There is no single source collecting comprehensive data on rules and rulemaking, and bodies that collect such information do not define or classify rules in the same way, making comparison and aggregation across different sources difficult. Perhaps in part for such reasons, data on agency rulemaking are surprisingly absent from most analyses of regulation.

Nevertheless, reliable generalizations about the scale of administrative rulemaking are possible: Generally speaking, administrative agencies together issue roughly 4,500 rules each year.[1] That is, over the past two decades, agencies have issued a yearly total of a certain class of "final rule documents" numbering in the middle 4,000s. This number includes independent agencies, which combined issue not quite 20 percent of all rules,[2] as well as executive branch agencies. Going back a couple more decades for the purposes of rough historical comparison, in the 1970s agencies' total yearly rules sometimes exceeded seven thousand. This comparison does not imply greater regulatory activity through rulemaking, however, as agencies through the 1970s likely issued smaller, piecemeal rules in greater numbers, whereas in more recent decades agencies often issue large, comprehensive single rules. For example, the total number of *Federal Register* pages published per year, an admittedly crude measurement of the volume of regulatory activity, has increased since the 1970s even though the yearly count of total final rules has decreased.

The calculation of over 4,000 yearly rules counts all final rule documents classified as such by the Regulatory Information Service Center (RISC), an information repository within the General Services Administration that collects information on agency rulemaking in connection with its publication of the *Federal Register*. The RISC is the best single source of data on rulemaking. It counts all agencies' "rule documents" that must, under either the Administrative Procedure Act or the Freedom of Information Act, be published in the *Federal Register*, which is how the RISC becomes aware of such documents in the first place. (To be clear, the 4,500 annual total does not include all documents published in the *Federal Register*, in which many other items besides rules are published.)

Because neither the APA nor the FOIA requires that every rule—that is, every rule satisfying the APA's definition of "rule"—be published in the *Federal Register*, however, the RISC yearly counts of total final rules documents do not quite capture all final rules. The APA exempts from its publication requirements several types of rules, including, for example, rules relating to agency management or personnel,[3] rules relating to property, loans, grants, benefits, or contracts,[4] and interpretive rules and policy statements.[5] On the other hand, the FOIA requires *Federal Register* publication of many types of final rules exempt from the APA's publication requirements. Yet the FOIA exempts from publication rules of particular rather than "general applicability,"[6] so those rules will not appear in the RISC totals.

Since 1982, the number of final rules documents counted by the RISC has changed from year to year by between 0.2 percent and 14.8 percent.[7] Since 1985, the total number has remained fairly steady, ranging from some 4,100 to some 4,800.[8] In other words, 4,500 is a decent yearly estimate of agencies' rulemaking volume over the last two decades. At the same time, looking for smaller trends, agencies issued annual rules in the high 4,000s in the middle to late 1990s, but issued rules totaling in the lower 4,000s in the years 2001–5, suggesting a slight decrease either in regulatory activity or in the use of the rulemaking process, or both, in very recent years.

The RISC data also tally agencies' yearly "proposed" as opposed to final rules. The volume of proposed rules provides another measure of rulemaking volume. Because the RISC's count of "proposed" rules excludes nonsubstantive rules that appear in the *Federal Register* only by operation of the FOIA (management and personnel rules, interpretive rules, etc.)—that is, rules that the FOIA requires to appear in the *Federal Register* show up in the RISC number for final rules but not proposed rules because the FOIA requires publication of only *final* rules—proposed rules may be a more reliable measure of more rulemaking activity. Agencies' proposed rules as counted by the RISC numbered in the low to middle 3,000s during the middle to late 1990s, and in the middle to upper 2,000s for the years 2000–2005. (Some proposed rules never see the light of final form, though most by far do.) By this indirect measure, then, agencies issue about 3,000 rules per year that are not "statements of general policy," "descriptions of [agency] organization,"and other nonsubstantive categories within FOIA's reach.[9]

Winnowing the count even further by focusing on truly substantive as opposed to nonsubstantive or less-substantive rules, the RISC distinguishes between what it calls "core" rules, on the one hand, and "routine and frequent" and "ministerial" rules, on the other. "Core" rules include "new" rules, "revision" rules, and "elimination" rules, each defined by RISC according to a rule's effect on the *Code of Federal Regulations* (CFR): New rules require a new section of the *CFR*; revision rules require a change in an existing section, and elimination rules require eliminating a section of the *CFR*. Rules the RISC classifies as "core" comprise roughly one-third of all final rules documents. In 1999, for example, core rules totaled about 1,410 out of about 4,700 final rules. In 2002, for another example, core rules made up 1,250 out of about 4,150 final rules. According to RISC, in other words, agencies issue almost 1,500 core rules in a typical year.

Among the approximately 1,500 core rules agencies issue each year, about one-fifth or one-sixth constitute "new" rules. Because this designation concerns merely how rules are codified, it is not terribly meaningful. Amendments to existing rules (RISC's "revision" rules) often have as much or more regulatory significance as new, stand-alone rules. Even so, it is noteworthy that agencies issue between 200 and 300 brand new core rules each year. Over the past decade, for example, the number of rules requiring new sections of the *Code of Federal Regulation* ranged from 180 in 2005 to 286 in 2000. Substantive rules amending (or eliminating a section of) the *CFR* instead numbered from about 1,000 to about 1,200.

Since the passage of the Congressional Review Act (CRA) in 1996,[10] the General Accounting Office (GAO), a nonpartisan legislative agency that monitors federal expenditures for Congress, also has maintained useful data about the volume of rulemaking. The GAO collects information about rulemaking in connection with keeping Congress informed of agencies' rulemaking activities, as required by the CRA.[11] According to the GAO,[12] agencies collectively issue between some 3,800 and 4,800 rules a year. The GAO's numbers are thus comparable to the RISC yearly totals, though they are lower by between a few dozen and a couple hundred for most years.

The GAO's separate count of total rules reinforces the RISC data, and vice versa, given that the total rules counts are so close between these two sources. The GAO's lower numbers partially reflect instances in which an agency does not consider one of its documents to be a rule that it must report to GAO, but where the RISC does consider the document some kind of rule. That is, unlike the RISC, the GAO depends upon agencies to report their rulemaking activities to it. Whereas the RISC simply uses data supplied to it by agencies upon publishing items in the *Federal Register*, and can thus make its own judgments about whether submitted items constitute rules, the GAO never learns about agency rules in the first place unless an agency submits a rule to it.[13] The threshold question of whether an agency undertaking constitutes a rule, and must therefore be submitted to the GAO, is thus left to the agencies, an occasional source of controversy between agencies and Congress.[14]

There is a second reason why the GAO's count of total rules is exceeded by the RISC's. Although the Congressional Review Act incorporates by explicit reference the APA's definition of "rule,"[15] it goes on to exclude from its scope "rules of particular applicability," rules "relating to agency management or personnel," and "any rule of agency organization, procedure or practice that does not affect the rights or obligation of non-agency parties."[16] Because all but the former types of these rules are published in the *Federal Register* under the FOIA, those rules are included in the RISC totals but not the GAO totals. This constitutes one advantage of the GAO data: The GAO's total numbers better estimate the number of more substantive rather than merely management, organizational, or procedural rules. For the years 2004 and 2005, for example, the GAO counted approximately three to six hundred fewer total rules than did the RISC, or approximately 3,700 and 3,400, respectively, as compared with the RISC's counts of about 4,000 for both years, suggesting that a majority of the RISC totals comprise more substantive rather than purely organizational or procedural rules. On the other hand, however, the GAO totals exceed the RISC's count of proposed rules because the CRA does not exclude from its scope every category of non- or less-substantive rule (such as "rules relating to property, loans, grants, benefits, or contracts") that is missing from RISC's tally of proposed rules.

Like the RISC, the GAO also distinguishes rules it considers to be more substantive from those it considers to be less or nonsubstantive, though the GAO employs different categories in making that distinction. Specifically, the GAO distinguishes between rules that are "economically significant," "significant," or "substantive," on the one hand, and rules that are instead "routine and frequent" or "informational" or "administrative," on the other.[17] Here again, the GAO data are comparable to the RISC data, each reinforcing the other. According to the GAO, agencies have issued from about 900 to about 1,500 significant or substantive rules per year since 1996, whereas again the RISC totals over the same period range from 1,100 to 1,800. One could average these sources to get rough yearly estimates of agencies' most substantive rules, in the ballpark of 1,300 or so rules a year.

Even among plainly substantive rules, however—whether by RISC or GAO criteria—there are rules, and then there are rules: Some substantive rules regulate in such a thoroughgoing way or across such a broad segment of society that they can be distinguished from more typical substantive rules. The GAO thus defines a "major" rule as one meeting certain criteria borrowed from executive orders requiring agencies to conduct cost-benefit analysis of their most significant rules. For example, a rule projected to have an annual impact on the economy of over $100 million constitutes a "major" rule. Under those same executive orders, in particular Executive Order 12866, agencies themselves must supply to OIRA cost-benefit analyses and other information concerning "significant" rules as also defined in the order. The RISC maintains on behalf of OIRA data concerning agencies' White House submissions under Executive Order 12866. In other words, the RISC maintains separate data summarizing the number of rules submitted for OIRA review, some of which is now available on OIRA's website as well.[18]

According to these RISC data, the White House has reviewed—in other words, agencies have submitted—between 73 and 111 "economically significant" rules, that is, rules meeting the $100 million threshold, each year for the past decade. This count is overinclusive and underinclusive, however. On the one hand, the RISC double counts proposed and final rules in its data, so that its number should roughly be cut in half to determine how many single economically significant rules the OIRA has reviewed. On the other hand, because Executive Order 12866 does not extend to independent agencies, independent agencies' major or economically significant rules are excluded from RISC's count.

The GAO counts "major" rules too, defined in terms similar to (though narrower than) those of Executive Order 12866. According to the GAO, agencies (this time including independent agencies, which are within the CRA's reach) have issued between 49 and 78 major rules per year over the past decade. In other words, out of agencies' roughly 1,300 "substantive" or "significant" rules issued each year, about 4 percent to 7 percent constitute very large scale rules with enormous economic consequences. Once again, the GAO's tabulation is consistent with the RISC's, numbering for most years somewhat more than half of the number of proposed and final economically significant rules submitted to OIRA by executive branch agencies.

Another measure of the volume of agencies' most important rules can be found by considering the number of rules executive branch agencies submit to OIRA under Executive Order 12866. That order requires agencies to submit cost-benefit analyses not only of rules that will have an annual effect on the economy of over $100 million, but also of rules that will adversely effect the economy or jobs, the environment, or public health, or will impede another agency's action, alter entitlements, or raise novel policy questions.[19] This data too is maintained by the RISC on behalf of OIRA. Since 1995, agencies have submitted for review between about 500 and 700 proposed or final rules per year meeting these criteria. In other words, each year executive branch agencies together issue several hundred rules that are substantive and significant enough to require White House scrutiny. This measure too comports with the RISC's own data as well as the GAO's data: The executive branch agencies issue a few hundred rules per year that meet Executive Order 12866's relatively restrictive criteria for significance, and thus number fewer than those counted by both the RISC's and the GAO's more expansive criteria for "significant"/"substantive" rules, but at the same time number more than those counted by the GAO's more restrictive, economic criteria for "major" rules.

Table 1 summarizes data on agencies' rulemaking activities from 1995 through 2005, providing a bird's-eye view of a recent decade of agency rulemaking.

To summarize the bean counting and emphasize the main point: Agencies issue roughly 4,500 rules per year, of which roughly 3,000 are substantive or procedural rules which must be published under the APA. Agencies issue about 1,100 to 1,500 annual rules—depending on the year and on who is counting—that are truly substantive, or "significant" or "core" rules. Executive branch agencies issue roughly 500 to 700 proposed or final rules a year that meet the high significance thresholds of Executive Order 12866 and therefore trigger closer White House oversight. And agencies, executive branch and independent agencies together, issue five or six dozen whopper rules a year each of which is estimated to have annual consequences in the hundreds of millions of dollars.

Details about which agencies issue how many rules are beyond the purpose of this discussion. Nevertheless, it warrants brief mention that among rulemaking agencies, regulatory agencies issue a lot. So while the above figures include agencies' nonregulatory rules as well—such as rules concerning benefits eligibility, for instance—regulatory rules constitute the lion's share of rules and certainly of the biggest rules. The Department of Transportation, for example, has issued the most final rules every year since 1982, and from 25 percent to 31 percent of all final rules for each year since 1996, based on the RISC's data.[20] During that same period, the Environmental Protection Agency issued the second most. The Federal Communications Commission, the Department of Health and Human Services, and the Department of the Interior come next, usually in that order, publishing from about 150 to about 350 rules per year each. This ranking references the agencies' rulemaking volume, not adjusted for the significance of their rules, however. Viewed by regulatory policy significance, the EPA issues the most significant rules most years, as will be illustrated later.

Adjudication

As chapter 5 explained, agencies adjudicate too. Unfortunately, there are no comprehensive data measuring the volume of regulatory adjudication.

One very rough measure of agency adjudication begins with the number of administrative law judges who conduct adjudications, approximately 1,350. Most ALJs adjudicate nonregulatory cases, however, allo-

Table 1
Agency Rulemaking, 1995–2005

	1995	1996	1997	1998	1999	2000	2001	2002	2003	2004	2005
Final Rules (RISC)	4,713	4,963	4,615	4,898	4,660	4,477	4,100	4,147	4,244	4,074	3,956
Proposed Rules (RISC)	3,339	3,266	3,035	3,169	3,414	2,850	2,635	2,758	2,732	2,631	2,552
Substantive Rules (RISC)	1,533	1,794	1,446	1,338	1,410	1,419	1,133	1,250	1,335	1,135	1,116
Substantive New Rules (RISC)	284	255	215	243	253	286	233	219	262	195	180
OIRA Rules (GSA and OIRA)	614–40	503–7	502–5	486–87	587	583	700	669	715	627	611
OIRA Econ Sig Rules (GSA and OIRA)	74–79	74–79	81–82	73–75	86	92–93	111	100–102	101	85	82
CRA Total Rules (GAO)	n/a	n/a	4,046	4,850	4,533	4,467	3,831	3,918	4,532	3,703	3,351
CRA Sig /Sub Rules (GAO)	n/a	n/a	1,491	1,439	991	1,084	918	1,032	1,035	1,011	941
CRA Major Rules (GAO)	n/a	n/a	60	78	49	76	72	50	54	66	56

cating benefits in Social Security, Medicare, and Black Lung cases, for example. Indeed, a majority of all ALJs, approximately 700, hear Social Security claims. Even so, twenty-eight other agencies, including many regulatory agencies, have one or more ALJs. In fact, most independent agencies rely heavily on formal adjudication. For example, the Federal Trade Commission, the Federal Energy Regulatory Commission, and the Securities and Exchange Commission, among others, each adjudicate dozens of regulatory cases each year. So do some executive branch regulatory agencies, such as the Department of Energy and the Department of the Interior.

While there are no data compiling the volume of formal adjudication across all regulatory agencies that employ the process, many such agencies maintain their own data. For example, in 2002 Department of Energy ALJs conducted 82 formal adjudications.[21] That same year, the Department of the Interior adjudicated 144 cases, while the Nuclear Regulatory Commission adjudicated 42. A reasonable estimate of formal adjudications with regulatory policy significance would number at a minimum in the several hundreds.

Apart from formal adjudication conducted under sections 554, 556, and 557 of the Administrative Procedure Act,[22] agencies also conduct "informal adjudications" in cases conducted by some kind of presiding officer but without all of the formal procedural requirements of the APA. In the most comprehensive studies of these informal adjudications, John Frye in 1992 estimated that agencies conduct approximately 343,000 such cases annually, and Raymond Limon in a 2002 update of Frye's study estimated that agencies conduct about 556,000 cases annually.[23] The Limon study, an agency survey undertaken through the Office of Administrative Law Judges within the U.S. Office of Personnel Management, estimates the number of administrative hearing officers (as opposed to ALJs proper, who conduct formal APA adjudications) to be 3,370. Whereas 1,350 ALJs conduct formal adjudications on a full-time basis, however, some hearing officers perform that task on a part-time basis.

Here again, most informal adjudications, by far, involve nonregulatory matters. Many involve law-enforcement questions or issues concerning the administration of civil penalties, including passport denials and security clearance disputes. Other informal adjudications, like formal adjudications, concern certain social welfare benefits, including veterans' benefits and certain Medicare cases, and thus do not count toward agencies' regulatory decisionmaking volume. But here too, agencies employ informal adjudication processes to conduct regulatory business as well, such as in the areas of nuclear power regulation and certain environmental regulation. In 2002, for example, the EPA conducted over 300 quasi-formal enforcement adjudications.[24] Some percentage of informal adjudications thus constitute real regulatory work, although exactly how much is not documented. Here again, though, an estimate of several hundred cases a year would be conservative.

INFORMAL AGENCY ACTION

As also explained in chapter 5, informal agency action constitutes a residual category of agency decisionmaking which, for that reason, is virtually impossible to quantify. Informal agency decisions—neither rules nor adjudications—would number in the tens if not hundreds of thousands per year. A numerical count, however, would not be very meaningful, as many—most—informal agency decisions are mundane.

Many, however, are not. Often, agencies regulate informally, issuing documents not satisfying the statutory definitions of rules or formal orders but nevertheless carrying important regulatory policy consequences. That such decisions—in recent years collectively labeled agency "guidances"—usually follow no prescribed procedures, notwithstanding the important policy consequences they sometimes carry, has long been a concern of Congress, the courts, and academic lawyers[25]—so much so that in 2000 the House Committee on Government Reform issued a report on the status and effect of agency guidance documents.[26] The House report concluded that agencies sometimes use guidance documents in order to "bypass the rulemaking process and expand[] an agency's power," describing some guidances as "backdoor regulation."[27] In an attempt to measure the volume of agency guidances, the committee asked several regulatory agencies to catalogue their guidance documents issued between March 1996 and December 1999. The House committee found, for example, that the EPA issued 2,654 guidance documents during that period, while the Occupational Safety and Health Administration had issued 3,374. An unrelated study of guidance documents issued by the Food and Drug Administration found that the FDA issued slightly more than twice as many guidance documents as rules during the period 2001–3.[28] While guidance documents typically are not legally binding on regulated parties, as the majority of the House committee explained, they are often binding as a matter of practice because they provide "safe harbors" for the behavior or performance of regulated parties.

Exactly how often agencies truly regulate through guidance documents or other informal means is an unsettled and controversial question. On the one hand, because Congress has not required agencies to conduct rulemakings or other prescribed procedures for every regulatory decision they make, some policy-relevant decisions properly take informal forms. On the other hand, as the House report expresses, agencies may sometimes regulate through guidances or other informal processes when they should instead use the rulemaking process. This worry finds further support in several important judicial decisions invalidating various guidance-type documents on the grounds that the agencies issuing them improperly bypassed the rulemaking process.[29] While it is unclear just how often agencies use guidances as a substitute for rulemaking or some other process, the answer is clearly not never.

Prompted by concerns about informal regulation, the Office of Information and Regulatory Affairs within the Office of Management and Budget in late 2005 issued a draft bulletin on "Good Guidance Practices."[30] The draft bulletin, on which OIRA solicited public comments, defines "guidance document" as any document issued not pursuant to a section 553 rulemaking or section 554 adjudication prepared to describe an agency's "interpretation of or policy on a regulatory or technical issue." The draft bulletin goes on to distinguish among different types of guidance documents and to propose that agencies solicit public comments on draft guidance documents before they are finalized and, for certain guidance documents, to seek White House approval for them as well. The most revealing feature of OIRA's proposal is that it identifies a class of guidance documents the consequences of which are expected to affect the economy by $100 million or more each year, raise highly controversial issues, or make changes in policy. In other words, OIRA's draft bulletin reflects an understanding that some agency guidance documents are not only substantive and significant, but as consequential as the most major of agency rules. Among the tens of thousands of guidance documents agencies issue, some unknown number have great regulatory significance.

REGULATORY LITIGATION

Agencies' regulatory decisions are often enforced or challenged in federal court, in cases involving an agency as a party plaintiff or defendant to a case. Most often, questions about the legal validity as well as the practical scope and force of agencies' regulatory decisions are settled by the courts.

Administrative litigation is therefore part and parcel of the regulatory process, as will be well illustrated later below in part 3. What is more, agency personnel, regulated parties, and others with a stake in agencies' regulatory decisions all understand this perfectly well, and thus the possibility—often, probability—of administrative litigation influences administrators from the very inception of regulatory initiatives. For this reason, agency litigation also constitutes part of the volume of agencies' regulatory activity generally, indicating among other things how many agency decisions are not only legally controversial but also significant enough to warrant the resources necessary to litigate.

Of the approximately 50,000 civil cases filed in U.S. district courts in which the United States is a party,[31] some unknown number involve decisions of regulatory agencies. Many agency cases do not involve regulatory decisions, however. The biggest category of such cases are Social Security cases, totaling about 15,000 cases annually. That leaves approximately 35,000 cases in which the United States is a party. Tens of thousands of those cases involve nonregulatory matters, government contract, tort, employment, or civil rights claims, for example. Cases filed in the district courts that in one way or another concern agencies' regulatory decisions almost certainly number in the thousands but certainly not tens of thousands.

The U.S. Court of Appeals also adjudicates agency cases. First, administrative cases are routinely appealed from the district courts to the Court of Appeals. In addition, several regulatory statutes provide for judicial review of agency action to commence in the appellate court. That is, parties seeking to challenge certain agency decisions file their cases directly in the Court of Appeals.

While there are no data measuring the total number of administrative law cases filed in the federal district courts, or the number of administrative law cases appealed from the district courts to the Court of Appeals, data on appellate filings from administrative agencies is maintained by the Administrative Office of the U.S. Courts. According to that data, agency appeals to the U.S. Court of Appeals typically number in the low 3,000s for most years. For example, in the years 1999, 2000, and 2001, administrative appeals filed in the Court of Appeals numbered 3,280, 3,237, and 3,300, respectively.[32] Recently, these numbers have increased dramatically due to an increase in nonregulatory appeals from the Board of Immigration Appeals (BIA), in response to a reorganization of the BIA that instituted new case review guidelines and standards for case-processing time, prompting thousands of new appellate filings. In prior years, BIA appeals constituted just over half of administrative appeals. In other words, about 1,500 non-BIA appeals are filed each year in the U.S. Court of Appeals. Of those, roughly 200 are tax cases.[33] Excluding those as well leaves about 1,000 cases from regulatory agencies, including the Department of Labor, the Federal Communications Commission, the Federal Energy Regulatory Commission, the Federal Trade Commission, and the Environmental Protection Agency, among several others.[34] Thus, up to 1,000 cases a year constitutes a responsible estimate of regulatory litigation brought directly in the appellate court. Because the U.S. district courts have general federal-question jurisdiction, whereas agency cases filed in the Court of Appeals require specific jurisdictional statutes, and given that there are about seven times as many district courts as appellate circuits, in all likelihood the number of agency cases filed in the district courts is several multiples of that. So again, agency litigation concerning regulatory issues probably totals a couple to (at most) a few thousand cases a year.

Administrative versus Legislative Regulation

But what is the measurement baseline against which administrative agencies' regulatory activities are determined to be a little or a lot? Certainly claims that agencies regulate too much are common in everyday political discourse, usually accompanied by calls for deregulation. Yet the criteria according to which such claims are made remain elusive. On the rare occasion where a comparative baseline is made explicit, it turns out to be the past: Agencies are said to regulate too much simply because they regulate more than they used to, never mind that how much they used to regulate is never established to be the socially desirable amount, or that measures of regulatory volume over time consist of dubious indicators like *Federal Register* page totals.

The volume of Congress's regulatory workload provides one interesting point of comparison. Although such a comparison has a certain apples-and-oranges quality, and sheds no light on normative questions about whether agencies regulate too much or too little, it nevertheless tests the proposition that regulation is mostly the work-product of administrative regulation. If agencies do far more regulatory work than does Congress, then the twin claims that most regulation is administrative regulation and that theories of regulation which abstract away administrative procedure thus leave out most of what they purport to explain are justified.

114

In addition, measuring agencies' regulatory workload against Congress's begins to shed light on the question whether Congress can keep up with its regulatory delegatees, that is, on the plausibility of the legislative dominance claim. Congress's task here becomes considerable, especially in light of the relative size of Congress and the regulatory agencies. First and most obviously, a single Congress is outnumbered by almost sixty agencies (including subdivisions of the executive departments) with significant regulatory authority. In fact, whereas the legislative branch of the federal government—including the Congressional Budget Office and the Government Printing Office as well as all other arms of Congress—employs just under 30,000 persons total, the executive branch, excluding the Department of Defense, and the Postal Service, employs well over 1,000,000.[35] Subtracting large, nonregulatory agencies like the Department of State, the Department of Homeland Security, and the Department of Health and Human Services, still leaves almost 1,000,000 agency employees.[36] Indeed, the number of all House and Senate employees combined—approximately 17,200—is less than the number of employees at the Environmental Protection Agency alone, approximately 17,800.[37] Abstract discussions of Congress's ability to monitor and discipline the regulatory agencies seldom confront such realities.

Perhaps not surprisingly, then, given the relative human and institutional resources of Congress and the agencies, Congress's workload is dwarfed by the regulatory workload of agencies. Whereas every year agencies issue several thousand rules, conduct several hundred policy-relevant formal adjudications, take untold numbers of informal actions with regulatory significance, and litigate a couple thousand cases to enforce or defend regulatory decisions, Congress enacts only between about one hundred and four hundred public laws each year. Granted, Congress does a lot besides legislate. Legislators introduce legislation (several thousand bills a year). They also pass resolutions (a couple hundred a year), confirm executive branch and judicial nominees (several hundred a year) as well as military nominees (tens of thousands a year), issue reports (several dozen a year), ratify treaties (a dozen or so a year), and pass private bills (a handful each year).[38] Legislators also perform unquantified volumes of constituent casework, communicate with voters and the press, and campaign for reelection. In addition, legislators on occasion join agency litigation—almost always on the side of parties challenging agency action—as will be seen below. In short, legislators keep busy.

But legislators do not spend countless hours on regulatory policymaking. Naturally, the most important form of congressional regulation consists of passing regulatory legislation including regulatory appropriations. Indeed, absent legislation, there is no regulation at all, as agencies' regulatory authority derives from congressional delegations in the first place. That simple fact does not answer, however, whether Congress plays a dominant role in regulatory decisionmaking once it has delegated regulatory authority to agencies, or how Congress's regulatory business compares with agencies' regulatory business.

Considering the volume of Congress's legislative workload over the past decade, Congress has not legislated at a breakneck pace. On average, it has enacted 218 public bills into law a year since 1995.[39] Congress has enacted not even half as many pieces of legislation over ten years as the average number of rules agencies issue in a single year. Put differently, it enacts only about one-fifth as many bills each year as the number of significant substantive rules agencies issue, and fewer than the number of rules important enough to be scrutinized by the White House, fewer than even brand-new "core" agency rules, and finally only a few times as many bills as the number of $100 million rules. All this to say nothing of the sundry other significant regulatory decisions agencies make each year besides rules.

What is more, these figures represent the total number of public laws enacted each year, no matter the subject matter of the legislation. But the subject matter of much legislation concerns such issues as national defense, trade and foreign affairs, tax, rivers and harbors, or social welfare. The above totals count budget bills as well. Only a subset of legislation constitutes "hands-on" regulatory legislation.

Finally, when Congress passes regulatory legislation, seldom does it regulate through legislation that substitutes for, much less overrides, agency decisionmaking. In other words, even where Congress itself regulates, it usually does so through legislation that increases rather than decreases agency authority. Only a small fraction of legislation displaces agency authority.

To be sure, Congress "regulates" in ways besides passing regulatory legislation. In particular, legislators monitor agencies to whom they have delegated regulatory authority. They hold oversight hearings, solicit testimony from administrative regulators, and issue reports about agency initiatives. They also pass appropriations bills that affect agencies' activities and influence their agenda. But whether these other forms of congressional regulation are enough for Congress to maintain control over agencies is an open question, and the central question at that. That Congress engages in these activities does not establish it effectively controls agencies and or enjoys dominant influence over regulatory policymaking.

On that note, the fact that Congress's regulatory work-product is dwarfed by administrative agencies' means that if Congress does have substantial influence over regulatory policymaking, it must be because its oversight mechanisms work very effectively indeed. That is, given the volume and scale of agency decisionmaking, Congress sure has a lot to keep track of. So, if Congress can really ensure that the agencies to whom it has delegated regulatory authority use that authority in ways that satisfy its members' preferences and intentions, it must be that the nonlegislative devices Congress employs to monitor and influence agencies work very well.

Chapter 8 considers that question. First, however, the next chapter considers who might participate in the processes of agency decisionmaking that generate these thousands of annual regulatory decisions.

Chapter Seven

Participation in Administrative Decisionmaking

BUT WHO'S BEHIND THE WHEEL? Having considered the specific procedures of regulatory decisionmaking and the frequencies with which those processes are used, an important question remains concerning the *subjects* of regulatory decisionmaking. In addition to agency personnel, who exactly participates in regulatory decisionmaking?

OPPORTUNITIES FOR PARTICIPATION

Examining the opportunities for participation that the regulatory decisionmaking processes afford provides clues about likely patterns of participation. For example, any party can participate in the ordinary rulemaking processes. As section 553 states: "After notice required by the section, the agency *shall give interested persons* an opportunity to participate in the rulemaking through submission of written data, views, or arguments."[1] Concerning who may respond to a notice of proposed rulemaking with comments about an agency's proposed rule, there are no restrictions or limitations. Doing so requires parties only to keep abreast of an agency's proposed rules.

Moreover, participants' comments need take no particular form. Formally at least, rulemaking is open and inclusive, and parties can participate on their own initiative and directly with the agency. In fact, any party can seek to initiate a rulemaking by petitioning an agency to issue a rule.[2] This openness is often touted by rulemaking's proponents. It is also emphasized by courts as a justification for greater judicial deference towards rules relative to decisions reached through less inclusive processes.[3]

What is more, rulemaking agencies commonly take affirmative steps to make the process accessible. For one, an agency's notice of proposed rulemaking or, better, advance notice of proposed rulemaking typically includes the name and telephone number of a contact person at the rulemaking agencies to whom questions and comments can be addressed about the proposed rule. They also provide citations to relevant studies or data on which a proposed rule is based, and interested parties can request copies of the same from the agency. In recent years, agencies have made considerable information concerning their rulemaking activities accessible on their official web pages, and have accepted comments electronically as well. And for especially important pending rules, agencies often hold hearings, regional meetings, and a variety of other public meetings. In short, agencies routinely provide more process in the course of ordinary rulemaking than what section 553 minimally requires. As a result, participation in agency rulemaking is neither formally nor as a practical matter limited only to parties with considerable economic and political resources.

How much influence any party's comments may have upon an agency's decision in any given case is a separate question, and as seen below one more difficult to answer. But undoubtedly this depends in part on the quality of the arguments and information that the party provides. Certainly agencies cannot safely ignore compelling, high-quality comments that are clearly apropos to an agency's proposal. Ignoring arguments or information bearing on an agency's rule will jeopardize that rule when challenged in court.

Participation in formal rulemaking is also open. The distinctions between formal and informal rulemaking, in other words, do not extend to who may participate in those processes. More is required of participating parties in the formal rulemaking mode, to be sure. Furthermore, participating parties are prohibited from communicating with the agency outside of the formal rulemaking procedures during the pendency of a formal rule. Such additional burdens render the process more cumbersome for agencies as well, which is why agencies have used formal rulemaking only when required to do so by statute. Even so, any party may participate in the process. And, in further contrast to informal rulemaking, those who do so are entitled to a response by the agency—to be included in the record of the formal rulemaking—to all proposed findings, conclusions, and exceptions they submit to the agency for its consideration,[4] although the agency may exclude irrelevant and repetitious evidence.[5]

As with ordinary and formal rulemaking, any party may participate in the public hearings carried out under a hybrid rulemaking statute as well. From a participant's point of view, hybrid rulemaking thus resembles informal rulemaking, though the former entails public, oral commentary rather than written commentary. In addition, agencies may limit the amount of public commentary any participant may supply, whereas there are no limits on the amount of written commentary a participant may send an agency in the ordinary rulemaking process. Beyond that, however, the obstacles to participation are practical rather than formal, as participation in a hybrid rulemaking may, as in formal rulemaking, require travel.

Because the Negotiated Rulemaking Act incorporates the Federal Advisory Committee Act, participation in a negotiated rulemaking requires membership on a federal advisory committee chartered under the FACA. Thus, a party seeking to participate in a negotiated rulemaking must seek appointment to an advisory committee by the agency, which the FACA and its implementing regulations allow parties to do. Although the FACA does not require an agency to select any party who seeks advisory-committee membership to an advisory committee, agencies have every incentive to select parties with distinct stakes in the development of a rule who could contribute meaningfully to a negotiation. Because the very purpose of a negotiated rulemaking is to find a consensus about a proposed rule before the rule is proposed, agencies will not want to alienate interested parties eager to participate, who could subsequently raise objections during the notice-and-comment process and potentially challenge the rule in court.

Although some agency adjudicatory decisions can have regulatory consequences as broad as those of substantive rules, the adjudication process is less inclusive. Whereas any interested party may participate in a rulemaking, participation in formal adjudication is limited to parties to the case as well as to those who can qualify, under the relevant statute or agency rules, as intervenors. A party will be allowed to intervene in a formal adjudication if it can show that the adjudication directly affects its interests or that its intervention is otherwise in the interest of justice. Courts have generally held that intervenor participation is a matter of agency discretion, so long as such determinations are not arbitrary. While some agencies once funded public intervenor programs in an attempt to widen participation in adjudications with broad implications, most have not, and those that did have since dismantled them.[6] Thus, participation in the formal adjudication process remains limited. In contrast to rulemaking, formal agency adjudication is a relatively closed procedure.

That observation runs in two directions. On the one hand, the adjudicating agency simply is not accessible to outside parties. Agencies do not welcome views or information presented by the public. Indeed, even the parties to the adjudication cannot communicate with the agency ex parte. Not only is information not solicited by a wide range of parties, then, but the flow of information from participating parties is tightly controlled. At the same time, however, the process is not easily penetrable by parties who might seek to influence the agency or affect the outcome of the adjudication. In other words, the adjudication process provides for interest groups or for legislators to influence agency decisionmakers. The very procedural aspects of the process that render it inaccessible generally also insulate the adjudicating agency from outside influences. Put differently, the formal adjudication process is evenhandedly closed.

In addition, while the process is not generally open to any party who might wish to participate, neither is it clandestine. Formal hearings are, with narrow exceptions, open to the public in the sense that anyone may attend. In addition, agencies' formal orders following the adjudication process, containing the agency's factual and legal conclusions, are promulgated in accessible public sources. Formal adjudication is transparent, in other words, allowing interested parties to monitor and respond to agency decisions, even though they may not participate directly in the decisionmaking process itself.

Because informal agency decisions and nonsubstantive rules are governed by no APA-prescribed procedures, it is difficult to specify the avenues of participation for these types of agency decisions. But to generalize, participation in the most informal of agency decisionmaking processes takes the form of direct communication with agency personnel. Approaching agency staff concerning an informal regulatory decision is the most common means of participation. Any interested parties may provide staff with comments, ideas, policy analyses, or technical data. In addition to interacting with agency staff, parties seeking to influence an informal agency decision might also contact political appointees at higher levels of an agency, where some of the most important informal decisions are made.

Communicating with the White House constitutes another possible avenue for participation in administrative decisionmaking more generally. As noted above, during all recent presidential administrations, the White House has established specific institutional structures for making regulatory policy and coordinating agency decisionmaking. As all major rulemaking by executive agencies now takes place under the supervision of the White House Office of Information and Regulatory Affairs specifically, parties with an interest in a rule pending OIRA review may approach OIRA staff. Such communication might shape the White House's treatment of a rule under review, or the rulemaking agency's regulatory policy direction or enforcement agenda more broadly.

For another example, any party interested in the regulatory issue facing a FACA-chartered advisory committee may participate in its deliberations rather than communicate with the chartering agency directly. That is, any interested party may participate in the development of advisory-committee recommendations through appearances before a committee, or by supplying a committee with relevant commentary or data. The transparency requirements of the FACA further promote participation in agency decisionmaking because committee deliberations and data are easily available to any interested parties, who can use that information to support or challenge the committee's recommendations to the agency.

Finally, parties seeking to influence the course of agency action can sue the agency in federal court. Indeed, regulatory litigation is a common form of participation in regulatory decisionmaking. The APA broadly states a cause of action by any party "adversely affected or aggrieved" by agency action. Such a party must satisfy the usual jurisdictional and standing requirements on which judicial review rests. But those obstacles are usually surmountable, and any party that satisfies them can challenge an agency's decision as beyond the agency's statutory authority, or not supported by the evidence in the agency's decisionmaking record, or arbitrary, or otherwise unsupportable and therefore in violation of the APA.

As noted, in most regulatory contexts (by far), litigation over agency decisions is a routine part of the general regulatory decisionmaking structure, in other words, part and parcel of administrative procedure. Judicial review is neither the last chronological stage of agency decisionmaking, nor does it imply a failure of decisionmaking processes. Rather, regulatory litigation constitutes a common feedback mechanism requiring agencies to withdraw or reconsider their decisions. Remanding a decision back to the agency is a common judicial remedy following a legal challenge of agency action. Thus, parties seeking to affect regulatory outcomes may and often do bring litigation, an ability that leverages their participation in earlier decisionmaking stages.

However parties may seek to participate in agency decisionmaking, the openness requirements of the FOIA, Sunshine Act, and FACA allow interested parties to keep abreast of agencies' regulatory activities. Such statutes thus promote participation. Any party can request information on which most agency decisions are based, and agencies as a general matter must conduct their business in a transparent manner. By executive order with purposes consonant with the FOIA and Sunshine Act, agencies are also required to publish their yearly agenda in a *Unified Agenda of Federal Regulatory Activities* and in *Regulatory Plan*, each published yearly by the Regulatory Information Service Center. Agency websites complement these sources by providing voluminous information about their agenda. Given these many sources of information, parties who would participate in agencies' regulatory decisionmaking processes can do so with the benefit of essential information about agencies' agenda. Insofar as parties can gather such information without large investments, the opportunities for participation provided by the APA and other statutes become meaningful.

POTENTIAL PARTICIPANTS

That agency decisionmaking processes are largely open answers who might participate, but not who in fact shows up. Apart from agency personnel, organized interest groups constitute the most common participants in agency decisionmaking. This is true across all decisionmaking processes. Often, such groups mobilize around business, trade, and professional interests directly affected by certain regulatory policies. Because such interests are typically self-interested and narrow, such groups are commonly labeled "special interests." Special interest groups are a familiar part of legislative decisionmaking, and they are widely perceived to enjoy considerable influence in the legislative arena. Their participation is felt on the administrative level as well, although to a smaller extent and for different reasons, as will be explored shortly.

The early 1970s saw the emergence of a new breed of interest group, however, the "citizens group" or "public interest group," names that seek to distinguish such groups from special interest groups. Interestingly, their origin owes to the very same criticism of regulation made by public choice theory. In words that could well have been used by public choice theorists, early organizers and leaders of public interest groups complained that regulatory agencies serviced narrow interests to the detriment of the general public.[7] Accordingly, public interest groups explained that they would protect diffuse interests against the powerful influences of special interests—responding to the phenomena predicted by public choice theory.[8] Common Cause founder John Gardner, for just one example, making reference to Mancur Olson, explained upon that group's formation in 1970 that it "would uphold the public interest against all comers—particularly against the special interests that dominate our national life today."[9] There are now of course dozens of such organizations.[10] According to many, they have played a significant role in regulatory policymaking, at both the legislative and administrative levels.[11]

Notwithstanding the conventional focus on organized interest groups as *the* relevant unit of analysis for understanding participation in regulatory decisionmaking, however, interest groups are not alone. First, individual firms also participate, on their own behalf. As shown in chapter 3, the public choice theory's reliance on the logic of collective action is unsatisfying in part because that logic does not fully account for the existence of organized groups. One answer is that interest groups are not as central as is commonly understood. Instead, large entities advocate for themselves, because the private benefits of doing so outweigh their own costs. As a result, many (privileged) interests "groups" may in fact be represented by particular members for whom the regulatory stakes are large enough to justify bearing the costs of participating in regulatory decisionmaking, which incidentally benefits others with similar regulatory interests. And the higher the regulatory stakes, the more often will individual firms deem it in their interest to participate in agency decisionmaking without cooperation from others.

In this light, understanding agency decisionmaking requires attention to the individual participation of various entities, as well as to coordinated participation by fully organized groups. In fact, what sometimes passes for an organized interest group may in fact be a loose affiliation of a very few large entities each individually motivated to participate in regulatory decisionmaking on its own. Although researchers have commonly categorized participants in regulatory decisionmaking according to different types of interest "groups," as will be seen shortly below, the label "group" can be rather capacious, and may include participation by single firms or other entities who advocate on behalf of others only incidentally. In short, not all *interests* participate in regulatory decisionmaking as *groups*.

Finally, individual citizens, not only organized groups and single entities, sometimes participate in administrative decisionmaking as well, though the dynamics of their participation are different and their influence is often less significant. Specifically, for high-profile regulatory decisions generating considerable public attention, individual citizens often participate in agency decisionmaking—in notice-and-comment rulemaking in particular—by sending comments to agencies concerning a proposed rule or other initiative, much as citizens sometimes write their legislative representatives. They do so at times also during the earliest, prerule stages of agency consideration of an issue, and at times outside of the rulemaking context entirely when an agency is considering an informal initiative that will not lead to the issuance of a substantive rule.

Citizens participate in agency decisionmaking on their own initiative or, more commonly, as a member of an ad hoc group seeking to influence deliberation on a specific issue by communicating their opinions or factual information to agency personnel. Sometimes, individuals are prompted to do so by organized interest groups who coordinate individual efforts, blurring the distinction between group and individual participation. Other times, private citizens act independently. Often, they are in one way or another prompted by agencies directly soliciting their participation. Either way, they are ideologically motivated to do so; in contrast to individual firms, the material benefits of participation for individuals is never worth the private costs. Participation in administrative decisionmaking by individual citizens therefore reflects noninstrumental motivations. In any event, understanding agency decisionmaking fully requires consideration of citizen participation too, especially in cases where individual participants are numerous enough to raise the political salience of a regulatory issue.

STUDIES OF PARTICIPATION AND INFLUENCE

Empirical questions remain, however, concerning who participates in the mostly open administrative decisionmaking processes agencies employ, how often those participants do so, and with what effect. Notwithstanding the topic's immediate relevance to fundamental questions about modern government, such questions have attracted surprisingly little research.

One dated but interesting examination of participation in regulatory decisionmaking was undertaken by the U.S. Senate Committee on Governmental Affairs. Its 1977 report, *Public Participation in Regulatory Agency Proceedings*, summarized findings based on an agency survey that sought to estimate "the extent of public participation in agency proceedings."[12] Specifically, committee researchers asked the Civil Aeronautics Board, the Federal Communications Commission, the Food and Drug Administration, the Federal Power Commission, the Federal Trade Commission, the Interstate Commerce Commission, the Nuclear Regulatory Commission, and the Securities and Exchange Commission to identify the most significant ten of each agency's last thirty rulemakings, and similarly the most significant ten of each agency's last thirty adjudications. The researchers then examined the dockets for each of the identified proceedings to determine the incidence of participation in each proceeding by both regulated and outside parties.

The Senate committee found that while many private parties participate in agency decisionmaking processes, parties representing broad outside interests either did not participate at all, or else participated in processes in which they were significantly outnumbered by parties representing regulated interests. There was no organized public participation in 75 percent of the FPC rulemakings, for example, notwithstanding "the clear consumer and public impact"[13] some of the examined dockets had. In the remaining 25 percent of FPC rulemakings, the ratio of regulated industry to public participation ranged from 4:1 to 12:1. Similarly, in the FDA rulemakings examined, fewer than 50 percent involved participation by parties outside of the regulated interests, again notwithstanding the "considerable public impact" some of those decisions had.[14] In FDA rulemakings where public-interest representatives had a presence, the ratio of industry to public interest participation ranged from 12:5 to 122:4.[15] This general pattern held for rulemaking by the other agencies studied as well.[16]

As for adjudication, the committee found similar patterns, with parties representing broad-based interests participating somewhat less. Such parties participated in fewer than 50 percent of the FPC adjudications, and where they did participate, they were outnumbered from 4:1 to 66:1. For another example, the FCC indicated to committee researchers that parties representing public interests participated in 10 percent of the commission's previous thirty adjudications. In the CAB's, NRC's, and FDA's adjudication processes, however, parties representing public interest groups participated more often, from 40 percent to 66 percent percent of the time. But here again, the ratio of participation by regulated parties to participation by nonregulated parties was comparable to those in rulemaking proceedings, ranging from 1:1 and 8:2 (FDA) to 43:13 and 82:6 (CAB).

Such findings suggest that, at least until the mid-1970s, large regulated parties enjoyed much greater presence in agency decisionmaking processes than did public interest groups and other broad-based interests. One exception to this general conclusion was found in requests to agencies under section 553(e) of the APA to initiate a rulemaking. The Senate committee found that for the FTC, NRC, and CPSC, petitions to commence a rulemaking submitted by representatives of those outside of the industry approached or exceeded petitions made by regulated industries.[17] Although broad-based groups did not participate in rulemakings once under way to an extent anywhere near that of regulated interests, such groups did propose that an agency undertake a rulemaking about as often as groups representing regulated interests.

More recently, other researchers have reached comparable though somewhat less dramatic conclusions. In one recent effort to measure participation in agency rulemaking, Cary Coglianese studied twenty-five significant EPA rules issued between 1989 and 1991 pursuant to the

Resource Conservation and Recovery Act (RCRA), which governs hazardous and solid waste disposal.[18] Coglianese found that in those rulemakings, parties representing businesses participated 96 percent of the time, while national trade associations participated 80 percent of the time, and environmental and citizen groups (categorized together) participated 12 percent of the time. Coglianese further found that groups representing regulated industries constituted 59 percent of all participating groups, while groups representing environmental and citizen interests constituted 4 percent of all participating groups.

In another study beginning in the early 1990s, Scott Furlong measured the incidence of participation in agency rulemaking by different types of interest groups by surveying rulemaking agencies.[19] Specifically, he surveyed one hundred agency personnel, five from each of twenty federal agencies, asking respondents to score the frequency of participation in their agency's rulemakings by different types of interest groups, on a scale of 0 ("never") to 10 ("always"). Furlong found that trade associations on average scored 6.7, followed by business groups, which scored 5.9, and closely thereafter by public interest groups, which received an average score of 5.7.[20] Furlong's study suggests that, at least according to the recorded perception of agency personnel, public interest groups may participate in rulemakings almost as often as business and trade groups do, although outnumbered within a given rulemaking. Furlong's results cast a more positive light on the results others have reached: Public interest groups are present in rulemakings about as often as other types of interest groups are, though fewer of them participate in rulemaking at all and those that do are outnumbered by other interests.

But estimates of the frequency with which various parties participate in agency decisionmaking processes and the amount of resources those parties commit to their participation are meaningful only inasmuch as they provide reliable markers of parties' abilities to affect the substance of agency decisions. Ultimately, it is efficacious participation, not mere participation, that affects regulatory outcomes. Measurements of participation quantify the efforts different types of interests make to influence agency decisionmakers, but whether those efforts spell proportionately more influence is a separate question.

The efficacy of participation—influence—though very difficult to quantify, might be measured in several ways. For one, participants could be asked about their own perceptions of the type and amount of influence they enjoy as a consequence of participation. Taking this approach, Furlong's survey asked different types of interest groups how often they were "successful" in "getting what they wanted" from agencies during the course of the rulemaking process. He found that different types of interest groups accessed their own success similarly: 76 percent of trade groups reported that they were successful more often than not, while 68 percent of business groups, 64 percent of public interest groups, and 60 percent of unions indicated the same.

Furlong's study also measured group influence with reference to agencies' perceptions of interest-group influence across different group types. Here he asked one hundred agency respondents to score the overall "influence" that different types of interest groups had within the respondents' agencies, on a scale of 0 ("none") to 10 ("substantial"). Trade associations scored highest, 5.73, followed by public interest groups, 5.39, business groups, 5.33, and unions, 5.20.[21] Furlong also asked agency personnel to score their agencies' tendencies to make changes to proposed rules in response to comments they receive from different types of interest groups during the notice-and-comment period of a rulemaking. Here Furlong found that agency personnel again gave trade associations the highest average score, 4.58, followed again by public interest groups, 4.55, business groups, 4.35, and unions, 4.16. Furlong's results suggest that the disparities between the frequency with which different types of interest groups participate in rulemaking and disparities between the amount of resources different types of interests commit to participation do not translate neatly into the same disparities in influence between different types of groups, at least according to agency personnel.

Other scholars have resisted relying on survey data of groups and agencies due to the obvious shortcomings of that approach, seeking instead to measure influence by analyzing the differences between agencies' proposed rules and their corresponding final rules against written comments the agencies received in the interim. Indeed, while there remains a dearth of empirical study of rulemaking, a small body of interesting and important work in this vein has emerged just within the last several years. In one such study, Jason and Susan Webb Yackee sampled forty rules from four executive agencies and examined the rulemaking dockets for each of those forty rules, categorizing the rules according to their salience and coding over 1,600 rulemaking comments according to their source by interest group type.[22] Yackee and Yackee then measured the differences between proposed and final rules, and analyzed whether rules commented on mostly by business interests were correlated with more extensive differences between proposed and final rules. They concluded that interest groups representing business interests did have a measurable and disproportionate influence on the development of rules, and in particular that business-interest comments predicted a greater likelihood that the rule-making agency's final rule would provide less extensive regulation than its proposed rule. At the same time, though, Yackee and Yackee also found that while citizens' and public interest groups' comments on proposed rules were outnumbered by those from business interests, both citizens and public interest groups submitted comments in over half of the rules they examined.

In a two closely related studies focusing only on lower-salience rules and not distinguishing among types of commenting interest groups, Susan Yackee also found that interest-group comments on proposed rules had a measurable effect on the form of final rules. In one study, Yackee found agencies to be somewhat influenced by commenting interest groups in the sense that they moved the rulemaking agency towards "less" regulation in its final rule.[23] She further found that the more congressional attention a proposed rule generated the less influence commenting interest groups had, while increased presidential attention did not seem correlated with interest-group impact on the studied final rules. In a companion study, Yackee again concluded that interest groups had a measurable influence on rulemaking agencies, and furthermore that a rulemaking agency's final rule is most likely to reflect comments by interest groups where there is a high level of consensus among commenting groups.[24]

Marissa Golden also analyzed written comments submitted during the rulemaking process for eleven randomly selected rules issued by the EPA, NHTSA, and HUD in an attempt to measure influence in the rulemaking process by different types of interests and groups.[25] She too compared the content of written comments to changes between the agencies' proposed rules and final rules. Though her conclusions are limited by the small sample size of analyzed rules—only eight of the examined rules were issued by regulatory agencies (the other three by HUD)—Golden found, like other researchers, that business and trade interests participate far more than citizens groups, except in the case of HUD rules, where citizens' groups participated much more than business groups.

But according to Golden, that disparity of participation did not translate into a disparity of influence between different types of participating groups. In fact, Golden found no "undue business influence" in the examined rules, among other reasons because business interests did not present a united approach to the proposed rules in question. That finding resonates with Magat, Krupnick, and Harrington's well-known study of EPA rulemaking in the 1980s,[26] from which they concluded that business groups were generally not effective during the notice-and-comment period at influencing EPA rules. Golden also concludes that no type of interest groups enjoys greater influence than any other type, in part because no type of group enjoys very much influence at all. In only one of her studied rules did the agency alter its proposed rule "a great deal." Otherwise, changes between the proposed rules and final rules were modest, and did not alter the core of what the agencies had proposed. Golden further concludes, like Yackee, that whether an agency will modify a proposed rules depends on whether there is consensus among those commenting on the rule that the rule should be altered. Where participants are divided over the merits of a proposed rule, the agency is unlikely to modify it significantly. Finally, Golden concludes that agencies tend to respond to a rule's critics much less than they do to a rule's supporters, and relatedly that agencies do not simply react to interest group comments but rather demonstrate independent motivation for their proposed rules.

William West reaches similar conclusions concerning agency responsiveness to interest-group influence during notice-and-comment rulemaking.[27] West examined forty-two rulemakings by fourteen different agencies, conducting in-depth interviews with agency staff most closely connected to those rulemakings to determine the extent to which agencies alter their proposed rules during rulemaking and why they do so. West found that, among the forty-two rules he examined, twenty-eight generated significant conflict giving rise to both critical and supportive comments by outside interests. Of those, the agency changed its proposed rule in a "meaningful" but not "fundamental" way 57 percent of the time; 43 percent of rules generating controversy were not meaningfully changed following their proposal. West concludes that while agencies make changes to proposed rules "frequently enough" during notice and comment, those changes "tend to be small and painful." In addition, like Susan Yackee, West finds that changes in final rules take the form of eliminating a portion of the proposed rule rather than adding to it or adopting an innovative change. West attributes a substantial portion of those changes to executive or legislative involvement rather than to influence by groups responding to proposed rules.

As explained above, rulemaking processes do not exhaust the avenues for participation in agency decisionmaking, although they are especially important in that regard. But data on participation and measures of influence in other fora are even more sparse. Kay Schlozman and John Tierney's famous survey of Washington-based interest groups provides some information about group participation in federal advisory committees and advisory committee processes. They found that 95 percent of union groups, 74 percent of business groups, 74 percent of trade groups, and 67 percent of citizen groups reported that their organizations serve on advisory committees.[28] As Schlozman and Tierney point out, the extent of overall business participation is higher than these percentages suggest, given first that business groups are far more numerous, and second that they may be more likely to have multiple seats on a given advisory committee. Nevertheless, it is noteworthy that citizens groups report that they frequently serve on federal advisory committees and that the percentage of business, trade, and citizens' groups reporting that they participate on advisory committees is roughly the same.

A survey of all government agencies that use advisory committees suggests citizens groups and environmental groups are in fact represented on most agency advisory committees. Thirty-four percent of responding agencies indicated that four-fifths or more of their agency's advisory committees "have at least one member who is also a member of a citizens interest group, consumer interest group, or environmental interest group."[29] In addition, 32 percent of responding agencies indicated one-fifth to four-fifths of their advisory committees have such a member, while 34 percent of responding agencies indicated that one-fifth or fewer of their committees have such members.[30]

Agency perceptions of the composition of federal advisory committees do not exhaust the sources of information on that issue, however. Pursuant to the FACA and its regulations, the General Services Administration maintains records of all agencies' advisory committees, including committee rosters with names and affiliations of all members. In another study of some twelve hundred advisory committee members from a random sample of fifty advisory committees, representatives of business and trade groups composed 23 percent and 12 percent of all members, respectively, while members of broad-based interests groups such as consumer and environmental groups and academicians or other policy experts comprised a comparable 15 percent and 11 percent of all members. Members from the government were the most populous group, composing 28 percent of all members, while representatives of labor unions and other unidentified groups composed 5 percent each. Taking the committees as a whole rather than their individual members, 74 percent of the sampled committees had at least one member representing a business interest, while 66 percent of committees had at least one member representing broad-based interests. Fewer, 50 percent of the committees, had members representing a trade group, while 56 percent and 24 percent of committees had at least one academic and union member, respectively.[31] These findings suggest that broad-based interests are often represented on federal advisory committees.

Communication with the White House in conjunction with executive oversight of agency rulemaking is another possible forum for participation in administrative decisionmaking for which some data exist. Data recording meetings held between the White House's OIRA staff and outside parties concerning agency rules under OIRA review fit the general pattern of the above studies. There too, business-oriented interests outnumber public interest and citizens' groups. But there too, the latter are regularly represented, though not as often. In a study of all OIRA meetings with persons outside government from 1993 through 2000, OIRA staff met with representatives of narrow, business-oriented interests 56 percent of the time, but jointly with representatives of broad-based as well as narrow interests 28 percent of the time, and with representatives of broad-based organizations alone 10 percent of the time. The same data also suggest that changes to proposed rules required by OIRA are not correlated with the types of interests that attend or request meetings with OIRA. That is, the type of interests with whom OIRA met concerning a given rule was not correlated with any increase in the probability that the rule would be changed during the review process.[32] As Golden found for the rulemakings she examined, neither business groups nor public interest groups enjoy more measurable influence in the OIRA rule review process, if either has much influence at all.

To generalize from available studies, then, business or industry interests participate in agency decisionmaking processes significantly more than other, broad-based types of interests, especially as measured by the frequency and volume of their participation. At the same time, however, citizens' groups and public-interest organizations are often also present in agency decisionmaking processes, though substantially outnumbered. With respect to the influence participants have on agency decisionmaking—as opposed to mere presence in various decisionmaking fora—the available evidence taken as a whole is inconclusive. On the one hand, some studies conclude that interest groups have only a limited influence on the development of agency rules. Other studies conclude instead that interest groups in general do have an influence on the development of final rules, and that business interests in particular have an influence on agency decisionmaking, at least for lower-salience rules from a few agencies. Even so, however, some studies concluding that interest groups influence rulemaking find influence in the form of curtailing the scope of a proposed rule rather than altering the rule's content. To that extent, interest groups do not get what they want from agencies, but merely less of what they do not want.

Beyond these rough and qualified conclusions, little else can be confidently generalized about participation and influence in agency decisionmaking. Contextual analysis of particular agency initiatives would therefore advance understanding of this issue, at least pending additional global studies. Accordingly, part 3 will look closely at several specific instances of regulatory decisionmaking, as soon as chapter 8 draws on this chapter and the previous two to develop further the administrative process theory of regulation first presented in chapter 4.

Chapter Eight

The Administrative-Process Approach Expanded: A More Developed Picture

IN THE LIGHT OF CLOSER consideration of how agencies regulate, with what possible motivations, in what institutional environment, and with whose participation—and especially given deeper understanding of the procedural channels of regulatory decisionmaking—it is now possible to develop further the claims of the administrative process theory of regulation introduced in chapter 4, in part by calling legislative dominance into further question.

ADMINISTRATIVE VERSUS LEGISLATIVE DECISIONMAKING

In partial contrast to decisionmaking by legislators, the processes of regulatory decisionmaking by administrative agencies promote the consideration of the arguments and information supplied by a range of interests, even though typically those interests are not equally powerful or equally well represented. As observed in chapter 3, although the mere presence of broad-based interest groups does not alone defy the logic of collective action, upon which the public choice theory constructs its case against regulation, their existence at least requires qualifications of strong versions of the public-choice tenet that narrow, rent-seeking interest groups always dominate the regulatory process. For example, where some producer sought a regulation that would simply create a barrier to entry into that producer's market, public-interested consumer groups might provide a countervailing force sufficient to prevent agency capture by the producer. Where a special interest group might seek through regulation to externalize the environmental costs of its production onto a diffuse public, again a public-interested environmental group might combat that effort by exposing the potential externality. More generally, publically oriented interest groups might also promote welfare-enhancing regulation that addresses serious market failures. In addition, they might also monitor firms to enhance compliance with existing socially beneficial regulation.

The claim here is not that broad-based interest groups pursue the public interest, nor that there is any single identifiable public interest, nor even that such groups necessarily represent *the public* in the deepest sense. All the same, the presence of public interest organizations in regulatory decisionmaking processes can significantly stymie the ability of special interests to secure what is for them alone favorable regulation. By supplying agencies with alternative sources of analyses and information, by monitoring as well as participating in agency decisionmaking, and by initiating litigation to challenge agency action that may undermine general interests or to enforce beneficial regulation, public interest groups serve as an antidote to special-interest participation in administrative decisionmaking. In short, their presence renders administrative decisionmaking multidimensional, complicating any simple function that makes regulatory outcomes the result of special-interest domination.

Information as the Currency of Administrative Decisionmaking

But the point is bigger. For much the same can be said about public interest groups' presence in the legislative sphere as well. There too, such groups lobby Congress, providing alternative sources of expertise, policy analysis, and information. Public interest groups also monitor Congress and legislative committees, and hold press conferences and generate press releases to draw attention to what they consider to be illicit interest-group influence on the legislature. In other words, public interest groups undertake activities in the legislative arena similar to the ones they undertake in the administrative arena. And to some extent they have similar effects, for as noted above, many students of legislative politics see broad-based groups as a politically relevant force in legislative decisionmaking today.

Yet the differences between legislative and administrative decisionmaking processes make broad-based interest groups much more relevant—potentially more influential—in the administrative context. First, the currency of administrative decisionmaking is information, not votes or potential campaign contributions. That is, in rulemaking and other administrative procedures, agencies depend upon information to do whatever they aim to do. Those with the most information, with the most credible and verifiable information, will have a greater opportunity to influence administrative decisionmakers. Relatedly, those with the strongest arguments about regulatory alternatives—that is, those who can most convincingly marshal information about the consequences of regulatory alternatives—again will tend to command more attention by administrators than will those with weaker arguments.

135

Moreover, information and argumentation are not fungible, as votes and campaign dollars are. Whereas from a legislator's perspective one vote is about as valuable as another, and ten dollars of campaign contributions are about ten times as valuable as one, from an administrator's perspective information is not valuable in proportion to its volume. Instead, the arguments and information participants in administrative decisionmaking provide are worth either a great deal—because they earn administrators' careful consideration—or they are worth very little—because they do not. Wholly redundant arguments and duplicative sources of data are worth almost nothing. In short, in contrast to most legislative decisionmaking, administrative decisions are not determined by which side of an issue voices its views more often or more loudly or persuades a decisionmaker that it represents more constituents.

Take notice-and-comment rulemaking. Because the value of comments received during a proposed rule's comment period is not closely proportional to their volume, a single organization with relevant and credible information can have about as much influence on a rulemaking as many organizations on the opposing side of the regulatory issue. Interest groups with fewer resources than others thus can have an effect on a rulemaking vastly disproportionate to the relative size of their budgets. Indeed, a single interest group submitting unique arguments during a rulemaking can have more marginal influence on an agency's final decision than many groups presenting the same opposing argument duplicatively. To be sure, participating in a rulemaking at all requires some organizational and financial wherewithal, but again the costs of participation are not so overwhelming that only very well funded interests can participate, and formally any party may participate in the process. Thus, relative to decisionmaking by congressional committees, whose members are very likely to be more influenced by a greater volume of constituent letters and interest-group support, agency rulemaking is less susceptible to the same kind of influences, as administrators have less reason to respond to interest-group pressure. Rulemaking, therefore, to some extent levels the interest-group playing field.

Mechanical application of the logic of collective action to the rulemaking process overlooks this important point. In the particular context of administrative rulemaking, the "group good" toward which a group's members may or may not contribute is usually information. But here, information has a radically diminishing marginal utility. Thus, the collective action problem is not as severe as in other settings where every member's contribution accrues to the benefit of the group. In the paradigmatic settings of pollution prevention or maintaining a cartel, for example, a single group member's decision not to pollute or to keep prices high does not make much difference until many other members decide not to pollute or to keep prices high; providing those group goods requires considerable cooperation. But in the context of administrative rulemaking, in contrast, once one group member supplies information, then other groups members will benefit without ongoing cooperation. Indeed, once one member provides an agency with information or advocates a particular point of view about that agency's proposal, there is not much value to other group members doing the exact same thing.

To put the point differently, cooperation is just not as necessary or as fragile in the specific context of agency rulemaking. In Olsonian terms, in the rulemaking context many groups are "privileged," and therefore the group goods in question—information and the representation of a particular point of view—might often be supplied by single group members. Given that the collective action problem is not always acute in the context of administrative rulemaking, groups that can best overcome the problem in other settings will not enjoy the same comparative advantages in the rulemaking context. Interest group activity and the ability of a group's member to cooperate matter, just not as much as they do elsewhere. Thus, glib application of the generic logic of collective action to administrative rulemaking might not illuminate very much.

Federal advisory committees provide another example of how the centrality of information in administrative decisionmaking attenuates the connection between how much advocacy a given point of view enjoys, on the one hand, and the likely influence that same point of view carries, on the other. The percentage of federal advisory committee members representing different types of interests on a given committee is unlikely to translate neatly into influence on advisory committee advice or recommendations, certainly not in any linear fashion. As suggested above, numerically underrepresented interests may enjoy more influence at the margin than overrepresented interests. The deliberations of an advisory committee consisting of ten members representing similar business interests and no members from public interest groups are likely to be very different from the deliberations of an advisory committee with eight members from business groups and two members of broad-based groups. As federal advisory committees often comprise members from different viewpoints, advisory committee advice is often pluralistic, even though committee members representing business-oriented interests outnumber members representing other kinds of interests.

The general point here is missed by those who too loosely analogize administrative decisionmaking to legislative decisionmaking, or administrators' decisionmaking calculus to those of legislators. No doubt, interest groups are pervasive in both legislative and administrative fora. And agency rulemaking is often commonly described as decisionmaking modeled on a legislature, and indeed ordinary rules are called also "legislative rules." In addition, interest groups themselves sometimes employ tactics well suited to attract the attention of legislators, such as mass mailings, in the administrative arena where they are much less effective.

As a result, assumptions about the similarity of interest group influence across on legislators and administrators are easy to make. But they are too quick. Given that information rather than political-electoral support fuels agency decisionmaking, what works for interest groups in the legislative arena may not in the administrative arena, at least not in the same way or to the same degree.

Because the relationship between participation and influence is more attenuated in the administrative than in the legislative arena, data on the frequency of different parties' participation and on their relative resources can mislead. For example, a public interest group or a small-business group vastly outnumbered in a particular agency proceeding may nevertheless enjoy some influence with the agency and find that its views are considered more closely than are the views of its regulatory adversaries, especially if the presence of such groups is taken to reflect broader constituencies. In fact, it seems likely that agencies routinely give more weight to the views of interests that are underrepresented precisely because they are underrepresented. Indeed, it may be difficult not to do so, as unique points of view tend to stand out by definition.[1] Because agencies do not merely count votes or consider interest-group muscle in their decisionmaking processes, measurements of the incidence of participation and of the resources various parties commit to agency decisionmaking processes will understate the influence of those who participate less frequently and with fewer resources.

Participation as an Entitlement

What is more, as already explained, most agency decisionmaking processes are, relative to decisionmaking by a legislative committee, more open. Rulemaking is open; adjudication is transparent; and information underlying proposed agency action is readily and cheaply available to any interested party. Notice-and-comment rulemaking in particular is designed exactly to solicit participation from any party who seeks to influence agency action. In contrast to legislative or even judicial decisionmaking, participation in agency rulemaking is a statutory right, to

138

be exercised without invitation or permission. And whereas legislative committee hearings are often highly choreographed events involving invited witnesses, agency hearings are by comparison open and inclusive. Because administrators hear the views expressed by parties who choose to express them, rather than only those who can command attention because of their electoral importance, again administrative decisionmaking mutes differences of interest-group strength that often characterizes legislative decisionmaking.

Decisionmakers with Job Security

Moreover, agency personnel themselves often determine how much weight to attach to comments, arguments, and information supplied by participants in a rulemaking. Thus, administrators who believe a certain position or perspective merits particular importance can give that position special weight. Again, administrators do not simply measure the volume of reactions that alternative regulatory proposals might generate, as legislators cognizant of how alternative legislative proposals might play before their voters sometimes do. Similarly, and also unlike legislators, administrators do not monitor the polls. Instead, agency personnel can sift through the comments and reactions sparked by regulatory initiatives and judge those reactions according to their worth, whereas legislators cannot discount voters' views contrary to their own, at least not without greater political risk.

Of course, this implies a danger. Administrators who would like to favor one group or another, even for illegitimate reasons, would have the ability to do so, for example, by assigning greater decisionmaking weight to that group's position. So much turns on administrators' motivations. But to the extent many administrative regulators are committed to the fundamental mission of their agencies or feel bound to administer regulatory statutes in a neutral or publically interested way, it seems plausible that administrators would tend to attach more or less weight to different interests' reactions to regulatory proposals on their assessment of the merits of those reactions. At any rate, they do not simply count them.

Executive Oversight and Competing Loyalties of Administrative Decisionmakers

The White House's oversight of agency decisionmaking—and authority over executive agencies—also undermines any simple picture of congressional control. Because most agencies answer to the president, whatever pressures agencies feel from legislative constituencies may be balanced against competing commands from the executive. As a result, powerful legislative constituencies may have to secure White House support for their regulatory points of view, without which interest groups may be unable to secure their preferred regulatory course. In this light, legislative support alone is no longer sufficient to predict regulatory favoritism. Furthermore, agencies politically supported by the White House may be able to withstand considerable pressure from legislators and legislatively important interests. Some interests may be powerful enough to enjoy White House favor as well, but often legislators and the White House have different regulatory priorities. Enlisting both the Congress and the White House to move a regulatory agency in the same direction requires political capital that few interests can frequently muster. Thus, executive-legislative tension can attenuate legislative control over agencies.

JUDICIAL REVIEW AND THE LEVERAGING EFFECT OF PARTICIPATION IN ADMINISTRATIVE DECISIONMAKING

There is more to the administrative-process story, however. Crucially, the availability of judicial review leverages public participation in administrative decisionmaking. As explained above, judicial challenges to agency action are in many cases common, and in other cases inevitable. Subject to standing and similar requirements, any interest, group, or person aggrieved by agency action can seek judicial relief upon bringing suit against the agency.

Parties that do so commonly highlight information or arguments contained in an agency's decisionmaking record that the agency did not adequately consider. Comments received during the notice-and-comment period of rulemaking, for example, become part of the agency's docket— the rulemaking record—which parties objecting to agency action can subsequently make part of a reviewing court's record on review. The openness of rulemaking together with the availability of judicial review thus helps to ensure that agency decisionmakers consider all relevant information concerning proposed agency action.

Like rulemaking, the institution of judicial review thus works to level the interest-group playing field. One dissatisfied interest group can trigger judicial review of an agency's decision about as well as any other group can; judicial review can be initiated by any party that can afford to file a brief—a significant but not insurmountable hurdle. Differences in economic or political-electoral resources therefore do not translate to different interest groups' relative ability to subject agency action to judicial review. Therefore, such disparities in interest group resources or political clout do not translate into equal disparities in regulatory influence in the way they may in the legislative arena. Given that judicial review is available widely to any party aggrieved by agency action, agency personnel have another incentive to consider the views, arguments, and data supplied by all participants in administrative decisionmaking. Even where the agency may ultimately prevail, litigation is costly enough to be avoided where agencies can do so by adequately considering the views expressed by all interests affected by agency action.

And judicial scrutiny of agency action radically distinguishes agency decisionmaking from legislative decisionmaking. Legislative action is subject to judicial review only rarely, in the unusual case of possible constitutional defect; legislators' decisions are not subject to judicial scrutiny as a matter of course. Administrators' decisions, in contrast, are routinely reviewed by courts. Judicial review is often deferential, but agency decisions must show not only consistency with the scope of their delegated statutory authority, but also rationality, reasonableness, lack of arbitrariness, and due consideration of relevant data and arguments. Agencies are limited to the defensible.

Judicial review levels the interest-group playing field also by holding agencies faithful to the participatory rights and opportunities associated with agency decisionmaking. That is, where an agency has excluded some party from the decisionmaking process by cutting procedural corners, a reviewing court will invalidate or, if the agency is lucky, remand the agency decision ordering the agency to observe proper procedures. In this way, courts protect parties who might otherwise be excluded from decisionmaking processes, to the extent agencies would seek their exclusion. Just as courts safeguard democratic participation rights such as voting from legislatures and political parties who might exclude weak or underrepresented voters, so too in administrative law do courts safeguard the participation opportunities of the APA and related statutes, making procedural favoritism by agencies difficult.

Of course, participants and potential participants in agency decisionmaking, especially administrators themselves, are well aware of all of the above. As a result, judicial review operates as a feedback mechanism informing agency decisionmaking long before any party challenges a given decision in court. For instance, those commenting on a proposed rule are aware that the comments or data they supply to an agency can, if relevant to the agency's proposal and if ignored, provide a strong basis for a subsequent judicial challenge. Such parties therefore have a stronger incentive to supply important information in the very first place.

Administrators, for their part, are aware of the same, and they therefore have a stronger incentive to consider relevant facts and information supplied by comments. But then those commenting on the proposed rule know that administrators have a stronger incentive to consider their information, and so in turn have a still stronger incentive to supply important information bearing on the rule: They realize not only that their comments will provide a basis for judicial review, but also that their input therefore is more likely to be taken seriously by the agency. This leveraging effect again helps to ensure that the views of all participating in a rulemaking, not only those with considerable electoral resources, are adequately considered. Access to regulatory justice may not be equal among all interests—certainly it is not—but judicial review dilutes the economic and political disparities among participants in agency decisionmaking.

LEGISLATIVE DOMINANCE RECONSIDERED

Up to now the discussion has entertained the assumption that legislators consistently seek to appease their politically powerful constituencies' regulatory preferences by pressuring agencies to deliver favorable regulatory outcomes, or empowering their interest-group constituencies to do the same. The arguments above attempt to show how certain procedural and environmental features of administrative decisionmaking seriously attenuate legislative control.

But the initial assumption may be wrong: The conventional wisdom attributing such motivations to the legislator may be misguided, at least oversimplified. It may be that legislators do not, or not always, seek to control agencies in order to deliver favored regulation to politically important constituencies. Legislators might instead resist interest-group pressures, at least where they think that the regulatory outcomes an interest group seeks would not advance social welfare.

In addition, although some have argued forcefully that Congress uses administrative procedure as a device to monitor and control agencies, the opposite conclusion is at least as likely. That is, it seems more plausible upon examination of the details of administrative procedure that Congress employs the administrative process to promote agency independence. Agencies' procedural autonomy begets legal and political autonomy. This thesis inverts the legislative dominance premise: Congress does not dominate agencies through administrative procedure, but rather liberates them. And in so doing, Congress insulates itself from interest-group pressures by empowering partially autonomous administrators to do politically difficult regulatory work.

While too few students of regulation focus on the details of the administrative process directly, majority wisdom among those who do supports the public choice theory's legislative dominance claim. In other words, most scholars considering the question argue that administrative procedure serves as a disciplining device that Congress uses to control agencies. The collaborative works of Mathew McCubbins, Roger Noll, and Barry Weingast ("McNollgast") provide the most thoroughgoing and intelligent treatment of this view.[2] After persuasively arguing that the repertoire of congressional tools most commonly mentioned as sources of legislative control—budget powers, committee oversight, and so on—do not go very far to solve Congress's principal-agent problem, McNollgast argue that most of administrative law "is written for the purpose of helping elected politicians retain control of policymaking."[3] Indeed, according to McNollgast, administrative procedure is the indispensable solution to Congress's otherwise insurmountable bureaucratic compliance problem. What the public choice theory postulates, then, McNollgast attempt to demonstrate. Their conclusion thus provides critical support for the public choice theory's picture of the relationship between Congress and regulatory agencies.[4]

Specifically, McNollgast argue that administrative procedure facilitates legislative control by reducing the costs of congressional monitoring and thereby ensuring that agency decisions reflect congressional will. They argue, for example, that by standardizing agency decisionmaking procedures in the APA, Congress enabled itself to keep abreast of what agencies are doing. Because all agencies use the same basic procedures, the costs to Congress of following agency action are lower. For another example, McNollgast suggest that by requiring agencies to provide notice of their proposed rulemaking and to solicit commentary on proposed rules, Congress made it easier for affected constituencies to register directly with Congress, as well as with agencies, their opposition to pending agency action. Thus, the notice-and-comment rulemaking process gives Congress advanced warning of agencies that may be attempting to thwart congressional wishes and threaten important legislative constituencies. Administrative procedure therefore makes it hard for agencies to surprise Congress with decisions Congress would not like. By simultaneously slowing agencies down and providing affected interests with opportunities to express opposition to agency action, McNollgast argue that Congress solves its monitoring problem by exerting "ex ante control" over agencies.[5]

But close consideration of the circumstances of regulatory decisionmaking demonstrates the contrary. Administrative decisionmaking procedures as well as agencies' institutional position vis-à-vis the executive and judicial branches actually foster agency autonomy and independence from the legislature. The legislative dominance claim, and the McNollgast thesis that supports it, have it backwards.

For example, while it is true that notice-and-comment rulemaking enables regulated interest groups and Congress to monitor agencies more easily, the rulemaking process also allows other types of groups—public-interest law firms, the media, the public, government watchdog groups—to keep abreast of agency action more easily as well. Relative to these groups, Congress and regulated parties would certainly have a comparative advantage at monitoring agencies, if agency rulemaking processes were not standardized. Thus, the question is really not, as McNollgast suggest, whether standardized processes make it easier for Congress and powerful congressional constituencies to monitor agencies, but whether, all things considered, standardized processes make it easier for those constituencies to get the regulation they want. If standardized rulemaking processes are even more useful to broad-based interests, watchdog groups, and so on—if they do more to subject agencies to pressures and influences beyond the legislature and legislative constituencies—then their existence does not support the view that administrative procedure facilitates congressional control.

Recall the specifics. As outlined in chapter 5, an agency commencing a rulemaking is required by the APA to provide notice of its proposed rule that includes the rule's basic scope, purpose, justification, and authority. Thereafter, the agency is obliged to solicit commentary on its proposed rule from any interested party. Following the comment period, the rulemaking agency is to take into account all relevant facts, arguments, and other information gathered during the rulemaking process—both by the agency itself and as generated from the comments the agency receives—and render a judicially reviewable final rule that reflects all relevant considerations. To ensure that interested parties have the benefit of whatever information the agency deems especially important to its rule, the agency is prohibited from withholding from the public any such information during the rulemaking process.[6] Section 553 further requires the agency to promulgate, along with its final rule, an explanation for why the rule took the final shape it did.[7]

It is hard to see how section 553 rulemaking, the dominant procedural form of agency regulation, is especially amenable to powerful congressional constituencies or, therefore, especially well suited for legislative monitoring and control of agencies. Any party, weak or powerful, can petition the agency to begin the rulemaking process.[8] An agency must provide public notice of any rule it intends to develop, and receive comments from any party, no matter how well or poorly funded, who undertakes to contact the agency. Of course, the rulemaking agency may choose simply to ignore some comments, but it may do so at its peril if a party supplies relevant data or argument that a subsequent court determines the agency's rule unjustifiably failed to consider.

Nor does the adjudication side of administrative procedure seem especially well designed as a congressional control device. In fact, it seems even less well suited for that purpose. For example, section 554's separation-of-powers requirement forbidding ALJs from being supervised by others in the same agency who bring cases before the ALJs ensures some measure of decisionmaking independence. Such independence may work to the advantage of regulated parties against regulatory zealousness on the part of an agency, but it is far less clear how intra-agency separation of judicial and executive functions would benefit groups whose interests the agency was, as the public choice theory holds, trying to advance. In short, ALJ independence also complicates any claims about formal adjudication's susceptibility to regulatory rent-seeking—an important point apparently overlooked by public choice theorists who suggest that regulation through the common law is preferable to public-law regulation because judges are independent whereas legislators are not.[9] Legislators seeking to ensure favorable regulatory treatment of their favored constituencies would not likely find formal adjudication ideal for the task.

The APA's adjudication provisions prohibiting ex parte communications between the adjudicator and parties to the adjudication also stymie congressional influence.[10] The same is true for the APA's requirement that evidence forming the basis of the adjudication be introduced formally, and that wherever fairness requires, opposing parties enjoy the benefits of cross-examination of adverse witnesses.[11] Finally, ALJ decisions must include written rulings on material factual questions and statements of applicable agency policy and law,[12] which constrain decisionmakers from arbitrariness, as written opinions similarly constrain courts.

Intra-agency appeals (appeals through the agency's own "judiciary") are similarly formalized. And while agency heads can ultimately overrule ALJs and appellate adjudicatory bodies, agency adjudications are subject to the "substantial evidence" test upon appeal to a federal court.[13] A reviewing court will affirm the agency's ultimate decision only for reasons supported by the adjudication record.[14] Though higher levels in an agency may reverse an ALJ decision, reviewing courts require some explanation for why they have done so.[15]

As in the case of rulemaking, then, it is difficult to see how the formal adjudication process serves as a useful vehicle for ensuring that agencies supply desired regulation to important congressional constituencies. The formalized process does not lend itself to interest-group manipulation, nor is it very susceptible to congressional pressure. In fact, courts have held that the prohibition against ex parte communications during an adjudication extends even to members of Congress.[16] Granted again, the costs of participating in formal adjudication, which include the cost of counsel, are greater than those typically associated with rulemaking, and to that extent the process is less inviting to many interests. More importantly, formal adjudication is not open to any interested party, as rulemaking is. But while the exclusivity associated with formal adjudication may raise worries that those involved have special access to the agency that translates into regulatory favoritism, in fact the very trappings that make this procedure expensive and quasi-judicial—the semi-independence of ALJs, the submission of evidence, the opportunity to challenge contrary evidence, the promulgation of written decisions that explain the facts and the law underlying the agency's decision—also make the process unwieldy for delivering regulatory favors.

Apart from rulemaking and formal adjudication, other procedural mechanisms also appear to further promote openness and agency independence. For example, the FACA insulates agencies politically by providing an external, neutral source of expert policy recommendations that can be difficult for legislators and interest groups to ignore or discredit. The FACA's requirements that any agency seeking policy advice or recommendations from a group of persons outside of government, which agencies do often in the development of regulatory policy, charter that group as a federal advisory committee and then open its meetings to the public, announce them in advance, keep minutes of its meetings, make available to the public any documents on which the committee relies in rendering advice to an agency, and similarly make available its own documents and reports, all stymie special-interest control of agencies. And again both the

FACA and its implementing regulations require that the membership of an advisory committee represent diverse points of view concerning the issue at hand.[17]

Given these many good-government requirements, advisory committees chartered under it are not easily captured by narrow interests; advisory committees whose meetings and records are open and accessible make inconvenient vehicles for delivering biased advice to an agency. Of course, the transparency of advisory committees does not speak to the issue of who actually serves on them. If the FACA required openness while advisory committees' memberships were nevertheless dominated by special interest groups, then the institution might provide an effective avenue for interest group domination of agencies. But as summarized above, empirical evidence suggests that the FACA procedures for establishing and running an advisory committee go reasonably far to ensure balanced representation among many different types of interests. By providing a source of expert advice that aids agency record-building and can form a strong scientific or technical basis for agency action, through procedures that do not seem vulnerable to overrepresentation by special interests, the FACA seems to promote agency independence and evenhandedness more than it facilitates congressional or interest group control.

Much the same is therefore true of the Negotiated Rulemaking Act, as the same openness requirements apply. In fact, much like the FACA, the passage of the NRA reflected concerns about the dangers of agency communications with parties interested in the development of a rule prior to the publication of a proposed rule's notice. Thus the NRA requires agencies that assemble private parties to write the text of a negotiated proposed rule to do so in an open, inclusive, evenhanded manner. The negotiation process then promotes discussion, argumentation, and compromise among those interested in a negotiated rule's development.[18] Negotiated rulemaking, as a procedural institution, thus does not resonate very well with the public choice theory, although less turns on that observation given that negotiated rulemakings are, unlike advisory committees, uncommon.

Like the FACA and the NRA, the other important good-government appendages of the APA similarly present serious obstacles to, and moreover deter, regulatory favoritism. The FOIA's requirement that agencies publish their rules of procedure, contact information through which the public may obtain information or make requests for agency decisions, statements of general policy, and interpretations of general applicability formulated and adopted by an agency do not facilitate regulatory rent-seeking.[19] Nor do the FOIA's requirement that agencies provide any requesting party any information pertaining to any other agency records not falling within an exempted category of information. Similarly, the Sunshine Act's requirement that multimember agencies hold open, publicized meetings helps to ensure that agency decisions are transparent. To the extent that making regulatory decisions benefiting favored congressional constituencies is facilitated by administrators who operate outside the awareness of the public, the media, and broad-based interest groups, here again the good-government procedural ground rules impede the kind of regulatory decisionmaking the public choice theory contemplates.[20]

It is similarly difficult to understand how the NEPA's requirement that agencies prepare and publicize environmental impact statements for major federal actions constitutes a useful procedural constraint for ensuring that agencies serve only important congressional constituencies. On the one hand, one might argue that a statute like NEPA may advance the interests of some polluters by creating a barrier to entry. On the other hand, however, NEPA is clearly costly to polluters in that it forecloses certain regulatory outcomes available to polluters because those outcomes have an adverse impact on the environment. It is hard to say how these offsetting effects stack up. To be sure, NEPA may be easy to understand if attributed to Congress's desire to achieve some level of environmental protection,[21] but that assumption undermines the public choice theory's legislative motivation claim, according to which legislators promote the regulatory interests of narrow but powerful groups, not environmentalists.

That leaves interpretive rules, procedural rules, "guidances," and sundry other informal decisions for which there are few or no prescribed decisionmaking processes. One might argue that agencies are best able to supply the regulation sought by powerful congressional constituencies through informal decisionmaking. But on the other hand, this is just to say that administrative procedure as such does not facilitate regulatory rent seeking, but rather that, contrary to the McNollgast hypothesis, the absence of procedure does so; procedure itself can no longer be a device to control agencies if informal—that is, a-procedural—decisionmaking is where all of the interest-group action is. Moreover, if delegation itself is the worry, it is worth emphasizing that now much turns on administrators' motivations in predicting or explaining regulatory outcomes. If an agency has strong incentives to provide illicit benefits to some particular interest group, informal, off-radar decisionmaking may well help it do so. If on the other hand administrators are motivated to promote general interests, then informal decisionmaking power would seemingly help them do that. Thus, wherever agencies regulate by exercising raw discretion rather than according to statutorily prescribed procedures, much turns on what administrators' motivations really are. Meanwhile, examination of many of the specific provisions of the APA and related parts of Title 5 suggests that administrative procedure itself is not so well suited for congressional or, by extension, interest-group domination of agencies. Nor, relatedly, is the administrative process inaccessible to groups representing more general, public-oriented interests.

A final difficulty with the McNollgast view is its implicit suggestion that agencies defy Congress only through action, not inaction. But most often implementing a legislative-interest group deal requires affirmative agency action. Thus, an agency can thwart congressional will by failure to regulate, just as it may do so by regulating. Yet existing administrative process rules do little to allow interest groups, or Congress, to compel agency action that is not forthcoming. If Congress really intended the administrative process to hold agencies faithful to congressional will, it should have provided mechanisms (beyond simply allowing parties to ask for a rule) to overcome recalcitrant inaction as well as recalcitrant action. The fact that Congress did not provide such mechanisms further suggests that legislative control is not the primary purpose or effect of administrative procedure.

The empirical findings summarized in chapter 7 support the argument here that administrative process rules promote participation by a range of interests and organizations. Broad-based interests are present in most decisionmaking fora. And although interest groups representing more narrow, business-oriented interests overpopulate most agency decisionmaking processes, the sum of the empirical data concerning their influence suggests that they do not dominate those processes, much less control agencies' final regulatory decisions. Were the legislative dominance thesis correct, one would expect to find broad-based interests unable or unmotivated to participate in administrative regulatory decisionmaking, and at any rate to find that narrow interests together with Congress employ the administrative process to generate the regulatory outcomes they prefer. Yet the empirical record does not vindicate such expectations.[22]

To consider this issue from another angle, it is not difficult to imagine an administrative process regime much better suited to the degree of congressional control contemplated by the public choice theory and McNollgast than the regime set forth in the APA. For example, one can well imagine a world without an APA—such as the United States before 1946, most local governments to this day, and all but some dozen countries—in which each agency made decisions in various ways not easily discernable by those outside of regulated industry or otherwise most directly affected by an agency's work. Such a world would be harder for the public, the press, public interest groups, and even courts to navigate. Such a world would also be more costly for those seeking to participate in many agencies' decisionmaking processes or to influence many different agencies' decisions. In the absence of procedural consistency across agencies, such parties would have to learn each agency's procedural practices anew. Those regularly seeking rents from a single, familiar agency, on the other hand, would enjoy an informational advantage. Indeed, efforts to render agency decisionmaking processes more open and accessible by making them more consistent across agencies are largely what motivated the passage of the APA.

But even with an administrative procedure statute, decisionmaking processes more consonant with the public choice theory are easy to imagine. For one example, rulemaking provisions might allow agencies simply to announce a final rule following a comment period without any explanation about why the agency settled on the rule it did. On the adjudication side, allowing ex parte communications concerning the merits of a pending decision, as the APA did until an amendment in 1976[23]—one of the very few substantive changes to the act in its nearly sixty-year history,[24] prompted by worries that some agencies were unduly influenced by powerful interests on one side of a case—would make it easier for agencies to understand and satisfy the regulatory preferences of powerful constituencies. More generally, the APA could require agencies to seek congressional approval before their decisions become final, as might be possible through some version of a "negative veto" (as opposed to the affirmative veto famously invalidated by the Supreme Court in *INS v. Chadha*).[25] Better still, Congress could make it clear through the APA that members of Congress could communicate directly with agency personnel concerning any pending agency decision. Instead, various prohibitions on congressional influence on agency decisionmaking processes call into further question the idea that administrative procedure is largely a tool of congressional control. Finally, the APA might provide for judicial review that instructs courts to invalidate agency decisions only for blatantly ignoring APA-prescribed procedures, rather than for the more expansive "without observance of procedure required by law" standard under APA section 706.[26]

On that latter note, Congress could have provided for very limited, bare-rationality review, with no judicial inquiry into matters such as the adequacy of an agency's factual record supporting its decision, which would have had procedural implications relating to agencies' factual record-building practices. After all, while it is true that the federal courts have imposed many administrative process norms through the course of ruling on APA cases, to some extent Congress invited them to do so by supplying the terms of APA review and including inflatable words like "capricious" among them.[27] Thus, the APA's judicially articulated procedural requirements are not really *entirely* court-imposed. In any event, different conceivable processes would promote legislative control more than existing APA procedures do.

For example, aspects of the Model State Administrative Procedures Act seem better designed to promote legislative control than does the APA. For instance, the Model Act provides for the establishment of a legislative Administrative Rules Review Committee, which allows for legislative review of rules, including proposed or possible future rules,[28] and provides that the legislative committee may certify that an agency's rules are in the legislature's view contrary to the agency's authority.[29] Many states make approval by a legislative committee the final step in a rulemaking before a rule becomes final, although some state supreme courts have held that such requirements violated state constitutional separation of powers principles by in effect giving the legislature a veto over executive decisions.[30] The point remains, though, that relative to Congress, state legislatures typically enjoy more control over state agencies. Compared with some state acts, the APA seems less suited for ensuring that agencies heed legislative will. If Congress intended the APA primarily to secure congressional dominance, its choice of provisions seems in many respects puzzling.

But wait. If federal administrative process rules really liberate agencies from the legislature and from powerful legislative constituencies, one must wonder why Congress, or for that matter those interest groups that would benefit from tight legislative control over agencies, would ever allow such a state of affairs to develop. If Congress prefers to control agencies, and given that Congress creates administrators' decisionmaking processes in the first place, why wouldn't Congress devise administrative process rules that make certain agencies do what Congress and its powerful constituencies want?

This compelling question has several compelling answers. First, as explained above, Congress is not the sole source of the basic ground rules of administrative procedure. Rather, the president and especially the courts have supplemented or refined the text of the APA in ways that give the act its bite. Thus, to some extent, Congress itself has limited authority in the matter.

Second, it is less clear than many apparently believe that Congress would be able to adopt administrative procedures that give it tight control over agencies' regulatory decisions. For one thing, doing so would require legislators to overcome their own collective action problem, and an intergenerational one at that. Devising rules that will preserve a future legislature's dominance over agencies may not be something very many legislators in the present care much about. In the abstract, legislators presumably care about the extent to which they will be able to influence agencies in the future, but determining which administrative process rules would most accomplish that requires substantial legislator investment in the future, at the opportunity costs of focusing on immediate interest group demands—and various other demands on legislators' time—in the present. Structuring such rules would also require difficult ex ante calculations about whether and how different kinds of interest groups might participate in alternative processes, and how courts will interpret and apply statutory procedural rules. To the extent considerable uncertainty would surround those questions, the expected returns from legislative attention to administrative procedure will be small. An anthropomorphized legislature might care very much about future agency control, but for a legislature composed of hundreds of individuals whose own time horizons are limited and who have many conflicting demands on their time, it is not clear that administrative process rules will command the attention that ensuring future legislative dominance would require. The same is true for regulated interest groups: In the abstract, interest groups that would benefit from close legislative control over agencies would have an incentive to lobby for administrative process rules that promoted legislative control, but any given interest group's incentive to invest in securing a set of such rules for the benefit of all other similarly situated groups, especially given the uncertainty that would inevitably surround such an undertaking, is less clear. Powerful interest groups too might prefer to focus instead on more immediate and self-serving gains.

More importantly, however, Congress might well prefer instead to use administrative procedure to insulate itself from interest groups, rather than to control agencies and deliver demanded regulation. That is, by prescribing generally open and accessible rules of administrative procedure, such as those embodied in section 553—and devising open and accessible rules is a much simpler task than determining which rules would in the future best exclude certain interests but not others—Congress might use administrative procedure to resist interest group demands for favorable regulation. After all, why would legislators be motivated simply to act as interest group agents, if they could avoid doing so without sacrificing whatever interest group support they require to remain in office? It is one thing to hold, as the public choice theory does, that legislators are solicitous of special interest groups' demands. It is quite another to hold that they enjoy meeting those demands. By delegating substantial regulatory powers to agencies, which do not require the same type of political support from interest groups that members of Congress themselves do, and then by creating a set of rules that raise the costs of regulatory rent-seeking, legislators may employ the administrative process as a defense against interest group demands even while they can appear to champion their interest group supporters. They can always later deflect blame toward agencies, and the courts that vindicate agency decisions, for regulatory outcomes their interest group supporters do not like. They can growl at agencies too, under the eye of powerful constituencies. But individual legislators who are motivated at least in part to advance general interests might not regret much that agencies enjoy sufficient autonomy to do what Congress itself can do directly only at great political cost.

This account of congressional motivation and administrative process thus turns the legislative dominance premise upside down: Congress may well use the administrative process to enable agencies to pursue regulatory outcomes not favored by the most politically powerful interest groups. Interest groups' ability to pressure Congress to influence agencies is diminished rather than strengthened by the administrative process. At the same time, Congress thereby insulates itself too, politically, from special interest groups who would seek to enlist legislators to ensure that agencies deliver favorable regulation: If legislators cannot do all that much to force agencies to deliver favorable regulation, then they cannot be blamed all that much for failing to do so.

Overlooking this possibility, the public choice theory too quickly assumes instead that a Congress dependent on the support of interest groups that have only their narrow and self-regarding regulatory interests in mind can do nothing to limit the malignant consequences of that dependence. But if Congress can properly be anthropomorphized at all, maybe Congress is more resourceful than the theory gives it credit for. To be sure, interest groups might prefer that Congress not use administrative procedure to liberate agencies, and therefore to some extent liberate itself, but again it would take an unusually focused and far-sighted set of interest groups to prevent Congress from doing so. In short, serious questions about legislators' institutional incentives to devise administrative procedures that successfully control agencies lend further support to the conclusion that existing administrative process rules seem ill-designed to promote legislative control and regulatory rent-seeking.

But there is a relevant history here, which casts still further doubts on the public choice theory's legislative dominance claim and on the legislative dominance school represented by McNollgast more generally. At the time leading up to the Administrative Procedure Act's passage in 1946, efforts to standardize and codify agency decisionmaking processes were born largely out of a concern that, in the wake of the New Deal, federal agencies enjoyed too much power and discretion over regulated industries.[31] In response, those subject to agency power sought decisionmaking procedures that were open, accessible, and fair. Today, concerns about agency power are very different. The modern worry is that agencies and regulated industries will cooperate in ways that sacrifice public interests. The difficulty for the public choice theory, however, is that the very same procedural rules that were adopted to protect industry in the 1940s make it harder—because they are generally open, accessible, and fair—for industry to capture agencies today. Historical circumstances, in other words, produced a procedural regime that makes regulatory rent-seeking difficult.

In fact, in the late 1930s industry lost in its effort to secure alternative legislation that would have limited agency power (and thus the potency of New Deal reforms) considerably, a historical fact inconvenient for the public choice theory. It got, instead, an act that preserved agency power over industry—specifically, one that legislatively sanctioned agency rulemaking—but conditioned the use of that power on conformity with certain good-government decisionmaking procedures. Those procedures, helpful to regulated parties in an era that pitted industry against the government, undermine regulated parties' attempts to secure favorable regulation to the detriment of broad-based interests in a later era. And since the passage of the APA, the congresses that passed the FACA, FOIA, NEPA and Sunshine Act during the good-government reform era of the mid-1970s also did so explicitly to promote open and accessible regulatory government. There again, the legal-procedural structure of agency decisionmaking does not comport with process-based legislative control.

A final point remains. Recent congresses have perceived a need to exercise greater control over agencies, suggesting that Congress itself doubts its own capacity to control agencies on regulatory matters. For example, the 104th Congress passed legislation, part of the Small Business Regulatory Enforcement Fairness Act of 1996[32] (in turn a piece of the Contract with America Advancement Act of 1996), that amended Title 5 to require agencies to submit all of their new rules to Congress and to the General Accounting Office for review. This new procedure stays the effective date of major rules under congressional review for sixty days, and further provides for Congress to enact a joint resolution disapproving rules it considers to be undesirable.[33] The same Congress also established a legislative "Corrections Day" in the House,[34] a mechanism for fast-track consideration of bills that would "correct" agencies' decisions that Congress deemed misguided. While these developments have not changed the relationship between Congress and agencies significantly—for they have almost never been used—and while they certainly do not change the fact that Congress must pass legislation to undo what an agency has legally done, such efforts reflect some amount of legislative frustration about its own ability to influence agencies.

To sum up, the view that Congress uses administrative procedure to control agencies by ensuring that agencies provide favorable regulatory outcomes to important legislative constituencies seems, on close analysis, far-fetched. That view is at odds with the details of administrative procedure, which are at best clumsily suited to promote legislative control and intervention, and which promote openness and participation by a broad range of regulatory interests. The view also, like much of the public choice theory of regulation, abstracts away much of executive and judicial influences on administrative behavior. Perhaps more fundamentally, the legislative dominance claim assumes that Congress is able to solve its own public-good problem of devising a successful monitoring scheme, but then assumes Congress is powerless to solve its public-good problem of deflecting interest groups pressures and overcoming regulatory rent-seeking and other special-interest regulatory outcomes. But maybe Congress is resourceful enough to create a regulatory decisionmaking regime that provides agencies with considerable autonomy. Alternatively, maybe the existing administrative regime is largely the product of particular historical circumstances surrounding the passage of the APA as well as of the subsequent good-government statutes that have become part of administrative decisionmaking. Either way, administrative decisionmakers are not tightly constrained by legislators and their interest-group constituencies.

This is not to say, however, that legislative pressures and interest-group preferences cannot influence agencies in socially undesirable ways. The claim is rather that those pressures and influences do not seem, from a process point of view, irresistible. Rather, the administrative process appears instead to foster considerable decisionmaking autonomy and regulatory evenhandedness, especially to the extent administrators are themselves motivated to pursue general rather than narrow regulatory interests. Part 3 substantiates this claim with examples.

PART III

PUBLIC INTERESTED REGULATION

Introduction to Part 3

So grant this much: However uneven interest group pressures on Congress may be, and however often legislators may seek to use their powers over agencies to generate regulatory policies that favor narrow congressional constituencies, it is still plausible that administrative decisionmakers nevertheless often pursue regulatory policies designed to serve broad interests. It is plausible that agency regulators are motivated to do so as a result of their own commitments to the common good, which might after all account for why they became regulators in the first place. It is similarly plausible that agencies' decisionmaking procedures promote agency autonomy because they require some level of openness, notice, and accountability in regulatory decisionmaking, and thus are not well designed for interest-group favoritism. It is also plausible that presidential oversight and judicial review further promote agency autonomy by providing separate sets of incentives for agencies to consider all relevant facts, arguments, and policy consequences in the course of their decisionmaking processes. At the very least, whether the administrative process promotes agency independence rather than regulatory capture seems—considering the question purely in the abstract—up for grabs.

But what is plausible in the abstract may prove false in fact. Whether regulatory decisions ever advance broad-based interests over narrow interests is of course an empirical question. Whether regulatory decisions advance broad-based interests over narrow interests often enough, especially when the regulatory stakes are high, to offset whatever regulatory rents agencies otherwise provide—and thus whether regulation on the whole promotes rather than imperils public interests—is a separate empirical question. Unfortunately, questions concerning issues such as what motivates administrative decisionmakers, how the administrative process limits congressional control over agencies, and the extent to which judicial review reinforces congressional control or instead liberates agencies to pursue general interests are issues difficult to tackle, much less resolve as a matter of theory. As there is no measuring stick by which to resolve such questions, it is often hard to know just what to conclude. One can develop a theoretical argument in most any direction, which is not to say all arguments are equally compelling, only that it is never clear what a decisive test of any given argument might look like.

Consideration of actual examples of regulatory decisionmaking cannot solve this problem. But it sure helps. Accordingly, this chapter and the three that follow explore several sets of real regulatory decisions—regulatory initiatives that both reveal the limitations of the public choice theory of regulation and illustrate the promise of an administrative process approach. They include the Environmental Protection Agency's decision to develop stricter regulations governing ozone and particulate matter, the Food and Drug Administration's decision to regulate tobacco products, and the Forest Service's decision to limit the construction of roads in national forests, among others. These initiatives are noteworthy because each appears to be an instance where regulators sought to advance diffuse interests over organized opposition representing powerful, concentrated interests, and furthermore used their legal-procedural autonomy to do so. To that extent, these cases shed light on whether and under what circumstances administrators regulate in the public interest.

To risk stating the obvious, the case studies that follow are not offered as a random selection of regulatory cases with which to adjudicate decisively between competing accounts of regulation, or for that matter to evaluate once and for all the legislative dominance claim. Indeed, the examples in question were chosen in part precisely because they appear to be instances of administrative regulators advancing broad-based interests at the expense of concentrated, mobilized interests (and in part because of their sheer regulatory significance). On the other hand, while these regulatory case studies were not selected randomly, neither are they inconsequential regulatory developments whose discovery required long search—minor exceptions in a vast sea of special-interest regulation—nor do they exhaust examples of regulatory action that advance broad-based interests and social welfare.[1] To the contrary, each involves enormously important regulatory decisions that sparked intense national debates and implicated billions of dollars. Indeed, the EPA's regulatory action concerning ozone and particulate matter, the FDA's with respect to tobacco, and the Forest Service's "roadless" rule would all unquestionably make a short list of some of the most significant regulatory activity in more than a decade. Thus, while the case studies considered here cannot provide grounds for rejecting any theory of regulation, except one that admits no variation, they are nevertheless suggestive about whether and how the administrative state is capable of advancing social welfare.

Each of these regulatory initiatives provides an interesting story line. They will be analyzed with the following questions in mind: (1) First, are these examples instances of public-interested regulation, or not? Do they

deliver net social benefits or impose social costs? And how are those benefits and costs distributed? (2) Second, what made the initiatives possible?
In particular, what motivations did the relevant administrators appear to
have? What administrative processes did they employ, and which interests
participated in those processes? And what role did the agencies' institutional relationships with the president and the courts play? (3) Finally,
how did important legislative constituencies line up in favor of or against
the regulatory actions in question? How did Congress react to interest-
group responses? What monitoring and sanctioning techniques did Congress use in response to agency action? And with what effect? Later, part 4
will identify the common features of these and other regulatory initiatives,
consider what they reveal about the relative strengths of the public choice
and administrative process theories of regulation, and what conclusions
they support about the possibility of good regulatory government more
generally.

Chapter Nine

The Environmental Protection Agency's Ozone and Particulate Matter Rules

IN ONE OF THE MOST significant environmental regulatory initiatives in decades,[1] the U.S. Environmental Protection Agency in July 1997 issued final rules under the Clean Air Act tightening restrictions on ozone (O_3)and particulate matter (PM).[2] The EPA's rules—one rule for ozone and one for particulate matter, issued simultaneously—constituted a revision to the agency's National Ambient Air Quality Standards (NAAQS), which establish maximum levels for listed pollutants.[3] Sections 108 and 109 of the Clean Air Act require the EPA to identify air pollutants that threaten human health and welfare, and to specify maximum allowable levels of those pollutants.[4] The Clean Air Act also requires the agency to monitor areas of the country for compliance with allowable levels of listed pollutants, and further to update maximum levels at least once every five years to reflect changes in science and technology concerning the effects of listed pollutants and changing costs of their prevention.[5] Ozone (formerly known as "smog") and particulate matter ("soot" or "haze") are two of the six NAAQS-listed pollutants.

The EPA had last reviewed its restrictions relating to ozone in 1993, and to particulate matter back in 1987.[6] In December 1996, the EPA initiated rulemakings under section 553 of the Administrative Procedure Act by issuing notices of proposed rulemakings concerning its ozone and particulate matter limits.[7] In its notices, the EPA explained that, on the basis of intervening scientific research since 1993 and 1987, the agency had come to believe that its existing standards were inadequate to protect human health and welfare. The EPA identified the grounds on which it found existing standards inadequate, and made available to the public scientific studies the agency considered in reaching that conclusion. It also presented proposed rules to replace existing standards and invited comments on its proposals as well as on the issue of the adequacy of existing standards,[8] all pursuant to section 553 of the APA. While the EPA's decision took the procedural form of ordinary rulemaking, however, its decisionmaking process in this case was far from ordinary. To understand why, a bit more background is necessary.

Ozone and particulate matter are not themselves emissions, not usually (particulate matter can be). Rather, they are the by-products of emissions from a wide range of sources, which begins to explain why the EPA's actions here were so significant. Ozone, specifically tropospheric (ground level) ozone—not to be confused with stratospheric ozone, which protects the earth from harmful ultraviolet rays and differs from tropospheric ozone only in its location—results from atmospheric transformations ("cooking") of volatile organic compounds, nitrogen oxides, and oxygen in the presence of heat and sunlight. Particulate matter is a generic term for tiny liquid and solid particles of varying size and composition that lodge in the lungs and other parts of the body, such as the head, after inhalation. Much like ozone, particulate matter results from transformations of gaseous emissions such as sulfur oxides, nitrogen oxides, and volatile organic compounds.

Both ozone and particulate matter are indisputably harmful to human health and welfare, though debatable questions remain about what the tolerable level of each is. Both are more harmful in greater concentrations and less so in smaller amounts, but there is no clear breaking point above which either is exponentially more dangerous and below which either is far more safe. Both are also particularly threatening to young children, older persons, and asthmatics, as well as to a subset of the otherwise "normal" population that just happens to be more susceptible to health problems from these pollutants. Particulate matter is also especially threatening to individuals with heart or lung disease, as is ozone to completely healthy persons who regularly perform moderate physical work out of doors, and to those who exercise out of doors.

Prior to the EPA's 1997 rules tightening acceptable levels of ozone and particulate matter, the agency had set ozone limits at 0.12 parts per million (ppm), measuring ozone based on a one-hour averaging period, and particulate matter limits at 150 micrograms per cubic meter and 50 micrograms per cubic meter, based on twenty-four-hour and one-year average measurements respectively. Reacting to hundreds of research findings published in the early and mid-1990s concerning the health effects of particulate matter—and thousands of studies concerning the health effects of ozone—including studies reporting serious adverse health consequences at levels below existing standards, the EPA undertook to revise them. As one would expect, the agency's revision process had begun long before it formally announced its proposed rules in December 1996, or even long before the EPA in June 1996 published in the *Federal Register* an advance notice of proposed rulemaking (ANPR) for each rule identifying the main issues under the agency's consideration and presenting its decisionmaking timetable.[9] Indeed, the agency initiated possible revision of the ozone and particulate matter standards in the early 1990s when it began reviewing the latest scientific research on the health and welfare effects of the pollutants. In response to studies showing associations between premature death and particulate matter exposure at levels below then-existing standards, for example, the EPA facilitated confirming reanalysis of those studies by the Health Effects Institute, a respected research organization funded jointly by the agency and several motor vehicle and engine manufacturers. By February 1994, the EPA published in the *Federal Register* a notice of the agency's schedule for continued review of the science and possible revision of its standards.

Following that review, the agency at the end of 1996 proposed a rule reducing levels of permissible ambient ozone levels from 0.12 ppm to 0.08 ppm, though calculated using a more liberal eight-hour rather than one-hour average standard.[10] It similarly proposed a rule to reduce levels of particulate matter first by distinguishing between "fine" particulate matter, up to 2.5 microns in diameter ($PM_{2.5}$), and "coarse" particulate matter, from 2.5 to 10 microns (PM_{10})—10 microns being about one-seventh the diameter of a human hair—and then by limiting newly defined $PM_{2.5}$ to twenty-four-hour and annual average concentration maximums of 65 micrograms per cubic meter and 15 micrograms per cubic meter respectively, while retaining existing annual limitations of 50 micrograms per cubic meter and twenty-four-hour limitations of 150 micrograms per cubic meter for PM_{10}, though modifying the measurement methods for the latter.[11] In simpler terms, the EPA proposed to reduce acceptable levels of ozone and fine particulate matter, measuring the levels of each by average concentrations within specified measurement periods, and to revise its measurement methodology for course particulate matter. The agency invited comment not only on its proposed rules, but also on several specific alternative standards to those it proposed.[12]

The EPA's revisions to the ozone and particulate matter standards were prompted by more than scientific understanding of the pollutants' health effects, however. In the early 1990s, the agency was sued in federal court in Arizona by the American Lung Association for not updating its NAAQS at least as often as every five years, as required by the Clean Air Act.[13] The plaintiffs observed that since 1977 the agency had conducted only one review of its particulate matter standards and had revised them only once, in 1987. They sought to compel the EPA to perform its statutory obligation to review and, as appropriate, revise its NAAQS for particulate matter, relief opposed by several intervenors in the suit, including the American Mining Congress, the American Iron and Steel Institute, and the Hearth Products Association. In response, the EPA conceded that it was in violation of its statutory mandate but sought several years to conduct its review on the grounds that controversial issues were at stake, requiring consensus-building research at the frontiers of scientific knowledge of the health and welfare effects of particulate matter. Granting the plaintiff's motion for summary judgment in part and denying it in part, the court in October 1994 ordered the EPA to begin the process of reviewing and revising its particulate matter standards pursuant to a time line proposed by the EPA but slightly shortened by the court.[14]

Prompted, then, both by judicially mandated deadlines and by intervening scientific studies concerning the health effects of ozone and particulate matter, the EPA published its proposed rules at the end of 1996. (The agency's notice of proposed rulemaking for the particulate matter rule noted its judicially imposed deadline.) Upon publishing its proposed rules, the EPA estimated that its proposed new limitations would yield a number of benefits in various forms, including fifteen thousand lives saved annually; one million fewer annual incidences of significant decreases in children's lung functions requiring medical treatment, medication, or reduced activity; hundreds of thousands fewer annual incidences of aggravated asthma; hundreds of thousands fewer annual cases of aggravated coughing and difficult or painful breathing by children; tens of thousands fewer annual cases of symptoms associated with chronic bronchitis; thousands fewer hospital and emergency-room visits and admissions by individuals with asthma; reduced risks of illnesses such as inflammation of the lung, impairment of the lung's defense mechanisms, respiratory infection, and irreversible changes in lung structure leading to emphysema and chronic bronchitis or premature aging of the lungs; reduced risks of susceptibility to childhood diseases; between $50 and $120 billion annual savings in reduced medical expenditures and lower absenteeism from work; $500 million worth of avoided yield losses of major agricultural crops; reduced damage to other vegetation; and improved visibility over large regions of the eastern United States and over urban areas.[15] The EPA estimated that compliance costs would range from $6 to $9 billion annually for ten years.[16] While estimates of these benefits and costs varied, by any of the agency's measures the benefits of the proposed rules exceeded their costs by orders of magnitude. Thus the new rules appeared desirable as a matter of public policy, as well as necessary for the EPA to fulfill its responsibilities under the Clean Air Act.

While the EPA is charged under the Clean Air Act with updating the NAAQS, however, the agency does not implement those standards directly. Rather, the act requires the states to develop their own "state implementation plans" (SIPs),[17] to be submitted to the EPA for the agency's approval.[18] The EPA's role, then, is one of assistance to states in developing SIPs that will achieve compliance with the NAAQS and thus meet EPA approval. By the time the EPA proposed new ozone and particulate matter rules in 1996, some parts of the country had achieved compliance with the existing limits while other regions had not, reflecting differences in pollution concentration levels as well as in the effectiveness of SIPs in different parts of the country.

Because ozone and particulate matter are not typically discharged themselves, the important consequence of the proposed new limitations was that SIPs would have to restrict further the levels of pollution sources whose emissions contribute to their formation. This is where the case gets interesting. Pollution sources that would feel the squeeze of stricter SIPs included chemical plants, construction operations, factories, incinerators, oil refineries, motor vehicles manufacturers, power plants, and various other industrial and fuel-combustion sources. In short, numerous large industries were implicated, as the new NAAQS limits would require many major enterprises to make significant new investments in emission-reduction technologies. Not surprisingly, those forces mobilized aggressively against the proposed new standards.

But that gets slightly ahead of the story. Fully anticipating that its rules would generate enormous political resistance given the size and strength of those who would have to reduce emissions, the EPA went to great lengths to solicit public input concerning its proposals. It established a national toll-free telephone hotline (1-800-TELL-EPA) to facilitate public commentary on the proposed rules. It also solicited electronic comments via the Internet (before this practice was completely common). In addition, the EPA held several public hearings at major cities across the country, where dozens of industry representatives, local governments, and individuals responded with commentary on the proposed rules. Several of the EPA's regional offices held their own public meetings and workshops on the proposed new rules as well. The agency also participated in numerous meetings on the proposed rules organized by the Air and Waste Management Association, a nonprofit, nonpartisan professional organization that promotes environmental research and education. Finally, the EPA also held two national satellite telecasts to answer questions on the proposed standards. In other words, the EPA unveiled its proposed rules not merely by publishing them in the *Federal Register* and reacting to unsolicited comments, but by proactively soliciting feedback through various media and by creating several fora around the country for discussing the proposed rules and their justification. The agency's efforts to subject its proposed ozone and particulate matter rules to commentary and criticism were, in a word, unprecedented.

The agency also made available two crucial documents for each proposed rule that grounded the agency's analyses of them, a "criteria document" and a staff paper. In fact, these documents had been developed, made available for public comment, and revised even prior to the EPA's notices of proposed rulemaking, while the agency conducted its review of existing NAAQS. The multivolume criteria documents (one for ozone, one for particulate matter) summarized and evaluated all epidemiological and other scientific studies of the health effects of ozone and particulate matter. Those documents also reflected the independent expertise of the EPA's Clean Air Scientific Advisory Committee (CASAC), which reviewed and evaluated over 250 studies for the agency's benefit.[19]

Required by the Clean Air Act itself, and chartered under the Federal Advisory Committee Act, the Clean Air Scientific Advisory Committee is composed of nongovernment experts representing the academy, public health organizations, research institutes, and industry. A "standing" committee established to advise the EPA on scientific matters relating to clean air, the CASAC's membership is augmented with scientific and technical consultants with special expertise relating to particular NAAQS pollutants. For the purposes of reviewing the particulate matter standards, the CASAC had twenty-one members, and sixteen members for review of the ozone standard. The CASAC played a vital role in the EPA's decision to revise the NAAQS by reviewing and commenting upon the latest scientific data and studies on ozone and particulate matter.[20] For example, from 1994 through 1996 the CASAC held several public meetings (pursuant to the FACA) to review drafts of the criteria documents for ozone and particulate matter. These built upon workshops held by the EPA's National Center for Environmental Assessment to discuss new information about the health effects of each. That office prepared the criteria documents initially. The CASAC's task was then to provide independent review of the studies reflected in the criteria documents, and to draw conclusions from all available evidence. To that end, the CASAC reviewed successive drafts of the criteria documents through the mid-1990s. In 1995 and

1996, the CASAC concluded its reviews of the criteria documents and formally advised the EPA administrator concerning the state of scientific knowledge of the health effects of the two pollutants.

The staff papers for each proposed rule were authored by the EPA's Office of Air Quality Planning and Standards. In contrast to the criteria documents, the staff papers provided greater in-house review and assessment of relevant scientific and technical information for each pollutant. Otherwise like the criteria documents, they too provided comprehensive information about scientific studies. Also like the criteria documents, the staff papers were made available for public comment, and their final versions incorporated public comments received in response to earlier drafts. They were also reviewed by the CASAC, again in the name of outside expert review of the conclusions reached by the Office of Air Quality Planning and Standards. The staff papers also advised the administrator concerning the regulatory policy implications of the most important studies contained in the criteria documents, identifying for the administrator what the agency's staff believed to be the administrator's policy options. The staff papers and criteria documents, together with public commentary on them and with the CASAC's own conclusions and advice to the administrator, formed the basis of the EPA's determination to tighten the ozone and particulate matter standards beyond the levels established in 1993 and 1987. As the EPA administrator later summarized the scientific analyses underlying both proposed new standards, the agency benefited from "literally peer review of peer review of peer review."[21]

But interest-group opposition to the proposed rules was intense. The rules' opponents included automakers, coal producers, electric companies, oil companies, and other major industries. The National Association of Manufacturers fought against the new rules, for instance, as did the American Petroleum Institute. Unintimidated by the exhaustive analyses leading up to the EPA's proposed rules or by the some 270 studies that formed the basis of the agency's decision to revise the ozone and particulate matter standards, all of these forces combined to form the Air Quality Standards Coalition to contest the proposed rules. They were joined in further alliance by, for example, the small business community, farm groups, and the U.S. Conference of Mayors.

The proposed rules' opponents spent millions of dollars opposing the standards through lobbying and publicity.[22] They contested the soundness of the agency's proposals, including their scientific bases and the agency's assessments of the rules' economic consequences. And they made their objections known during the notice-and-comment stage of the EPA's rulemaking process, ensuring that their objections became part of the rulemaking records.[23] In all, the agency received fourteen thousand phone calls, four thousand e-mail messages, and fifty thousand sets of oral and written comments pertaining to the rules, many of which criticized rather than defended the proposed rules.

Not that opposition to the new rules was universal. Various academic researchers and medical research groups, including the American Lung Association and the Association of State and Territorial Health Officials, supported the proposed new standards, though they argued that the rules did not go far enough to protect human health adequately. The government of Canada took the same line, also arguing that the state of the scientific research counseled in favor of standards stricter than those the agency proposed. Environmental groups like the Natural Resources Defense Council and private citizens such as Olympic marathon winner Joan Benoit Samuelson also supported the proposed regulation, again arguing that the proposed standards did not go far enough. Such support notwithstanding, the proposed rules' mobilized opponents vastly outnumbered and outspent their organized supporters; interest-group resistance to the rules far outweighed interest-group support.

Because ozone and particulate matter travel well, small particulate matter especially, states and local governments also entered the controversy. On one side, northeastern states—that is to say, downwind states—supported the EPA's proposals, while Midwestern states—upwind states—and many local governments joined the rules' opponents. Perhaps not unexpectedly, Midwestern states reached the conclusion that the science underlying the proposed rules did not unambiguously support what the EPA contemplated and relatedly that the resulting costs imposed on industry would outweigh the rules' uncertain health and welfare benefits, while northeastern states found the evidence concerning the proposed rules and their expected net benefits overwhelming. More interestingly, this geographic division transcended partisan alignments: Republican governors from Massachusetts, New Jersey, and New York rushed to the EPA's defense,[24] long before the Democratic president decided whether to support the agency, while many Democratic governors, mayors, and members of Congress from the Midwest sharply criticized the agency and urged the White House to slow the EPA down.[25]

While the rules' opponents argued directly with the EPA, they did not count on the notice-and-comment process to alter the EPA's proposed course of regulatory action. They took their complaints to Congress as well. In turn, Congress exerted heavy pressure on the agency to abandon, soften, or delay implementation of its new standards. While Congress did not quite speak with one voice about the proposed new rules, congressional opponents of the rules expressed themselves far more often and more loudly than did congressional supporters.[26] Just for example, Congressman Joe Barton, chairman of the House Commerce Oversight and Investigations Subcommittee, sent a letter to the EPA administrator in December 1996 questioning the agency's authority to implement its proposed standards. Shortly thereafter, Senator Lincoln Chafee, chair of the Senate Environment and Public Works Committee, sent the administrator a letter, circulated for signatures, also questioning the agency's rules. The following June, the House Science Committee's Subcommittee on Energy and Environment issued a critical report of the EPA's initiative, alleging that, as one member put it, the agency had put "the regulatory cart before the scientific horse. "[27] In the letter of transmittal accompanying its report, the chair and ranking member of the subcommittee explained that the EPA's rules were a matter "of great concern to the Committee and to many Members of Congress," because the rules "will have far-reaching impacts on the U.S. economy, but may yield little in benefits to the American public."

That report followed and reflected congressional oversight hearings. Led largely by legislators from states housing industries with potentially high compliance costs—Democrats as much as Republicans[28]—both houses of Congress held several hearings in the spring of 1997.[29] In April, the House Commerce Committee's Subcommittee on Health and the Environment and the Subcommittee on Oversight and Investigations held lengthy joint hearings. The subcommittees invited four former or then-current chairs of the EPA's CASAC to testify, seeking their individual views of the agency's proposed rules.[30] Although as explained above the agency's proposals reflected the analysis and advice of the CASAC as a whole, some of its former chairs testified largely against the proposed rules, the PM rule in particular. For example, George Wolf—CASAC chair from 1993 to 1996 and then principal scientist of General Motors Environmental and Energy Staff—testified that deadlines did not allow the CASAC time to reach a consensus on the $PM_{2.5}$ standard and that therefore the EPA's proposed level reflected a policy judgment, not a decision based on science. Similarly, Roger McClellan, chair of the CASAC from 1988 to 1992 and then president of the Chemical Industry Institute of Toxicology, a nonprofit research organization funded principally by thirty leading industrial firms, testified against the $PM_{2.5}$ standard on the grounds that the causal link between exposure to particulate matter and adverse health responses required further study.

In May, those subcommittees held three more days of joint hearings, this time hearing testimony in strong opposition to the proposed rules from state and local officials, and admitting into the record prepared statements by, among others, Chicago's mayor (and then-president of the U.S. Conference of Mayors) Richard M. Daley and Ohio governor George Voinovich. Mayor Daley, for example, argued that the EPA's proposed rules would threaten rather than advance public health because the loss of jobs associated with their implementation would reduce access to health care and good nutrition. On the last day of the May hearings, the subcommittee members, now armed with the objections and arguments raised by all other witnesses as well as by congressional constituencies opposed to the rules, questioned administrator Carol Browner, who had testified earlier before the Senate as well.

The oversight hearings were no picnic for Browner. Indeed, subcommittee members themselves remarked on the unusual grilling they gave the administrator, before what they self-described as a "deeply skeptical audience."[31] One committee member remarked that Browner had "a credibility problem," while another noted the congressional "hostility toward your proposals."[32] Some accused her of being out of touch with the scientific and policy assessments of other agencies in the Clinton administration. She was accused also of ignoring all relevant science, of mischaracterizing the CASAC's advice, exaggerating the scientific bases of the rules, misstating her obligations under the Clean Air Act, failing to comply with Executive Order 12866, ignoring regulatory alternatives, and overstating the health benefits and understating the economic costs of the new rules. One member observed that Browner was "berated" by the subcommittees.[33] Another member added: "I don't believe you have been berated. Browbeaten, maybe, but not berated."[34] Some members suggested that the EPA's proposed rules would go so far as to require "lifestyle" changes by individuals who would have to reduce their use of barbeque grills and fireplaces, and sharply criticized the administrator for failing to acknowledge as much.[35]

At times, the rules' opponents made it personal: Some in Congress went so far as to charge that Browner from the very beginning took a results-oriented approach to the rulemakings with no intention of being influenced by comments and reactions to her agency's proposed rules, and that she therefore refused to consider in earnest the uncertainties surrounding the rules' benefits or the great burdens the rules would create. Congressman Coburn, for example, expressed his concern "that philosophy is driving science, and science is not driving philosophy,"[36] while Congressman Klink stated that "there are a lot of us that think that your decision is a fait accompli."[37] This charge echoed certain interest groups that also vilified the administrator,[38] including the Washington Legal Foundation, which took the highly unusual step of formally petitioning the EPA seeking Browner's recusal from the rulemakings on the ground that she could not give meaningful, open-minded consideration to the proposed rules because she had already determined to tighten the ozone and particulate matter standards.[39]

Others accused the EPA of withholding relevant factual information, not only from the White House but from Congress. In the April joint hearings, for example, Commerce Committee chairman Tom Bliley set the tone of the hearings by characterizing himself as "a vocal critic of EPA's repeated attempts to shield the proposals from legitimate Congressional scrutiny,"[40] a tone resounded in the May hearings as well.[41] Still others threatened to utilize the legislative "Corrections Day" or other congressional review procedures to invalidate the new standards legislatively given that the agency was so out of touch with congressional will.[42]

Nor did moderate congressional voices come to the Browner's rescue. Instead, they urged the EPA to loosen rather than abandon its proposed standards.[43] Very few legislators supported without qualification what the agency had proposed. Meanwhile, critical congressional reactions were bolstered by lobbying and testimony from the rules' many opponents, including industry representatives and Midwestern governors.

But the administrator defended the agency's proposals and its decisionmaking processes steadfastly before an unsympathetic Congress, as she had more generally before the public. She testified at length that the EPA, its CASAC, and all of the agency's working groups took into account all of the relevant science, as the Clean Air Act's emphasis on public health required her to do. She also explained that the agency had taken unprecedented measures to include all interests in its decisionmaking process, and deliberated at length with other agencies as well as the White House, which was satisfied with the agency's process. She further explained that implementation of the rules would require years of cooperation among the EPA, the states, and industry, and that areas out of compliance with the proposed standards could achieve compliance by focusing on utility emissions, as opposed to the activities of small business, much less of individual citizens.

Even so, given the strength of congressional and interest-group opposition to the proposed new standards, it was unclear during the months between publication of the EPA's proposed ozone and particulate matter rules and publication of the final rules in July 1997 whether the agency would adopt the standards it contemplated. This was true in part because during much of that time the White House equivocated about whether to support the agency. Some within the White House supported the EPA's stricter limits, while others focused on their costs.[44] According to several reports, the proposed rules were particularly controversial within the White House's National Economic Council and to some extent within the Office of Management and Budget (OMB).[45] As a result, until as late as June 25, when the White House decided to support the EPA's proposed rules rather than to advocate softening modifications as some had predicted, Administrator Browner found herself defending her agency's proposed rules before many strong enemies, with the help of few allies, and under the awkward cloud of a conspicuously silent White House.[46]

Though undecided until late in rulemaking process, the White House was not at all a passive participant in the EPA's decisionmaking. Beginning in 1993, the OMB and the EPA set up an interagency working group, later divided into an interagency policy group and an interagency technical group, in which the Departments of Interior, Treasury, Commerce, Agriculture, Defense, Transportation, and Justice, together with the Small Business Administration, the White House's Office of Science Technology and Policy, and its Council of Economic Advisors, all participated. Through the mid-1990s, the EPA and OMB convened numerous meetings to discuss the science and EPA's scientific review documents. By February 1997, those meetings became weekly. In addition, the White House's Office of Information and Regulatory Affairs reviewed the rules as mandated by Executive Order 12866, subjecting them—to the extent permitted under the Clean Air Act—to cost-benefit analysis as well as to consistency with the administration's regulatory policies and priorities. In conjunction with its review of the rules under Executive Order 12866, OIRA convened several meetings with interest-group representatives to discuss the rules pending review. Not only was the OIRA administrator (at that time, Sally Katzen) very familiar with the science and policy underlying what the EPA proposed to do, but detailed understanding extended up the executive-branch hierarchy to Vice President Gore and President Clinton as well. In short, the White House was neither unaware of nor apathetic towards the EPA's rules, but rather bitterly ambivalent given the rules' substantial costs. By the middle of 1997, however, that ambivalence gave way to support.

In the end, over intense objections from many powerful interest groups and members of Congress—though with a late-breaking boost from downwind senator Alfonse D'Amato (four of whose seven grandchildren suffer from asthma)[47]—and with last-minute political help from the White House, the EPA issued final rules that resembled its proposed rules very closely. The final ozone rule limits ozone to 0.08 ppm, as proposed, calculated using a three-year average of the annual fourth-highest (rather than third-highest, as originally proposed) daily maximum eight-hour concentration.[48] The final particulate matter rule limits $PM_{2.5}$ to 15 micrograms per cubic meter calculated on an annual basis, and 65 micrograms per cubic meter calculated on a twenty-four-hour basis (rather than the stricter standard of 50 micrograms per cubic meter on a twenty-four-hour basis, as originally proposed), and PM_{10} to 50 micrograms per cubic meter annually and 150 micrograms per cubic meter on a twenty-four-hour basis, just as proposed.[49] Upon announcing the final rules, the EPA responded at great length to comments the agency had received on its proposed rules and provided comprehensive explanations of the agency's justifications for the final form of the rules. The *Federal Register* entry for the final ozone rule ran 34 pages, while the agency explained its particulate matter rule in 109 pages. In another 135 *Federal Register* pages on the same day, the EPA provided additional information and solicited comments on measurement methodologies for the new $PM_{2.5}$ standard.

But promulgation of the final ozone and particulate matter rules did not end this regulatory saga. Not even close. Shortly after the EPA promulgated its final ozone and particulate matter rules, bills were introduced in both houses of Congress to impose four-year moratoria on the new standards.[50] On the House side, Representative Ron Klink introduced a bill to prevent implementation of the new rules and providing for several years of additional research on the necessity of the stricter standards before the rules could come into effect. In the Senate, Senator James Inhofe introduced a similar bill. Both bills reflected efforts to avoid or postpone the costs that compliance with the new rules would create for industry, utilities, and transportation. Between them, the House and Senate bills had over two hundred cosponsors.

Neither bill passed. But they upped the ante. Maintaining pressure on the agency even after its rules had been finalized, these bills expressed many legislators' continued resistance to agency action. Either bill might very well have passed, but neither was scheduled for markup because

175

they appeared to lack enough congressional support to overcome a likely presidential veto. Having just provided strong if late support for the EPA's initiative, President Clinton was not prepared to sign legislation undermining the agency's new rules. Thus the branches remained divided over the new standards for about a year after their issuance, creating uncertainty about when and how (and especially with what funding) the new rules would be implemented.

That impasse gave way to compromise the following year. With the support of the EPA, the White House, and the bipartisan leadership of the Senate Environment and Public Works Committee, Senator Inhofe (chair of the Clean Air Subcommittee) added an amendment to a transportation reauthorization bill that preserved the EPA's new standards but addressed some of the concerns raised by some of the rules' opponents. The Inhofe amendment became law in the middle of 1998. It requires, for example, that the EPA differentiate among different types of $PM_{2.5}$ so as to spare farmers from targeted regulation, based on farms groups' concerns that agricultural activities such as plowing and burning would be considered sources of $PM_{2.5}$ by the agency. The amendment also calls for federal funding of fine particulate matter monitoring networks required by the new PM standard to be established in every state, alleviating states' concerns about having to pay for the monitoring networks themselves. In addition, the amendment codified the EPA's implementation schedule, which gave the agency until July 2000 to designate ozone nonattainment areas and until December 2005 to designate $PM_{2.5}$ nonattainment areas. Upon promulgating the final rules, the EPA and the president announced an implementation schedule longer than that mandated by the Clean Air Act, but opponents of the rules worried the agency might be forced through litigation under the statute to act more quickly. By codifying the agency's schedule, the amendment preempted any judicial injunction to implement faster.

While the executive and legislative branches tussled over when and how the new rules would be implemented, the rules' interest-group opponents moved their fight to the courts as well. In fact, part of the reason Congress did not act even more aggressively to slow the EPA down following promulgation of the final rules was that the rules' opponents had already initiated litigation calling the rules' implementation into question.[51] Indeed, the implementation of the new standards was thrown into considerable doubt judicially in 1999. In a case brought by the American Truckers Associations (along with businesses and Midwestern states), the U.S. Court of Appeals for the D.C. Circuit ruled that the portion of the Clean

Air Act on which the EPA based its rules constituted an unconstitutional delegation of legislative power.[52] In a surprising turn, the court did not strike down the Clean Air Act as unconstitutional, but rather explained that the EPA's construction of the act in effect rendered it unconstitutional because that construction provided no intelligible principle cabining the agency's discretion in setting NAAQS standards to protect public health. The court invited the agency to reinterpret the act by supplying some specific criteria to limit its own discretion. The court also held that the EPA wrongly failed to consider the health benefits of ground-level ozone as a shield for ultraviolet radiation, and that the agency's measurements of PM_{10} were arbitrary and capricious.

That decision was reversed by the Supreme Court.[53] The Court explained that if the Clean Air Act were unconstitutional because its delegation to the EPA too broad, the agency's interpretation or reinterpretation of the statute could not rescue it. But, the Court held, the act's language instructing the EPA to develop NAAQS standards at levels "requisite to protect public health" provided a principle sufficiently intelligible for constitutional purposes. On remand of the case, the appeals court subsequently rejected all remaining legal challenges to the new standards, but not until almost five years had passed since the new rules' promulgation.

Even the EPA's ultimate litigation success did not imply that the new rules would take immediate effect, however, given the nature of this regulatory issue. For while the new standards became officially "effective" a few months after promulgation of the final rules—subject at that time to possible judicial invalidation and under congressional threats of moratoria—their effectiveness merely initiated a long processes of determining which areas of the country were in violation of the new rules and establishing implementation plans for improving air quality within those areas. In other words, it was clear from the very beginning, even among the rules' most committed proponents, that it would be years before the new ozone and particulate matter rules changed the practices of states and polluters on the ground. As Carol Browner testified before the impatient House subcommittees:

> The most important thing I think, to note is at the time I set the public health standard, there is not a single business, there is not a single State in the United States required to do anything, anything at all, nothing happens by the mere fact that I set the standard. Anything that does happen, happens over an 8, 10, 12-year period with public comment, with cost/benefit analysis, with review in Congress if appropriate. It all plays out in a very measured sensible manner.[54]

Because the new standards first require determinations of exactly which areas of the country are not in compliance with them and by how much, and then require the creation of SIPs that will bring those areas into compliance, operationalization of the new ozone and particulate matter rules would take at least several years.

Thus the 1997 ozone and particulate matter standards called for the EPA to designate areas not in compliance over the course of the next six to seven years. Areas not in compliance with established NAAQS levels are designated by the EPA as "nonattainment" areas. Today, most nonattainment areas are such because of the level of ozone and particulate matter in those areas. Approximately thirty-six EPA-designated areas containing about 86 million people were not in compliance with maximum ozone levels even before the new rules, while sixty-one designated areas containing about 25 million people were out of compliance with previous particulate matter limitations.[55] Upon implementation of the new ozone and particulate matter rules, the number of nonattainment areas for these two pollutants was expected to roughly double. Put in terms of counties rather than EPA-defined "areas" not in compliance with the old ozone and particulate matter rules, the number of counties out of compliance with the new limits was expected to triple.

Once the Supreme Court resolved most uncertainties concerning the legality of the new rules, the EPA requested all states and tribes to provide their recommendations concerning the designation of areas within their borders as attainment or nonattainment areas by July 2003, to pave the way for additional substantive rulemaking governing implementation of the rules. In 2004, the EPA made its compliance determinations, based on state and tribal recommendations and following some give-and-take between the agency and the states and tribes. Among other things, those determinations led the EPA to shift from one-hour to eight-hour ozone measurement designations.[56] During this same period, states began to modify their state implementation plans to reflect the new standards. The substantial time necessary first to collect data measuring ozone and particulate matter—especially data measuring the newly defined category of fine particulate matter, not collected before the new standards—and then to review that data, and finally to consider state designations and review state implementation strategies meant that it was not until 2004 that states turned in earnest to bringing nonattainment areas into compliance.

Implementation of the new standards is, then, still under way. The EPA gave states three years from the time the agency designated nonattainment areas to develop new pollution control plans to bring their areas into compliance. That is, states have had several more years to develop their compliance strategies, not to achieve actual compliance. As for compliance, the agency has set a timetable allowing states to reach attainment within ten years (with the possibility of two one-year extensions under certain circumstances) of the date of approved implementation plans, reflecting the agency's cost-benefit analyses of implementation alternatives. In other words, the time horizon for bringing states into compliance with the new standards extends to at least 2012. At their option, states could also enter into "early action compacts" with the EPA by submitting plans to meet the new ozone standards, according to which attainment deadlines for those standards would be deferred so long as participating states met specified "milestones" towards attainment.

Thus will this story continue for years to come. As of early 2005, for example, the EPA was still in the process of determining the finer points of the rule it promulgated for implementing the ozone standard, while opponents and defenders of the ozone rule continued to litigate the details concerning the timing and form of its implementation. But then technical and controversial solutions of complex regulatory problems are commonly implemented over long periods. In that light, it is to be fully expected that the benefits and costs of the ozone and particulate matter rules will be realized well in the future.

In the meantime, there is no question that the EPA's new rules shifted the regulatory baseline considerably: By tightening ozone and particulate matter standards substantially, the EPA triggered a long process of implementation, requiring stricter state plans for reducing air pollution, inspiring more regional cooperation to reduce emissions, and spawning technological advances to curb emissions more efficiently. The EPA did so notwithstanding the great strength and concentration of those opposed to the new rules, and notwithstanding strong opposition from Congress as well. It did so, moreover, employing robust administrative decisionmaking processes—including, among others, notice-and-comment rulemaking with advanced notice and extensive outside participation, advisory committees, peer review, and cost-benefit analysis. And it did so led by a determined administrator, with indispensable help from the White House, and with vindication from the federal courts. The full significance of these observations is saved for part 4.

Chapter Ten

The Food and Drug Administration's Tobacco Initiative

Exhibit two:

In August 1996, the federal Food and Drug Administration took what can only be described as an astonishing step, issuing a rule regulating cigarettes and smokeless tobacco products.[1] The FDA's rule, some 219 *Federal Register* pages long, regulated tobacco comprehensively. It governed the advertising, sales, and distribution of cigarettes and smokeless tobacco products. The tobacco rule constituted the FDA's most ambitious rulemaking initiative ever, one that responded to a problem of enormous social and economic proportions.

The effects of smoking present one of the biggest public health issues of our time. The basic facts are now well known: In the United States, smoking claims well over four hundred thousand lives annually, that is, about 20 percent of all deaths.[2] By comparison, tobacco results in more deaths every year than do alcohol, illegal drugs, auto accidents, violent crime, and AIDS combined. Smoking is causally responsible for 30 percent of all cancer deaths. Smoking is also responsible for 87 percent of all lung cancer deaths, 82 percent of deaths from chronic obstructive pulmonary disease, 21 percent of deaths from coronary heart disease, and 18 percent of deaths from a stroke.

Of course, those who die from smoking would have died of other causes. But on average, smokers who die from a disease induced by smoking lose between twelve and fifteen years of life. Moreover, short of death (and otherwise prior to death), smoking causes numerous serious health conditions, including, in addition to those already mentioned, cancers of the larynx, mouth, esophagus, and bladder, as well as peptic ulcer disease and low birth weight. On top of that, secondhand or "passive" smoke inhalation results annually in another several thousand deaths and hundreds of thousands of cases of respiratory ailments. Deaths and illnesses directly related to smoking therefore account for tens of billions of dollars in health expenditures and tens of billions of dollars in morbidity costs and lost earnings every year.[3]

Yet for decades, the health consequences of smoking were not well understood, especially by smokers themselves. As a result, in previous generations cigarettes were not perceived to warrant regulation of any kind. Indeed, for decades in the early middle of the twentieth century, cigarette manufacturers often advertised the beneficial health effects of smoking. Not widely perceived as detrimental, smoking became exceedingly common by the end of World War II.

The earliest serious attempts to "regulate" smoking—that is, through private-law mechanisms—did not much come until the 1980s, after the adverse effects of smoking became better documented and more widely known. For the first time, health experts then drew sustained public attention to the dangers of smoking. In the wake of resulting public health campaigns about smoking and ill health, and especially of greater understanding of smoking's consequences, plaintiffs' lawyers brought private litigation against tobacco companies. Smoker plaintiffs had litigated against tobacco companies earlier, but it was not until the late 1980s, when the adverse health effects of smoking became incontrovertible, and also when the deceptive practices of cigarette manufacturers were first revealed, that private litigation was even slightly successful.

Until the FDA's tobacco rule, however, the federal government had not regulated cigarettes or tobacco to a significant degree, with the important exception of legislation in 1965—as amended in 1969—that requires the now familiar warning labels on cigarettes and other tobacco products. Among regulatory agencies, the FDA would be the agency most likely to regulate, given that it regulates foods, drugs, cosmetics, and similar products that are ingested by or applied to the body. From that perspective, it comes as no surprise that the FDA would regulate cigarettes, if any agency ever would.

On the other hand, the FDA's authority derives from the Federal Food, Drug, and Cosmetics Act and its amendments (FDCA).[4] And under the FDCA, the FDA's jurisdiction over drugs extends to "drugs" and "devices" including "drug delivery systems." Because cigarettes are obviously neither food nor cosmetics, the agency's authority to regulate cigarettes depends on whether nicotine constitutes a drug and cigarettes therefore a drug delivery system for the purposes of the statute. Under the statute, a product is a drug or device if it is "intended to affect the structure or any function of the body."[5]

Significantly—as subsequent events would prove—the FDA had considered regulating cigarettes on previous occasions. It had assumed regulatory jurisdiction over cigarettes in a couple of instances in the 1950s where manufacturers marketed their products by making specific claims about beneficial therapeutic effects. Otherwise, though, the agency had repeatedly concluded that it lacked jurisdiction over cigarettes and tobacco as ordinarily marketed, even when the FDA was repeatedly prompted to regulate by a public health organization in the late 1970s.

But things changed, dramatically, by the mid-1990s. Reflecting not only a decade of overwhelming evidence about the effects of smoking, but also new evidence about the addictiveness of nicotine, the manipulability of nicotine levels in cigarettes, and the marketing strategies of cigarette manufacturers, especially with respect to minors, the FDA in August 1995 proposed an ambitious new rule. The rule sought above all else to reduce the incidence of youth smoking. The FDA explained in its introduction to the proposed rule that, because the cigarette industry loses approximately 1.7 million customers each year—1.3 million of whom quit and the rest of whom die—cigarette manufacturers target young smokers to replace lost customers. As a result, approximately three thousand young persons begin smoking each day in the United States, and young smokers constitute the industry's major source of new smokers. The FDA noted further that while the prevalence of smoking among adults had declined in recent years, the prevalence of smoking among minors had risen in the 1990s. The agency explained that its proposed rule would, by limiting the appeal of and access to cigarettes and smokeless tobacco for minors, reduce the number of young smokers and in turn reduce the overall death and disease rates of tobacco generally.[6]

The proposed rule thus aimed first to restrict access to cigarettes sales by minors.[7] For starters, the proposed rule prohibited the retail sale of single cigarettes, and required cigarette packages to contain at least twenty cigarettes, forbidding the manufacture of "kiddie packs." It also eliminated vending machine sales, mail-order sales, self-service displays, and free tobacco samples, again all to reduce minors' access to cigarettes and tobacco products. The proposed rule also limited certain tobacco advertising in the media.[8] For example, it required text-only, black-and-white written advertisements in magazines and other publications with a youth readership of more than two million. The proposed rule also prohibited the distribution of nontobacco promotional items such as clothing, hats, pens, and desktop toys that carried tobacco brand names.[9] It also prohibited tobacco corporate sponsors of sporting and other events from using their brand names or any other brand identifying symbols during such events.[10] Finally, the proposed rule required tobacco manufacturers to finance a national public education program aimed to reduce youth smoking.[11]

As in the case of the EPA's ozone and particulate matter rules, the FDA's tobacco rulemaking process started before the agency published its notice of proposed rulemaking. In early 1994, for example, prompted by petitions submitted by the Coalition on Smoking or Health—a public interest group representing the American Cancer Society, the American Heart Association, and the American Lung Association—and others,[12] the FDA undertook examination of its regulatory jurisdiction over products containing nicotine. About the same time, the agency also began investigating whether cigarette manufacturers controlled the levels of nicotine in their products in ways that create and sustain addiction. And a year before the FDA published its proposed rule, the agency's Drug Abuse Advisory Committee, established under the FACA, held an important public hearing on the addictiveness of cigarettes and reported findings concluding that tobacco products contain nicotine at levels that create and sustain addiction.[13] (It was another FDA advisory committee, the Advisory Committee on Smoking and Health, that back in 1964 provided advice that informed the 1964 surgeon general's report highlighting the ill-health effects of smoking and the pharmacological effects of nicotine, an important impetus behind the labeling legislation in that decade.) The FDA's proposed tobacco rule thus followed the agency's recent investigations of the medical and social-scientific evidence concerning patterns of smoking among adults and children, as well as of the addictive qualities of nicotine, and the marketing, sales, and distribution practices of tobacco companies.

Because the FDA's proposed rule was clearly a "major" rule under Executive Order 12866, the agency provided a cost-benefit analysis of it. The FDA estimated that the rule would impose an initial cost on the tobacco industry of between $174 and $187 million, and thereafter annual costs of between $149 and $185 million.[14] The agency also estimated that the rule would generate between $28 and $43 billion in annual benefits, mostly due to savings in health-related expenditures.[15] As the FDA explained, the intangible nature of some of the benefits of smoking—including the utility smokers get from smoking—as well as the difficulties of converting health improvements into precise economic benefits, made cost-benefit analysis of the proposed rule partly speculative. Even so, however, the projected benefits exceeded the projected costs by a large multiple. The benefits from avoided health care costs alone exceeded the domestic revenue of the major tobacco companies, a fact that underscored the core problem—that cigarettes impose large social costs that are internalized neither by cigarette manufacturers nor smokers themselves.

Following publication of the proposed rule, the FDA accepted comments from August until November 1995. At the close of the initial comment period, given the controversy surrounding its proposal and the resulting volume of commentary the agency received, the FDA extended the public comment period until January 1996. Thereafter, it reopened the comment period for another month that spring.[16]

Comment on the proposed rule was indeed voluminous: The rule generated seven hundred thousand pieces of written commentary. Although three hundred thousand of those comments came from one particular mail campaign—a form letter expressing concern that the rule's limitation on corporate sponsorship would have a negative effect on auto racing, mostly delivered by a single law firm representing opponents of the rule—even discounting those, the agency received the most comments in the history of FDA rulemaking.[17] Ninety-five thousand individuals mailed the agency their individual views. The FDA also received five hundred different form letters. The vast majority of unduplicated comments supported the agency's proposal.

The sheer magnitude of the FDA's rulemaking was not its only distinguishing feature. Unconventionally, the agency also solicited comments on the question of its regulatory jurisdiction over cigarettes and other tobacco products.[18] It did so even though it was under no obligation to do notice-and-comment concerning its regulatory authority specifically. The FDA might have, for example, promulgated an interpretive rule concerning its statutory authority prior to issuing its proposed tobacco rule, making its intentions known.[19] Or the agency might have issued its proposed rule and included a short statement simply identifying the statutory authority under which the agency was operating and explaining why the agency determined that its authority supported its rule, as the APA requires and as agencies routinely do. But anticipating the political significance of what it proposed to do, and expecting forceful opposition by tobacco companies and other powerful interests, the FDA instead invited commentary on the threshold question of its statutory authority, and indeed later committed considerable space to that issue in its voluminous final rule.[20]

The FDA also sought, prior to promulgating its proposed rule, an order from the White House directing it to initiate a tobacco rulemaking. Here again, this maneuver was unconventional. For one thing, the FDA legally did not need White House prompting to regulate. If the agency had jurisdiction over cigarettes, it could have initiated the rulemaking on its own. While informal communication and coordination between agencies and the White House are very common prior to a notice of a proposed major rule, such coordination does not usually result in a command from the White House formally instructing an agency to undertake regulatory action. Moreover, if the FDA lacked jurisdiction over nicotine or cigarettes, then a White House directive could not empower the FDA with authority it lacked. Either way, the White House's command was meaningful only politically.

But it was exactly political support that mattered in the early stage of this case. The political significance of the FDA's proposed rule, and the agency's accurate expectations of strong opposition by tobacco companies and many legislators, led FDA commissioner David Kessler not only to clear his agency's plan with the White House informally, but also to get from the White House official instructions to move ahead.[21] As a result, following confidential communications between the FDA and the White House concerning possible regulatory steps to be taken by the FDA—during which time Democratic governors and legislators from tobacco states who were aware of the FDA's potential activity urged the White House to prevent FDA regulation of tobacco—the president issued an executive order announcing that he was "directing" the FDA to adopt regulations aimed to limit children's access to tobacco.[22] Without such White House support, the FDA certainly would not have gone forward.

The FDA's proposed tobacco rule enjoyed support from several quarters. First, consumer groups such as Public Citizen and the National Center for Tobacco-Free Kids supported the rule. So did many medical researchers, health professionals, and public health organizations. For example, the American Medical Association—which had filed an amicus brief in tobacco litigation before the Supreme Court in the famous *Cipollone v. Liggett Group* case[23] (arguing that the 1965 and 1969 cigarette labeling acts should not be interpreted to preempt state common-law suits against tobacco manufacturers)—strongly supported the rule, for which it had petitioned in the first place. Other health organizations supported the rule as well, including among others the American Academy of Pediatrics and the American College of Preventive Medicine. In addition, educational organizations such as the National Parent-Teachers Association, the National Association of Elementary School Principals, and the National Association of Secondary School Principals also strongly supported the rule. Finally, thousands of individual citizens also commented in support of the rule on their own behalf, as did tens of thousands of children through their parents.

Notwithstanding such support, the FDA faced stronger opposition from several powerful interests. Because the economic stakes were very high for the rule's opponents, they too mobilized, submitting thousands of pages of comments objecting to the proposed rule.[24] Tobacco farmers and cigarette manufacturers in particular had a lot to lose. If the rule were finalized and its intended effects realized, cigarette makers and in turn farmers would face a substantial drop in the demand for their products. In addition, cigarette manufacturers faced compliance costs as well, including for example the costs of changing their cigarette distribution practices. In fact, the tobacco industry estimated the annual costs of the rule for it to be approximately $1 billion—more than five times higher than the FDA's estimates of the proposed rule's costs—excluding the losses from reduced sales.[25] Thus the Tobacco Institute threw its substantial weight against the proposed rule.

Tobacco farmers and cigarette makers were not the rule's only organized opponents, however. Advertisers too had a lot at stake, given the proposed rule's limits on tobacco advertising. Because the proposed rule severely limited cigarette manufacturers' ability to advertise in publications read by minors, advertisers too faced losses in revenue. They too mobilized against the rule, spending considerable resources focusing on issues relating to advertisement and their First Amendment rights. Tobacco retailers—grocers and convenience stores—did the same, again motivated by potential lost sales.

Smokers themselves also opposed the rule. The National Smokers Alliance and other smokers' groups submitted comments to the agency protesting the proposed rule on the grounds it interfered with their autonomy. Finally, organizations representing automobile race tracks also submitted comments critical of the FDA's proposal. Because of the proposed rule's limitations on cigarette corporate sponsorship of sporting events, and given the importance of brand sponsorship of auto races, race cars, and drivers, race fans and track advocates opposed the rule on the grounds that it would unduly interfere with their business and recreational activities.

While both supporters and opponents of the rule thus mobilized in response to the FDA's proposal, the rule's opponents outspent its supporters. The cigarette industry, for example, submitted a single "comment" objecting to the proposed rule that consisted of some two thousand pages of written commentary and another forty-seven thousand pages of supporting documents. In addition to opposing the FDA's proposed rule through the notice-and-comment process, the rule's opponents also called on Congress to stop the FDA, whereas supporters of the rule—lacking many legislative allies—voiced their support largely through the rulemaking process. The rule's opponents protested in the media and other settings as well. As in the case of the EPA's ozone and particulate matter rules, opposition to the tobacco rule extended beyond the FDA's publication of its final rule. For example, following the agency's promulgation of the final rule in August 1996, and just before the 1996 election, hundreds of tobacco farmers demonstrated in Vice President Al Gore's hometown, protesting the rule and promising to vote against Gore in the election.[26]

Again as in the case of the EPA rules, congressional opposition to the FDA's proposed rule both far outweighed congressional support and crossed party lines. Just as Democratic legislators from Midwestern industrial states opposed the ozone and particulate matter rules, so too Dixiecrats from tobacco states opposed the tobacco rule. Senator Wendell Ford of Kentucky, for one example, introduced a bill, aimed to reduce minors' access to cigarettes and exposure to cigarette advertising, that specifically prohibited the FDA from regulating tobacco.[27] Senator Ford—the Senate's second-ranking Democrat at the time—characterized his bill as a moderate alternative to the FDA's proposed rule, which he described as the work of "zealots."[28] Southeastern Republicans also strongly opposed the FDA's rule. Senator Jesse Helms, for example, stated that "[t]he president is in effect declaring war on 76,000 North Carolinians who gain their livelihood in one form or another from tobacco."[29] Toward the close of the rule's public comment period, thirty-three senators, including both the majority and minority leaders, signed a letter strenuously objecting to the FDA's proposal.

On the House side, Speaker Newt Gingrich proclaimed that the "FDA had lost its mind," stating that "[i]f you want an example of big government interfering, it would be the FDA picking a brand new fight when we haven't won the far more serious fights about crack and cocaine and heroin."[30] That sentiment was echoed by Representative Howard Coble of North Carolina, who complained that "the FDA continues to play its role as the officious intermeddler, inserting its nose into an area where it doesn't belong," notwithstanding that "tobacco is legally grown, legally produced, legally processed and legally marketed."[31] Even House minority leader Richard Gephardt joined a coalition of lawmakers actively opposing FDA regulation. Still others in Congress warned the FDA that there would be a congressional "response" if the agency went ahead with its proposed rule over congressional objections.[32] House Democrat Rick Boucher, among many others, cosponsored legislation providing that the agency lacked authority to regulate tobacco.

Many of the FDA's critics targeted Commissioner Kessler personally. For example, Senate majority leader and presidential candidate Robert Dole made clear not only that he opposed FDA regulation of tobacco but also that, if elected, he would immediately fire Kessler,[33] making Kessler the first FDA commissioner in history to make a presidential platform. Other legislators commonly characterized the FDA's proposed rule as the work of a runaway commissioner, calling Kessler "out of his mind,"[34] "out of control,"[35] the "National Nanny,"[36] a regulator who never "held a real job,"[37] and whose "regulatory glee is more than a little frightening."[38] Interest-group opponents of the agency's proposed rule joined legislators in personalizing their opposition. The president of the Tobacco Growers Association, for instance, declared that "David Kessler's plan is ridiculous."

Notwithstanding strong congressional resistance to the FDA's proposed rule, and somewhat ironically given that resistance, Congress itself had already entered the controversy surrounding smoking and the marketing of cigarettes. Indeed, congressional action nearly rendered the FDA rule irrelevant. In 1994, Kessler testified repeatedly before the House Energy and Commerce Committee's Subcommittee on Health and the Environment—a subcommittee much more friendly to Kessler before the 1994 midterm elections than after—about the evidence his agency was gathering from former tobacco employees concerning cigarette companies' manipulation of nicotine levels in their product.[39] At that time, Congress was investigating reports that cigarette companies adjusted nicotine levels to create addiction to their products. In response to such reports, Congress was considering legislation expanding the FDA's authority over cigarettes. In fact, during Kessler's congressional testimony, he expressly requested guidance from Congress about how the FDA should proceed given the evidence it had gathered about the composition of cigarettes, manufacturers' practices, addiction, and the health effects of smoking.[40]

Later that year, the same House subcommittee also heard now-famous testimony from the CEOs of seven large tobacco companies concerning the industry's views on addiction and its practices with respect to altering nicotine levels in their products.[41] (That testimony later led to a Justice Department perjury investigation.) Former tobacco company scientists and other employees also testified about tobacco company research establishing the addictive qualities of nicotine, further exposing questionable industry practices. Concerned about such practices, some in Congress thought legislative action might be necessary. That possibility evaporated, however, following the midterm elections in 1994, when Republicans adverse to regulation gained control of Congress.

The midterm elections did not change public opinion, however. In fact, public opinion turned increasingly against the tobacco industry through the mid-1990s, following revelations about nicotine addiction, the manipulation of nicotine levels in cigarettes, and tobacco marketing aimed at minors. Significantly, that shift in public perceptions of cigarette makers made them increasingly vulnerable to private litigation. For example, whereas cigarette manufacturers had previously relied on juries that were unsympathetic to smoker plaintiffs, negative public opinion of cigarette makers altered jury sympathies. Relatedly, legal doctrines that had protected cigarette manufacturer defendants from successful lawsuits—such as the "assumption of risk" defense—no longer protected defendants as well in light of evidence that defendants altered nicotine content without smokers' knowledge. Similarly, the high hurdles smoker plaintiffs faced following the *Cipollone* case that required plaintiffs to show misrepresentation no longer seemed so high. In short, public perceptions, and with such perceptions the legal landscape, changed quickly and dramatically against tobacco manufacturers.

Meanwhile, the attorneys general of many states had entered into negotiations with the major tobacco companies to resolve suits against the companies brought on behalf of the states seeking reimbursement for state expenditures on health care for smokers. Given new evidence about not only the health consequences of smoking but more specifically about the financial burden those consequences placed on states, states brought litigation to recoup their expenditures. Following months of intensive negotiations between the states and the industry, both sides looked to Congress to pass legislation essentially "ratifying" an agreement between dozens of states and the major tobacco companies. For months during 1996—and again even as late as the summer of 1997 after the FDA's rule was finalized—it appeared that Congress would ratify an unprecedented $369 billion agreement, according to which tobacco firms would contribute heavily to funds covering past and present medical costs of treatment for smoking-induced illnesses as well as funds financing antismoking educational campaigns, while getting in return substantial restrictions on the types of lawsuits that could be brought against them to recover for injuries caused by their products. That nationally ratified settlement would have specifically provided for legislative codification of several aspects of the FDA's rule, in particular its restrictions aimed to reduce smoking by minors, but also would have restricted the agency's ability to regulate, and certainly to ban, nicotine directly.[42] In other words, the legislation passed to codify the proposed national settlement would have in one way or another largely mooted the FDA's rule.

But while the two sides had agreed in principle to the proposed national settlement, it was never enacted legislatively. Ultimately, tobacco companies opposed legislative revisions of the agreement that had increased the dollar amounts they would have to pay.[43] And some within the industry, including Philip Morris, held out for an agreement that specifically prevented all FDA regulation. On the other side, some health advocates also opposed the national agreement. For example, the American Cancer Society, the American Lung Association, and C. Everette Koop (who first brought sustained public attention to the ill-health effects of smoking during his tenure as surgeon general in the 1980s) opposed the settlement on the grounds that under it the FDA would be too restricted and that tobacco companies' responsibility under the proposed settlement to reduce teen smoking did not go far enough.[44] Because the mega-settlement unraveled while pending in Congress, the FDA's rule was never preempted legislatively. The FDA held center stage alone after all.

The FDA therefore pushed ahead on its own. And notwithstanding the strong opposition generated by its proposed rule, the FDA's final tobacco rule—like the EPA's final ozone and particulate matter rules—closely resembled its proposed version. For example, like the proposed rule, the final rule prohibited free samples of cigarettes and the distribution of cigarette "kiddie packs."[45] It also prohibited billboard advertising within one thousand feet of school playgrounds,[46] advertising in publications with significant youth readership,[47] and the distribution of gym bags, hats, and other clothing items printed with tobacco brands or logos.[48] The final rule also prohibited brand-name sponsorship of sporting events and, going further than its proposed version, brand-sponsored automobile races and racing teams in particular.[49] On the other hand, whereas the proposed rule would have banned cigarette vending machines and colored billboard and in-store advertising altogether,[50] the final rule permitted both in "adult only" facilities such as nightclubs.[51] The final rule also required the six tobacco companies with the most significant shares of sales to minors to educate young people about the health risks of their products,[52] whereas the proposed rule would have established a $150 million annual fund, financed by tobacco manufacturers, to conduct a national education campaign.[53] Even so, the final tobacco rule was very similar to its proposed version, and the differences were in off-setting directions.

The FDA also issued what it labeled an "annex" to its final rule, a "Determination of Jurisdiction" over cigarettes and smokeless tobacco as nicotine delivery devices under the FDCA.[54] In the final rule's six-hundred-page annex, the FDA explained its determinations that cigarettes and smokeless tobacco affect the structure and function of the body given that nicotine causes and sustains addiction, causes other mood-altering effects, and affects weight. The agency also explained that, for the purposes of the FDCA, manufacturers of cigarettes and smokeless tobacco "intend" those effects on the body. The FDA reached that conclusion on the grounds that the addictive and other pharmacological effects of nicotine are widely known and accepted, that consumers use cigarettes predominantly for pharmacological purposes, that manufacturers know that nicotine causes such effects in consumers and design their products to provide consumers with an active dose of nicotine, and finally that an inevitable and foreseeable consequence of the design of cigarettes and smokeless tobacco is to sustain consumers' addiction.[55]

The FDA further observed in support of its jurisdiction over cigarettes that although the agency had in the 1970s concluded it lacked authority to regulate tobacco, it reached that conclusion on the basis of its then-current understandings of tobacco's effects and cigarette manufacturers' practices.[56] The FDA pointed out that decades ago it asserted regulatory jurisdiction over a brand of cigarettes intended to reduce body weight. Its decision to regulate tobacco more broadly now followed from a much deeper understanding both of the effects of tobacco on the body and of manufacturers' intentions with respect to those effects.[57] In other words, the agency had not simply changed its mind about its authority to regulate tobacco, but rather acted in response to new evidence about tobacco, nicotine, and cigarette manufacturer practices.

Also like the EPA's ozone and particulate matter rules, the FDA's final tobacco rule relied heavily on scientific evidence and expert consensus. The FDA referenced some 190,000 pages of materials to ground its rule in the latest medical, psychological, scientific, and social-scientific evidence.[58] The agency relied both on its own expertise and especially on the best evidence available from the scientific and medical communities. Each of the rule's major substantive provisions was accompanied by extensive references to the relevant literature. As a result, critics were hard pressed to deny that the rule showed adequate technical understanding of the issues. As the agency explained upon publishing its final rule, it had "provided over 1,000 endnotes and footnotes directing readers to each and every document, including every study, Government report, journal article, industry document, and agency record" on which it relied to justify its rule.[59]

Expertise and scientific evidence did not persuade the FDA's industry or congressional critics, however. Immediately following the agency's promulgation of its final tobacco rule, some in Congress resisted providing appropriations to the FDA for the purposes of enforcing the new rule.[60] Others proposed legislation nullifying the rule or otherwise curtailing the agency's jurisdiction.[61] Nor did Congress quickly forgive and forget. For example, in late 1998 Senate majority whip Don Nickels blocked consideration of Jane Henney, the president's appointee to succeed Kessler as commissioner of the FDA, in part on the grounds that Henney, then head of the University of New Mexico Medical Center, indicated she supported the tobacco rule.[62]

But litigation, not legislation, posed the bigger threat to the tobacco rule. In fact, litigation had surrounded the FDA's rule from its very inception. The day before the FDA published its *proposed* rule in the *Federal Register*, numerous tobacco companies, advertising firms, and the National Association of Convenience Stores filed lawsuits against the agency. They sought declaratory relief on the grounds that the FDA's rule exceeded the agency's regulatory authority under the FDCA.[63] Yet the importance of these legal challenges to the FDA's tobacco initiative were of questionable relevance until after the national settlement negotiations broke down following the FDA promulgation of its final rule. Once the FDA finalized its rule and it became apparent that legislation would not preempt it, the litigation suddenly loomed large.

The legal challenges to the FDA's rule were first adjudicated by a federal court in 1997, by which time several separate cases against the agency brought by different plaintiffs—tobacco, advertisers, grocers, and convenience retailers—had been consolidated. Also by that time, the rule's supporters, including many states and state attorneys general together with public health organizations, educational groups, and other organizations such as the National Association of African Americans for Positive Imagery, had joined the litigation as amici curiae in support of the FDA. The rule's opponents, including House and Senate legislators from tobacco states and tobacco states themselves, had also joined the litigation as amici against the agency. And just as the proponents of the EPA's ozone and particulate matter rules had enlisted a celebrity—Olympic marathoner Joan Benoit Samuelson—to testify in favor of the EPA rules as a representative of those who exercise out of doors, so too the opponents of the tobacco rule enlisted race care driver Mario Andretti to join the litigation challenging the tobacco rule as a representative of auto-racing interests.

The plaintiffs chose North Carolina as their forum in which to challenge the rule. But that choice proved unsuccessful, at least initially. The U.S. District Court for the Middle District of North Carolina ruled that the FDA had not exceeded its statutory authority.[64] In particular, the district court held that the FDA had properly responded to new evidence concerning nicotine, smoking, addiction, and tobacco company practices, and that such new evidence brought tobacco products within the scope of the terms "drug" and "device" as unambiguously defined in the Federal Food, Drug, and Cosmetics Act, given among other things tobacco's intended effects on the body. With respect to provisions of the FDA's rule regulating advertising and promotion of tobacco products, on the other hand, the court held that the agency lacked authority under the statute for those. The district court thus largely vindicated the FDA, though it invalidated the important advertising portions of the tobacco rule as beyond the agency's statutory reach (and therefore did not need to consider the First Amendment challenges to the advertising parts of the rule).

Both sides appealed. This time, however, the rule's opponents prevailed. In a divided (two to one) decision, the U.S. Court of Appeals for the Fourth Circuit reversed the district court, holding that the FDA's statutory authority did not extend to tobacco.[65] According to the appellate court, the FDCA could not be read to extend to tobacco products for several reasons. For example, if the statute were understood to extend to tobacco products, the court reasoned, then under the act those products would have to be approved by the FDA prior to being marketed. Similarly, because the FDCA prohibits the introduction into commerce of any drug or device that is dangerous when used as suggested, the court argued that the FDA would have to ban cigarettes if they were drugs or devices.[66] Such considerations led the appellate court to conclude that, as a matter of statutory interpretation, the FDCA could not be read to extend to tobacco. Also in contrast to the district court, the appellate court concluded that Congress's failure to enact legislation authorizing the FDA to regulate tobacco in previous decades when the agency had repeatedly concluded it lacked such authority constituted evidence that Congress did not interpret the FDCA to encompass tobacco.[67]

The FDA appealed, and a divided Supreme Court affirmed. In March 2000, the Court held in a five-to-four decision that the FDA's authority under the FDCA did not extend to nicotine and cigarettes.[68] Like the appellate court, the Supreme Court majority concluded that, viewing the

FDCA "as a whole" rather than focusing on only its terms "drug" and "device," cigarettes and tobacco did not fit within its framework. Also like the appellate court, the Court concluded that Congress had "effectively ratified" the FDA's previous position that it lacked regulatory jurisdiction over tobacco given that Congress had passed legislation concerning tobacco yet had not extended the agency's authority. While the Supreme Court agreed with the FDA that its rule addressed "perhaps the single most significant threat to public health in the United States," it nevertheless determined the agency lacked jurisdiction to confront that problem.[69]

The FDA's tobacco initiative ended there, short one high court vote. Even so, by promulgating its final tobacco rule over intense industry and legislative opposition, the agency had won an epic battle. And while the rule was ultimately invalidated judicially, the FDA's tobacco initiative provided a major pivot point towards greater regulation of cigarettes. First, the FDA's efforts had a profound effect on public awareness of and sentiment towards cigarette advertising and distribution practices. That awareness and sentiment has prompted some amount of self-regulation by several cigarette companies, which now undertake advertising campaigns to reduce youth smoking. New public awareness and changed public sentiment has also, again, affected potential jury responses to cigarette defendants in private litigation, as evidenced dramatically, for example, by the Florida class action litigation, *Engle v. Liggett Group*, in which a jury in 2000 rendered a $145 billion judgment against the major tobacco companies for a nationally certified class of smokers.[70]

Second, although the national tobacco settlement was not enacted into law by Congress, many states later negotiated their own billion-dollar settlements with the major tobacco companies.[71] Those settlements were facilitated by the medical and social-scientific facts the FDA gathered and publicized in its tobacco rulemaking. In other words, the agency's tobacco initiative provided inertia for the state settlements. The tobacco rule had changed the political as well as the legal climate surrounding tobacco regulation.

Finally, the FDA's efforts also fueled the Justice Department's efforts to recover the federal government's expenditures for health costs attributable to smoking. That is, for years following the FDA's tobacco rule, the Justice Department sought $279 billion from the major tobacco companies. The United States brought an action under the Racketeer Influenced and Corrupt Organizations Act seeking disgorgement of the industry's ill-gotten gains during several decades of falsely promoting its products as harmless. But in early 2005, a divided appellate court held that the United States could not seek civil penalties that would not "prevent or restrain" future corrupt conduct. As a result, the Justice Department initially sought $130 billion to finance twenty-five years of smoking cessation programs and advertisements, but subsequently (and controversially) modified its request seeking only $14 billion for such programs.[72] The point, however, is that the facts underlying FDA's tobacco rule and the publicity and political salience that the agency's rule generated strengthened the federal government's claim and thus facilitated the Justice Department's suit as well.

In short, the FDA's tobacco rule in several important ways helped to shift the regulatory baseline beyond mere labeling regulation and towards various other forms of regulation that placed more of the costs of smoking on cigarette manufacturers. These continuing aftershocks of the FDA's tobacco initiative give it enduring significance. That the FDA was able to promulgate a cost-justified final rule to advance the interest of diffuse beneficiaries and over the objections of strong and concentrated opponents makes the tobacco rule a compelling example of benign regulation, as detailed later below.

Chapter Eleven

The Forest Service's Roadless Policy for National Forests

In its most ambitious regulatory initiative in modern times—an initiative variously called "one of the most significant conservation efforts in United States history,"[1] "the most significant land conservation initiative in nearly a century,"[2] and an "epic initiative"[3]—the U.S. Forest Service in January 2001 issued its final "roadless rule."[4] The effect of the roadless rule was to limit substantially road construction in over 55 million acres of designated national forests. The affected area constituted almost one-third of the 194 million total acres of national forest land. The Forest Service's rule both reflected and further perpetuated an intense national debate about appropriate uses of the country's national forests. That debate pitted very different types of interests against one another, and involved all three branches of government, in addition to the agency itself.

First, some context. The Forest Service is an agency within the U.S. Department of Agriculture (USDA) whose chief, a presidential appointee, answers to the secretary of agriculture as well as to the president. The Forest Service's mission is to safeguard and manage all "national forests" as well as "national grasslands," designated as such by presidential proclamation. The national forests taken together comprise the National Forest System, containing approximately one-half of the entire country's softwood timber and providing habitat for about one-third of the species listed under the Endangered Species Act. In statutes including the National Forest Management Act (1976)[5] and the Multiple-Use Sustained-Yield Act (1960),[6] Congress has instructed the USDA to manage the national forests for multiple purposes, including recreation, timber cultivation, watershed protection, wildlife and fish management, and resource conservation. According to these same statutes, the national forests are to be managed for those purposes in a manner that preserves them in perpetuity.

Congress has also authorized the Forest Service to issue such regulations as may be "necessary and desirable"[7] to fulfill its mission of management and preservation of the national forests. Congress has furthermore required the agency to create a "land management plan" or "forest management plan" for every individual national forest, of which there are 155. In so doing, however, Congress provided only very general principles and criteria for the development of such plans.[8] As a result, the management of any particular national forest is left largely to the discretion of that forest's own "supervisor," an employee of the Forest Service who is the head manager of the forest.

With respect to forest road development specifically, Congress also delegated to the USDA the authority to issue regulations concerning the construction of roads, including the authority to build roads and to grant easements for roads and road building. These statutory delegations require only that the department exercise its road-building and road-permitting authority consistent with applicable forest management plans. Roads through national forests are necessary to accomplish all of the forests' purposes. For one thing, roads provide access to facilitate management of forests and their fish and wildlife. Roads also provide access necessary for recreational activities—motorized as well as nonmotorized recreation—and conservation activities as well. Roads are also necessary to extract minerals from some national forests. Not least of all, roads are necessary to harvest timber. Indeed, timber harvesting constitutes the most demanding use of national forest roads.

Traditionally, USDA rules delegated to individual forest supervisors the responsibility to assess road needs, permit road construction where necessary or desirable, select road locations, and negotiate the details of road construction and use. Individual forest supervisors exercised their authority in various ways, reflecting both individual supervisors' management differences and the different needs of and demands across different national forests. While forest supervisors ultimately possess considerable regulatory authority over their forests, local pressures upon them to shape management plans to meet local needs are not always inconsequential, as captured for example in Herbert Kaufman's famous study.[9] Forest supervisors sometimes yield to local pressures, generally and with respect to road development in particular, a fact that eventually motivated a national policy on forest road development.

At the present, the National Forest System currently contains approximately 380,000 miles of roads. Those roads carry some nine thousand Forest Service vehicles each day. Forest Service vehicles enable the agency to perform all of its responsibilities—preserving wildlife habitat, maintaining recreational infrastructure, preventing fire, and conducting search-

and-rescue activities, among others. The national forest system's roads are also used by approximately another fifteen thousand private vehicles each day for harvesting timber and extracting other natural resources.

Notwithstanding the hundreds of thousands of forest roads supporting tens of thousands of vehicles, millions of acres of national forest land remain classified as "inventoried roadless areas." Some of these areas—a couple dozen million acres—are roadless because Congress has designated them as "wilderness areas" under the Wilderness Act. The Wilderness Act,[10] passed in 1964 to create the National Wilderness Preservation System, designated about 10 million acres of national forests as wilderness areas in which permanent road construction and commercial activities are therefore prohibited. Since, Congress has in smaller, state-specific legislation designated another nearly 12.5 million acres of the national forests as wilderness areas.

Apart from legislatively designated wilderness areas, though, the Forest Service has exercised its statutory authority to manage the national forests to classify another couple dozen million acres as "roadless," meaning that although roads are not prohibited in those areas by statute, the Forest Service itself determined that road construction is not appropriate in most of those areas, subject to narrow exceptions made on a local basis. But even areas officially inventoried as "roadless" by the agency, either because of legislative designation or as a result of the agency's own determinations, still contain some roads. In fact, some inventoried "roadless" areas contain roads for logging and other commercial enterprises. The difference between roadless and nonroadless areas is considerable, but one of degree: Inventoried roadless areas have few roads, and though some timber harvesting occurs in some of them, they are largely primitive, undisturbed forests. Combined, such areas—most in parcels of five thousand acres or more—constitute about 2 percent of the total land mass of the United States. They provide unique opportunities for dispersed recreation, house rare plant and animal species, and by safeguarding watersheds protect water supplies.

In May 2000, the Forest Service published in the *Federal Register* a proposed rule to bar road construction in most of the inventoried roadless areas within the national forests.[11] The agency's proposed rule followed a published notice of intent (NOI) to issue a proposed rule and to prepare an accompanying environmental impact statement for that rule, as required by NEPA.[12] The agency's notice of intent in turn immediately followed a presidential directive to the Forest Service to devise a plan to protect roadless areas within the National Forest System: On October 13,

1999, President Clinton directed the Forest Service to develop and propose for public comment rules to provide for long-term protection of roadless areas.[13] Referencing President Theodore Roosevelt's establishment of the National Forest System a century before, the president's memorandum to the secretary of the USDA stated that it was "in the best interest of our Nation, and of future generations, to provide strong and lasting protection" for roadless areas.

The Forest Service's NOI followed six days later. In it, the agency appealed to "strong public sentiment" for protecting national forest roadless areas and the clean water, biological diversity, wildlife habitat, and recreational opportunities they provide. The agency also invited public comment on its not-yet-proposed roadless rule.

The roadless rule itself was but the heart of a larger regulatory initiative, however, begun a couple of years before, prompted in part by calls in late 1997 for greater protection of the roadless areas of the national forests.[14] This initiative manifested itself first in January 1998, when the Forest Service issued an advance notice of proposed rulemaking (ANPR) in which the agency explained it planned to revise its regulations relating to the national forest transportation system as a whole.[15] That closely related ANPR stated that while the national forest road system had been funded and built to facilitate timber harvesting, in recent decades the national forests were used increasingly for recreation. By 1997, for example, the Forest Service's twenty-three thousand recreational facilities accommodated 860 million visitors (counting repeat visitors of course). The agency further explained that it had new scientific information about the environmental costs associated with existing roads, and more specifically that the adverse ecological impacts of the roads were greater than it had previously understood. The agency identified increased flooding and landslides, increased stream sedimentation, degradation of fish and wildlife habitat, and the increased presence of invasive species as a consequence of existing roads. At the same time, the Forest Service emphasized that the funding it received to maintain forest roads so as to minimize these undesirable effects were severely inadequate. As a result, the agency explained, it planned to "aggressively decommission" unnecessary forest roads in order to minimize ecological harm.

In conjunction with its ANPR to revise its national forest transportation system, the Forest Service on the same day in January 1998 proposed and invited comments on a moratorium on road construction in the roadless areas of the national forests, a precursor to the roadless rule itself.[16] The agency explained that ecological concerns regarding run-off from the roads justified a moratorium, which would allow it to develop a sensible global rule concerning road development. The Forest Service further observed that it lacked resources even to maintain its existing road system, which further justified a moratorium on new road construction so the agency could determine how best to manage roads already built. Forest Service chief Michael Dombeck estimated that his agency suffered from a $8.4 billion road maintenance and reconstruction backlog, and received only about one-fifth of the annual funding from Congress necessary to maintain existing forest roads to current environmental and safety standards.[17] Accordingly, the Forest Service announced that its moratorium would extend to reconstruction as well as new road construction, freezing road development until the agency could finalize a general plan. The agency's proposed moratorium was to last eighteen months from its effective date. In February 1999, the agency made the proposed road moratorium effective by issuing it as an "interim rule" under the APA, subsequently characterizing the moratorium as a "timeout" to allow the agency to develop a new "road management policy and the analytical tools to provide a more ecological approach to existing and future road needs."[18]

In addition to its roadless and transportation-system rules, the Forest Service in October 1999 solicited comments on yet another closely related proposal under the National Forest Management Act to centralize amendments and revision to national forest management plans by creating a special designation for roadless areas.[19] As with the other rules, the agency again stressed "more effective integration of science into forest planning and management," and indeed this rule was developed based on the recommendations of an advisory committee of twenty scientists, created in 1998 to advise the USDA on forest management. It justified its proposal to adopt a "national direction" for local forest land managers on the grounds that the economic and noneconomic costs of its current approach to road construction was high, and also on the grounds the "strong public sentiment" existed for greater protection of roadless areas.[20] Notably, Forest Service chief Dombeck himself was listed as the "responsible official" on the agency's notice.

This management rule was finalized in November 2000, while the roadless rule proper was still pending in proposed form.[21] The final version of the planning rule explained that the planning process would now consider explicitly the designation and preservation of roadless areas, and although roadless areas would not be withdrawn from active management, responsible officials should evaluate inventoried roadless areas as well as unroaded areas and consider the level of protection to be afforded to them.[22]

The Forest Service's roadless initiative, then, included not only the road-less rule itself but also a reorientation of its national forest transportation priorities and new planning mechanisms at the national level to ensure that forest supervisors would give explicit attention to roadless areas. The agency's efforts generated enormous attention and public reaction, much of it solicited. For example, the Forest Service created a website with information and updates concerning its roadless initiative, and invited comments by mail, fax, and email. Throughout 1999, the agency also hosted public meetings on the subject of forest road development. In all, the agency organized about two hundred such meetings around the country, and in all fifty states, including as well ten "national meetings" in addition to local meetings hosted by each of the agency's national forest offices.

These meetings were publicized in advance, and members of the public were invited to be heard. The national meetings were characterized by the Forest Service as "structured listening sessions" during which members of the public were invited to give comments on the agency's roadless initiative.[23] Participants' comments were taken by a court reporter present at each meeting, and then entered into the rulemaking record. The agency also provided background information and instructions about where and how to send comments for those who preferred to attend a meeting and express their written reactions later. The point of the meetings was to gather information and public views about what form a proposed road-less rule should take. The Forest Service's deputy chief for the National Forest System explained that the agency was attempting "to give every interested person an opportunity to comment" on the roadless issue.[24]

Following a year of public vetting of its roadless initiative, the Forest Service in May 2000 then issued the text of its proposed roadless rule, together with a draft environmental impact statement (DEIS) of the same.[25] The agency's notice of proposed rulemaking stated that its proposed rule sought a desirable balance among environmental and wildlife preservation, recreational uses such as hiking and hunting, and commercial uses of the national forests. Its proposed rule prohibited new road construction or reconstruction in inventoried roadless areas of the national forests, except where necessary to protect health and safety, to conduct environmental clean-up, to prevent irreparable resource damage caused by an existing road, or to respect "existing rights" of access. The proposed rule did not explicitly state that timber harvesting would be prevented in the roadless areas. But the rule's implication was clear. Interestingly, however, the agency's proposal exempted the large Tongass National Forest in Alaska—which alone makes up about 10 million of the total 58 million acres of roadless areas in the entire National Forest System—until 2004, by which time that forest's plan could be reviewed and appropriate action then taken if necessary.

In a press release announcing the proposed rule, Agriculture secretary Dan Glickman explained that the Forest Service would conduct "an aggressive public outreach campaign" on its proposal, and that public comments on the proposed rule would be "absolutely critical" as the agency crafted a policy that balanced "national and local interests and adequately protects roadless areas for present and future generations."[26] The secretary noted that the Forest Service had by the time of its proposed rule already held over 180 public meetings and collected more than 365,000 comments on its roadless initiative. Chief Dombeck issued his own press release, as well as a letter to all employees on the day the agency published its proposed roadless rule.[27] Dombeck, too, emphasized public involvement in developing a final roadless rule. He explained that the Forest Service would hold 300 more public meetings "to explain this proposal and garner public input" because the proposed rule "can, and will, be improved based on public involvement and review." Dombeck justified the thrust of the proposed rule, though, by pointing to the public benefits associated with the roadless areas of the National Forest System and the agency's lack of funding adequate to maintain its existing road system. Finally, the forest chief observed that the agency's proposal responded to the president's directive to develop ways to preserve for future generations "some of the last, best, unprotected wildland anywhere in our nation," and furthermore that because more than "25 years of local planning, lawsuits, and controversy have failed to resolve the roadless area issue" new direction and leadership were necessary. By clear implication, the Forest Service's proposed rule aimed to provide that missing direction and leadership.

As the agency did following its earlier notice of intent, the Forest Service scheduled another round of public meetings across the country and solicited additional public comments. By the time the agency issued its final environmental impact statement (FEIS) on November 13, 2000, it had held over six hundred public meetings, attended by hundreds of thousands of people. The agency had also collected 1.6 million comments on its roadless plan—taking written and oral comments together—the vast majority of them favorable.[28] The Forest Service then invited further commentary on its four-volume, four-hundred page FEIS, distributed via the web and in hard copy at all Forest Service offices and at over ten thousand public libraries.

The roadless rule embodied in the FEIS closely resembled the proposed rule, but with three changes. First, the rule's prohibition on new road construction permitted a few more exceptions, allowing road construction to rectify existing hazardous road conditions, to complete a Federal Aid Highway project, or to respect rights created by statute or treaty. Second, the rule explicitly prohibited timber harvesting in roadless areas. This prohibition too came with rather narrow exceptions, permitting timber harvesting that would improve the habitat of threatened or endangered species, reduce the risk of wildfire, or restore part of an ecological system. Finally, the FEIS also provided that the prohibition on road construction and timber harvesting would go into effect for the Tongass National Forest as well—not simply be considered for application to the Tongass Forest—in April 2004.

Notwithstanding broad public support, however, the roadless rule was no sure bet. As Chief Dombeck summarized in an op-ed piece in December 1999 explaining and defending his agency, "Many are pleased with the roadless initiative: many are not."[29] To be more specific about that, the timber industry strongly opposed the roadless rule. Because the rule would prevent expanded timber harvesting by prohibiting road construction at a pace in absence of the rule estimated to be 232 miles per year, and because the rule would to some extend impede existing harvesting by preventing road reconstruction, timber interests objected. They foresaw, correctly, reduced timber production and fewer timber harvesting jobs as a result of the rule.

Politicians from several western states also opposed the agency's initiative. Sharing the timber companies' concerns, they argued that forest management decisions should continue to be made by local forest managers, who were more responsive to local issues. Several Indian tribes also opposed the roadless rule. Like the states, they argued that the roadless initiative deprived them of desirable local control of national forests within their boundaries. Finally, the rule's opponents also included part of the motorized recreational industry, including for example the American Council of Snowmobile Associations, as well as cattle companies such as the Highland Livestock and Land Company.

In absolute terms, supporters of the agency's roadless rule far outnumbered its opponents.[30] But as in the case of the EPA and FDA rules, whereas the rule's opponents were concentrated and well financed, its supporters represented mostly small and diffuse interests. Apart from the agency and countless individuals who voiced support for the rule, several leading environmental groups weighed in on the side of the roadless rule.

Until the middle of 2004, when several major sportswear manufacturers such as Nike and Columbia Sportswear sent a letter to the USDA expressing their support for the roadless rule, the environmental groups constituted the rule's only organized defenders. On the other side, the rule's opponents included members of the Senate from several western states and several western state governors and attorneys general. The Kootenai Tribe of Idaho mobilized against the roadless rule, as did for example the Boise Cascade Corporation, parent corporation of timber interests and distributors of building supplies and paper office products. Such entities marshaled substantial organizational and political resources to the debate surrounding the Forest Service's rule. Indeed, Boise Cascade bused individual loggers to some of the Forest Service's public meetings on the proposed roadless rule so that the loggers could express their opposition.[31]

Such opposition notwithstanding, however, the Forest Service issued its final roadless rule on January 12, 2001—in other words, eight days before the end of the Clinton administration and beginning of the administration of George W. Bush—with an effective date of March 13, 2001. Like the EPA's ozone and particulate matter rules, the final roadless rule resembled its proposed rule and FEIS closely. The final rule provided for a couple of additional narrow exceptions to its prohibitions on road construction and timber harvesting. In particular, it allowed for road construction necessary to respect existing mineral leases, and allowed for "infrequent" timber harvesting of small-diameter trees to improve roadless area characteristics or when incidental to forest maintenance. On the other hand, the final rule went farther than its proposed incarnations by including the Tongass National Forest within its scope, barring road construction and timber harvesting there too immediately.

Yet its fate was still far from certain. For Republican occupation of the White House brought nominees for a new secretary of agriculture, Ann Veneman, and a new Forest Service chief, Dale Bosworth. More importantly, the incoming president had during the recent presidential campaign indicated his disagreement with the Clinton administration's roadless policy, a disagreement amplified during the first months of the new administration.[32] In short, an important partisan shift occurred before the new rule's ink had dried, placing its future in doubt.

And so, on February 5, 2001, under new leadership, the Forest Service published in the *Federal Register* a new "rule" extending the effective date of the roadless rule to May 12, 2001.[33] The agency characterized its rule as a "rule of procedure" under section 553 of the APA, and therefore not subject to notice and comment or, in the alternative, as a rule under the "good cause" exception in section 553 on the ground that seeking public comment would be "impracticable, unnecessary and contrary to the public interest." The purpose of postponing the effective date of the roadless rule was to allow the new administration to review the rule and decide what it would do.

That June, Chief Bosworth issued a "guidance" to Forest Service managers explaining that they should continue efforts to protect roadless areas, but that he personally would reserve all authority to determine whether road construction and timber harvest would be permitted in roadless areas. To implement this guidance, he issued an accompanying directive to amend the agency manuals to reflect his new reservation of authority. The guidance also called for mapping of existing national forest roads and for further consideration of a long-term plan for roadless areas, including the possibility of making recommendations to Congress for wilderness area designations. Shortly thereafter, the Forest Service published an advance notice of proposed rulemaking, requesting public comment anew on the issue of management and protection of roadless areas of the national forests. The agency's revived effort eventually generated eight hundred thousand public comments, again most favoring protecting the inventoried roadless areas from road construction and timber harvest.

At the same time, the roadless rule was also challenged in the courts, eventually the subject no fewer than nine separate lawsuits contesting the rule's legality. For example, the State of Wyoming sued in federal court in Wyoming.[34] Likewise, the State of Idaho, 17 percent of which constitutes inventoried roadless area, brought suit in the federal court in Idaho four days following the Forest Service's promulgation of the final roadless rule (and several months before its effective date).[35] Separately, the Kootenai Tribe of Idaho together with plaintiffs representing the timber, cattle, and snowmobile industries brought a parallel suit in Idaho the day before, later combined on appeal with Idaho's case.[36] Suits challenging the rule were also brought in Alaska, North Dakota, and Utah, while the American Forests and Paper Association filed two suits in federal court in the District of Columbia. Montana officials later joined the Idaho plaintiffs as amicus curiae, as did U.S. senators Larry Craig and Mark Dayton, and the Washington Legal Foundation.

Those challenging the rule in a court brought two main claims. First, they argued that the agency did not fully comply with the National Environmental Protection Act on the grounds that the Forest Service's environmental impact statement was insufficient. In particular, plaintiffs such as Idaho, the Kootenai Tribe of Idaho, and timber and snowmobile interests argued that the agency had not provided sufficiently detailed maps of the potentially affected roadless areas and furthermore that the agency had added several million acres total to its inventoried roadless areas between its draft environmental impact statement and its final environmental impact statement, and as a result potentially affected parties were not given enough opportunity to respond to and participate in the development of the final environmental impact statement. Those challenging the final rule also argued that the Forest Service's decision to allow for only sixty-nine days for public comment on its draft environmental impact statement similarly deprived them of meaningful input.

Other challengers argued that the final rule also violated the Wilderness Act. According to this legal theory, the Forest Service overstepped its statutory jurisdiction and usurped congressional power by issuing a roadless rule that created de facto wilderness areas, notwithstanding that under the Wilderness Act only Congress has the power to designate them. The State of Wyoming, for example, which also brought NEPA claims against all three of the rules comprising the Forest Service's roadless initiative, argued that the agency created wilderness areas without congressional action by (re)naming them "roadless forests" and permitting only those uses of roadless areas that are permitted in congressionally designated wilderness areas. To support this argument, Wyoming pointed out that many of the areas the agency designated as roadless were based on surveys originally done for the purpose of making recommendations to Congress about wilderness designations.

The plaintiffs succeeded, initially. In May 2001, the U.S. District Court for the District of Idaho granted a preliminary injunction prohibiting the Forest Service from implementing "all aspects" of the roadless rule. The district court concluded that the plaintiffs demonstrated a likelihood of success on the merits of their case against the rule, and that irreparable harm could result in the meantime, and on those grounds granted a preliminary injunction against the rule. That court furthermore opined that the Forest Service's decision not to extend the forty-five-day period for public comment on the agency's environmental impact statement to beyond sixty-nine days suggested that the agency's action "was a political decision pre-determined in its outcome."[37] On appeal, however, the U.S. Court of Appeals for the Ninth Circuit reversed and remanded the case.[38] Disagreeing with the district court's conclusions concerning the plaintiffs' likelihood of success on the alleged NEPA violations, the appellate court ordered the district court to dissolve its preliminary injunction against the rule.

Wyoming's case also found success before the district court. The Wyoming court found what it considered to be several NEPA violations, including the Forest Service's failure to consider enough alternatives to its roadless rule. That court remarked that the agency rushed "to satisfy a predetermined directive by Chief Dombeck, which eliminated competing alternatives out of consideration and existence."[39] The Wyoming court also agreed with the state that the Forest Service's roadless rule violated the Wilderness Act by short-circuiting congressional designations of wilderness areas. Accordingly, that court permanently rather than preliminarily enjoined the implementation of the roadless rule.

The party defendant in the litigation against the roadless rule was, of course, the Forest Service, and the U.S. Department of Justice therefore represented the government as the agency's lawyer. Interestingly, however, the incoming presidential administration determined it would not defend the rule in court. That is, the Justice Department's briefs responding to the legal challenges to the rule did not defend it on the merits. For example, in the Idaho litigation the federal defendants took no position on the merits of the plaintiffs' case, arguing simply that injunctive relief was not yet necessary because the agency would on its own initiative revisit the rule. The litigation was defended on the merits instead by several environmental organizations, as well as group of self-organized agency employees called Forest Service Employees For Environmental Ethics.

Nor did the Justice Department appeal the Idaho district court's injunctions prohibiting the Forest Service from implementing the roadless rule, once that court granted a preliminary injunction against the rule. The appeals of those injunctions were litigated instead by environmental groups permitted to intervene on behalf of the agency. In fact, the Justice Department not only did not defend the rule, but went even farther by taking the unusual position that the rule invalidated by the Idaho district court was invalid throughout the many states composing Ninth Circuit, rather than only in Idaho within the geographical reach of that district court's jurisdiction. Nor finally did the Justice Department appeal the Wyoming district court's permanent injunction against the rule, again leaving the appeal to the environmental-group intervenors, without whom the rule would have found no defenders in court.

In another case brought in Alaska concerning that state's Tongass National Forest, the government entered into a settlement agreement that in effect exempted that forest from the roadless rule. According to the terms of the agreement, the USDA agreed to publish a proposed rule exempting the Tongass National Forest from the roadless rule's prohibitions while the department considered its options with respect to roadless policy. In December 2003, the agency issued a final rule doing just that, sparking criticism by hundreds of small gun clubs and sportsmen's groups opposed to exempting Tongass. As a result of the settlement, the court in that litigation granted the parties' motions voluntarily dismissing the case.

Through the early months of 2001, when the rule's fate was very much uncertain given executive-branch reconsideration as well as pending litigation, Congress made its own views known, providing a fresh wind of support for the rule. Although the roadless rule from its inception found vocal critics in certain western legislators, including Representative Larry Craig of Idaho perhaps most of all, the center of congressional gravity clearly favored the rule. In fact, during several oversight hearings held during the development of the roadless rule, Congress provided its consistent blessing for what the agency was doing. That support was reiterated, at times forcefully, in the year following the presidential election.

Congressional support for the rule reflected public sentiment. While public sentiment within small, logging-dependent towns in Idaho ran against the roadless initiative, the roadless rule enjoyed strong support not only nationally but even generally within states with high concentrations of roadless areas.[40] Congress then responded on behalf of those constituencies supporting the rule.[41] Nor was congressional support neatly partisan, for many Republican legislators publically defended the roadless initiative and called on the White House to support the original roadless rule.[42]

On the House side, for example, some two hundred representatives cosigned a bill introduced in 2002 that would have legislated the roadless rule into law, expressing the House's strong support for the rule.[43] Indeed, several such bills were introduced in Congress, including companion House and Senate bills introduced by members of the State of Washington's congressional delegation,[44] even though—or perhaps because of the fact that—Washington contains large tracts of inventoried roadless areas. Some in Congress also supported legislation that would have undone the settlement reached in the Alaska litigation exempting the Tongass National Forest from the roadless rule.[45]

Meanwhile, the Senate's Committee on the Judiciary held a confirmation hearing for Thomas Sansonetti, the newly nominated assistant attorney general for environment and natural resources—the Justice Department's top environmental lawyer—a presidential nomination requiring confirmation. Sansonetti had previously lobbied on behalf of coal-mining interests and that connection drew concerns from Senate Democrats and others.[46] During his confirmation hearing, committee members supportive of the final roadless rule questioned him about his position on the rule. He answered that he would enforce the rule. Washington senator Maria Cantwell, whose frustration about the administration's reluctance to enforce the roadless rule and other environmental laws led her to request to chair the hearing, pointedly asked Sansonetti whether, if confirmed by the Senate, he would pledge to enforce the roadless rule.[47] Their colloquy illustrates the importance some legislators attached to its enforcement:

SENATOR CANTWELL. So . . . if you are confirmed [will you] defend the roadless rule on its merits and instruct the attorneys to begin a substantive participation in the case?

MR. SANSONETTI. . . . . [O]nce I get into the building is concerned, I am going to say what is the status of the roadless rule? What is the law right now as it exists? Then I will say our job is to defend that—

SENATOR CANTWELL. And defend it substantively?

MR. SANSONETTI. And to defend it substantively, yes, ma'am.

SENATOR CANTWELL. And does that change at all if, in fact, the administration is pursuing a new rulemaking during that same time period?

MR. SANSONETTI. No, because as long as the law in effect is the law in effect, just because there is perhaps either an attempt here in the legislative branch of the government or in the executive branch of the government to change that does not mean that the law is not in effect. . . .

SENATOR CANTWELL. Thank you.[48]

Combined, the House and Senate held many oversight hearings on the roadless initiative, beginning in 1998 and continuing for several years after the change in administration following the 2000 elections.[49] Although some western legislators continued their opposition to the roadless initiative, on the whole the legislative hearings provided occasion for Congress to express its support for the roadless rule to the Clinton administration and to communicate the same to the new Bush administration. Eventually, the new administration's position reflected public and congressional support for the initiative. Thus, for example, Agriculture undersecretary Mark Rey, a central official in the new administration's reanalysis of the roadless rule, testified in early 2004 before the Senate Energy and Natural Resources Committee that the administration would be "significantly modifying" its draft planning regulations in response to critical reactions to its proposed changes from the public and members of Congress.[50]

Thus the Bush administration's opposition to the roadless rule softened significantly, though the rule's legality remained the subject of pending litigation. Responding to continued public support for the roadless rule and recognizing bipartisan congressional support as well, and notwithstanding the timber industry's lasting opposition, the White House determined that it would let at least some version of the final rule stand and would no longer oppose its enforcement. By mid-2004, Secretary Veneman reinstated the 2003-expired Bosworth directive protecting inventoried roadless areas in order to preserve the roadless-rule status quo until the agency could complete yet another, substitute rule. Days later, the agency issued a notice of proposed rulemaking and accompanying proposed rule effectively revising the final roadless rule of January 2001.[51] By this time, the U.S. Court of Appeals for the Ninth Circuit had reversed the Idaho district court's preliminary injunction against the rule,[52] making the rule effective for the first time since its issuance (though other litigation continued). In response to that appellate decision, in the middle of 2003, the USDA announced it would implement the rule. In fact, apart from the Tongass National Forest, the roadless rule's prohibitions against road development had been enforced through the Bosworth and Veneman directives freezing road development pending resolution of the controversy surrounding the rule.

Simultaneously, however, the agency solicited comments on its proposed substitute rule. After twice extending the public comment period, the Forest Service finalized its new rule in May 2005.[53] The new rule provided that governors in states with inventoried roadless areas may, within eighteen months of the effective date of the rule, petition the USDA to make one-time modifications of forest management plans created under the roadless initiative that would allow road construction or reconstruction within a petitioning governor's state. If the department granted a petition, those state-specific modifications would take the procedural form of a new notice-and-comment rulemaking, with the accompanying public participation and preparation of environmental impact statements that the law requires.

The new rule also contained a provision requiring the establishment of a new federal advisory committee to provide advice and recommendations to the department concerning the state modification process.[54] Accordingly, upon publishing the new rule, the agency announced that it would charter an advisory committee under the Federal Advisory Committee Act and solicited membership nominations. The advisory committee would review each petition seeking modification of a forest management plan and provide advice to the agency concerning the merits of such petitions, and for petitions granted, would provide advice and recommendations also during the subsequent rulemaking processes.

While the new rule was described in some press accounts as a complete reversal of the Clinton administration's roadless rule, in fact the substitute rule did not undo all of the Clinton roadless initiative. First of all, the roadless rule itself was not the sole piece of that larger initiative, which as already explained included new forest land-planning and management rules that require greater consideration and protection of inventoried roadless areas by forest managers. Those separate rules remain. In addition, the USDA extended its directive prohibiting road construction through at least mid-2007,[55] a possibility the Forest Service left open upon announcing its new rule.

Furthermore, while the new rule[56] allowed for the possibility of state-specific modifications of roadless management plans, again those modifications would be subject to separate rulemaking and advisory-committee processes. Because the newly established national advisory committee must under the FACA include representatives representing diverse points of view, a point emphasized in the Forest Service's promulgation of its final new rule, the environmental organizations that have defended the roadless rule will find membership on the new advisory committee. Thus, state petitioning process will not allow narrow interests to revise forest management plans all by themselves.

Thus the story of the roadless initiative continues, and will for some time. Recently, the U.S. Court of Appeals for the Tenth Circuit vacated the judgment of the Wyoming district court enjoining the original roadless rule's enforcement, on the grounds that the new roadless rule rendered the appeal of the Wyoming decision moot.[57] Even so, litigation concerning the roadless initiative will continue.[58] In fact, contemplating that its newest rule would itself become the subject of legal challenge, the Forest Service included a "severability clause" in the Bush rule providing that if some of it is judicially invalidated, the other parts of the rule shall remain as law.[59] That concern proved correct, if not enough to save the rule, when more recently the U.S. District Court for the Northern District of California held that the Bush rule was unlawful for failure to provide an adequate environmental impact statement. That court reinstated the Clinton roadless rule, which will undoubtedly prompt new rounds of litigation. And even assuming some version of the Bush replacement rule is resuscitated, only time will tell what the scope of state-specific roadless management modifications will look like, and how many there might be.

However the final details fall out, there is no question that the roadless initiative shifted the relevant regulatory baseline considerably. Spawned by calls for greater forest protection, and instigated by an intrepid administrator, the Forest Service's roadless rule and its sibling forest planning and management rules drastically changed the baseline concerning road development in over forty million acres of the national forests. And given that serious political and legal challenges to the rule did not in the end go very far to stop it, in all likelihood the roadless rule has changed the regulatory status quo for generations.

The roadless initiative effectuated significant regulatory change in part as a result of wide public participation in its development. Utilizing expanded notice-and-comment and public hearing processes, the Forest Service both created and relied upon strong public support for its initiative. In addition, by appealing to scientific and economic analyses of its regulatory alternatives, relying on expert scientific advice, and providing voluminous data about its proposals, the agency also preempted easy legal or political reversal. Such procedural institutions—including notice-and-comment rulemaking, expert analyses, and the federal advisory committee process—will also determine whether and how road construction in the national forests will be permitted in the future. In the meantime, those same processes allowed the agency to undertake an ambitious initiative over the objections of concentrated, well-funded local interests.

That latter point warrants emphasis. Whereas beneficiaries of the roadless initiative are diffuse, and include future generations, its opponents represented a small handful of industry groups on whom the costs—which after all take the form of reduced national subsidies of their businesses—of the roadless rule fell almost exclusively. Those opponents found representation in state and national politicians, including powerful legislators, and eventually found a sympathetic audience in the White House. But given the momentum created by processes culminating in the roadless rule, even organized opposition was not enough. Concentrated and well-represented local interests and their legislative allies could not undo what the Forest Service—with the help of one White House, support from most of members of Congress as well as the public, and substantial vindication from the courts—had done.

Chapter Twelve

Socially Beneficial Administrative Decisionmaking: Additional Evidence

THE PREVIOUS THREE CHAPTERS document several ambitious regulatory initiatives that advanced public interests by generating substantial net benefits, broadly distributed, over the strong opposition of concentrated and organized interests. What such cases suggest about the limits of the public choice theory of regulation, and what they illustrate about the relevance of the administrative process, will be considered shortly.

Getting there, however, requires anticipating one objection to the direction of the general argument: Perhaps the examples just narrated constitute exceptions that prove the rule. That is, if regulatory initiatives like those presented above are few and infrequent, then perhaps one can draw no conclusions from them one way or another. Or worse, if such cases are rare, then maybe their very infrequency demonstrates the power of the public choice theory's conclusions after all.

Thus the inherent limits of any case study analysis, or indeed of any argument by induction: A skeptic can always claim that the examples offered do not stack up high enough. On the other hand, the very fact that one can *always* make such an objection means that the objection is not always compelling. Of course, ultimately the question how many examples it takes to draw conclusions is not answered by science or logic; the power of any argument by induction is, instead, a matter of judgment.

So, what conclusions may be drawn from the case studies of chapters 9, 10, and 11 may be subject to debate—excepting, again, debate about whether the case studies disprove any theory holding that public-interested regulation is not possible, which they do. Still, more examples are more powerful than fewer. And, more examples lend strength to the significance of each example (for the stronger the pattern, the more likely each example is part of a pattern in the first place). With those observations in mind, this chapter provides several additional vignettes—more abbreviated case studies of still more examples of public-interested regulation—which will reinforce the conclusions to be drawn from the preceding three chapters. These examples include the establishment of the Federal Trade Commission's "Do Not Call" registry, the Securities and Exchange Commission's rules on attorney conduct, and the Office of the Comptroller of the Currency's expansion of activities in which national banks may engage. As will be seen, these examples share many features of the regulatory initiatives presented above. At a minimum, then, they establish that the regulatory initiatives of the EPA, FDA, and the Forest Service are not unique. Each also tells another very interesting regulatory story.

THE FEDERAL TRADE COMMISSION'S "DO NOT CALL" REGISTRY

In January 2003, the Federal Trade Commission issued a final rule announcing the establishment of a national telephone registry that allows individual telephone customers to prevent incoming phone calls by most telephone marketers.[1] This new rule constituted an amendment to an earlier and important FTC rule, known as the "Telemarketing Sales Rule," promulgated by the agency in 1995.[2] The Telemarketing Sales Rule, in turn, implemented the Telemarketing Act,[3] in which Congress specifically directed the FTC to issue a rule to prevent deceptive and abusive telemarketing practices, including among other things practices that abused consumers' right to privacy. That legislation reflected congressional concerns, heightened through the 1990s, about telemarketing fraud.

Telemarketing is a $300 billion a year industry, according to estimates.[4] Most of that figure reflects legitimate business activity—the solicitation of bona fide sales of goods and services by reputable companies. But as much as $40 billion annually is estimated to be lost due to fraudulent activity conducted or initiated over the telephone.[5] Major credit card companies report hundreds of millions of dollars per year in losses as a result of telemarketing fraud, for example. And the National Consumers League has estimated that over five million people have purchased something over the telephone they subsequently believed was a fraud. Fraudulent transactions involving bogus health care products marketed to senior citizens is considered one especially important example of the problem. By its very nature, however, fraudulent telemarketing activity is difficult to measure, undertaken by fly-by-night operations that move quickly and avoid detection by law enforcement organizations. Even so, in the early 1990s the problems of telemarketing fraud and abusive telemarketing activities were widely perceived to be on the rise, largely as a result of technologies and techniques that made telemarketing abuse easier to undertake and harder to detect—including for example predictive and automated dialing, caller-identification blockers, and quick hang-ups.

These concerns manifested themselves legislatively at both the state and national levels. Throughout the 1990s, many states passed statutes aimed both to curb telemarketing fraud and to protect consumer privacy, following Congress's lead in 1991 with the passage of the Telephone Consumer Protection Act. The Telephone Consumer Protection Act directed another independent agency, the Federal Communications Commission (FCC), also to consider ways to protect residential telephone subscribers' privacy rights. In addition, that legislation limited the use of automatic dialers and banned unsolicited commercial faxes, among other things. Pursuant to the Telephone Consumer Protection Act, the FCC initiated its own rulemakings and promulgated regulations to enforce that statute.

One of those FCC rules required telemarketers to remove a telephone subscriber's phone number from a marketer's calling list whenever the subscriber requested.[6] In other words, the FCC regulations provided that in response to a given seller's call, a consumer could ask to be taken off the seller's list of telephone numbers and that request was to be respected by the seller, who was not to call again. This prohibition was—and remains—enforceable by consumers through private rights of action created in the Telephone Consumer Protection Act, which provides that any consumer who receives two or more calls by the same telemarketing entity within a twelve-month period can recover the greater of actual damages or five hundred dollars. Needless to say, such small-damage consumer suits, by themselves, do not make for very strong regulatory enforcement.

Congress took a second swing at the problem in 1994 with the Telemarketing Act and the more narrow Senior Citizens Against Marketing Scams Act, the latter of which increased prison sentences for certain types of telemarketing fraud. Besides directing the FTC to consider ways to protect consumers' privacy, the Telemarketing Act also directed the agency to issue a rule restricting the time of day during which telemarketers could place calls and requiring sellers to identify themselves at the beginning of a sales call. The Telemarketing Act furthermore instructed the FTC—whose general mission includes preventing unfair trade practices—to consider a rule that would create certain record-keeping requirements on the part of telemarketers, and to prohibit activities that "assist or facilitate" deceptive telemarketing practices as well as those practices themselves.

The FTC's Telemarketing Sales Rule was the result. It required telephone solicitors to identify themselves promptly upon placing a call, to identify the call as a sales call stating the good or service offered, to disclose the full costs for goods or services before a consumer agrees to pay, and to initiate calls no earlier than 8:00 A.M. or later than 9:00 P.M. in the time zone of the person receiving the call. Just like the FCC's rule, the FTC's Telemarketing Sales Rule also required telemarketers to remove from their calling lists any consumer who so requested, a provision of the rule known as the "Do Not Call" provision.[7]

By 2000, however, the FTC determined that the regulatory prohibitions of its original rule did not go far enough. The agency reached that conclusion upon reviewing the efficacy of the original review. Like the Clean Air Act's requirement that the EPA revisit National Ambient Air Quality Standards every five years, the Telemarketing Sales Act specifically required the FTC to perform a five-year review of the rule it adopted to carry out the act.[8] Accordingly, at the end of 1999 the commission initiated a "Rule Review" proceeding by announcing in the *Federal Register* that in January 2000 it would hold a "public forum" to discuss the "Do Not Call" provisions of its Telemarketing Sales Rule.[9] The commission's notice further explained that it intended to request written comments and academic studies concerning its rule and the telemarketing industry more generally, and that it would hold additional fora in the near future. The agency also invited public participation in its first scheduled forum, hosted at the FTC's offices in Washington. One month later, the FTC published in the *Federal Register* another, similar notice of another public forum for the purpose of discussing all other provisions of its original rule besides the "Do Not Call" provision.[10] This second notice also invited public comments concerning the efficacy of the original Telemarketing Sales Rule.

Commenters responding to the commission's request for comments included consumer groups, law enforcement organizations, and industry groups. Commenters generally praised the original rule for reducing telemarketing fraud and providing a law-enforcement tool for combating telemarketing fraud, for Congress had provided that the Telemarketing Act (and thus its implementing regulations) would be enforceable not only by the FTC but by private citizens bringing private rights of action in court and more importantly by state officials as well. On the other hand, most commentators also suggested that the rule was not very effective in protecting consumers' privacy.

Responding to reactions to what the agency named its "Do Not Call Forum" as well as to the comments it received on the Telemarketing Sales Rule generally, the FTC held a second forum in July 2000. As a result of the views expressed by members of the public at those fora and in written comments, and based as well on the agency's own law enforcement expe-

216

rience, the FTC determined to retain its original rule but to strengthen it by amendment. The amendment would take the form, however, of an independent substantive rulemaking. Accordingly, in January 2002 the FTC issued a notice of proposed rulemaking (NPRM) proposing a number of changes to the Telemarketing Sales Rule, including a new ban on disclosing to any third party a customer's billing information, a prohibition on telemarketer use of caller-identification-blocking technologies, restrictions on the use of novel payment systems, and most importantly for present purposes the creation of a national "Do Not Call" registry maintained by the FTC allowing consumers to prevent calls from most telemarketers without specifically requesting to be taken off each telemarketer's calling list separately.[11]

The agency's NPRM generated about sixty-four thousand comments in response to its proposed rule. Commenters represented industry, consumer groups, privacy groups, and law enforcement. Many individuals commented on their own behalf as well. Further to air the issues surrounding its proposal, the commission held another public forum, this time over three days, to discuss its proposed revision and comments it had received in response. Like its first two public forums, this one was transcribed and placed on the public record, as were many of the written and electronic comments the commission received, and placed on the FTC's website. The agency also briefly extended the period for commenting on its proposed rule.[12]

The constellation of interests supporting or opposing the proposed amendments to the rule was predictable enough. On the one side, consumer and privacy groups together with law enforcement organizations supported strengthening the rule, and strongly supported the proposed "Do Not Call" registry specifically. These interests—including organizations such as American Association of Retired Persons, Consumers Union, the Privacy Rights Clearinghouse, and the National Association of Attorneys General, for example—argued that the existing company-specific "Do Not Call" prohibitions were too burdensome on consumers, difficult for consumers to confirm, and ignored by sellers. They added that the Telephone Consumer Protection Act's private right of action was far too burdensome for individual consumers to seek meaningful redress for violations of the company-specific "Do Not Call" prohibitions, and that even consumers who took the trouble to bring suit found the difficulties compounded upon trying to enforce a favorable judgment.

In opposition, industry groups—including the Direct Marketing Association, the Direct Selling Association, and individual firms like Best Buy and Celebrity Prime Foods, among many others—resisted, voicing several objections. In the first place, they contested the FTC's statutory authority to create a national registry. They argued that because the Telemarketing Act does not mention a national registry, and because Congress had in the Telephone Consumer Protection Act directed another agency (the FCC) to consider the possibility of creating such a registry, Congress must not have intended the establishment of a registry to be within the FTC's statutory authority.

In the alternative, industry groups argued that a national registry would interfere with state registries, creating coordination problems among national and state registries and thereby engender confusion. Thus, they argued, if the FTC were to establish a national "Do Not Call" registry, it would have to preempt similar state regulation, a position strongly resisted by the National Association of Attorneys General and other state officials. Opponents further argued that the proposed registry would interfere with their First Amendment speech rights, by impeding their ability to communicate with potential customers. In addition, opponents of the national registry argued that the economic costs of this aspect of the rule would be significant and undesirable, including a drastic reduction in telemarketing revenues and a loss of jobs, particularly for women, minorities, and rural workers, all of whom the Direct Marketing Association suggested were overrepresented among telemarketing employees. Some of the registry's opponents argued, most creatively, that the FTC should have but failed to conduct an environmental analysis required under NEPA, on the grounds that a reduction in telemarketing sales would result in increased consumer travel to shopping malls and other retail destinations, causing increased air pollution.

Finally, industry groups argued that the national registry was unnecessary because they had, through self-regulation, already established a system that did what the proposed registry would do. That is, the Direct Marketing Association had already created a "Telephone Preference Service" (TPS) that allows telephone customers to remove their numbers from telemarketing lists. Thus, opponents argued, a national "Do Not Call" registry was not necessary, notwithstanding that the TPS service is voluntary on the part of sellers, limited to the sellers who are members of the Direct Marketing Association, and enforced if at all only by the association.

Charitable organizations—such as the Childhood Leukemia Foundation, the March of Dimes, and the Red Cross—fell somewhere in between industry and consumer groups concerning the proposed rule in general, though they forcefully resisted being included within the scope of a national registry in particular. While curbing telemarketing fraud would benefit their legitimate activities, they opposed application of a national "Do Not Call" registry to them on the grounds that such a registry would cripple their efforts to raise money for charitable causes, which depend heavily on telephone solicitations. They too argued that First Amendment values should protect them from the scope of a national registry, and that their political, charitable, or otherwise noncommercial speech was entitled to greater First Amendment protection than was the commercial speech of ordinary telemarketers.

While industry argued that the proposed amendments went too far, some of the amendments' supporters argued that the commission's proposals were too weak. Most notably, certain consumer and privacy groups argued that the FTC should create instead an "opt in" national calling registry through which consumers could agree to receive telemarketing solicitations. According to their alternative, consumers would have to take an affirmative step to put their telephone numbers on a list making them eligible for telemarketers to call, rather than take an affirmative step to avoid unwanted calls. These groups argued that a no-call default would best protect consumer privacy as well as reduce telemarketing fraud.

Supporters and opponents of the proposed national "Do Not Call" registry advanced their arguments at the FTC's public forums and especially through written comments and email comments submitted during the rulemaking's notice-and-comment process, which the FTC catalogued extensively. The vast majority of the total comments received on the commission's proposed rule addressed the issue of a registry, and written and email comments supporting the registry outnumbered those opposing by a ratio of three to one.[13] Although comments submitted by individuals overwhelmingly supported the national registry, arguing repeatedly that the company-specific "Do Not Call" provision of the existing rule did not go far enough to protect their privacy, the proposal's opponents also organized commentary by individual telemarketers who expressed pride in their work and worries about their personal economic futures if their telemarketing activity were reduced.

In the end, the final amended rule preserved all of the main strictures of the original Telemarketing Sales Rule, adding to them. Explicitly balancing all competing interests, and emphasizing implicated First Amendment interests, the FTC decided to create the "opt out" national "Do Not Call" registry contemplated in its proposed rule, and not to preempt similar state registries, and to exempt charitable organizations. One year after publishing its proposed rule, then, the commission in January 2003 issued its final rule, responding to the comments it received during the rulemaking process in exhaustive detail far above that required by the Administrative Procedure Act. The final rule was adopted unanimously by all five FTC commissioners.

The FTC justified the need for a new, national registry on several grounds, including most especially the limited effectiveness of the company-specific "Do Not Call" provision of the original rule. The commission concluded that, telemarketing industry objections notwithstanding, its rulemaking record demonstrated "overwhelmingly" that the company-specific approach "is seriously inadequate to protect consumers' privacy from an abusive pattern of calls . . . . [and that] consumers continue to be angered by and frustrated with the pattern of unsolicited telemarketing calls they receive from the multitude of sellers and telemarketers."[14] Although the commission concluded that a national registry "should contain few exemptions in order to provide consumers with the most comprehensive privacy protection possible,"[15] it exempted calls between parties with "established business relationships" and calls by charitable solicitors, in the former case relying on cost-benefit considerations and in the latter acknowledging implicated First Amendment interests.[16]

Those narrow exemptions aside, industry opposition to the "Do Not Call" registry otherwise yielded completely to the FTC's rulemaking effort to protect consumers. Seeking to implement a new registry system "with the lowest possible costs,"[17] the FTC then solicited quotes from private parties capable of operating a national registry, completed another rulemaking to establish fees for telemarketers' use of the registry,[18] and established telephone and web-based interfaces for individuals to add their numbers to the registry. The commission's final rule, effective as of January 2005, requires telemarketers to "scrub" their calling lists once a month by removing from their lists telephone numbers that appear on the national registry.

Not surprisingly, however, the telemarketing industry did not give up there. Rather, upon the commission's publication of its final rule in January 2003, industry groups represented by Mainstream Marketing Services, TMG Marketing, and the American Teleservices Association filed suit in the U.S. district court in Colorado. At the same time, Global Contact Services, InfoCision Management Corporation, and the Direct Marketing Association, among others, brought similar challenge in the U.S. District Court for the Western District of Oklahoma. Both groups of plaintiffs prevailed, winning summary judgment against implementation of the "Do Not Call" portion of the FTC's rule. In the Colorado case, the court held that the registry violated the plaintiffs' commercial speech rights under the First Amendment.[19] In the Oklahoma case, the court concluded instead that the FTC lacked authority under the Telemarketing and Consumer Fraud and Abuse Prevention Act, but reached that conclusion upon explaining that it was interpreting that statute in a way that avoided the question about its constitutionality.[20]

But those cases proved to be only a short setback for the FTC. Within a month of the decision in the Colorado case, the U.S. Court of Appeals for the Tenth Circuit granted a stay against the district court's judgment,[21] which the FTC had sought pending its appeal of that case. The appellate court's decision to grant a stay implied that the FTC was likely to prevail on appeal. And indeed, following consolidation of the Colorado and Oklahoma cases on appeal, the Tenth Circuit in February 2004 reversed, holding that the FTC had statutory authority to issue the "Do Not Call" rule, that it had not acted in violation of the APA, and that the final rule did not violate the First Amendment.[22] The appellate decision thus resolved any question about the FTC rule's legality, and the only other court to consider the issue since—the U.S. district court in Maryland—similarly held that the FTC's rule was a valid exercise of its statutory authority and did not violate the First Amendment.[23] The "Do Not Call" rule has since gone into full effect. At the present, approximately fifty-nine million consumers have placed their telephone numbers on the registry.

THE SECURITIES AND EXCHANGE COMMISSION'S ATTORNEY CONDUCT RULE

A series of large-scale corporate scandals during the last several years—involving major corporations such as Enron, Tyco, and WorldCom, and costing shareholders hundreds of billions of dollars—brought great attention to the issue of executive misfeasance and, eventually, to the role that lawyers may play in abetting, facilitating, or discouraging corporate misconduct. A major result of that attention was the well-publicized Sarbanes-Oxley Act of 2002,[24] the most important corporate governance legislation in decades, aimed to protect investors and enhance corporate responsibility by, among other things, requiring new corporate financial disclosures, providing new measures to reduce accounting fraud, and creating the new Public Company Accounting Oversight Board to oversee the auditing profession. Section 307 of Sarbanes-Oxley, "Rules of Professional Responsibility for Attorneys,"a small and open-ended section in an otherwise long and detailed statute, directed the Securities and Exchange Commission (SEC) to issue rules establishing minimum standards of professional conduct governing all attorneys who represent a securities issuer before the commission.[25] Section 307 instructed the agency to devise rules "in the public interest" and "for the protection of investors," requiring that such rules at a minimum oblige an attorney to report evidence of a material violation of law or fiduciary duty. Reflecting the unusual political importance Congress attached to addressing corporate scandal, section 307 required the commission to promulgate its rules quickly, within 180 days of the act's passage—by January 2003.

The SEC got busy. In November 2002, the agency proposed a rule giving flesh to section 307.[26] The commission's rule proposed to alter the relationship between attorneys and their securities-issuing clients, and indeed the relationships among attorneys, those clients, and the commission itself. In a nutshell, the commission sought to enlist attorneys practicing before it to combat corporate fraud by disclosing evidence of material fraud to senior personnel within the corporate issuer. Put differently, the commission sought to prevent attorneys from facilitating and then concealing corporate misconduct on the grounds that they could not disclose their clients' confidential information.

The central features of the SEC's proposed rule were two. First, the commission proposed that any attorney practicing before it on behalf of a securities issuer who becomes aware of a "material violation" of securities law by the issuer (or agent of the issuer) be required to report evidence of that violation to the issuer's chief legal officer or chief executive officer or, for attorneys working under the supervision of another attorney, to the supervising attorney who would in turn report to the CLO. If the attorney did not believe the CLO or CEO responded or was likely to respond appropriately, the attorney would then be required to report evidence of the violation to the issuer's audit committee or nonemployed directors or, if the issuer's board of directors had no nonemployed committee, to its board of directors. The proposed rule contained an alternative reporting requirement for corporations electing to establish an independent "Qualified Legal Compliance Committee," to whom the attorney could report a material violation and in so doing completely fulfill the reporting requirement without taking further action. Together, these provisions of the commission's proposal became known as the "up the ladder" requirement, for attorneys were in essence required to report evidence of material violations of securities laws up the corporate hierarchy of their issuing client.

In addition to the "up the ladder" requirement, the other main component of the commission's proposed rule became known as its "noisy withdrawal" requirement. This requirement was triggered whenever an attorney reporting a possible material violation of the law received no satisfactory response up the corporate legal-executive chain of command. In such a case, which the commission contemplated would be fairly rare given the likely deterrent effects of the rule's "up the ladder" provisions,[27] the attorney would have to resign from the issuing client and notify the commission in writing that he or she had withdrawn from representing the issuer. In addition, the attorney would have to disaffirm any opinion, document, or other disclosure the attorney prepared for the commission on behalf of the client that the attorney believed might be materially false or misleading. Such notification would be "noisy" because it would alert the commission that something might be amiss, even though the withdrawing attorney would not disclose specific facts to the commission apart from identifying potentially false or misleading disclosures, if any.

Upon proposing its rule, the SEC explained that the rule would satisfy the requirements of section 307. The commission first observed that while section 307 did not require all the particulars of its proposed rule, Congress authorized the rule by delegating to the agency responsibility for devising minimum standards. The commission also argued its proposal would serve the public interest and protect investors—the criteria of section 307—because it would reduce corporate fraud and misconduct. Its proposed rule would deter such conduct in the very first place by increasing the likelihood that fraud would be detected, and provide a channel minimizing the harm of corporate misrepresentations by addressing them early and internally where they arose. Its rule would furthermore give "the investing public" more confidence that corporate disclosures submitted to the Commission contained accurate information. Increased investor confidence, in turn, would promote investment in, and the efficiency of, capital markets. The SEC thus justified its proposal not only on the basis that it responded to congressional instruction, but also in public-policy and cost-benefit terms.[28] On those grounds, the rule seemed socially desirable, a sensible device to combat serious fraud.

But the SEC faced stiff opposition from the profession it aimed to regulate: Bar organizations quickly and aggressively mobilized against it. The rules' opponents included the American Bar Association (ABA), most importantly, as well as the American Corporate Counsel Association, the American College of Trial Lawyers, the Association of the Bar of the City of New York, the Los Angeles County Bar Association, the Federal Bar Council, and the Attorneys' Liability Assurance Society. In addition, dozens of the largest and best corporate law firms also mobilized to oppose the rule. Bar groups and law firms argued publically against the commission's proposal, and submitted lengthy written comments to the SEC arguing against the rule.

Lawyers objected to nearly all aspects of the SEC's proposal, not least its "noisy withdrawal" provision. Apart from contesting the commission's statutory authority to issue a rule containing such a provision, lawyer groups objected to the merits of the commission's proposal on the grounds that such a rule would conflict with state ethics requirements. They argued, in other words, that an attorney would be forced to choose between observance of the rule and observance of ethical obligations created and enforced at the state level. Opponents also argued that the rule would have perverse consequences because clients would begin to exclude their attorneys from meetings and other communications involving information about a possible material violation, thereby reducing attorneys' ability to prevent or remedy violations. According to this argument, the proposed rule would create undesirable distance between corporate clients and their lawyers.

The core objection to the "noisy withdrawal" provision, however, focused on attorney ethics. Codes of ethical conduct, part of state law and state professional rules, in general prohibit attorneys from disclosing confidential client information, not only once an attorney-client relationship has been established but even after that relationship is terminated. Professional codes of ethical conduct similarly prohibit attorneys from entering into or facilitating any conflict of interest between themselves and a client. The SEC's proposed "noisy withdrawal" provision thus threatened, bar groups argued, lawyers' basic understandings of their role as corporate counsel.

But then state law and ethics rules can be trumped by a federal agency carrying out congressionally delegated authority, and the SEC certainly can establish its own rules of conduct for attorneys practicing before it. So bar groups' objection was not centrally a legal one, though sometimes cast in those terms, but a normative objection that the SEC should not alter the relationship between corporate counsel and their clients. In short, the bar mobilized for the purpose of protecting the corporate-counsel status quo.

Yet the SEC and indeed the legislative sponsors of section 307—which was added to the Sarbanes-Oxley Act as a floor amendment over the objection of the ABA in the first place—perceived that that status quo contributed to the problem of corporate misconduct. The intent behind section 307 and its implementing regulations was precisely to change established attorney practices.[29] Thus the senators proposing section 307—Senators John Edwards (a plaintiff's attorney), Michael Enzi (the Senate's only accountant), and Jon Corzine (the Senate's only investment banker)—repeatedly expressed their view that attorneys had facilitated recent corporate scandals and that while greater attention should be paid to accountants and corporate executives, lawyers too deserved regulatory attention.[30]

Moreover, the SEC's proposal was not as radical as some opponents suggested. As the commission and supporters of its proposal pointed out, the vast majority of state ethical codes of attorney conduct permitted though did not require disclosures of securities violations where an attorney's work-product would be used by a client to advance that violation. And where a violation would constitute a crime, many states required an attorney to disclose the violation, again if the attorney's work would be used by the client to facilitate the crime. In addition, some state ethics committees were, at the time the SEC released its proposal, revisiting the issue of attorney-client relationships in the context of corporate misconduct. In other words, the SEC's proposal, although undoubtedly significant, was not as revolutionary as some of its opponents suggested.

Furthermore, even the bar itself perceived at least part of the problem of lawyers' role or possible role in major corporate scandals. In mid-2002, the American Bar Association's Task Force on Corporate Responsibility released a preliminary report that acknowledged that corporate attorneys bear some of the blame for the failed system of corporate governance.[31] Then, after unsuccessfully opposing section 307's passage, the ABA established a task force to work "with" the SEC to develop implementing rules. The ABA thereafter recommended changes in the Model Rules of Professional Conduct to address lawyers' roles in facilitating or preventing corporate misfeasance. Meanwhile, state organizations also examined the issue of attorneys' role in corporate misconduct, on the basis of which the Council of Chief Justices submitted comments urging the SEC to postpone regulating in the area to see what would happen at the state level. Ultimately, however, the ABA task force's recommendations were not adopted, nor did the bar make other relevant changes to affect corporate attorney conduct.

On the other side of the debate, in support of the SEC's proposal, sat legal academicians. In fact, interestingly, the organized proponents of the SEC's proposal consisted almost entirely of law professors, some of whom had called for stricter regulation of corporate attorney conduct before Sarbanes-Oxley was passed. Responding to the commission's proposed rule, a group of fifty law professors submitted comments supporting the SEC. Several other prominent legal academics also submitted letters and comments to the agency on their own behalf. While a few of the proposal's supporters urged the SEC to go even farther than it proposed, the majority of academic commenters—most experts on the subject of corporate attorney ethics—argued that the agency's proposals responded appropriately and adequately to the issue of attorney conduct and corporate misfeasance. The commission relied on the academics' comments extensively, referring to and quoting from them in detail, both in the course of explaining its proposals and later upon announcing its final rule.[32]

After several months of the notice-and-comment process following the release of its proposal, the SEC in January 2003 adopted its proposed "up the ladder" requirements and most other aspects of its proposed rule as well, except the "noisy withdrawal" requirement.[33] In addition to excluding the "noisy withdrawal" provision, the final rule made several smaller but significant changes in response to the comments the commission had received, both from bar groups and from foreign lawyers. First, the agency clarified the objective standard triggering an obligation to report evidence of a material violation. According to the final rule, an attorney is obligated to report a potential material violation whenever "it would be unreasonable, under the circumstances, for a prudent and competent attorney not to conclude that it is reasonably likely" that a violation has or is likely to occur.[34] Second, the commission eliminated its proposed requirement that an attorney document communications made concerning a potential material violation. Although the proposed rule required an attorney reporting such a violation to document his or her report, and similarly for an attorney hearing such a report to document a response, the commission explained it was persuaded by nearly universal comments in opposition that such a requirement would reduce managers' willingness to be honest with attorneys and create a conflict of interest between lawyer and client by forcing the lawyer prepare a written file that might be used later against the client, while trying to advise and advocate for the client at the same time.

Finally, the commission also excluded foreign lawyers from the reach of its rule, provided that they appeared before the commission only incidentally or in consultation with domestic council and did not hold themselves out to be practicing securities lawyers. Non-U.S. lawyers along with domestic attorneys had argued against the commission's proposed rule, on similar grounds that its application to them would interfere with their professional obligations in their home jurisdictions and interfere as well with international comity. Solicitous of such concerns, the SEC in December 2002 hosted a "roundtable" for the purpose of discussing the impact of its proposed rules on foreign lawyers. The roundtable invited foreign participants to express their views on the application of the commission's rules to lawyers licensed outside of the United States, views also expressed in more than forty written comment letters the agency received. In the end, the SEC determined that members of foreign bars should not, simply by virtue of that fact, be exempted from the scope of its rule, but on the other hand that "non-appearing foreign attorneys" would not be encompassed by the rule.

When the SEC finalized its rule excluding the "noisy withdrawal" provision, it resolicited comments on that aspect of its original proposed rule. In other words, upon finalizing most other portions of its proposal, the commission kept the "noisy withdrawal" proposal alive by extending the comment period on that aspect of the proposal and requesting another round of comments. At the same time, the SEC summarized and addressed many of the comments it had received on that part of its original proposal, both pro and con, in effect inviting comments on those comments.

In addition, the commission simultaneously proposed and solicited comments on an alternative to its original "noisy withdrawal" provision.[35] According to this alternative, when an attorney withdraws from representing an issuer as a result of not receiving an appropriate response to his or her "up the ladder" reports of material violations of securities laws, the issuer—rather than the attorney—could report to the commission and disclose publically that an attorney had withdrawn. The attorney would still be required to withdraw from representing the issuer, and to notify the issuer in writing that the withdrawal is based on "professional considerations," but need not disclose anything to the commission directly, nor disaffirm any documents or disclosures the attorney helped to prepare. Such a withdrawal would therefore be quieter than the commission's "noisy withdrawal" proposal. Upon releasing its alternative proposal, the commission argued that it would mute bar groups' criticisms of "noisy withdrawal," those concerning the attorney-client privilege in particular, while at the same time providing protection to investors by helping to ensure issuers respond appropriately to reports of material violations.

That trail ends there: The SEC has not adopted the "noisy withdrawal" proposal or its alternative. Nor has the SEC completed its rulemaking by deciding conclusively against either proposal. Instead, the commission has listed its "noisy withdrawal" proposal in the annual *Regulatory Agenda* as a pending "Long Term Action" that it may or may not act upon within twelve months. In fact, it has so listed the proposal in the *Regulatory Agenda* for the past three years, in nearly identical statements each year, which strongly suggests that the commission has no intention of finalizing that part of its original rule.[36] In a speech at the Rocky Mountain Securities Conference in May 2003, SEC commissioner Paul Atkins also suggested that the commission may be unlikely to pursue "noisy withdrawal" or its alternative, in his view because the ABA might develop its own ethical standards to address the issue, a prediction that to date has not proven prescient.[37]

However that may be, the rule governing attorney conduct that the SEC did finalize and codify was unprecedented even without the "noisy withdrawal" provision. In the process of implementing legislation that Commissioner Atkins described as a previously "unimaginable [before recent scandals] incursion of the U.S. federal government into the corporate governance area,"[38] the SEC went one historically significant step further. For the first time, a federal agency directly regulated the ethical conduct of attorneys. And the "up the ladder" and related requirements of the commission's new rule have in fact changed the practice of corporate lawyering significantly. In addition, the new rule focuses future attention on the role of the corporate bar in facilitating or instead combating corporate misconduct. Notably, the SEC accomplished these changes over the objections of well-organized, persistent, and powerful bar organizations, including the ABA and dozens of prestigious corporate law firms, exercising its independence with political help from no organized interest groups and with only the very modest support that academicians provide.

The Office of the Comptroller
of the Currency's Liberalization of National Banks

Not all important regulatory initiatives take the form of a rulemaking or, as in the case of the FTC's "Do Not Call" registry, a piece of a single rule. Some emerge instead through a series of formal and informal decisions that, collectively, change the regulatory landscape dramatically. Some of these initiatives provide additional examples of administrative regulators employing the administrative process to advance general interests. The Office of the Comptroller of the Currency's liberalization of national banks is one such case.

Over the last decade, the Office of the Comptroller of the Currency (OCC) completed an ambitious effort to expand the types of financial services that national banks may provide. Through a set of regulatory decisions with enormous economic and political consequences, the OCC allowed banks and their subsidiaries to compete with insurance companies and insurance agents—both among banks' archrivals—by selling insurance and annuities and to some extent by underwriting insurance. The OCC has also allowed a national bank's subsidiary to underwrite municipal revenue bonds—once an activity within the exclusive domain of securities firms—by inviting national banks to apply to the OCC for permission to conduct through their subsidiaries activities which the parent banks themselves could not conduct.

But the effects of the OCC's liberalization extended even beyond radically altering the regulatory field on which financial services providers compete. No less importantly, the OCC's actions also helped prompt equally significant liberalizing decisions by the Federal Reserve Board ("the Fed") relating to permissible conduct by bank holding companies (as opposed to banks and their subsidiaries).[39] On top of that, the OCC's liberalization of national banks also prompted Congress to enact financial services reform legislation, after many years of being unable to do so given interest-group deadlock over proposed legislative change. Indeed, recent legislative reform in the financial services area was widely considered necessary due to mammoth mergers in the financial services markets that were inspired by the OCC's and the Fed's regulatory actions.[40] Yet the OCC and the Fed had already largely upstaged Congress. At the very least, Congress copied as much as led these agencies by ratifying many administrative developments. The following explains.

The OCC has primary regulatory authority over national banks (of which there are approximately twenty-eight hundred)—that is, banks chartered by the federal government rather than by one of the states, and banks as opposed to bank holding companies, over whom the Fed has primary regulatory authority. The OCC's mission is to provide a safe, sound, and competitive national banking system. To that end, the agency supervises national banks and enforces federal banking laws. Its functions include, for example, approving new bank charters and national bank merger applications. The agency performs such functions procedurally by undertaking rulemakings relating to activities that are permissible for national banks, ruling on applications by banks to engage in certain activities, and conducting adjudications to enforce banking statutes and its own regulations.

As the primary regulator of national banks, the OCC implements the National Bank Act of 1864,[41] the predecessor of which (the National Currency Act of 1863)[42] created the agency. A critical section of the National Bank Act outlines what national banks may and may not do, providing among other things that they can "exercise . . . all such incidental powers as shall be necessary to carry on the business of banking."[43] The identification of such powers rests with the OCC, giving the agency considerable power over the banking business and, therefore, its competitors. Until recently, the Glass-Steagall Act and other federal banking laws had prohibited banks from engaging in nonbanking businesses, and likewise prohibited nonbanking businesses from engaging in banking.[44] The National Bank Act's "incidental powers" clause was one of the two escape hatches from that general prohibition, the other being a crucial analogous section of the Bank Holding Company Act[45] providing that a bank holding company may engage in a nonbanking activity considered "to be so closely related to banking or managing or controlling banks as to be a proper incident thereto."[46]

In the last decade, the OCC has used the National Bank Act's escape hatch in an increasingly aggressive way, thereby permitting more nonbanking functions to be performed by national banks, generating considerable resistance from national banks' competitors. One of the first major examples occurred in 1990, when the OCC determined that sales of fixed or variable annuities qualified as "part of, or incidental to, the business of banking." On that occasion, NationsBank and its brokerage subsidiary sought permission from the OCC for the subsidiary to act as an agent in the sale of annuities, which the OCC granted on the grounds that banks are empowered to broker a variety of comparable financial investment instruments when carrying out their traditional role of financial intermediaries. The Variable Annuity Life Insurance Company and other insurers challenged the agency's authority to give NationsBank permission to sell annuities by bringing several lawsuits under the Administrative Procedure Act.[47] They argued that the agency misinterpreted the National Bank Act by allowing a bank subsidiary to engage in an activity Congress intended to prohibit. But the U.S. Supreme Court ultimately deferred to the comptroller's reading of the statute, and thus national banks may now sell annuities.

In December 1997, the OCC took a similar approach, this time permit-ting a bank to sell crop insurance as "incidental" to its business. In its response to an application to do so by the Iowa Bankers Association, the agency reasoned that selling crop insurance constitutes an "incidental" power "necessary" to carry out the business of banking because selling that kind of insurance helps a bank to secure its loans—with the loans secured by the now-insured crop.[48] While perhaps sensible enough, this reasoning too had dire consequences for insurance sellers, for it strongly suggested that any insurance sold in connection with a bank loan that helps the bank secure its loan may be permissible. Because many types of insurance may aid in securing a bank loan, the agency's reasoning implied that banks might be able to sell many other types of insurance, an implica-tion not missed by insurance groups, who forcefully criticized the OCC's decision.[49]

As mentioned, the OCC also recently allowed a national bank's op-erating subsidiaries ("op-sub") to underwrite municipal revenue bonds, as part of the agency's so-called "Part 5 initiative"—a reference to the part of Title 12 of the *Code of Federal Regulations* governing the rules, policies, and procedures for banks' corporate activities, one important provision of which concerns activities that are permissible for a national bank's subsidiary.[50] Permissible activities for an op-sub were long thought to piggyback on activities permissible for the parent bank itself,[51] but in 1994 the OCC began a notice-and-comment rulemaking proposing to change the rule to encourage banks in good regulatory standing to apply for permission for one of their op-subs to engage in an activity that its parent bank could not.[52] The proposal's critics, which included insurance and securities associations, opposed on several grounds, arguing that the OCC lacked authority to allow subsidiaries to do what banks could not, and furthermore that doing so would be inconsistent with OCC prece-dent, inconsistent with the Glass-Steagall Act and the Bank Holding Com-pany Act, and would subject national banks to unacceptable safety and soundness risks.[53]

In the end, however, the OCC did much of what it proposed to do. Upon issuing its final Part 5 rule, the agency explained that while it had usually taken the position that banking laws applicable to a national bank should also apply in the same way to a bank's operating subsidiary, that rule of thumb never represented "a legal determination that an operating subsidiary may never permissibly conduct activities different from those allowed its parent bank. "[54] In support of its case, the OCC traced the history of rather minor instances where the OCC approved activities by subsidiaries different from those allowed banks.[55] The agency also provided an analysis of the Glass-Steagall Act, the Bank Holding Company Act, and other banking laws, arguing that none foreclosed the possibility of op-subs performing activities not permissible for banks, and furthermore that its new rule did not authorize any new activities but rather allowed for the possibility of them, adding that the agency would not approve any applications that ran counter to federal banking statutes or presented safety and soundness risks.[56] Finally, the OCC stressed that subsidiaries' activities still must qualify as part of the business of banking or be incidental thereto, or else be permissible for national banks or their subsidiaries under statutory authority besides the National Bank Act.[57]

In its commentary on the final Part 5 rule governing subsidiaries, the agency explained:

> [A] national bank operating subsidiary remains limited in its activities to those that are part of or incidental to the business of banking as determined by the OCC, or otherwise permissible for national banks or their subsidiaries under other statutory authority. The final rule confirms, however, that this may include activities different from what the parent national bank may conduct directly, if, in the circumstances presented, the reason or rationale for restricting the parent bank's ability to conduct the activity does not apply to the subsidiary.[58]

The agency's Part 5 initiative thus made clear that it would entertain applications by banks or their subsidiaries to engage in activities not otherwise permissible for a bank, on the grounds that such activities were part of or incidental to and necessary to carry out the business of banking. In so doing, the OCC explained that its case-by-case evaluations of op-sub applications would focus on the form and specificity of the restriction applicable to the parent bank, the rationale underlying that restriction, and whether granting an application would frustrate the congressional purpose underlying the restriction.[59] Even so, the agency's position was unquestionably innovative and significant.

The OCC's temerity, on that issue and similar liberalizing efforts, owed largely to its comptroller, Eugene Ludwig. A visionary head of the OCC, who enjoyed White House and Treasury Department encouragement, Ludwig pushed national bank liberalization as far as possible within the OCC's statutory framework. Though criticized by some, and strongly opposed by the insurance industry and often by the Fed as well,[60] Ludwig defended the OCC's Part 5 initiative on the grounds that technological and economic changes required changes in national bank practices allowing banks to compete with other financial service providers. The comptroller argued that the stability of the national banking system depended on such changes. According to some reports, Ludwig's OCC postponed the Part 5 rule pending possible congressional action on the same front, but ultimately promulgated its final rule once it became clear that no legislative reform was forthcoming.[61] Defending his agency's initiative, Ludwig argued that the very safety and soundness of the banking system required decisive action allowing op-subs to engage in new activities.[62]

Following promulgation of the final Part 5 rule in late 1996, then, the OCC in 1997 authorized Zion First National Bank to use one of its subsidiaries to underwrite municipal revenue bonds.[63] Following Zion First National Bank's application to do so, the OCC published notice of and requested public comment on Zion's "application to commence new activities."[64] Interestingly, although the agency's decision with respect to an application concerning corporate activities is not itself a rule (but rather the application of one), the OCC's new Part 5 provisions established a notice-and-comment-type procedure—a miniature rulemaking of sorts—for all applications submitted to the agency for permission to conduct activities not previously approved. Following receipt of an application, then, the OCC provides "notice" and invites "comments," after which the agency explains the decision it has reached with reference to supporting and opposing comments.[65]

The agency's notice with respect to Zion's application generated opposition from the Securities Industry Association, the Securities and Exchange Commission, the Fed, and Consumers Union.[66] These opponents argued, among other things, that a subsidiary of a national bank should not be permitted to engage in any activity that is not permissible for a national bank. The OCC rejected this argument, however, observing that underwriting and dealing in revenue bonds is "a functional equivalent or a logical outgrowth of" activities banks are already engaged in, and concluding that an activity not permissible for a bank may nevertheless, and under appropriate circumstances, be performed by a bank's subsidiary.[67] The agency has reaffirmed that general position several times since, as for example when it approved an application by Fleet National Bank to allow one of its subsidiaries to underwrite credit life insurance as "part of" and "incidental to" Fleet's credit card activities.[68]

The OCC's liberalizing initiatives have not been limited to interpretations of the "incidental powers" language of the National Bank Act, however. The agency also recently approved a bank's proposal to use a subsidiary in a small town to facilitate insurance sales through any of the bank's branches. While long-standing authority provided an exception to statutory prohibitions against banks selling insurance for towns of fewer than five thousand residents, state insurance laws nevertheless largely prevented banks from selling insurance even in small towns. But in 1996, the Supreme Court made clear that state laws purporting to prohibit national banks from selling insurance had to yield to federal law, a ruling that opened the way for insurance sales by national banks.[69] The OCC subsequently took the underutilized small-town exception and ran with it, allowing a national bank to use the exception to support insurance sales by the bank's other units. What sounds like a technicality had far-reaching implications: Now a national bank can open a subsidiary in a small town, and then market insurance sales anywhere throughout the country, so long as it processes all of those insurance sales through its small-town subsidiary, as for example the OCC has allowed in connection with Mellon Bank's application to sell title insurance through a subsidiary's joint venture. Here again, the agency was met with intense objections, this time from insurance agents.

But insurers and securities underwriters have not been the OCC's only critics. Many in Congress—where insurance companies and insurance agents have traditionally enjoyed considerable influence[70]—also loudly criticized the agency's liberalizations, on the grounds that the OCC overreached and thwarted congressional will. For example, Senator Alfonse M. D'Amato, then the Senate Banking Committee chair, captured congressional frustration by stating:

> We should not sit idly by while the Comptroller of the Currency attempts to unilaterally redesign the financial system and alter the state and federal regulatory framework established by Congress. . . . The Comptroller is deliberately consolidating power within his agency by first approving new powers for national banks and then asserting the authority to regulate such activities.[71]

For another example, Representative John Dingell, an influential member on the House Energy and Commerce Committee, repeatedly criticized Ludwig and the OCC during the mid-1990s over the agency's approval of bank sales of "retirement CDs"—an investment product combining features of the traditional CD and an annuity—its general treatment of op-subs, and its de facto regulation of insurance products. Dingell pulled no punches, calling Ludwig's actions "arrogant, high-handed, stupid and dangerous."[72] In 1994, Dingell, along with D'Amato and other House and Senate members, sent a letter to the OCC promising to introduce legislation that would kill the retirement CD if the agency allowed its sale by banks, which the OCC nevertheless allowed without repercussion.[73] In 1996, Representative Gerald Solomon, then chairman of the House Rules Committee (and incidentally a former insurance agent), introduced a bill that would have blocked OCC funding if the agency authorized national banks to sell any new products or services.[74] And some versions of draft legislation finally modernizing financial services included moratoria on the agency's ability to expand banks' insurance powers.[75]

But while many within Congress were highly critical of the OCC, Congress was able to do little to slow the agency down, in part because the federal courts sanctioned agency-sponsored reform. In the face of repeated judicial challenges to the OCC's actions brought by banks' competitors, the agency's decisions allowing national banks and their subsidiaries to do more and more met with consistent judicial favor.[76] Indeed, in several cases the U.S. Supreme Court sanctioned OCC interpretations of the statute unanimously.[77] Showing considerable deference to OCC interpretations of the National Bank Act, the Supreme Court and lower federal courts have emphasized the agency's expertise concerning banking matters as a justification for judicial deference.

Ironically, judicial affirmation of the comptroller's liberalizations paved the way for Congress finally to enact reform legislation. This is true in large part because insurance groups, having "lost" at the agency level and in the courts, eventually came to support rather than oppose legislative reform, overcoming legislative gridlock. Concluding that bank-supplied insurance products were an unavoidable reality, insurers sought reform legislation that would give them broader financial services powers too, allowing them to compete with banks, and that would preserve state regulation of insurance, considered more friendly to insurers.[78] As a result, banks, insurers, and securities underwriters ultimately came together in favor of reform, ending long years of legislative inaction over financial services reform. In truth, Congress had little choice, barring statutory invalidation of what the OCC had done by resurrecting the firewalls separating banking from insurance and securities, but to codify much of what the OCC had done. Following skirmishes concerning matters such as the applicability of the Community Reinvestment Act[79] to a reformed financial services world, Congress then passed modernizing legislation, following the path the OCC blazed.[80]

By all accounts, the reforms both undertaken and instigated by the OCC advanced general interests. They did so most generally by increasing efficiency and competition in the financial services market. By allowing banks to compete with other financial service providers, and in turn them to compete with banks, consumers benefit in the form of greater access and lower cost of financial service products. Such competition also allows financial service providers to exploit economic and technological advances, further promoting efficiency in the financial services markets, with benefits again redounding to consumers. In short, the financial services world had outgrown Glass-Steagall, and the OCC's initiative to modernize national banking helped shed an ill-fitting regulatory regime. Thus was the expert consensus in support of regulatory and legislative reforms broad and deep.

But the OCC's steps did not come easily, notwithstanding academic consensus in support of its efforts. For in the short run, the agency's liberalizing steps produced clear winners and losers, including among the latter organized insurance underwriters, insurance agents, and securities dealers. These powerful interests did not accept the OCC's actions without resistance, nor did their congressional allies. Yet the OCC was not greatly influenced, much less controlled, by such interests or their legislative supporters. Rather, through rulemaking and informal decisionmaking, and with judicial blessing of the agency's interpretation of national banking laws, the OCC and its entrepreneurial administrator were able to carry out an ambitious and socially beneficial regulatory agenda.

Part 4 answers the question "So what?"

PART IV

PUBLIC CHOICE AND
ADMINISTRATIVE PROCESS

INTRODUCTION TO PART 4

To take stock: Part 1 of this study called into theoretical question the power of the dominant public choice theory of regulation, the main conclusion of which is that agencies deliver socially undesirable regulation to politically powerful interest groups. Part 1 argued that, considered on its own conceptual terms, that theory seems in several ways imprecise, and in other ways precise but question-begging. Part 1 speculated that some of its nevertheless enduring influence may owe to the lack of any satisfying alternative theory. Part 1 then sketched an alternative "administrative process theory of regulation." The administrative process account emphasizes the central feature of regulatory decisionmaking that the public choice theory abstracts away, that is, the ground-level legal procedures through which agencies regulate.

Part 2 unpacked that feature by showing in detail how agencies regulate—what particular decisionmaking processes they employ and when, with what opportunities for outside participation, and under whose oversight. Having examined regulatory decisionmaking procedures in detail, part 2 then developed further the administrative process theory of regulation, according to which regulatory outcomes are a function of—and therefore explicable only with reference to—the formal and informal administrative process rules agency employ, as well as administrators' motivations and the institutional environment in which administrators make regulatory decisions. The administrative process account demotes Congress and organized interest groups in explaining regulatory outcomes, positing instead that agencies's decisionmaking procedures provide them with sufficient autonomy to advance general interests where they are motivated to do so, especially where they find political or legal support from the other branches, and even over the concentrated opposition of legislatively influential interests. The administrative process theory therefore contemplates regulatory outcomes at odds with the predictions of the capture-oriented, interest-group-centric vision of regulatory government supplied by the public choice theory.

Part 3 then offered three cases studies of regulation, and then a few more, to facilitate further evaluation of the two theories. To complete the square, this chapter and its twin that follows specify how those case studies call into question the power of public choice theory, on the one hand, and provide support for the administrative process approach, on the other. The final chapter considers some objections to the conclusions reached in the next two chapters, and offers additional general conclusions.

Chapter Thirteen

The Public Choice Theory Revisited

The Process Critique

THE REGULATORY initiatives presented in part 3 contravene the public choice theory's process expectations. The point is subtle but important, subtle because on the one hand a core defect of the public choice theory is exactly that it elides the processes of regulatory decisionmaking—so how can the theory have process expectations?—and yet important because the theory nevertheless implies regulatory processes consonant with its substantive regulatory predictions—for agencies can deliver the kinds of regulatory outcomes the theory predicts *only if* they possess procedural tools appropriate for that task. Put differently, while the public choice theory is not very specific about regulatory decisionmaking processes, at the same time it unambiguously implies processes capable of generating some kinds of regulatory outcomes (regulatory rents to favored groups) and not others (regulation that promotes general interests).

Recall that the public choice theory finds the most conceptual support from the legislative dominance hypothesis, which holds that legislators can ensure that agencies deliver favorable regulation to important constituent groups, and that they accomplish such control through administrative procedural rules. Chapter 8 called that premise into doubt, arguing that upon careful consideration the regulatory regime's process rules do not seem well designed to facilitate congressional control or regulatory rent-seeking. Rulemaking in particular seems rather at odds with the public choice theory's expectations, given the openness of that process. And much the same can be said for agencies' other informal and even formal decisionmaking processes. Chapter 8 concluded, then, that regulatory decisionmaking processes carried out under the Administrative Procedure Act and related requirements seem poorly suited to the purposes attributed to regulatory decisionmaking by the public choice account.

The details of the cases studied above provide support for that process critique. Indeed, the details of the studied examples cast doubt on all of the public choice theory's core claims identified in chapter 3. To begin with, recall what, procedurally speaking, prompted the studied regulatory initiatives in the first place. The EPA's ozone and particulate matter rules, the FDA's tobacco rule, the Forest Service's roadless rule, and the FTC's "Do Not Call" rule all were originally prompted not by special interests seeking regulatory rents, but by public sentiment and the support of public interest organizations. In the EPA case, part of what prompted the agency to regulate was a successful lawsuit—in a cause of action brought under the APA—by a public interest group (the American Lung Association) alleging that the EPA had failed to fulfill its obligation under the Clean Air Act by updating its National Ambient Air Quality Standards on time. Thus the EPA explained in its notice of proposed rulemaking that its rule responded not only to a statutory deadline but also to a judicial order following the lawsuit.

Similarly, the FDA's initial inquiry into its authority for regulating tobacco products was precipitated by a public interest group's petitions under APA section 553 formally requesting the FDA to consider a tobacco rulemaking. As noted in chapter 5, section 553 provides for any party to request that an agency initiate a rulemaking, and in the FDA case the Coalition on Smoking or Health petitioned the agency under that section. The creation of the FTC's registry was also prompted by consumer concerns about fraud and privacy, not by either the industry regulated by that rule or that industry's competitors. Following feedback from consumers the FTC received in the wake of the fora it hosted on the efficacy of the original Telemarketing Sales Rule, the agency undertook to revise its rule to provide for a national registry in addition to the seller-specific prohibition against unwanted telemarketing. So was the SEC's initiative fueled by academic calls for regulation of corporate attorney conduct. The SEC was prompted to regulate most immediately by a statutory deadline, but on the other hand academic calls for such regulation predated the legislation under which the SEC regulated and put the idea of regulating corporate attorney conduct in circulation. Less formally, environmental groups urged the Forest Service to reevaluate its roadless policy as well.

The OCC's initiative, in partial contrast to the other agencies', was not prompted by public interest groups, much less public sentiment, but then neither was it triggered by rent-seeking interest groups. The OCC's liberalization of national banks was prompted in part by economic and technological changes in the financial services market, as well as by the comptroller's resulting belief that some of the legal barriers separating financial service providers had outlived their usefulness. Although national banks undoubtedly welcomed and even advocated for the OCC's initiative, the

OCC's efforts are not plausibly reducible merely to the wishes the banking industry, for among other reasons national banks had advocated for liberalizations long before the OCC acted, and thus that advocacy alone cannot account for the comptroller's actions.

Thus the studied agencies' initiatives resulted not from special interest groups prompting the agencies to deliver favorable regulation to them, but rather in large part from the mobilization of broad-based interests. This fact not only contravenes the public choice theory's predictions about the origins of regulatory initiatives, but also illustrates the weakness of the theory's "interest group motivation claim," according to which interests mobilize only to advance the economic interests of their members. The difficulty for the theory is that those groups that supported, or in a few of the cases advocated for, the agencies' initiatives were not motivated to advance the economic interests of their members. To be sure, in each case public interest groups, public health advocates, environmental lawyers, and academicians met the opposition of interest groups seeking to advance their economic interests. Such groups were present too. But the point remains that agency initiatives triggered in part by broad-based organizations are at odds with the public choice theory's model of interest group behavior.

Once prompted to regulate, the agencies in all of the studied cases regulated through the notice-and-comment rulemaking process. This comes as no great surprise given the policy significance of the decisions, but it warrants emphasis that none of the agencies in question attempted to affect significant regulatory change through off-record, informal, or purely discretionary decisionmaking processes. In other words, none of the agencies sought to regulate in the dark. That is slightly less true with respect to the OCC, which liberalized in part informally through interpretations of the National Bank Act and the approval of applications to conduct certain activities following procedures the agency established through a rulemaking. Even there, however, the OCC did not circumvent the rulemaking process but, to the contrary, established its own rulemaking-like process for considering what activities it would allow national banks' subsidiaries to engage in under its Part 5 rule. In short, in no case did an agency seek to regulate in a manner that skirted the openness requirements of notice-and-comment rulemaking. Because the public choice theory contemplates that agencies will avoid transparency and instead use their discretion to deliver regulatory rents, the fact that the studied agencies did not seek to regulate in procedural secrecy also disappoints the theory's expectations.

The studied agencies' reliance on rulemaking thus raises the crucial question whether that administrative process successfully alerted Congress concerning what would be burdensome regulation—from the point of view of legislatively important interest groups—and thereby allow Congress to slow the agencies down, as the public choice theory's "legislative dominance claim" suggests. Here the theory encounters two serious problems. First, the notice-and-comment rulemakings did not in fact alert Congress to pending agency action in any of the considered cases. For in each case, the agency began exploring and gathering data about its yet-to-be-proposed rules far in advance of publishing its notice of proposed rulemaking in the *Federal Register*. And while all of the agencies' initiatives preceded initiation of the section 553 process, none of the agencies' prenotice activities was clandestine. Instead, the agencies publically announced their regulatory intentions in advance of formally initiating their rulemakings. The EPA began publically studying the health and welfare effects of ozone and particulate matter a few years before it published its notices of proposed rulemaking. The FDA began inquiries into the health effects of smoking, nicotine addiction, and the marketing and sales practices of tobacco companies over a year before its notice of proposed rulemaking. In fact, both the EPA and the FDA chartered advisory committees under the Federal Advisory Committee Act in advance of proposing regulation, making its initiatives even more public. And the OCC articulated its interpretations of the federal banking laws before it undertook its Part 5 revision.

Both regulated interests and members of Congress were therefore keenly aware of what the agencies might do before the commencement of section 553 rulemaking in all of the studied cases. Indeed, in the case of the FDA's tobacco rule, opposing interest groups prepared lawsuits before the agency issued even its proposed rule.[1] And in the EPA and Forest Service cases, the agencies issued an advanced notice of proposed rulemaking or a notice of intention to propose a rule, voluntarily announcing their future rulemaking intentions. In no case did the agencies' compliance with the APA inform legislators who would have otherwise been unaware of an agency's regulatory agenda.

More fundamentally, Congress, once fully aware of the agencies' regulatory initiatives—though made aware by the agencies themselves rather than the strictures of section 553—could do rather little to slow the agencies down in any case. It is true that the notice-and-comment process provided an opportunity for legislators to react to the agencies' proposals. And that happened in the case of the EPA, FDA, and USFS rulemakings, where Midwestern, southeastern, and western legislators respectively voiced strong opposition to the agencies' proposed rules. But their opposition did not derail the proposed rulemakings, nor were legislators opposing the agencies' rules able to use the rulemaking process itself to reign those agencies in. To the contrary, opposing legislators participated in the rulemaking process much like any other party, providing written comments during the notice-and-comment process (just as they would later challenge final agency decisions judicially much like any other party, by joining others' lawsuits and filing briefs).

Not only that, but all of the studied agencies went to considerable lengths to solicit participation in their rulemakings beyond what section 553 requires: The EPA hosted numerous public meetings. The FDA invited questions about its jurisdiction. The Forest Service held meetings in every national forest implicated in its rule. The FTC and SEC hosted public forums. The OCC established its own rulemaking process. And all of these agencies were forthcoming with the data and analyses underlying their regulatory initiatives to an extent well beyond the requirements of the APA. Yet the heightened participation these efforts prompted did not lead to tighter congressional control of the agencies. Indeed, if greater participation in the rulemaking process were a source of greater congressional control, one would wonder why the agencies went out of their ways to solicit even more participation and input than section 553 requires. For example, if establishing rulemaking procedures that mobilize potential opponents against agency action is how Congress controls the EPA, for example, why did the EPA on its own initiative attend conferences, hold regional meetings, and provide satellite telecasts to explore its revised ozone and particulate matter standards? And why did the agency provide advance notice of its initiative, giving all concerned additional time to mobilize against what the agency contemplated?

The claim that openness and accessibility binds agencies to congressional preferences seems completely contradicted by the studied examples. Interest group opposition and congressional disapproval of the EPA's action could not have been much stronger, and yet the EPA undertook to do what according to McNollgast's legislative dominance theory should have decreased, not increased, the agency's regulatory autonomy. By the same token, if notice and comment serves to keep otherwise errant agencies faithful to congressional will, one would wonder why the FDA undertook a separate notice-and-comment process concerning its statutory jurisdiction, or why the OCC established its own notice-and-comment procedure for considering op-sub applications, or why the Forest

Service solicited so many comments on its proposed rule. Again, if Congress uses the notice-and-comment process to ensure that agencies further the interests of important congressional constituencies rather than pursue their own agendas, such agency efforts to solicit broad and deep participation are difficult to understand.

More generally, even when Congress as a whole was largely hostile to agency action, as it was towards the EPA and FDA rules and to some extent the OCC's initiative, again Congress was unable to block the agencies' initiatives. Congress repeatedly threatened to use or used various agency disciplining devices—hearings, reports, budget power, moratoria, or repeals—in response to the agencies' proposals. In several cases, some legislators characterized the head administrators as outcome-driven ideologues and accused them of overstepping the bounds of their statutory authority, an ironic critique of administrators controlled by legislators. In fact, the head administrators were the object of such criticisms in every case involving executive-branch agencies—the EPA, FDA, USFS, and OCC; only in cases involving multiheaded, independent agencies—the FTC and SEC—were those criticisms not made. Interestingly, such criticism transcended party lines, reflecting some legislators' first priority to defend their constituencies—upwind pollution sources, tobacco farmers, timber interests, and insurance companies—from what would be for those constituencies unfavorable regulation.

Yet even strong congressional criticism and disapproval did not discipline the administrators or their agencies very effectively. In each of the studied cases, the agencies undertook their regulatory initiatives largely uninhibited by adverse congressional reaction. Indeed, legislators' inability to block agency action is one of the striking features of the studied examples. Neither party affiliation in the EPA case, nor deference to regional legislative preferences in the FDA and Forest Service cases, nor legislative seniority in the OCC case was sufficient to forestall the agencies' efforts. In no case did Congress control the agencies to the extent contemplated by the legislative dominance claim.

Part of the explanation for Congress's apparent inability to stymie agency action may be that congressional protest and threats are intended to appease important constituencies as much as to control agencies, as suggested in chapter 8. The EPA case seems suggestive here, casting some doubt on the public choice theory's "legislator motivation claim," according to which legislators always seek to trade favorable regulation for interest group support. Consider for example, Representative Dingell's posture expressed in a speech before the National Association of Manufacturers, where he said, referring to the EPA's proposed rules: "Let me be clear. I don't want to have to fight the administration or the president, but if this decision is not handled wisely, I am fully prepared to go to war."[2] As ranking Commerce Committee member, Dingell might have done more to impede the EPA, had he really determined to do so. Yet ultimately he did not act to stop the EPA's rules. Some war. Perhaps Representative Dingell's bark is bigger than his bite.[3] How far one can generalize from that one example is not clear. But surely agency personnel discount the rhetoric of legislators to some extent, knowing that some congressional threats serve members' own political purposes and therefore need not always be taken too seriously. Because measuring legislators' sincerity may be impossible, as long as legislators from tobacco states and legislators from timber states protest the FDA's and the Forest Service's actions loudly, they might appease home constituencies without influencing the course of agency action. At any rate, given the ease with which legislators can voice objections without taking additional steps to discipline agencies—talk is cheap—the strength of the public choice theory's legislator motivation claim must rest on more than legislators' statements protesting proposed agency action.

Regulated interest groups themselves fared no better than Congress in using administrative procedure to secure favorable regulation or to prevent unfavorable regulation, calling into question the public choice theory's "agency favoritism claim" as well. In all of the cases in question, regulated interest groups participated actively in the administrative process leading up to the agencies' final rules. Yet their participation did not enable them either to derail or to co-opt the agencies' initiatives. In fact, none of the studied cases suggests that the notice-and-comment process is useful for narrow interests seeking to block an agency's proposed action.

The heavy interest-group opposition registered during the notice-and-comment periods of the EPA's ozone and particulate matter rules, for example, did not effectively undermine that agency's efforts. Nor did the hundreds of thousands of comments the Forest Service received in response to its proposed rule thwart that agency's initiative, even after the change in administrations when the agency solicited comments to reveal any demerits of its roadless rule. Similarly, the comments from the telemarketing industry concerning the FTC's proposed rule, which the agency recorded and responded to extensively, did not derail the new telemarketing sales rule.

For another example, the three hundred thousand letters from a single mail campaign and the hundreds of form letters that the FDA received in opposition to its proposed tobacco rule did little to influence the FDA. Mass-mailing campaigns during that rulemaking process were awkwardly transplanted from the legislative arena by interests accustomed to legislative politics. But unlike legislators, the FDA was not counting votes or potential votes in favor of and against its tobacco rule. Nor did the letter campaign communicate to the FDA something the agency did not already know. The FDA fully understood the political implications of what it proposed, as evidenced by, among other things, Kessler's prior requests for guidance from both the White House and Congress. And comments that duplicate other comments add nothing but weight to the agency's rulemaking record. Perhaps those organizing the mass-mail campaigns thought they would send an intimidating signal to the FDA about the political pressures Congress would be under to stop the agency, but if so, they had no such effect. The tobacco rulemaking thus illustrates not how an agency can be cowed by important congressional constituencies who mobilize during the rulemaking process, but rather how an agency may attempt to regulate on behalf of general interests even in the face of such opposition.

To be fair, this is not quite to say that the public choice theory finds no support whatever from the procedural dimension of examined cases. A defender of the theory could point to the sheer volume of activity on the part of organized interests opposing the agencies' proposals. Groups committing the most resources in pursuit of their regulatory goals were indeed concentrated interests advancing their own economic interests, lending some support to the theory's "collective action claim." Opposition to the EPA rules by the Air Quality Standards Coalition, the cigarette industry's multi-thousand-page comment during the FDA rulemaking, and Boise Cascade's busing of loggers to public meetings hosted by the Forest Service to comment in opposition to the roadless rule are all illustrative. The bar's opposition to the SEC's attorney conduct rule also illustrates the quick mobilization of economic interests against an agency's attempt to regulate in the public interest. On the other hand, all of the studied cases except the OCC case involved meaningful participation also by parties motivated to advance diffuse interests who favored the agencies' initiatives. Thus very strong versions of the public choice theory's collective action claim, as well as its interest group motivation claim, seem off the mark.

A defender of the public choice account finds additional support from congressional attempts to prevent or discourage the agencies from adopting regulations contrary to the interests of important congressional constituencies. In some of the cases, legislators were genuinely motivated to protect their interest group supporters. The importance of geography as the powerful predictor of how legislators resisted (or in a few instances supported) the EPA, FDA, and USFS may be especially revealing. In those cases, members of Congress were motivated to protect their political turf. In the OCC case, there appeared to be no strong congressional champions of the comptroller, which may be a measure of the insurance industry's influence on Congress, even though Congress itself enacted banking reform legislation once interest-group opponents to such legislation changed their views (which development itself suggests that some legislators opposed statutory reforms not in principle but rather because, and only as long as, their constituencies did). In other words, the public choice theory's legislator motivation claim finds some support from the evidence.

The more important point remains, however, that in every case Congress was unable to influence agencies to deliver the regulatory decisions sought by powerful congressional constituencies, notwithstanding congressional reliance on all of the tools available to Congress to discipline agencies. And none of the studied agencies' regulatory decisionmaking processes either facilitated the delivery of regulatory rents or stymied the efforts of public-interested administrators. Neither Congress nor rent-seeking interests groups successfully employed regulatory decisionmaking procedures to produce regulatory favors to narrow interests. On the whole, the studied cases therefore severely disappoint the public choice theory's procedural expectations.

THE SUBSTANTIVE CRITIQUE

The studied cases also disappoint the public choice theory's substantive expectations. Given that the theory aims expressly to explain the substantive effects of regulation, this result is even more damning than the process critique.

Substantively, each of the examined cases involved regulatory initiatives advancing broad-based interests over concentrated interests—industrial polluters, tobacco companies, timber, advertisers, the corporate bar, and insurers. And in each case, the agencies regulated over the objections of those same powerful interests. In each instance, in other words, the public choice theory's defining conclusion that regulatory outcomes advance the interests of the organized few at the greater expense of the diffuse many is unsubstantiated.

In the EPA and FDA cases, the political fault lines were drawn similarly: public interest groups, health professionals, public health organizations, academic researchers, and some state and local officials supported the EPA's and the FDA's proposals, while industry groups as well as other states and localities opposed them. Those who would bear most of the costs objected the most—the National Association of Manufacturers, the American Petroleum Institute, and other industry groups mobilized against the ozone and particulate matter rules, while tobacco, cigarette manufacturers, and advertisers mobilized against the tobacco rule.

In the EPA case, the regulatory beneficiaries include the public at large, especially citizens in downwind states, and most especially those who work outdoors, elderly persons, children, and asthmatics. Such interests were represented by organized groups like the American Lung Association and celebrity athletes, but as a general matter they were not highly organized. In the FDA case, the main regulatory beneficiaries include children, future potential smokers, and taxpayers, again represented by public-interest medical associations but not organized themselves. Indeed, the EPA and FDA cases are particularly noteworthy in this respect given that the primary regulatory beneficiaries—children and future generations—are not even voters, much less organized voters who could reward legislators or administrators for beneficial regulation.

Much the same is true of the Forest Service's roadless rule. The regulatory beneficiaries there too include future generations for whom natural forests areas are preserved, as well as environmentalists, hunters and fishermen, and citizens generally for whom preserving roadless areas holds environmental or aesthetic benefits. These interests were not highly organized, and most of the public participation in the Forest Service's rulemaking took the form of participation by individual citizens, although environmental groups did mobilize to defend the agency in the roadless rule litigation. On the other side, timber interests, Indian tribes, and part of the motorized recreation industry opposed. In contrast to the diffuse interests supporting the roadless initiative, these interests were organized. Here again, however, those organized interests, even in alliance with legislators from timber states, did not prevail over the many diffuse supporters of the agency's initiative.

The FTC's telemarketing sales rule with its "Do Not Call" register fits this same general pattern: Consumers, backed by privacy advocates and law enforcement organizations, supported the agency's initiative over the opposition of the telemarketing industry. As in the Forest Service case, the benefits to individual supporters of the FTC's proposed rule were rather small—the future benefits of avoiding unwanted telemarketing sales calls and the possibility of avoiding fraud. Although significant on a social scale, these benefits are small for any individual beneficiary of the agency's rule—especially considering the ex ante probability any individual consumer faces of falling victim to telemarketing fraud—and they do not provide the health and safety benefits of the EPA and FDA rules. On the other side, however, telemarketers opposing the rule depend heavily on their ability to communicate with consumers and make sales over the telephone. For them, the regulatory stakes were considerable indeed.

Here again, however, those who had the most individually to lose lost, while those who individually had the least to gain won. The FTC's rule advanced social welfare nevertheless, given that the regulatory winners outnumbered the regulatory losers, and given that fraud by its nature is not an activity towards which society is agnostic in the first place. Although the public choice theory explicitly predicts that the economic interests of the organized few will prevail over the individually smaller interests of the diffuse many, just the opposite happened again in the FTC case.

And in the SEC case too. The beneficiaries of the SEC's attorney conduct rule constitute an even more diffuse group, indeed a group practically unidentifiable—the general investing public and future investors. Not surprisingly, the investing public and future investing public did not participate in the SEC's initiative at all. In fact, no organized group as such supported what the SEC proposed. Instead, a few dozen law professors constituted the only participating supporters of the agency's proposals. In contrast, those who would bear the main costs of the SEC's proposal, the corporate bar, mobilized against the rule, aided by bar organizations and major law firms. Among organizations able to mobilize and influence political and regulatory decisionmaking, the bar ranks among the most effective. Notwithstanding the bar's opposition to the SEC's corporate attorney conduct proposal, however, the agency finalized most of its proposal.

There is one caveat, of course: The SEC did not finalize its "noisy withdrawal" provision of its attorney conduct rule, nor the agency's proposed alternative to that provision requiring issuers rather than lawyers to report a lawyer's withdrawal. Instead, the agency finalized its "up the ladder" requirements and other portions of the proposal, leaving the "noisy withdrawal" provision to wither on the vine. One could argue, then, that the bar mobilized effectively against the agency to prevail over the diffuse interests of investors, thus vindicating the expectations of the public choice theory.

Hard to know. On the one hand, the bar did succeed in stopping a regulatory proposal it opposed and which the agency at least initially thought would satisfy the criterion of Sarbanes-Oxley of advancing "the public interest." On the other hand, that outcome—preventing even more benign regulation—is not the paradigmatic rent-seeking the public choice theory envisions, which is instead securing regulatory rents rather than preventing socially desirable regulation (although as explained in chapter 7, weakening agency proposals is the only kind of influence that some political scientists have been able to identify empirically). More importantly, though, the public choice theory is not vindicated every time an agency modifies its proposal in response to opposition. After all, a major purpose of the notice-and-comment process is to consider analyses and objections from rulemaking participants. Accordingly, some modification of agencies' initial proposed rules is the norm, a norm illustrated by the above cases even though most of the studied agencies's changes were modest.[4]

Moreover, agencies may propose overly stringent rules in part for tactical reasons, because they anticipate objection and so that through subsequent revisions of proposed rules they can appear responsive. In the case of the SEC's attorney conduct rule in particular, the rule the agency ultimately adopted contained the important substance of the SEC's original proposal, including the "up the ladder" requirement. Although the bar prevailed against one aspect of the agency's proposal, it resisted the rest of the rule unsuccessfully. What was left still changed the regulatory landscape and affected corporate attorney conduct dramatically.

Expert opinion surrounding the SEC's original proposal provides one reasonable measure of whether the agency simply capitulated to the special interests it regulates by issuing its attorney conduct rule without the "noisy withdrawal" requirement. Interestingly, the academicians who both called for the SEC to regulate the corporate bar in the first place and provided support for the agency during its rulemaking did not, on the whole, advocate for the type of "noisy withdrawal" requirement that the SEC proposed. In other words, the SEC's original proposal went farther than even most of the agency's supporters, experts on the subject, would have gone. In that light, the SEC's decision effectively to abandon its proposal does not seem quite reducible to the agency weakening in the face of interest-group pressure. To be sure, had the SEC promulgated its rule as originally proposed, that would provide more evidence against the public choice theory, and therefore the fact that the agency changed course provides a little support for the theory. But then it is difficult to prove the negative that the SEC did not merely cave to interest-group pressure, and in any case the agency's weakening of a proposal that, in final form, remained so significant seems like slim vindication of the public choice theory.

That leaves the OCC. Unlike all of the other cases, the OCC's initiative did not quite pit the organized, economic interests of industry or professional groups against the diffuse environmental, health and safety, and consumer-protection interests of the public. Instead, a concentrated and organized special interest—the banking industry—clearly favored the OCC's regulations, while other concentrated and mobilized interests—insurers and securities firms—opposed them. To that extent, the OCC's initiative pitted the special interests of banks against those of their competitors. On the other hand, the OCC's liberalization also was widely considered to benefit consumer interests more generally; economists and public policy experts overwhelmingly believed that preserving old distinctions among banks, insurance companies, and investment companies would be contrary to public interests. By impeding healthy competition, innovation, and growth in the financial services sector, preserving all distinctions among different financial services providers would harm consumers' interests.[5] Thus the OCC case cannot fairly be characterized merely as an instance of an agency delivering regulatory rents to the industry it is supposed to regulate. After all, if the OCC were motivated simply to promote the interests of banks over their competitors, and at the expense of consumers, it could have done that long ago. Certainly the statutory authority on which the OCC relied was hardly new.

Instead, the OCC responded to contemporaneous technological and economic changes that counseled in favor of promoting competition and scale economies by liberalizing national bank activities. For example, banks' competitors had only recently started to market on a large scale products that competed with the savings and demand deposit services traditionally offered by banks, such as cash value life insurance (by insurance companies) and money market mutual funds with unlimited checkwriting privileges (by investment companies). Because the OCC further encouraged a benign competition that market forces had already generated, its efforts are best understood, like the EPA's and FDA's, as promoting public interests over the special-interest opposition of banks' competitors, even though banking interests also benefited. What is more, because the OCC's actions helped to break a legislative logjam that had impeded financial services reform legislation, legislation that benefited not only national banks but also their competitors, again the OCC's initiative is best understood as socially beneficial.

The studied cases illustrate the possibility of socially beneficial regulation because they involved regulatory initiatives the social benefits of which outweighed the social costs. According to conventional understanding, such regulation advances social welfare by definition. Having said that, there are other possible criteria for identifying socially beneficial regulation as well. Another measure considers not—or not only—the benefits and costs of regulation but also the distribution of its benefits and burdens. By this measure, regulation that improves the underlying distribution of resources (by reference to some normative distributive baseline) improves social welfare. From purely a distributive point of view, reallocation of social resources may be desirable even if a regulatory initiative's benefits are outweighed by its cost; the distributive improvement might justify such a loss. Alternatively, a distributive criterion could be added to the cost-benefit criterion such that only regulation that is both distributively desirable and produces net social benefits counts as socially beneficial.

Still other measures of socially desirable regulation are also possible. For example, where benefits and costs are not easily or uncontroversially quantified, expert opinion may provide a substitute test. By this measure, expert consensus about whether specified public policy goals would likely be advanced by a regulatory proposal, even though estimates about the benefits and costs of that proposal are uncertain or highly variable, would distinguish socially desirable from undesirable regulation. Finally, public acceptance might provide yet another measure of socially desirable regulation, especially from a perspective emphasizing democratic and political legitimacy. Here again, this measure could be used as an alternative to cost-benefit assessments such that only regulatory outcomes enjoying broad public acceptance would be desirable no matter how the (other) benefits and costs stack up, or instead as a complimentary measure such that regulatory outcomes that generated more benefits than costs would be desirable so long as they also enjoyed public support or at least did not engender broad opposition.

Among these measures for accessing regulatory outcomes, students of regulation usually favor cost-benefit criteria, for understandable reasons not examined here. The important point, though, is that the studied cases illustrate the possibility of socially beneficial regulation by *all* of these measures: Each case presented expected regulatory benefits exceeding regulatory costs. This is most obviously true of the EPA and FDA cases, for which the benefits and costs were most readily quantified, though the Forest Service and SEC also concluded that the benefits of their initiatives exceeded expected costs. So did the FTC, although, as an independent agency like the SEC, the FTC was not required to prepare for White House approval extended cost-benefit analyses. The OCC case did not lend itself to neat cost-benefit analysis, given the enormous range of activities affected by the comptroller's initiative. But in no case did the agency's regulatory initiative flunk any social cost-benefit test.

The distributive consequences of each case also seem at the very least defensible if not unambiguously desirable. As noted, in every case diffuse interests were benefited by the regulation in question—the general public (EPA, FTC), taxpayers (FDA), future generations (EPA, FDA, USFS), children (EPA, FDA), the infirm (EPA, FTC), the investing public (SEC), financial services consumers (SEC, OCC). To the extent the studied regulatory outcomes benefited narrower interests as well, those beneficiaries—such as the elderly (FTC) or asthmatics (EPA) or outdoor workers (EPA)—would by most accounts be more rather than less deserving of some redistributive regulatory consequences. At the same time, those who bore most of the direct costs of the regulations—industrial polluters, cigarette manufacturers, securities issuers—would by most accounts probably be considered less deserving of regulatory redistribution in their favor.

This is not to say that those who bore most costs are undeserving of regulatory benefits, or that they should always bear the burden of regulatory redistributions. The point is rather that, as least at first glance, regulatory initiatives that impose the costs of air pollution on industrial manufacturers, or the costs of roadless area protection on timber companies, or the costs of SEC compliance on securities issuers or corporate law firms, are not objectionable from a redistributive point of view. Certainly those who emphasize the distributive and redistributive consequences of regulatory outcomes as a criterion of desirable regulation do not have such interests in mind. The more important point is that the public choice theory does emphasize the illicit redistributive consequences of regulation, positing that regulation redistributes from the diffuse many to the undeserving few. The studied cases illustrate just the opposite.

Each case also enjoyed consensus expert support. Supportive scientific and medical expert opinion was extensive in the EPA and FDA cases. Those agencies relied heavily on expert advisory committees, the relevant scientific and medical literatures, and peer review of agency analyses and conclusions. Undivided expert opinion supported the SEC's initiative as well. In the FTC case, law enforcement groups, experts in the area of consumer fraud, unanimously argued that a "Do Not Call" registry was necessary over seller-specific prohibitions to combat fraud. And finally experts sided with the Forest Service and OCC too. In the former case,

Forest Service employees mobilized in support of the rule after a change in presidential administrations cast doubts on whether the agency would preserve the rule. Although not "experts" in the scientific sense, Forest Service personnel had the most experience and information concerning the regulatory issues in question. Finally, in the OCC case, experts widely supported the OCC's liberalizing moves, though they did not play the organized role that they did in the EPA, FDA, or even SEC cases.

Each initiative also enjoyed public acceptance, or at least generated no public opposition. In the FDA, Forest Service, and FTC cases especially, public support for the agencies was broad and deep. That was true in the EPA case as well, if to a slightly lesser extent given the more technical aspects of those rulemakings. Whereas the public very easily connected with cigarette-marketing practices, preserving national forest lands, and preventing unwanted telemarketing calls, the EPA's ozone and particulate matter rules were somewhat less accessible, although again the EPA (like the FDA, USFS, and FTC) generated substantial public support for its proposed rules through its many public meetings, telephone hotline, and website materials. The SEC and OCC initiatives did not generate such public support, in contrast, but neither did they generate public opposition. In those cases, public support and public opinion played no great role one way or another.

By any of several possible criteria for identifying socially beneficial regulation, then—cost-benefit analysis, distributive consequences, expert opinion, and public support—the studied cases demonstrate that regulation can advance public interests, vindicating the administrative process theory's "social welfare claim" while disappointing the public choice theory's defining predictions. Taken together, the examples well illustrate the possibility of good regulatory government.

Nor, finally, do the facts of any of the cases plausibly suggest that the agencies were in fact delivering regulatory rents dressed as public-interest regulation. Such a suggestion—regulatory rents in public-interest clothing—is sometimes advanced as a fallback argument for the public choice theory when confronted with seemingly contradictory evidence. According to it, regulation that appears to advance public interests merely appears to do so. Looking closer, however, one can find instead that some narrow interest or another benefits from what purports to be socially beneficial regulation and that those interests were instrumental in securing favorable regulation cleverly packaged.

None of the studied cases supports such an argument. First, apart from the agencies' defenders and opponents identified above, there were no other parties participating in the regulatory decisionmaking processes. There were, in other words, no offstage parties urging the agencies to regulate, or refrain from regulating, or to regulate in some other way. Those who supported and those who opposed the agency initiatives did so genuinely, and were extremely detailed with respect to the information, analyses, and arguments they provided to the agencies. They did not send the agencies astray by concealing part of their support or opposition or hiding any of the costs or benefits of the agencies' proposals.

And it strains the imagination to try to identify parties who somehow benefited incidentally from the agencies' decisions and whose invisible support therefore explains the outcome of any of the cases. There is no substitute good for cigarettes whose maker urged the FDA to propose its tobacco rule; its addictive nature justified the FDA's proposal. A very broad range of pollution sources are subject to the EPA's ozone and particulate matter rules, which is why the rules were so controversial. The Forest Service's roadless rule regulates a unique public good—the National Forest System. The FTC's "Do Not Call" registry was not the brainchild of on-site retail sellers or web marketers. The SEC's attorney conduct rule, affecting securities issuers generally, did not generate beneficial side-effects for some other industry. Finally, the OCC's initiative affected major industries—banking, insurance, and securities—but in well-understood ways that prompted members of those industries to participate in the OCC's decisionmaking (and all of whom were ultimately burdened and benefited in different ways). In short, there is simply no plausible "story behind the story" of any of the studied cases according to which a regulatory initiative that appeared socially beneficial in fact delivered hidden rents to hidden interests.

The far more concise, plausible, and factually grounded explanation for the studied cases holds instead that administrators, motivated to advance broad-based regulatory interests, used administrative procedure—with various degrees of help from public interest groups, the president, and courts along the way—to exercise their delegated authority in pursuit of regulatory policies that advanced public interests, as the following chapter details.

Chapter Fourteen

The Promise of an
Administrative-Process Orientation

T HE CASE STUDIES OF PART 3 not only cast further doubt upon the strength of the public choice theory of regulation. They also vindicate the administrative process theory. Specifically, the studied cases illustrate how administrative decisionmaking procedures can promote agency auton- omy and authority, and how autonomous agencies can undertake socially desirable regulation. They also show that administrative regulators are sometimes motivated to advance public interests, and how they might do so even over the objections of interest groups and legislators, especially when they secure the political or legal support of another institution of government.

THE CENTRALITY OF ADMINISTRATIVE PROCEDURE

First, the administrative process theory's "agency autonomy claim" seems well supported by the cases in question. As already seen, the studied agen- cies were procedurally generous: Each solicited outside participation, pro- vided information, and invited focused commentary on its proposed ini- tiatives as required, but to an extent far beyond that required, by administrative law. As the FDA correctly observed concerning its notice obligations under the APA for its proposed tobacco rule, for one example among many, "no court . . . had required the degree of public disclosure at the notice stage of a rulemaking proceeding that FDA undertook here.[1] The FDA, and all of the studied agencies, provided more notice, data, and opportunities for participation in its decisionmaking that the APA (or any other legal authority) demanded. The question becomes, then, whether and how agency procedures helped them achieve their regulatory objec- tives: Why did the agencies go to such lengths?

For several reasons. Most generally, robust administrative procedure enabled the agencies both to gather and to provide information about their regulatory proposals. First, the agencies solicited information about their initiatives from outside parties who knew something the agencies did not. This allowed the agencies to attract support for their proposals from parties sympathetic to the agencies' initiatives. Such parties could provide additional data supporting what the agencies had proposed, or new arguments justifying what the agencies had proposed. Such parties could also simply register their philosophical or political support for the agencies, which also bolstered the agencies' positions, especially when outside support was well informed.

At the same time, robust administrative process also allowed the agencies to measure the extent and nature of opposition to their proposals—to test their proposals, scientifically, economically, and politically. Relatedly, generous administrative procedure gave the agencies opportunities to alter their proposals in light of the information they received from both supporters and detractors. Put differently, robust procedure—in particular successive rounds of notice-and-comment accompanying various forms of public outreach—gave the agencies many opportunities to refine their proposals in response to support or opposition or both. Not that agencies merely responded opportunistically to feedback generated during the administrative process, although the agencies did prove themselves politically astute. Rather, the studied agencies employed the dynamic processes of administrative decisionmaking to establish, reestablish, modify, justify, and above all secure their proposals. Ultimately, the agencies' final decisions following robust decisionmaking processes were then far less vulnerable to attack, whether by disgruntled interest groups, legislators, or litigants.

The details of the studied cases substantiate this conclusion. But to begin with, recall again that those seeking socially beneficial regulation used procedural devices to help put several of the studied regulatory initiatives on agencies' agenda in the very first place. The American Lung Association's APA lawsuit against the EPA, creating an injunction requiring the agency to initiate its ozone and particulate matter rulemakings; the Coalition on Smoking or Health's petition for an FDA rulemaking under APA section 553; and attendees at the FTC's public fora on the efficacy of existing telemarketing rules all helped to prompt those agencies' efforts initially, providing support for the administrative process theory's "administrative neutrality claim" as well. That is, these agencies' proposals came not out of nowhere—much less were they prompted by special interests seeking regulatory rents—but rather showed agency responsiveness to public interest advocates acting through administrative process rules to affect the agencies' agenda.[2]

The impetus for regulation can and often does come from within an agency as well, however, and the studied cases also show how agencies themselves use administrative structures to develop well-grounded regulatory proposals initially. The EPA's reliance on its Health Effects Institute and the workshops convened by its National Center for Environmental Assessment before it issued its advance notice of proposed rulemaking, as well as the great weight the EPA placed on the findings of its Clean Air Scientific Advisory Committee, exemplify how an agency can solicit authoritative scientific and medical evidence concerning the benefits of a proposed initiative before it is fully introduced. So do the FDA's reliance on the advice of its Drug Abuse Advisory Committee, following that committee's public hearings on the addictiveness of cigarettes, and the Forest Service's reliance on a scientific advisory committee convened to provide the agency with advice on national forest management. By relying on advisory committees chartered under the Federal Advisory Committee Act, with its attendant good-government procedural requirements, these agencies enlisted independent yet publically scrutinized expertise from the relevant scientific communities and thereby preempted easy critiques of their initiatives on the grounds they were not well considered or scientifically grounded.

The EPA case is an especially powerful example of how an agency's advisory committee can leverage its regulatory authority. The EPA used its CASAC first to prepare a study of scientific and medical research relevant to its existing ozone and particulate matter standards, and also to review and evaluate the agency's own staff studies and literature reviews. Accordingly, the CASAC held public hearings, subject to the FACA, to consider drafts of its findings. Subsequently, in her defense of the EPA's proposed rules before Congress, Administrator Browner relied heavily on the CASAC's ultimate findings. And when congressional opponents enlisted former CASAC members to testify against the agency's proposed rules, Browner pointed out that the EPA relied on reports and recommendations of its advisory committee as a whole, not the views of any particular committee member, whose individual views should not count for very much.[3] Upon later promulgating its final rules, the EPA referred to its advisory committee's views and recommendations innumerable times, as it had in its commentary accompanying its proposed rules, to explain and justify its final decisions. In short, the EPA's advisory committee—upon which it relied more than any other source—enhanced its credibility and authority, especially against its congressional and interest-group critics.

The EPA's creation and public release of its criteria documents and staff papers did the same. The agency's reliance on exhaustive internal technical reviews enhanced its credibility and thus authority by making difficult the objection that the EPA's proposals were based on scientific misunderstanding. For example, Browner could credibly claim in defense of her agency's proposals that they reflected "peer review of peer review of peer review,"[4] and that the EPA had made great efforts to "go where the science takes us."[5] While explaining the findings of and reactions to the criteria documents and staff papers made for lengthy and complex proposed and final rules—being exhaustive and transparent in the context of NAAQS rulemakings is cumbersome—the agency's efforts insulated the EPA from credible claims that its rules were ill-considered. To be sure, some of the rules' opponents made such claims, but those objections were much less powerful given the extent to which the agency had done, and publicized, and invited criticisms of, its homework. The criteria documents and staff papers provided the EPA with ready answers to such objections.

Similarly, the FDA's compilation and public release of two hundred thousand pages of its factual materials relating to smoking, the incidence of smoking among subpopulations, smoking's health effects, and the marketing of tobacco products provided substantial grounding for its proposal. By providing exhaustive background materials forming the basis of its proposed rule, the FDA too preempted criticisms of its proposed rule as ill-considered or scientifically unjustified. Here again, the rules' opponents made those and many other arguments against the proposed rule. But because the agency had been exhaustively forthcoming about its own research and the findings of the scientific and medical communities, such criticisms did not stick. The FDA too had undermined its critics' credibility.

The SEC's attorney conduct rule did not present such technical or scientific issues, but here too the agency used administrative procedure to enlist expert opinion that grounded the SEC's proposal. Here again, the agency's proposal was not developed by the agency alone, but rather reflected policy proposals that academic commentators had already made. Thus, even though the SEC was under a tight statutory deadline to regulate, its initial proposal already reflected careful consideration of the issues at stake, and the SEC could and did appeal to the independence and neutrality of outside experts.

The SEC's reliance on academic experts not only grounded the agency's initial proposals, but also allowed it to draw from a base of informed support for its rule. Given that the SEC enjoyed consensus expert support about the merits of its attorney-conduct proposal, the agency's proposal was more tenable. Opponents had to show not only that the SEC was wrong, but also that the experts who had recommended and supported the agency's proposals were wrong as well. Put differently, those objecting to the SEC's proposal could not isolate the agency, because the agency did not stand alone, but rather had to engage its proposal on the merits and demonstrate why the collective expertise of the SEC's academic supporters was misguided.

The studied agencies used administrative decisionmaking tools also to generate affirmative support for their proposals, not only to defend them. The Forest Service's public meetings provide a dramatic example. By holding hundreds of meetings on its roadless initiative attended by thousands of citizens—local as well as national meetings, meetings in every state and every national forest, including some two hundred meetings before even proposing its roadless rule—the Forest Service greatly expanded the constituency supporting its proposals. In the agency's own words, the meetings were designed "to give every interested person an opportunity to comment" on its roadless initiative. And the effort seemed to succeed. While public sentiment favored and to some extent motivated the Forest Service in the first place, the agency's actions drew great attention to its regulatory agenda and as a result drew many more supporters, ordinary citizens and also legislators, for what the agency had proposed. Thus the Forest Service's "aggressive public outreach campaign," which included not only the open meetings but also its establishment of a roadless-rule website and agency assistance to parties seeking to participate in notice-and-comment, paid off. As a result, by the time a new administration sought to reverse that agency's course, it was largely too late. By then, the roadless initiative had too many supporters, evidenced by the hundreds of thousands of additional supportive comments the agency received after effectively reopening its rulemaking process to reconsider the roadless rule.

Likewise, the EPA's many public meetings, conferences, hotline, and telecasts about its ozone and particulate matter rules generated support for its initiative. While ordinary citizens did not play as great a role in the EPA rulemakings as they did in the Forest Service rulemakings, still the EPA's extensive road show enlisted agency supporters, including many citizens as well as health advocates and public health officials. No less, the EPA's public outreach attracted the attention of downwind beneficiaries of its proposed rules, providing them with the agency's own analyses of the benefits of its proposals which they could in turn use to advocate in favor of the EPA's initiative. The EPA's efforts thus illustrate one important effect of soliciting reaction to agency proposals: The agency not only airs its own proposal, but informs others who can in turn provide informed support of what the agency has proposed. The EPA's defenders were more credible and effective given the education they received from the agency itself.

The FTC's *Federal Register* notices announcing that it would hold public fora and soliciting requests for comments on the efficacy of the old Telemarketing Sales Rule also generated support for its initiative. That is, the FTC invited criticisms of the old telemarketing rule's limited "Do Not Call" provisions and thereby attracted consumer advocates, privacy advocates, and law enforcement groups as strong supporters for a new, more stringent rule. In turn, the FTC relied on that support, expressed in the recorded and transcribed public fora, both to resolve questions about its proposed rule and to justify its final rule. Here again, the agency created a dynamic process through which it informed outside parties about its proposal, drew objections but also enlisted support, and then benefited from many outside parties' solicited reactions to its initiative. Rather than announce a proposal and defend it against all comers, the FTC strengthened its position by inviting feedback to what it proposed and then relying on the support its proposal generated. In this case, the combined support of both privacy groups and law enforcement groups gave the FTC's initiative especially secure factual, political, and therefore legal footing.

The agencies' solicitation of written comments in particular during their rulemaking processes similarly solicited support of (as well as objections to) their regulatory agenda. The EPA's unprecedented efforts to solicit comments through the Internet and otherwise, and the FDA's and Forest Service's record-breaking volumes of written commentary, generated considerable support for those agencies. Indeed, the Forest Service solicited comments on its road construction moratorium and on a roadless rule—that is, the idea of a roadless rule—upon publishing its "notice of intent" to propose a rule but before proposing the rule itself. As a result, its proposed roadless rule had supporters by the time its text was first presented. The FTC did a version of the same, soliciting comments on a probable revision to the Telemarketing Sales Rule before proposing a specific new rule. Here again, the agency's notice-and-comment period produced tens of thousands of comments in response to the FTC's proposal, the overwhelming majority of which favored what the agency proposed. In each of these cases, then, written comments supplied to the agency during the rulemaking process provided various forms of support—factual, expert, political—for what the agency had proposed.

As argued in chapter 8, the absolute volume of commentary, especially duplicative commentary, received in response to an agency's proposed rule provides a misleading measure of how much influence commenting parties will have on the agency's proposal. At the same time, however, more voluminous commentary can provide the agency with more varied facts and arguments supporting its proposals, especially where one of the criteria informing the agency's consideration of its proposal is the degree of public support the proposal enjoys. For example, setting aside the five hundred form-letter comments and three-hundred-thousand-piece mail campaign the FDA received, the ninety-five thousand separate comments the agency received from individuals in response to its proposed tobacco rule, like the favorable commentary it received from the National Parent-Teachers Association, provided genuine support for its politically precarious proposal. For another example, the Forest Service explained in its proposed revision of the Clinton roadless rule that the agency carefully considered all of the comments it received, though it noted that each comment received was "considered for its substance and contribution to informed decisionmaking, whether it is one comment repeated by tens of thousands of people or a comment submitted by only one person."[6]

Finally, and no less importantly, the studied agencies' decisionmaking processes enabled them to identify all objections to their initiatives. Here once again, the EPA's use of its criteria documents and staff papers is illustrative. By making its scientific reviews and findings public, the EPA exposed and therefore tested the technical strength of its proposals, based on its review of hundreds of studies. Releasing the agency's scientific conclusions invited parties to identify any other studies or draw any alternative conclusions about the state of the science concerning the health effects of different levels of ozone and particulate matter. In fact, the EPA went farther by inviting comment on specific alternatives to its original ozone and particulate matter proposals. Wherever parties disagreed with the agency or supported alternative proposals instead, the EPA responded. In the end, opponents of the proposed rules did not always agree with the EPA's analysis, but by then the agency had had every opportunity to evaluate their objections and respond to them on the merits. In defending its proposed rules—within the White House (before the White House came to support them), against members of Congress, and against the objections of interest groups—the EPA defended against no surprises.

Similarly, the FDA actively solicited all possible objections to its proposed tobacco rule. First, like the EPA, the FDA provided exhaustive references to the medical and social-scientific bases of its proposal. In response, the industry's forty-seven-thousand-page objection identified for the agency all conceivable objections to what the FDA had proposed. Likewise, its separate "Annex" rulemaking procedure soliciting comments and objections specifically to its regulatory jurisdiction also exposed all legal objections outside parties had to the agency's proposal. The FDA was then as well positioned as possible to respond to any objections to its rule. By inviting all criticisms of what it had proposed, and by disclosing all scientific bases for what it proposed in order to ensure that its critics were well informed, the FDA too eliminated the possibility of unanticipated objections to its tobacco rule.

The Forest Service's disclosure of its draft environmental impact statement also solicited objections to its proposal. Those opposed to the agency's initiative could be very specific about what misguided findings and projections the Forest Service made. That specificity, like unfavorable comments the agency received during the notice-and-comment process, informed the agency of the grounds for opposition to its rule. As a result, the Forest Service was better able to justify and defend its rule against legal challenges.

The SEC also used the comment process to solicit criticisms of its "noisy withdrawal" proposal, including criticisms of arguments made in support of that proposal. For the SEC requested comments not only upon presenting its proposal originally, but again upon finalizing most other aspects of its attorney-conduct rule. At that time, the agency asked for a new round of comments on the "noisy withdrawal" provision and, by publishing many of the comments it had already received, solicited as well comments on previous comments. Like the EPA's request for comments on specific alternative ozone and particulate matter rules, the SEC also requested comparative comments on its own alternative to the "noisy withdrawal" rule, allowing issuers rather than attorneys to disclose to the commission that an attorney had withdrawn. Thus, the SEC was able both to measure further the level of opposition to its original "noisy withdrawal" provision, and to solicit information about the merits of its alternative.

For a final example, the OCC's rulemaking-like process for operating subsidiary applications to engage in nonbanking activities also operated to expose the grounds for objection that a national bank's competitor might have. That is, rather than grant an application and then face the prospect of defending its decision in a lawsuit, the OCC instead established a process for soliciting objections at the time the application was made. This enabled the agency to determine whether the objections were well founded, in which case it could deny the application, or instead motivated by anticompetitive interests, in which case it would grant the application. Opposing parties could and did still bring litigation challenging the OCC's decision to grant an application, but their legal objections had already been considered by the agency, whose successful record before the courts may be unmatched among federal agencies.

Thus in various ways did administrative processes empower the studied agencies to carry out their regulatory agenda. By gathering additional information, drawing from available expertise, soliciting support and educating supporters, inviting objections and evaluating their merits, and as a result of all of these by strengthening the final rules born of their proposals, the studied agencies maximized their ability to defend their initiatives—publicly, politically, technically, and legally—notwithstanding the considerable strength of organized interests opposed to them.

Still, the question may linger, what is it about *administrative procedure* exactly that empowers regulatory agencies? The question forgets what administrative procedure entails. Fundamentally, it entails (1) notice of proposed agency action; (2) disclosure of the bases of proposed agency action; (3) opportunities for public input about proposed agency action; (4) rational agency decisionmaking; and (5) transparent explanation of the reasons for agency action. The studied agencies engaged in the administrative process in just these ways. They did so, specifically, by (1) publishing many layers of notice of their regulatory agenda, including advance notices of proposed rulemakings, notices of intent, notices of timetable for future rulemaking, and proposed rules; (2) widely publicizing advisory committee reports, literature reviews, expert advice, and draft cost-benefit and environmental impact analyses underlying their proposed action; (3) aggressively soliciting public reaction to their regulatory proposals by convening and attending public meetings, inviting public comments, and facilitating and recording commentary; (4) conducting cost-benefit analyses, relying on external as well as internal expert advice and committee analysis, recording and responding to objections to agency proposals, and modifying agency proposals in light of meritorious objections; and finally (5) publically explaining the bases of agency conclusions at exhaustive length throughout the decisionmaking process. Having so thoroughly engaged in these processes of administrative decisionmaking, the agencies were then best positioned to defend their regulatory decisions, against powerful interest groups and legislative critics alike. This result vindicates the administrative process theory's agency autonomy claim.

There is a flip side as well, however: Agencies that provide robust administrative process—agencies that go to exceptional lengths to disclose the bases for their action, solicit feedback, and invite all objections to their proposals—most risk being forced to abandon their regulatory initiatives when sound analysis of them so counsels. In other words, robust decisionmaking procedures commit agencies to go wherever the best analyses of their proposals may lead. Where their proposals are not well grounded or well supported, their weaknesses will most easily be exposed, and the agencies will be most vulnerable politically and legally, as the very result of their robust decisionmaking procedures. Of course, agencies understand this, and thus have incentives to ensure that their regulatory decisions are carefully considered, fully aired, and well justified, which explains why agencies often provide more administrative process than minimally necessary. But this result affirms the general conclusion that the administrative process helps to promote sound regulation: The administrative process constrains agencies with poor regulatory proposals, as well as empowers agencies seeking to do what is socially beneficial.

PUBLIC-INTERESTED ADMINISTRATORS

Yet agencies are too easily anthropomorphized, here and elsewhere. In fact, what has been famously said of Congress—that Congress is a "they" not an "it"[7]—applies with equal force to administrative agencies: Agency actions are the combined behavior of many individual administrators. All the same, among those many individual administrators, lead administrators have the greatest influence on agencies' agenda.

In each of the studied cases, lead agency personnel were motivated to advance public interests, vindicating the administrative process theory's "administrator motivation claim" as well. That is, in each case the agencies' efforts were led by strong-willed and independent administrators who championed what they considered to be desirable regulatory policy. These administrators were often the object of intense congressional and interest group criticism. Yet they persisted.

EPA administrator Carol Browner is one compelling case in point. During the proposal stages of the ozone and particulate matter rules, commentators routinely attributed her adamant defense of the EPA's rules against industry criticism to her belief that good science and policy justified the EPA's proposals.[8] And for good reason. Given her response to criticism, she was certainly not influenced by her critics, much less motivated to please or placate them. In the face of protests like the Washington Legal Foundation's petition for her recusal from the EPA's rulemaking, Browner was unflappable, evidencing her commitment to her conception of the public interest.

Browner's resolve also meant she could not be pushed around by Congress either, even when "berated" or "browbeaten" by her legislative critics from industrial states and even given the scarcity of legislative supporters for the EPA's rules. While several legislators questioned Browner's authority to implement its proposed rules, and while several more accused her of withholding factual information concerning the rules' costs and benefits from Congress and of taking a results-oriented rather than a scientific approach to the ozone and particulate matter rules, Browner more than held her own against legislative critics. In fact, rather than allow Congress to bully the EPA into diluting its proposed rules, Browner argued at the oversight hearings that agency critics did not fully understand the science or else presented it incompletely. Given her command of the technical issues, Browner was a formidable witness before Congress, who at times inverted the usual relationship between legislators and agency regulators. As one legislative critic of the EPA's rules observed in (unintentionally humorous) frustration, for example: "Agencies used to live in fear of what Representatives Dingell and Waxman would say. Now, it's as if committees live in fear of what Carol Browner will say if we issue a resolution of disapproval."[9]

Browner showed public-interested independence from the White House as well. That is, although her relationship with the White House was obviously stronger than with Congress because she answered directly to the president, Browner's willingness to explain and defend the ozone and particulate matter rules before they had the unequivocal support of the White House demonstrated another dimension of commitment to her agency's initiative. That is, Browner's resistance to interest-group and legislative opposition could not have been motivated by expectations of political benefits, for her or her agency, coming from the White House. During the long pendency of the proposed ozone and particulate matter rules, before they enjoyed full White House backing, Browner's job was largely thankless. That she persisted in such a climate—earning no measurable personal or political credit—is further evidence of her public-interest motivations.

The sustained controversy and political opposition Browner endured was matched only by that FDA commissioner David Kessler faced. While Browner heard pointed and personal criticism of her leadership, criticisms of Kessler's leadership of the FDA were more pointed and personal. As observed above, Kessler was to his legislative critics a "zealot." Like Browner, Kessler had few legislative friends (although unlike Browner he enjoyed the support of the White House from the very beginning of his agency's initiative). And Congress responded to the FDA's proposal just like it responded to the EPA's—with threats of reductions in the agency's budget, bills to curtail its jurisdiction, and moratoria on implementation of its proposed rule. Not only did Kessler, like Browner, have legislative critics from both political parties, but those critics included the legislative leadership from both parties. As also observed above, Kessler had the distinction of making the platform of the Republican nominee for president, who promised if elected to fire Kessler.

To say Kessler too was unbowed by his legislative critics, or by the tobacco and advertising interests that so strongly opposed the FDA's rule, however, would grossly understate it. Like his critics, Kessler viewed himself and his FDA colleagues as mavericks. As he stated following the FDA's victory against tobacco and advertisers in federal district court: "A small group of very committed people at the agency took on the impossible. The President of the United States supported them, and a federal district judge in North Carolina in very large measure agreed."[10] He was neither motivated nor influenced by interest-group politics, part of no "iron triangle" or "issue network." The devices Congress employed to discipline him did not work. All to the contrary, he antagonized regulated interests, relying on the public-interest justifications for the FDA's initiative provided by the considerable weight of the medical and social-scientific literatures that formed the bases of the FDA's rule, as well as the largely unorganized public support for the rule.

As a result, FDA watchers argued that Kessler's battle to regulate tobacco would put him "into the history books,"[11] for the FDA's initiative under his direction was not only motivated to advance public interests, but politically daring, at least from the beginning, as even the White House recognized. Kessler's willingness to regulate tobacco notwithstanding the political strength of opposing interests constitutes further evidence of his public-interest motivations. His initiative advanced the interests of smokers and children, and yielded him no personal benefits apart from whatever satisfaction comes from undertaking politically difficult but socially beneficial regulatory initiatives. Although ultimately the FDA lost at the Supreme Court, still Kessler's efforts altered considerably public opinion and the larger the political landscape surrounding questions about how tobacco is marketed and distributed, paving the way for, among other things, several billion-dollar settlement agreements between cigarette manufacturers and the states. Interestingly but not surprisingly, when Kessler later announced his resignation from the FDA, tobacco stock prices soared.[12]

Forest Service chief Michael Dombeck also regulated against the strong current of critics. Although the stakes surrounding the Forest Service's roadless initiative were not nearly so high as those surrounding the EPA's and FDA's efforts, the rhetoric was at times comparable. Dombeck's congressional critics called him "arrogant" and "delusional."[13] Also like Browner and Kessler, regulated interests accused Dombeck too of regulating in bad faith. Groups representing timber and the Kootenai Tribe, along with western legislators from some timber states, sought to discredit him by arguing the roadless rule was hurried in the final months of the Clinton administration, a criticism echoed by the federal courts in Idaho and Wyoming, who suggested that the chief's final rule "was a political decision pre-determined in its outcome"[14] and a "predetermined directive by Chief Dombeck [that had] eliminated competing alternatives out of consideration and existence."[15]

That specific criticism, made of Browner and Kessler too, is difficult to understand from a public-choice perspective, but easy to understand if administrators are motivated to advance public interests, as the administrative process theory postulates. That is, critics accused Dombeck of giving insufficient attention to the arguments that regulated interests made against the Forest Service's roadless rule. On this view, Dombeck was not unduly solicitous of timber and recreational interests; he was rather not solicitous enough. His "political decision" was not a product of interest-group politics or legislative pressure, but rather a matter of conviction that protecting roadless areas of the national forests was important enough to be done before the end of the administration.

However one views the merits of Dombeck's effort to finish the roadless rule—and the Forest Service certainly did make a point to finish the final rule before the next administration took power, though in fairness the larger roadless initiative and the other rules encompassed by it had been under development for several years—his efforts manifested the very opposite of interest-group favoritism. He was motivated, instead, by what he perceived to be the substantial public-interest merits of the roadless rule. The critique of Dombeck—and Browner and Kessler—according to which he was too motivated by his own beliefs and therefore failed to consider the full costs regulated parties would bear as a consequence of his agency's initiative thus supports the administrator motivation claim. It is a critique incompatible with the public choice account. By a similar token, the praise that Dombeck (and Browner and Kessler) received from conservation interests (and environmentalists and public health advocates in Browner's and Kessler's cases) for his willingness to resist pressures from regulated interests also supports the administrator motivation claim.

Comptroller Eugene Ludwig fits the same mold. Characterized as "one of the most aggressive comptrollers in modern times,"[16] Ludwig did what Congress had been unable or unwilling to do, by expanding national banks' ability to compete with other financial service providers. Like Browner, Kessler, and Dombeck, Ludwig regulated unintimidated by the harsh criticism of those whose immediate economic interests were harmed, including securities issuers, insurance companies, and their legislative supporters. Also like the others, Ludwig too was accused of overstepping his regulatory authority, not only in lawsuits contesting the legality of OCC decisions but by legislators—who variously accused Ludwig of being a "rogue" regulator[17] and leading an "unseemly" and "misleading" campaign by banks against Congress[18]—who threatened to reign his agency in if it did not stop liberalizing national bank activities. Like the other administrators, Ludwig was subjected to the threat of congressional sanctions such as reduced agency funding and congressional moratoria on OCC decisions.

Congressional and interest-group opposition had the same effect on Ludwig it had on his counterparts at the EPA, FDA, and Forest Service, however: He continued to pursue his agency's liberalization of national banks without hesitation or apology. For example, when op-sub reform was stalled in Congress, Ludwig justified his agency's actions as required by the public interest: "We cannot wait, because a failure to move ahead prudently in the current dynamic environment is likely to create safety and soundness problems for the banking industry. . . . [A] regulator who identifies a safety and soundness issue—whether an issue of immediate concern or one off on the horizon with long-term implications—and does nothing is not doing his job or serving the public interest."[19] Ludwig argued that his agency's actions were justified because they advanced the public interest when no other part of government had undertaken them. As in the EPA, FDA, and Forest Service cases—only more so—in the OCC case the comptroller was able to fill gaps created by the legislature.

The FTC and SEC cases further support the claim that administrators are sometimes motivated to advance general interests, although as independent agencies headed by multimember bodies that essentially conduct their regulatory work by committee, they do so less dramatically: Neither quite involved a personalized battle between a lead administrator and powerful regulated interests. Even so, the FTC and SEC's actions at the commission level can show greater or lesser effort to advance social welfare, and similarly less or more solicitude of regulated groups pursuing their own narrow interests. Similarly, the presence of absence of division within a commission concerning a given regulatory decision provides a measure of the strength of its regulatory commitment. Not least of all, so can the position of their chairs.

In the case of the FTC's telemarketing rule, neither the commission as a whole nor individual commissioners exhibited any evidence of regulatory favoritism towards telemarketers or other firms whose goods were sold over the telephone. At the time the FTC adopted its final rule in January 2003, a majority of its commissioners were Republicans, including its chair, Timothy Muris. Muris had previously worked for the FTC and OMB during the Reagan administration, and was therefore expected to advocate limited regulation of commercial activities. Yet the FTC's adoption of the final telemarketing rule was unanimous and uncontroversial among its five commissioners. For Muris in particular, who defied expectations by developing a reputation for aggressively protecting consumers' interests, the creation of the "Do Not Call" registry over the opposition of the telemarketing industry and corporations that sell their goods and services through telemarketers constituted his most well known achievement, and one he was credited for spearheading and defending.[20]

It was also a majority-Republican SEC that unanimously adopted the final attorney-conduct rule. As in the case of the FTC, the chair of the SEC at that time, William Donaldson, was a Republican appointee and one of three Republicans among the five SEC commissioners. Former head of the New York Stock Exchange, Donaldson brought to the SEC extensive experience in business and investment banking. Given that background and his appointment by President George Bush, Donaldson, like Muris, was expected by many to be a regulatory caretaker for business and corporate interests.[21] Yet Donaldson's tenure also contradicted expectations. Far more often than not during his chairmanship at the SEC, Donaldson sided with investor and consumer interests and against corporate interests, joining the two Democrats to make a majority of three on the commission. He quickly developed the reputation as tough on issues of corporate governance, and under his leadership (and in the wake of Sarbanes-Oxley) the SEC issued more significant regulations, governing nearly all aspects of securities and mutual funds, than it had in decades.

Donaldson thus exemplifies the potentially transformative effect of assuming such an important regulatory position. He sought to advance what he considered to be a socially beneficial regulatory agenda, notwithstanding that doing so often conflicted with the interests most closely linked to his own background and experience. As one commentator put it, capturing the widespread view of Donaldson: "In Republican and business circles, William H. Donaldson has been viewed as the David Souter of the Securities and Exchange Commission, a disappointingly independent choice."[22] The SEC's attorney-conduct rule was but one of that agency's initiatives demonstrating Chairman Donaldson's independence.

Thus each of the studied cases supports the administrator motivation claim. And none undermines it. To be sure, there are two small shreds of evidence from the studied cases supporting the public choice theory's premise that regulated interests may be able to enlist *former* administrators to support their regulatory goals. First, the tobacco industry enlisted former FDA personnel to aid it in opposing the FDA's tobacco rule, lending some support to the revolving-door phenomenon and any mileage the public choice theory gets from that phenomenon.[23] Second, as already noted, two former members of the EPA's CASAC testified before Congress on behalf of industry groups against the proposed ozone and particulate matter rules, which suggests again that some interest groups can benefit from the experience of those closest to agency decisions, although former advisory committee members are not former administrators. But these shreds exhaust the evidence in the studied cases suggesting that (former) agency insiders might help advance the goals of powerful interest groups. In the overall scheme of the EPA's and FDA's initiatives, these are small footnotes that do not alter the conclusion that agency personnel present and past did not advocate on behalf of regulated parties.

Certainly none of the lead administrators, much less any of their subordinates, acted in any way that could be reasonably interpreted as favoring special interests. Neither Browner, Kessler, Dombeck, Ludwig, nor the commissioners of the FTC and SEC sought to deliver regulatory rents to regulated interests. Much to the contrary, even when Congress objected to their actions—because they threatened important legislative constituencies—these administrators marched forward. Similarly, in the one case where the White House objected to an agency's initiative already under way, Forest Service personnel again largely persisted. The claim that agency regulators are motivated to advance public interests thus finds considerable support in the studied cases.

Of course, this conclusion applies in particular to the head administrators of the studied agencies, not to line-level civil servants whose behavior is outside of the scope of the case studies (except in the case of the Forest Service). But this qualifies the result only slightly. For chief administrators are those best positioned—and by conventional wisdom most motivated—to deliver regulatory rents. Ordinary civil servants, in contrast, enjoy civil service protections, and thus cannot easily be sanctioned by politicians. Ordinary civil servants must follow, and are therefore used to following, the alternating priorities of the two political parties. And they do so while generally maintaining their own codes of professionalism and belief in their agencies' mission. In other words, civil servants are the most difficult agency personnel for rent seekers to co-opt. Indeed, political appointees' limited ability to control the behavior of the civil servants who serve beneath them is a cliché.

The real action is at the top. Political appointees have the closest links to legislators and the White House. Political appointees also have greatest authority over their agencies' missions. Given the nature of their positions, appointees also focus more than civil servants on their agencies' budgets, on shorter-term assessments of their agencies' performance, and finally on their own career futures once their administrative tenure ends. In short, lead administrators are most sensitive to the heat of political pressure, and have the greatest incentives to respond to it. Thus, the conclusion that the lead administrators in the studied cases not only resisted such pressures but sought instead to advance public interests in politically difficult circumstances says a lot about the nature of administrative behavior.

Institutional Environmental

Administrative procedure and independent-minded administrators were not all that promoted agency autonomy in the studied cases. In fact, it was not always clear that the agencies' regulatory efforts would be successful, and their ultimate success often depended on at least tacit support from the White House or the courts. Fortunately, executive oversight (for the executive-branch agencies) and judicial review in most cases further fostered agency autonomy from interest-group and legislative opponents of the agencies' initiatives.

For example, while White House support for the EPA's rules was slow to come, the White House's ultimate support for the EPA made it possible for the agency to issue final rules that closely resembled their proposed versions. And although the White House was reportedly divided internally over the proposed rules—a division that congressional opponents of the rules emphasized—the administrator of the White House's Office of Information and Regulatory Affairs testified before Congress to defend the EPA, explaining that White House scrutiny of, and questions about, agency rules is common and should not be used as evidence that the EPA's rules were misguided.[24] White House oversight of the EPA rules worked as it should, with the White House ultimately supporting an otherwise politically vulnerable agency. Had it chosen to do so, the White House could have instead stopped the EPA, or required the agency to modify its proposed rules substantially. It did not, but rather rescued the agency, politically, from a hostile Congress.

The EPA case also illustrates how presidents and vice presidents can sometimes better afford to support agency attempts to promote general interests than Congress can. According to many commentators, Clinton, and especially then-presidential candidate Gore, had much more to gain politically by courting Midwestern states and cities, which opposed the EPA's rules, than by further demonstrating their environmentalist credentials.[25] As one observer aptly put it shortly before the White House made clear—with decisive vice-presidential involvement[26]—that it was supporting the EPA: "Gore doesn't need to get any greener."[27] Nevertheless, the White House supported the EPA. Whereas the geographical politics of the ozone and particulate matter rules made them simply unsupportable by many legislative Democrats, a Democratic White House could afford to support them, even though a purely political calculus would have argued against such support.

The FDA case also illustrates that the White House can foster agency independence from Congress in ways that allow an agency better to pursue general interests, again especially where the White House itself is willing to take political risks. Although Clinton wanted electoral support from tobacco states in the 1996 elections, and although Democratic governors and senators from those states strongly urged him not to support the FDA's tobacco initiative, the White House nevertheless encouraged Kessler's efforts from the beginning. While the administration perceived that limiting access to tobacco by children could eventually become popular with the voters, the White House's initial support of the FDA over strong regional and intraparty opposition constituted, as commentators described, "a high stakes confrontation with the tobacco industry,"[28] and a political "mine-field."[29]

Reflecting back to the time his administration initiated the tobacco rulemaking, President Clinton stated:

> The first time [the vice president and I] began to discuss this was about the time the FDA opened their inquiry. And he looked at me and I looked at him and I said, well, you know what this might lead to? And he said, I certainly hope so. (Laughter.) And I said, well, you know—I shouldn't say this, this is our private conversation—I said, you know, it really isn't an accident that nobody else has ever tried to do this (Laughter.) It's not an accident. This is not going to be one of those freebies, you know. (Laughter.)[30]

The administration understood the potential political consequences from the start, before voters were made much aware of the issue, and yet it encouraged the FDA to go forward notwithstanding the political liability. Only with such support was the FDA able to undertake tobacco regulation, an initiative that otherwise would have been politically infeasible.

Like the FDA case, the Forest Service case also demonstrates how agencies can benefit from the momentum provided by political support from the White House. Here, too, the agency's efforts were prompted by a formal directive from the president, who stumped for the roadless initiative as well. This White House support raised public awareness of the Forest Service's initiative, and with that awareness came public support. As a result of White House backing, then, the Forest Service's roadless initiative was not easily resisted by powerful interests adverse to the roadless rule, neither in the early stages of that initiative nor once the agency finalized its rule.

At the same time, however, the Forest Service case also demonstrates that White House support, even for an executive-branch agency, is not indispensable where the agency's initiative already under way enjoys strong public and congressional support. For the White House's subsequent opposition to the roadless rule immediately following the 2000 elections was not enough to derail the rule. Of course, the White House had the authority to direct the agency to alter its regulatory course. But that authority was subject to two limits. Legally, the Forest Service could not undo its roadless rule without some factual record demonstrating that a reverse course was not "arbitrary or capricious" as interpreted under the APA. That is, the APA binds agencies to the administrative record they have developed, which is to say an agency can pursue contrary regulatory initiatives when, but only when, a new factual record justifies such a reversal. And politically, the White House could not easily direct the Forest Service to reverse its course given that the agency's initiative was by then strongly supported by the public and Congress. Thus, while White House support can go far to protect agencies against congressional opposition and even hostility, the Forest Service case shows that in some circumstances White House resistance to an agency's initiative already under way may not stop the agency where its efforts enjoy broad support from other quarters.

The OCC case also exemplifies how White House support can promote agency autonomy from Congress. There, the administration went on record publicly in support of the OCC's liberalizing efforts, on the grounds that it believed that reform of financial services regulation was overdue. And when the White House signaled to Congress its strong support for financial services reform legislation, it insisted, through the Treasury Department, that the OCC not be written out of any such legislation.[31] The OCC case does not illustrate a White House taking large political risks, but it too shows how the White House can bolster an agency's position relative to Congress and especially legislatively influential interest groups.

Then there are the courts. Given the nature of judicial review—which depends upon some party bringing litigation and is largely retrospective—judicial support for an agency's regulatory initiative is not a necessary condition of publically interested regulation. On the other hand, judicial invalidation of an agency's regulatory initiative is often fatal. And given that any regulatory action with significant economic stakes is likely to become the subject of litigation, judicial review of agency action is a routine part of the regulatory process. Thus, in practical terms, any agency undertaking significant regulatory action must earn the support of reviewing courts, at the very least concerning its authority to undertake that action.

The judicial challenges to the regulatory initiatives of the EPA, FDA, USFS, FTC, and OCC, all brought by regulated interest groups under the APA, shed light on the effects of judicial review on agency autonomy. (The SEC's rules have not been challenged in court.) As seen, judicial treatment of these agencies' regulatory initiatives varied. On one side of the spectrum, the courts completely vindicated the OCC from its congressional and interest-group critics by repeatedly sanctioning the comptroller's interpretations of federal banking laws. Having lost repeatedly in the courts, opponents of the OCC's actions had nowhere else to turn, and as a result turned their attention to legislative reform that largely codified what the comptroller had done. In short, the courts sealed the success of the OCC's initiative.

The courts also vindicated the EPA's controversial rules, although not until the Supreme Court's decision reversing the D.C. Circuit's invalidation of the EPA's rules. Ditto for the FTC; lower courts initially invalidated the "Do Not Call" rule, but were reversed by a higher court that upheld the rule. The Forest Service's roadless also met a mixed judicial reaction, with two lower courts invalidating the rule, and then one appellate court reversing one of those cases and another appellate court mooting the other case. Although the Forest Service's judicial success was not as clean as OCC's, the EPA's, or the FTC's, still the Ninth Circuit's decision upholding the roadless rule largely vindicated the agency and certainly undermined the Forest Service's critics. And as a result of the Tenth Circuit's decision mooting the Wyoming district court's decision against the agency, there is no undisturbed judicial decision invalidating the roadless rule. Meanwhile, the court in the Northern District of California revived the Clinton roadless rule upon invalidating its replacement. For these four agencies, then, there is no longer any serious doubt about the legality of their core initiatives, though in the EPA case litigation of some of the details of the rules' implementation is inevitable, and additional litigation concerning the roadless initiative is likely as well.

In contrast to all of the above, judicial review ended the FDA's regulatory effort, dead in its long tracks. Although congressional and interest-group opponents of the tobacco rule could not stop the FDA at the administrative or political level, ultimately they found success before the Supreme Court (though they had largely lost initially at the district court level). The FDA case thus illustrates that judicial review can be hazardous for agencies, not only for their critics and opponents. Sometimes agencies lose in court, and given that they do, judicial review provides opportunity for interests resistant to socially beneficial regulation—because it imposes high costs on them—to stop it.

Ironically, however, it is exactly this double-edged aspect of judicial review that enhances agency autonomy. Because agencies can and sometimes do lose when their regulatory actions are challenged judicially, judicial decisions upholding agency action provide powerful support for agencies whose decisions are vindicated. That is, given the possibility that courts will invalidate agency action that is "wrong," a judicial decision upholding an agency's action as "right" provides the agency with a strong endorsement that weakens the posture of the agency's opponents. Certainly legally, but also politically, the prevailing agency enjoys the legitimacy of having its decision tested by courts. Opponents have a more difficult time sustaining their opposition—and the sympathy of legislators, other interest groups, or the public—once an agency decision enjoys judicial blessing. Judicial review thus has the effect of muting agency opponents, and therefore of strengthening agencies vis-à-vis their opponents.

And agencies win far more often than not. That is, in most cases agencies' opponents do not succeed in invalidating agency action judicially. This is true in part because often those opposed to an agency's decision bring suit whenever that decision affects their interests adversely, whether or not they have a strong—as opposed to a plausible—claim that the agency acted illegally. In the studied cases, while the agencies in question did not always survive judicial challenges brought by regulated interests, the courts usually upheld agency action no matter how vehemently opposed by powerful interest groups and legislators. Judicial review helped the agencies because the reviewing courts generally concluded their decisions were, among other tests of legality, well supported by the agencies' record. Given the facts the agencies had gathered and the processes by which they had gathered them, the reviewing courts generally concluded the agencies had acted lawfully.

Moreover, when the studied agencies lost at the judicial level, they seldom did so for the reasons emphasized most by their interest-group opponents. In other words, sometimes the reviewing courts vindicated agency critics, but seldom vindicated their criticisms. For example, when the appeals court invalidated the EPA rules, it did so not on the grounds that the EPA had fashioned rules that were unjustified substantively, but rather on the grounds that the congressional authority was too vaguely interpreted. Indeed, the court in that same decision ruled in favor of the EPA against many of the substantive criticisms its congressional and interest-group opponents made against the rules.

In the FDA case, the Supreme Court similarly determined that the agency lacked the statutory authority to promulgate the tobacco rule. The Supreme Court did not conclude, however, that the FDA's rule made for bad public policy or was otherwise unjustified on the merits, notwithstanding the many arguments the rule's opponents had made along those lines. The Court did not call into question the agency's medical and social-scientific findings concerning the effects of smoking or the practices and demographics of tobacco marketing and distribution. In other words, with respect to the substantive justifications of the FDA's rule, judicial review did not undermine the FDA. To the contrary, the Court explicitly suggested that the agency's rule made for sound public policy. Indeed, the majority opinion invalidating the tobacco rule stated that the FDA had "amply demonstrated that tobacco use, particularly among children and adolescents, poses perhaps the single most significant threat to public health in the United States."[32] The agency lost instead on the grounds that it lacked sufficient statutory authority to regulate in the public interest.

The FTC also lost in the Oklahoma court on the grounds that it lacked statutory authority to issue its "Do Not Call" rule, not on the basis that the rule was contrary to public interests. But the court in that case emphasized that its interpretation of the FTC's power under the Telemarketing and Consumer Fraud and Abuse Prevention Act was informed by First Amendment considerations: It interpreted the act not to give the FTC authority to issue the "Do Not Call" rule because that interpretation would avoid the constitutional question. At the same time, the Oklahoma court explicitly rejected the telemarketing plaintiffs' other objections against the rule, including the claim that the agency had not provided them with adequate notice of the differences between the proposed rule and final rule as required by the Administrative Procedure Act.

The FTC's defeat in the Colorado litigation, where the court decided against the agency directly on First Amendment grounds, did not call into question the substantive policy benefits of the "Do Not Call" rule either. Rather, the district court there simply held that the rule violated telemarketers' speech rights. The appellate court's reversal of that decision, however, left the rule's opponents with no battle to fight. But the "Do Not Call" rule's opponents not only did not win on appeal; they lost something as well, given the more subtle effects of the Tenth Circuit's reversal. By ruling that the FTC had not violated telemarketers' commercial speech rights, the court justified the agency's decision not only legally but normatively, for the First Amendment analysis includes considerations of the reasonableness and legitimacy of purpose of the government's restriction on speech. Accordingly, the appellate court noted the "undisputedly substantial governmental interests" of safeguarding "the privacy of individuals in their homes" and avoiding "the risk of fraudulent and abusive solicitation," and concluded that the FTC's rule protected these interests in an appropriately tailored way.[33] Ultimately, then, judicial review legitimized the FTC's decision on policy grounds too. The court in effect held that the FTC's rule was justified given the interests at stake and the means by which the agency protected those interests.

The Forest Service was the only agency for which judicial review squarely called into question the substantive merits of what the agency had done. In ruling that the Forest Service had likely violated the National

Environmental Protection Act and the Wilderness Act, the Idaho and Wyoming district courts concluded that the agency had not adequately considered all costs or contemplated all alternatives to its roadless rule. On substantive policy grounds, in other words, the agency's rule had not yet been justified. But then neither of these decisions stood, and the Ninth Circuit specifically held to the contrary that the Forest Service in fact had taken costs and alternatives sufficiently into consideration and had given those opposed to the roadless rule sufficient time to identify its deficiencies. In the end, then, the Forest Service too was vindicated, at least in part. On balance, judicial review legitimized what the agency had done.

The roadless rule litigation further highlights just how an agency's supporters or opponents can use judicial review to bolster their own more general case for or against the agency's regulatory initiative. While the Wyoming district court appeal was still pending, but after the new presidential administration brought a new leadership to the Forest Service and a new view of the roadless rule, the Forest Service's website featured the Wyoming district court case invalidating the roadless rule prominently. Agency press releases and its roadless rule "time line" also emphasized the Wyoming case, which, the agency's official sources of information represented, showed the rule to be illegal. Such representations were not technically incorrect, but they failed to capture all of the legal circumstances, and other litigation, surrounding the roadless rule. In short, the Wyoming case got a billing out of proportion to its legal significance. The example illustrates how a judicial decision invalidating agency action allows critics—in this case, the new administration—to point to an independent authority to validate their criticism, just as judicial victory allows supporters and the agency itself to invoke independent authority to validate what the agency has done.

Thus does judicial review provide legitimacy to one side or the other in disputes over agency action. It also provides eventual closure on those disputes. For in a world without judicial review, the political tussle between agency detractors and supporters, and among their legislative allies, and perhaps involving the White House as well, could run on indefinitely. Judicial review avoids that result by providing finality to long-running regulatory battles. Given the deference courts show to agencies, coupled with agencies' efforts to developing factual records that will survive judicial challenge, judicial review tends to provide closure in a way that vindicates the challenged agency.

As a result, the judiciary's role in administrative decisionmaking, like the president's, attenuates Congress's ability to influence regulatory agencies. To control agencies, Congress must compete with the other branches of government. In all of the studied cases except the FDA case, judicial review promoted agency independence from Congress or regulated interests by vindicating what the agency had done over the objections of legislative and interest-group critics, just as in all the studied cases except the Forest Service case, the White House's support of agency action promoted agency independence from Congress or regulated interests by providing an alternative source of political support. To be sure, the studied cases also exemplify the potential influence Congress enjoys over agencies as well. Congress is far from irrelevant. But neither is it the only source of agency control.

Finally, the studied cases also illustrate the considerable access that groups besides regulated industries have to the courts, a point emphasized by the administrative process theory. Environmental and health organizations litigated in defense of the EPA rules, after the American Lung Association had already litigated to prompt those rules in the first place. Health organizations litigated as amici in the FDA case as well. The Association for the Advancement of Retired Persons supported the FTC as amici in that agency's defense of its regulation too. The most dramatic example, however, is the Forest Service case, where environmental organizations defended the roadless rule on appeal when the newly headed Department of Justice did not. In no case were public-interest litigants unable to press their case effectively—whether defending the agencies' substantive policy decisions or (in some cases) arguing that the agency could have gone farther—before reviewing courts. However limited their economic resources by comparison with regulated parties, that disparity did not translate to the same litigation handicap.

To summarize this long chapter briefly, the studied cases lend considerable support to the administrative process theory of regulation. In particular, they show how agencies employed various administrative procedures to inoculate themselves against interest-group criticisms and congressional sanctions, how public-interested administrators were motivated to pursue regulatory goals they believed advanced social welfare in the face of substantial opposition, and finally how presidential oversight and judicial review often secured agency independence against the opposition of powerful interests who bore much of the costs of socially beneficial regulation. The examined cases also show, therefore, how organized and well-funded interests—representing industrial manufacturers, utilities, tobacco producers, advertisers, timber, telemarketers, securities issuers, corporate lawyers, and insurance companies—were unable to use the administrative process to change the course of ambitious regulatory initiatives that advanced general interests but imposed costs on them. At the very least, the studied cases thus strongly suggest that administrative process rules, administrator motivations, and agency relationships with the White House and the courts can be as determinative of regulatory outcomes as is the constellation of congressional constituencies affected by regulatory choices. To understand regulation, emphasis on the administrative process is well placed.

Chapter Fifteen

Regulatory Rents, Regulatory Failures, and Other Objections

WHAT OBJECTIONS MIGHT BE raised against the conclusions of the last two chapters? Several seem likely, some defending the public choice theory and others attacking the administrative process theory offered in its place. In fairness, some likely objections are not wholly without merit. The remainder of this analysis considers likely objections and, notwithstanding the important differences between the public-choice and the administrative-process accounts of regulation, considers the extent to which they might be partially connected.

OBJECTIONS

In Defense of the Public Choice Theory

A STRAW THEORY

One possible objection to the critical assessment of public choice theory offered above holds that the assessment attacks a straw theory. According to this objection, the public choice theory is not as pessimistic as presented: Regulation does not inevitably result in the supply of regulatory rents to socially undeserving interest groups, but does so often enough to cast doubt on the efficacy of the regulatory regime overall. Thus, this objection goes, a few specific examples of successful regulation do not undermine the public choice theory. The theory should be expected to accommodate them.

This objection—expanding the theory to accommodate contrary evidence—is not compelling, however, for several reasons. First of all, such an objection forgets the critical evaluation of the public choice theory offered in part 1, which argued that the theory does not bear close conceptual scrutiny, quite apart from its empirical reliability. The case studies of part 3 lend support to the criticisms of earlier chapters. And in light of those criticisms, empirical results inconsistent with the public choice theory are not surprising: A weak theory's predictions are not unexpectedly unreliable. But those conceptual criticisms stand no matter how a public choice theorist might respond to the case studies above; the critique of the public choice theory offered here does not hinge on the case studies of part 3, or any others. It is just more powerful in light of them.

Second, the public choice theory of regulation encounters serious falsifiability problems if watered down to accommodate socially beneficial regulatory outcomes like those presented here, especially considering the regulatory importance of the studied cases. If examples of successful regulation are not inconsistent with the theory, then it is hard to know what *is* inconsistent with the theory. If it is hard to know what is inconsistent with the theory, then it is also hard to know what is consistent with the theory. To have any explanatory or predictive power, the theory has to rule some regulatory outcomes in and others out. The cases studied seem much at odds with the central expectations of the theory, and thus with its normative rejection of regulation.

In addition, the public choice theory as characterized here certainly is faithful to its presentation by its most influential proponents. George Stigler's challenge, quoted in chapter 2, both avoids the falsifiability problem and encapsulates the theory's core tenet: "[T]he theory would be contradicted if, for a given regulatory policy, we found the group with larger benefits and lower costs of political action being dominated by another group with lesser benefits and higher cost of political action. Temporary accidents aside, such cases simply will not arise: our extensive experience with the general theory in economics gives us the confidence this is so."[1] The case studies of part 3 are responsive to Stigler's challenge and thus to the considerable influence of the public choice theory.

And that influence extends to the present, if by inertia more than by studied acceptance. Thus Robert Tollison, for one example, concludes in an essay on theories of regulation that "one might state that opposing theories"—theories, Tollison explains, opposing specifically Stigler's theory as developed and generalized by Peltzman and Becker—"have been pretty thoroughly driven from the scene."[2] As Tollison and others observe,[3] there simply is no competitor. As explained earlier, casual students of regulation routinely invoke that same, unrivaled theory as a placeholder for the rarely questioned proposition that politically powerful interest groups secure from agencies regulation that is favorable to them and harmful to society. To object that the analysis here dissects a straw theory presupposes incorrectly that some better form of the theory exists.

ECONOMIC, NOT SOCIAL, REGULATION

Another possible objection to some of the conclusions above, in particular to the evidentiary weight of part 3's case studies, holds that the EPA, FDA, USFS, and FTC examples should not count very heavily against the public choice theory because those agencies are in the business of "social" regulation (addressing health, safety, and the environment) rather than "economic" regulation (regulating monopolies and other market conditions), and those who developed the public choice theory focused first on economic regulation. This objection is not compelling either.

First, proponents of the public choice theory in fact have not limited their logic to a particular type of regulation. Rather, they describe in general terms regulatory dynamics that, they argue, produced socially undesirable outcomes. Furthermore, although much of their early work addresses economic regulation, when they address post-1970 consumer-oriented regulation specifically, they expressly apply the theory to such regulation.[4] Moreover, there is no reason within the theory's conceptual framework why health and safety regulation should be different from any other type of regulation, or in other words why public choice theorists should restrict the scope of their theory. Most forms of regulation involve similar exercises of the state's monopoly on regulatory power, require application of the same basic decisionmaking rules, and are carried out by similarly situated regulators, no matter what the substantive regulatory field. So if regulation entails the advancement of some interests over others, that should hold true across different regulatory terrain.

Indeed, agencies like the EPA, FDA, and FTC are well positioned to deliver regulatory rents, were they so motivated.[5] Environmental regulation could be used by powerful interests as a barrier to entry to new firms, thereby protecting those interests' market power. This possibility seems especially strong to the extent that environmental standards can be applied, as in fact they often are, more strictly to new entrants in a market than to existing firms; old technology can be grandfathered in, while new pollution sources have to conform to stricter emission standards, for instance. Just as international environmental standards can be used to avoid competition for domestic firms, so too environmental law can be used to garner rents for existing firms by raising potential competitors' costs. And in famous instances of environmental legislation it has.[6]

Much the same could be said of food-and-drug regulation and consumer-protection regulation as well. The FDA and FTC are well positioned to give advantages to some firms or industries over others. For example, either could promote the interests of established firms over new market entrants by developing regulations more costly for new entrants to follow, and indeed it is possible that the FDA "protects" established firms even when it is motivated to regulate in a neutral way.[7] So again, the public choice theory's predictions should extend to their regulatory jurisdictions as well. FDA and FTC regulatory initiatives that seek instead to advance general interests, as well as the studied EPA rules, therefore fairly count against the theory.

Of course, regulation by the OCC and SEC fit comfortably with the paradigm of economic regulation, so those cases should count against the theory without objection. Had the OCC promoted the banking interests in some illicit way, or had the OCC instead supported banks' competitors' interests in some illicit way, either one following cues from Congress, then the public choice theory would have appeared stronger. But the OCC did not act at all following congressional prompting, but rather over congressional objection. And rather than deliver regulatory rents to banks, it advanced broad social interests, which largely happened to line up with banking interests. As for the SEC, its rule on corporate attorney conduct benefited investors over the objections of the profession it regulated, inverting the predictions of a theory according to which economic regulation advances the interests of those regulated. That the OCC and SEC successfully employed the same basic processes as the other studied agencies lends support to the argument that those cases too illustrate how agencies can use the administrative process to promote socially desirable regulatory policy.

OTHER EMPIRICAL EVIDENCE CONFIRMS REGULATORY RENT-SEEKING

Yet another objection counters that other empirical evidence corroborates the public choice theory's claims and predictions, notwithstanding the above criticisms. According to this objection, the argument above fails to consider the full range of studies relevant to evaluating the public choice theory against the more sanguine administrative process theory. On this view, the available evidence considered as a whole rescues the former, the case studies of part 3 notwithstanding. Such a response deserves careful attention. But it too proves weak.

First, it is important to distinguish special-interest legislation from special-interest regulation, given that sometimes they are treated as interchangeable, especially among those who conclude, as the public choice theory does, that agencies largely do Congress's bidding. Yet examples of legislation delivering rents to influential interests cannot rescue the public choice theory *of regulation*, which encompasses regulation by administrative agencies. Instead, a defender of the theory must identify instances of regulatory agencies employing the administrative process to deliver such rents. After all, administrative regulation might be an antidote to undesirable legislation.

Focusing, then, on the evidentiary basis of the public choice theory's claims about administrative regulation, the specific examples public choice theorists have identified in support of their theory are surprisingly few. Those who originally developed the theory enlisted studies of regulation of the airlines, securities, telecommunications, television, and trucking industries as their primary examples lending empirical support to its predictions. For example, Richard Posner identified regulation of the airlines, broadcasting, stock brokerage, and trucking, arguing that regulation of these industries "cannot be explained on the ground that they increase the wealth or, by any widely accepted standard of equity or fairness, the justice of the society."[8] For another example, Sam Peltzman pointed to the Civil Aeronautics Board's (CAB) fare structure prior to 1974 as an example providing "strong support" for the public choice theory.[9]

Stigler identified the CAB's refusal to approve new carrier lines, as well as certain trucking and securities regulations, as examples of regulatory outcomes promoting the interests of an industry at the expense of the general welfare.[10] Specifically, he argued that trucking weight-limit regulations show how an organized interest group can obtain favorable regulation that undermines efficiency and raises costs for consumers. With respect to securities regulation, Stigler also argued that a minimum commission structure on the sale of stocks, a requirement that a seller of mutual fund shares observe the offering price, and regulation of the selling expenses of mutual funds separately illustrate how the SEC has established or supported regulatory policies "inimical to the investor's welfare."[11] These examples were all offered as instances where regulatory outcomes benefited certain well-organized interests but undermined social welfare. Stigler summarized the position like this:

> What does the consumer owe to the ICC [Interstate Commerce Commission]? He owes for certain only two things: the support of a compulsory noncompetitive rate structure in the motor trucking industry . . . and the imposition of a nonviable rigidity upon the railroad industry which is helping to destroy it. . . . What does the consumer owe the CAB? Again, as with the ICC, very high barriers to the entry

of new firms, and the support of a rate structure seriously in conflict with competition. What does the consumer owe to the regulation of television? Mainly such things as an extraordinary campaign to prevent and hamper pay television—although the main channel of this obstructive influence . . . has been through the Congress acting upon the FCC.[12]

But while these examples arguably provided support for the public choice theory once upon a time,[13] they no longer do so. This is true for the simple reason that in nearly all of these regulatory areas, Congress and the relevant agencies themselves have deregulated, undoing any regulatory protections or subsidies these industries may have enjoyed. In fact, although Stigler relied so heavily on the ICC—the agency for which the term "capture" was first introduced[14]—the trucking industry was subsequently deregulated and the ICC eliminated over the strong objections of both the American Trucking Association and the Teamsters Union, and without the support of trucking's competitors or any other concentrated interests that would explain that deregulation in public-choice terms.[15] Similarly, the CAB under its chairman Alfred Kahn deregulated the airlines and recommended its own termination, on the grounds that doing so promoted efficiency and the public interest. Telecommunications and television both have also been deregulated. Thus, much of the evidence public choice theorists first identified in support of their theory now calls that theory into question.[16]

That difficulty might be minimized if only more recent studies provided substitute evidentiary support. The problem, however, is that other studies to which a defender of the public choice theory might point are modest or of doubtful relevance. For while the scope of the public choice theory quickly expanded from the "theory of economic regulation" to the "economic theory of regulation" to the "economic theory of government,"[17] the empirical evidence supporting that rapid expansion has not kept pace, not even close. Instead, much of the empirical side of the literature analyzes cases such as the British factory acts of the 1830s,[18] or English Corn Laws,[19] or the passage of the Sherman Act in 1890,[20] or turn-of-the-century state corporate chartering laws or other state regulation.[21] Such evidence, as historically interesting as it may be, provides scarce support for the public choice theory's indictment of the U.S. regulatory state in the twenty-first century.

On top of that, still other work calls the public choice theory into further question, not by providing scarce support but by reaching opposing conclusions. For just one example, one of the very few empirical studies of business-group influence in agency decisionmaking that considers agency budgetary concerns and the future private-sector employment prospects of agency personnel—pieces of the causal mechanism that according to the public choice theory can lead regulators to respond to interest groups' regulatory demands—concludes that such factors result in no systematic agency bias in favor of business interests.[22] Still other studies of the effects of regulation suggest that the public choice theory's conclusions are often difficult to square with actual regulatory outcomes.[23] For example, Mark Kelman analyzed several critical studies of the effects of safety regulation—including studies of automobile regulation (by Peltzman), consumer product safety, and workplace safety—all of which argued that such regulation rendered the general public less well off and benefited, if anyone, special interest groups.[24] But according to Kelman, any reasonable account of the evidence on which those studies relied—Kelman focused on each study's methodology and supporting data—leads instead to the conclusion that regulation in each case was on balance socially beneficial. The case studies offered here add to the body of work casting doubt on the empirical predictions of the public choice theory.

Not to overstate, some empirical work on the contemporary U.S. regulatory state concludes that agencies have provided regulatory benefits to narrow interests at the greater expense to society.[25] But all evidence considered, the public choice theory rests on a rather thin empirical foundation, leading many to conclude that the empirical evidence often offered in support of the theory is at best unsupportive and at worst inconsistent with the theory.[26] William Mitchell and Michael Munger, for example, reach this same conclusion upon surveying the evidence:

> The theory cannot . . . explain deregulation save for the tautology that the industry is now, for some reason, better off without regulation. . . . The theory can be applied to a variety of . . . economic regulatory policies, but in general its chief predictions are either tautological or are not borne out empirically.[27]

At least when measured against the public interest theory's enduring influence, the empirical evidence supporting it is shockingly modest.

RENT-SEEKING IN THE SHADOWS

Another objection to the conclusions above holds that although agencies might regulate to advance social welfare on important occasions—such as those in the studied examples—when the regulatory issues are well known, agencies still commonly provide regulatory favors when regulatory issues are under the radar. Moreover, this objection adds, most regulatory issues are under the radar. So most of day-to-day administrative regulation involves satisfying the preferences of narrow interests, even if in the most salient cases that is not true. Worse, by occasionally promoting public interests in marquee cases involving high regulatory stakes, the administrative regime inspires misplaced confidence in it, making the delivery of regulatory rents in the shadows easier.

The problem with this objection is that it is largely an assertion, not supported by either theoretical reasons or generalizable evidence.[28] Again, if regulation provides benefits to organized groups at the expense of the general welfare due to the incentives regulatory decisionmakers have and given the decisionmaking processes they employ, that should be true across different regulatory contexts. Whatever decisionmaking mechanisms produce benefits to favored groups in the shadows should be available in the light as well. The public choice theory holds not that the consequences of special-interest regulation are unknown, but rather that regulatory losers can do little about it.

Admittedly, one can distinguish between higher-salience and lower-salience regulatory issues, measured for example by the level of public attention or outside participation an issue generates. And it is imaginable that agencies are more likely to deliver regulatory favors to undeserving interest groups—assuming that they are so motivated in the first place—in low-salience settings where doing so is less likely to draw notice. On the other hand, this distinction cannot be taken very far. Today, information about administrative agencies's regulatory agenda, the basis on which they intend to regulate, how interested parties can track the development of proposed initiatives, and similarly about how interested parties can communicate their own views to agencies or otherwise participate in agency decisionmaking is easily and cheaply accessible. Agencies and numerous other organization have informative websites with user-friendly links to all of their regulatory initiatives. Copies of proposed rules and other proposed decisions, directions for filing electronic comments, summaries of others' comments, names of participants in a rulemaking—all of these are nearly costlessly available to anyone: Public interest groups, news media organizations, and curious citizens have ready access to regulatory agencies, their agenda, and their decisionmaking processes. As a result of the e-government revolution, administrative regulation is characterized by a level of transparency that would have seemed impossible two decades ago. While one can still distinguish among regulatory decisions according to the amount of public attention they generate or the number of outside participants they involve, few agency decisions with significant stakes escape public attention or participation completely. Regulatory decisionmaking is seldom done in the dark anymore.

But entertaining such distinctions, it is hard to know whether higher- or lower-salience regulatory initiatives provide greater incentives for agencies to favor special interests. In the former case, it seems likely that rent-seeking interests have the most to gain because the regulatory stakes are likely higher. They would therefore have greater motivation in those instances to exercise their influence with legislators or agencies directly, spending their political capital where it mattered most. Where, in contrast, regulatory decisions receive little notice, probably because the stakes are low, special interests have the least to gain. How these offsetting considerations—between the relative ease of rent-seeking, on the one hand, and the yields from doing so, on the other—might stack up is difficult to say.

The regulatory initiatives studied above illustrate the difficulty of establishing that lower salience (or lower stakes) leads to regulatory rent-seeking. First, the studied cases drew varying levels of public attention, outside participation, and support for the agencies' proposals and presented a range of regulatory stakes: While the EPA and FDA rules were high-salience and high-stakes regulatory initiatives almost without precedent, the Forest Service and FTC rules were very well publicized, especially the roadless rule, but involved far smaller, though significant, regulatory stakes. At the same time, among those participating in the EPA's and FDA's rulemakings, opposition to the agencies' initiatives outweighed support, especially in the EPA case, whereas in the Forest Service and FTC cases the agencies' supporters at least matched their detractors. Meanwhile, the SEC and OCC initiatives attracted little attention beyond the regulated parties in question. In the case of the SEC's attorney conduct rule, the only parties that mobilized in response to the agency's proposal, apart from academicians, were corporate attorneys resisting the rule. Public interest groups and individual citizens did not participate at all, whereas individual citizens did participate in the EPA, FDA, USFS, and FTC rulemakings. And while some policymakers defended the OCC's liberalization of national banks on the ground that it would promote public interests, again consumer groups and citizen groups did not participate much in the OCC's decisionmaking processes. Measured by the volume of participation in rulemaking, in other words, or by the public attention the initiatives generated, the SEC and OCC cases were not high-salience regulatory initiatives, although again the stakes were significant, especially in the OCC case. Taken together, then, the studied cases illustrate how agencies can promote general interests whether or not their decisions generate enormous public attention or outside participation, whether those who participate the most are critical or supportive of the agency, and whether the regulatory stakes are huge or merely substantial.

Finally, if rent-seeking somehow were accomplished in the shadows, and not in cases generating high attention and participation, the policy response to that finding would not in any case be deregulation. In other words, the objection that agencies deliver regulatory rents to favored interests only when no one else is looking does not support the public choice theory's normative rejection of regulation. Such a conclusion, were it tenable, would instead justify increased transparency and participation in agency decisionmaking processes.

REAL CAPTURE IS INFORMATIONAL CAPTURE

Still another objection invokes the theory of informational capture. It counters that real regulatory capture does not take the form of legislative or interest-group political coercion of agencies, but rather the more subtle form of influencing agencies by supplying biased information to them, on which they must inevitably rely. According to this objection—which supports the public choice theory's conclusions but is not faithful to its argument—agencies depend crucially on information to do their regulatory work, and regulated parties tend to possess the most information relevant to regulatory decisions implicating them. Because those parties control whether their information is revealed and how it is framed, they can use their informational advantages to shape regulatory outcomes in their favor.

This objection too offers assertion disguised as theory. For one thing, agencies are not unaware of information biases, especially the biases of mobilized interests who would bear most of the costs of complying with new regulation. Given the obvious biases regulated parties will often have, agencies are not likely to accept the arguments and information supplied by such parties uncritically. In fact, in theory agencies might well overcompensate for such biases by discounting the claims of regulated interests too much. In other words, the fact that regulated parties may be biased might lead agencies not to take their information seriously enough, and thus to regulate against such parties' interests more than they should, rather than regulate in such parties' favor. This equally plausible possibility is assumed away by the idea of informational capture.[29]

Second, agencies have very robust processes for gathering and evaluating information: They employ policy analysts, including economists, accountants, and scientists. They rely on peer review. They also solicit advice from experts and other consultants. They convene advisory groups. They publicize their findings and disclose other studies on which their proposals rely. In addition to all of that, agencies also often quantify the costs and benefits of proposed regulatory decisions, and invite interested parties to comment on the same. In short, regulatory agencies are not dependent upon regulated parties for either information or expertise. The idea that regulated interests can fool agencies fails to consider the considerable infrastructure agencies have developed to generate and process information.

At the same time, though, agencies do not have a monopoly on information relevant to proposed regulatory initiatives. Yet another problem with the suggestion that agencies favor special interests as a result of information problems overlooks the various levels of scrutiny that the data and arguments underlying agencies' decisions receive. If one group supplies an agency with incomplete or biased information, another group with adverse interests will have opportunities to challenge or rebut it. On top of that, as already seen, the other branches of government also scrutinize the quality of agency information. The White House requires cost-benefit analyses underlying executive branch agencies' decisions, and the courts to a lesser but significant extent also scrutinize the factual bases of agency decisions, especially when those challenging agency action bring claims specifically alleging that an agency's decision lacks an adequate factual basis. In short, not only are agencies themselves sophisticated producers and consumers of information, the scrutiny their decisions and even proposed decisions receive from interest groups and other branches of government further ensures that regulatory decisions reflect sound analysis. The point is not that all interested parties will agree about the evidentiary basis for any given decision—far from it—but rather that there is no reason to think agencies can be easily misled, informationally duped. The notion that agency decisions will reflect the biases of regulated interests assumes away agency oversight.

The studied cases illustrate vividly that agencies are not informationally captured, as the agencies in question relied on numerous channels to develop and evaluate information relevant to their initiatives. As seen, the EPA's ozone and particulate matter rules reflected exhaustive consideration of relevant scientific and epidemiological information. The FDA's tobacco rule did too, reflecting as well social-scientific information about issues such as teen smoking. Both rules generated much competing data and information about the agencies' proposals. Although those critical of the agencies' initiatives outnumbered supporters, still the EPA and FDA received information from a wide range of interests urging the agencies in very different directions. Not only did those agencies receive information from a wide range of sources, they solicited it as well. The Forest Service, too, went to considerable lengths to gather information, holding meetings throughout the National Forest System. And the SEC and FTC hosted fora to gather information, and provided extensive information to all interested parties about comments received from participants in those agencies' rulemakings. Finally, in all of these cases, the regulated interests argued that agencies did not give sufficient weight to the information they supplied. Thus the actual facts of agency decisionmaking in the considered examples shows how implausible informational capture can be.

Not to belabor the point, but here once again the objection offered in defense of the public choice theory does not lead to the theory's policy conclusions in any event. For even if agencies were informationally captured, such a result would argue for better agency techniques for gathering and evaluating data, techniques such as greater reliance on cost-benefit analysis and peer review (whose legislative advocates argue are useful to protect regulated interests from agencies, not the other way around). In short, even if agency decisions result from skewed information, that informational bias should be corrected. Deregulation would not follow.

Against the Administrative Process Theory

The above objections focus on the previous chapters' critical assessment of the public choice theory. That leaves possible objections to their defense of the administrative process theory. For even if the public choice theory is weak, that does not make the administrative process theory strong.

THE ADMINISTRATIVE PROCESS THEORY IS NOT WELL SPECIFIED

One type of objection to the administrative process theory rejects it as insufficiently developed. According to one form of this objection, the theory is difficult to assess because it does not yield crisp predictions. Instead, the administrative process theory hedges: It holds that agencies enjoy considerable autonomy which they *may* exercise to advance social welfare *if* they are motivated to do so and *provided that* they are not opposed by every branch of government. These qualifications mean that, in contrast to the public choice theory, the administrative process theory cannot make abstract predictions about regulatory outcomes that are independent of the facts of any regulatory case. Put differently, according to the administrative process theory, knowing whether or not an agency will advance public interests with respect to a given regulatory issue requires first answering ground-level empirical questions about the circumstances of that issue.

This criticism carries some force. Whereas the public choice theory purports to yield abstract predictions, the administrative process theory yields instead contingent predictions. The administrative process theory is, therefore, less elegant. On the other hand, the more general public choice theory is more elegant only because it makes empirical assumptions so strong that they are embedded in the theory implicitly rather than framed as contingencies explicitly. But those assumptions are crucial to the theory: Interest groups pressure legislators for favorable regulatory treatment *because in fact* that is what interest groups are mobilized to do. Legislators pressure agencies to deliver regulatory rents *because in fact* legislators respond to interest-group demands. Agencies exhibit regulatory favoritism *because in fact* they have little choice but to respond to legislative cues. And so on.

But the public choice theory could be framed in less general terms that acknowledged the contingency of its empirical premises and thus yielded qualified predictions: To the extent that special interests pressure reelection-minded legislators for favorable regulation, and insofar as legislators respond to those pressures by ensuring that administrative agencies cater to special interests' regulatory preferences, and provided that agencies cannot resist legislative influence or are not motivated to do so, agencies deliver regulatory rents to special interests. The public choice theory becomes less concise, but also more plausible. By the inverse token, the administrative process theory could be stated in unqualified terms yielding succinct predictions: Agencies exercise their legal-procedural autonomy created by administrative procedure to regulate in the public interest. The administrative process theory becomes more concise, but much weaker. The cumbersome quality of that theory is also its virtue, because it acknowledges the contingent nature of regulatory outcomes.

And although contingent, the administrative process theory does yield clear predictions. It predicts that regulatory outcomes will advance social welfare where its specified conditions hold. The theory is therefore also falsifiable. Instances where agencies undermine social welfare by providing rents to narrow interests counts against the theory (but does not disprove it given that it allows for such cases). So would, for example, evidence that Congress controls agencies, or that administrative procedure undermines agency autonomy, or that interest groups always sought regulatory rents, or that some types of interests are excluded from participating in regulatory decisionmaking. Admittedly, these issues can be difficult to measure. That fact is no defect of the theory itself, however, but rather a consequence of its complex subject matter.

THE ADMINISTRATIVE PROCESS THEORY IS TOO OPTIMISTIC

Another set of objections to the affirmative case reject it as simply too optimistic. One objection of this type holds that the theory overlooks that regulatory agencies perform poorly, positing that they are not so much corrupt as incompetent. They misunderstand consequences, grossly. And as a result, they often fail to accomplish their regulatory missions. They "overregulate" or "underregulate" or otherwise subvert their very purposes.

This objection is difficult to answer, although it is not very powerful. Agencies cannot predict in advance *all* of the consequences of their regulatory decisions. That much seems true. And in well-documented cases, especially in the context of health and safety regulation, agencies have overregulated or underregulated, in the sense that across different regulatory settings they have not always equalized the marginal costs or marginal benefits of regulation.[30] No doubt, agencies have sometimes thwarted their own goals.

Yet assessments of regulatory performance presuppose elusive criteria, and the baseline question remains: Compared to what? No organization or institution can anticipate completely the consequences of its actions, neither other institutions of government nor profit-seeking entrepreneurs rewarded for accurate predictions. Uncertainty, and partial failure, are ubiquitous. Given that truism, the issue becomes whether regulatory agencies perform so poorly that social welfare would be advanced either by leaving regulatory decisionmaking entirely to other branches of government or by abandoning regulation altogether. The alternatives are far-fetched.

Legislation, for example, also brings unintended and even ironic consequences, and indeed legislative debates often reduce to disagreements about the likely consequences of legislative proposals. The partial procedural evenhandedness and transparency of administrative decisionmaking processes seem likely to promote, though not guarantee, well-informed decisions at least as well as legislative procedures do. Participation in agency rulemaking by private parties seems more balanced than such participation in the legislative arena. And administrative decisionmaking is significantly more transparent than legislative decisionmaking, and increasingly relies on expert consultation. In addition, administrative decisions, unlike most legislative decisions, are subject at least to rationality review by courts and in most cases cost-benefit scrutiny by the White House. Add to all that the fact that administrators need not seek reelection and can therefore avoid at least crass political calculations when considering regulatory alternatives, and it is hard to see exactly what features of administrative decisionmaking render it unusually susceptible to irrationality or failure. The administrative process theory does not contemplate that administrative decisionmaking is perfect, just not worse than realistic alternatives.

Data on the performance of administrative regulation support an optimistic view of the social welfare consequences of major regulatory initiatives over the last decade. As required by the recent Regulatory Right to Know Act,[31] the Office of Management and Budget compiles, monetizes, and aggregates the costs and benefits of major regulatory programs. The OMB's reports required by that statute provide accounting statements that estimate total annual costs and benefits of regulatory rules in the aggregate, by agency and agency program, and by major rule. The OMB uses data provided by the agencies, but subject to OMB review under Executive Order 12866 and to public notice. The OMB's reports themselves are subject to peer review under the statute.

One recent (and representative) comprehensive report, *Informing Regulatory Decisions: 2003 Report to Congress on the Costs and Benefits of Federal Regulations and Unfunded Mandates on State, Local, and Tribal Entities*, issued by OMB's Office of Information and Regulatory Affairs,[32] provides estimates of the total annual costs and benefits of 107 rules reviewed by OIRA from 1992 to 2002 that generated costs or benefits of at least $100 million annually and for which a substantial portion of those costs and benefits was monetized by the issuing agency or by OMB. In the aggregate, those 107 rules generated annual benefits between $146.8 billion and $230.8 billion, and annual costs between $36.6 billion and $42.8 billion. Among those 107 rules, however, four particular EPA rules account for a large portion of the total aggregate annual benefits, rules for which the estimated annual benefits are between $101 and $119 billion. Excluding those rules and measuring the total benefits and costs of the remaining 103 rules, the benefits still exceed the costs, with total annual benefits between $41 and $107 billion, and costs between $29 and $34 billion.

The OIRA report categorizes the 107 analyzed rules by the agencies that issued them as well—USDA, Education, Energy, HHS, HUD, DOL, DOT, and EPA. For each agency taken separately, the estimated annual benefits again exceed the estimated annual costs. In fact, taking the lowest estimate of annual benefits and the highest estimate of annual costs for each agency, still for all agencies the benefits of their major rules exceed the costs. The report further considers the net cost-benefit effects of select regulatory programs and agencies within the executive departments. Here again, the rules of most select programs and agencies created total benefits far exceeding their total costs, in the extreme case of the EPA's Office of Air by over $100 billion annually. For another example, with HHS, the FDA's rules over the past ten years have generated between $2.0 and $4.5 billion annually, while imposing costs of $0.5 to $0.7 billion.

To be sure, the rules of some subagencies over the past decade have not produced benefits exceeding their total costs. For example, while the DOT's major rules have generated substantial net benefits, the OIRA report estimates the U.S. Coast Guard's major rules (that is, those included within the set of 107 analyzed rules) to have generated only $0.07 billion in annual benefits but $1.2 billion in costs. For another example, the Occupational Safety and Health Administration's rules relating to occupational exposure to asbestos issued between 1992 and 1995 imposed estimated costs exceeding their benefits. But on the whole, available data overwhelmingly support the conclusion that most major regulatory initiatives advance social welfare by generating benefits that usually far exceed their costs.[33] In that light, the case studies presented in part 3 do not constitute exceptional cases, and the administrative process theory's "social welfare claim" seems vindicated.

A weaker version of the "too optimistic" objection responds that agency decisionmaking does not generate socially optimal regulation. This objection is apt, but not powerful. The administrative process theory advanced here—and its partial defense of the regulatory state—do not require that agencies generate *optimal* regulatory results. On occasion they may; the theory does not rule that possibility out. But that is a high standard, and not one against other institutions are fairly measured either. Seldom will agency decisionmakers have all of the information necessary to ensure that regulatory outcomes are optimal, though that is an ideal point towards which regulatory decisionmakers should strive.

That the market does not always deliver optimal social outcomes, for example, is not a powerful critique of the market, so long as the market generates outcomes that generally advance social welfare. A defender of administrative regulation need not demonstrate that agency decisionmaking leads to optimal social outcomes any more than a defender of the market must demonstrate that the market generates optimal outcomes. The crucial question is whether the institution improves rather than optimizes social welfare. A defender of the market need show only that the market, notwithstanding its imperfections, tends to advance social welfare. If administrative regulation passes the cost-benefit test, because all things considered it tends to render society better off, that is a sufficient defense of the regulatory state even though further social-welfare improvements—and decisionmaking procedures designed to promote them—would be desirable too.

A more specific version of the "too optimistic" objection focuses on the administrative process theory's suggestion that legislators might resist interest-group pressures by empowering autonomous regulatory agencies and then delegating to those agencies substantial regulatory power. According to this objection, the theory is just too convenient. By suggesting not only that agencies can resist interest-group pressures but also that, by deferring to administrators and removing themselves from direct regulatory decisionmaking, legislators can too, the theory asks too much.

Maybe so. The extent to which legislators employ the administrative process to promote agency autonomy and to distance themselves from otherwise influential interests is difficult to know. It is possible that agencies exercise autonomy completely contrary to the wishes of Congress, and that if only Congress could, it would dominate agencies unfailingly. On the other hand, legislators seem unlikely to be so one-dimensional; as suggested in chapter 3, their goals must be complex. Moreover, it seems unlikely that administrative autonomy through administrative procedural rules is a matter entirely beyond Congress's control. If that is right, then Congress has at least acquiesced in administrative decisionmaking that is considerably independent of Congress. (If that is wrong, then agency autonomy is beyond congressional control.) In that event it seems plausible that, for reasons identified in chapter 8, individual legislators could use delegation for political protection by attributing regulatory outcomes that advanced general interests but disappointed politically important constituencies to the efforts of independent administrators.

This suggestion is not, however, original to the administrative process theory, though it is consonant with it. To the contrary, the idea that delegation provides political protection to legislators is an old chestnut of the traditional administrative law literature.[34] It probably captures legislative motivation accurately, at least in part, but it may not. In any case, the administrative process theory does not require it. With or without tacit legislative blessing, agencies can use administrative procedure to regulate in the public interest.

PARTIALLY RECONCILING COMPETING THEORIES

To say that regulators are sometimes motivated to pursue public-interested regulation, and that they have the procedural and institutional decisionmaking tools to do so even where some legislators and well-organized interest groups oppose agency initiatives, is not to deny the importance of legislative preferences or the relevance of well-organized interests. The cases examined here do not show, for example, that congressional preferences concerning regulatory outcomes are irrelevant; Congress exhibited considerable pressure on some of the agencies, just not enough to alter fundamentally their respective courses. Nor do those cases show that interest groups are irrelevant to understanding regulation. Again to the contrary, opponents of the regulatory initiatives in some of the studied cases showed considerable strength in the administrative arena, nearly prevailed in the legislative arena, and sometimes prevailed in court. The main claim of the administrative process theory is simply that there is more—not less—to the story of regulation than legislative control and interest-group influence, notwithstanding the inordinate explanatory weight these factors are usually thought to carry. The theory thus identifies circumstances under which social-welfare-enhancing regulation is possible, and even likely.

But that same identification implies circumstances under which such regulation is not so likely, specifically, where the conditions favoring public-interested regulation do not hold. Where they do not, the administrative process theory contemplates regulatory outcomes that may well not advance social welfare. From this point of view, the difference between the two theories is not whether one allows for regulatory outcomes that advance narrow interests of some to the greater detriment of the rest of society, but instead how often that result occurs.

Regulatory outcomes will tend to advance public interests most where administrators are motivated to advance public interests and undertake initiatives they believe will do so; at least some interests actively support rather than oppose an agency's initiative; congressional discipline in response to agency action is not undertaken or proves ineffective in changing agency behavior; an agency uses administrative procedure to create public visibility and to solicit participation from a range of regulatory interests; an agency uses administrative procedure to develop a factual record providing scientific and economic justification for their initiatives that enjoys consensus support from the relevant scientific field; the White House deems an agency's initiative worthy of political capital; and the agency's initiative finds legal basis and therefore judicial support. The coincidence of such conditions constitutes the environment most conducive to public-interested regulation. Actual results may vary.

By implication, one would least expect to find public-interested regulation where administrators exhibit no commitment to such regulation; opposition to an agency's initiative is universal; congressional discipline in response to agency action proves effective; an agency does not use administrative procedure to create public visibility or solicit participation from a range of implicated interests; an agency does not use the administrative process to develop a factual record providing scientific or economic support for its initiatives; the White House does not support an agency; and the legal basis on which an agency regulates renders the its initiative judicially vulnerable. The coincidence of these alternative conditions constitutes the hardest case for public-interested regulation. Where they are met, public-interested regulation is most unlikely, and regulatory outcomes may instead advance narrow and socially undesirable interests.

To generalize a bit further, it is clear that the conditions most conducive to public-interested regulation are not all necessary conditions. In a couple of the studied cases, for example—the EPA, FDA, and OCC cases and to some extent the USFS case as well—Congress attempted to prevent the agencies' initiatives. Yet congressional disapprobation did not slow the agencies down much. Thus, congressional opposition to agency proposals will not prevent public-interested regulation if enough other conditions conducive to such regulation hold. For another example, none of the studied agencies was always supported by the courts when interests adverse to the agencies brought judicial challenges. Thus, perfect judicial vindication is not a necessary condition of benign regulation.

On the other hand, some of the conditions promoting public-interested regulation probably approach necessary or contingently necessary conditions. For example, agencies will advance public-interested regulation only where administrators themselves are motivated to do so. Unless agencies advance general regulatory interests inadvertently, they do so only because agency decisionmakers aim to further their own conceptions of the public interest in the first place.

The studied cases also suggest that White House support is necessary, at least where congressional and interest-group opposition is otherwise substantial. In the Forest Service and OCC cases, the agencies' initiatives may not have been possible without presidential support. Certainly neither the tobacco rule nor the ozone and particulate matter rules would have been possible without White House support. Where congressional and interest-group opposition is so strong, as in those cases, the president's support is crucial. Where, in contrast, opposition to an agency's initiative is not overwhelming, as in the FTC and SEC cases for example, direct White House support may not be necessary. And the facts of the Forest Service case illustrate that even White House opposition may not stop an agency initiative already under way if that initiative enjoys congressional support, as the roadless rule eventually did. Public-interested regulation does not require the support of both the executive and legislative branches, though the studied cases do suggest that such regulation is possible only if agencies have the support of at least one of them.

For another example, although agencies need not always prevail in court, on the other hand judicial confirmation that a challenged agency's initiative falls within its statutory authority, especially from an appellate court, is necessary. The Supreme Court's invalidation of the tobacco rule illustrates vividly how little agency independence from regulated interests and even White House support will matter if a court determines that agency's decision exceeds its authority.

The simple point is that publically interested regulation is not inevitable according to the administrative process theory, but rather requires the convergence of several alternative conditions. Otherwise, the administrative process theory and the public choice theory that it challenges may predict similar regulatory outcomes and, to that extent, can be connected. The big difference (made clear by now, one hopes) is that the latter sees social-welfare-enhancing regulation as unrealistic—because contrary to the very corrupted purpose of regulation—whereas the former sees such regulation as entirely within reach. Both in theory and in fact.

Conclusion

The Regulatory State and Social Welfare

O<small>N THE OCCASION OF VETOING</small> the Walter-Logan Bill,[1] Congress's alternative to what later became the Administrative Procedure Act of 1946, President Franklin D. Roosevelt stated:

> Wherever a continuing series of controversies exist between a powerful and concentrated interest on one side and a diversified mass of individuals, each of whose separate interests may be small, on the other side, the only means of obtaining equality before the law has been to place the controversy in an administrative tribunal.[2]

Too strong. Yet there is an element of truth in Roosevelt's claim, and it is that element which this study has sought to emphasize. Administrative agencies do not achieve equality between powerful, concentrated interests, on the one hand, and small, diffuse interests, on the other. (How could they?) Nor are administrative agencies a panacea for all market failures, much less all difficult economic and social problems. Nor are all agencies equally efficacious in addressing complex economic and social challenges.

That said, it is also true that, under certain circumstances, administrative agencies can and do vindicate the regulatory interests of "a diversified mass of individuals." More specifically, administrative regulation can and does advance social welfare, where social welfare is measured especially in cost-benefit terms but also with reference to regulation's distributional effects, popular support underlying it, and expert consensus behind it. Administrative agencies can advance social welfare in cases where lead administrators are motivated to do so in the first place, where agencies employ decisionmaking procedures not easily susceptible to undue influence by "powerful and concentrated" interests, and where agencies find political and legal support from another branch of government. With respect to agencies' decisionmaking processes in particular, agencies have on important occasions proven themselves adept at using APA and non-APA procedures—including, among others, successive rounds of rulemaking, aggressive solicitation of public comments, hosting of nonrequired public hearings and other public meetings, and reliance on expert advisory committees and peer review—in ways that maximize their regulatory autonomy. Such processes can simultaneously generate support for an agency's regulatory initiative, test the scientific and political grounds for that initiative, and air all objections to the agency's proposal. As a result, agencies can emerge from the administrative process stronger, that is, stronger both politically—less vulnerable to critics' claims their initiatives are ill-considered—and legally—more likely to survive judicial challenges.

Thus the disanalogy between legislative regulation and administrative regulation. In contrast to legislators, administrators as far less dependent upon the types of political resources so valuable to members of Congress. They are therefore less easily enlisted to advance the regulatory preferences of rent-seeking interests offering legislatively valuable resources. (As also seen above, the extent to which the conventional wisdom oversimplifies legislative behavior too is another worthy topic.) Relative to legislators, administrative regulators are more liberated to follow where sound science and good policy may lead. Their decisionmaking processes not only promote but to some extent require notice of pending agency action, disclosure of the factual and policy bases for that action, and informed and rational decisionmaking that includes full consideration of the consequences of alternative decisions. These methods and norms of administrative decisionmaking are reinforced by executive oversight and judicial review, further attenuating rent-seekers' potential influence on agency decisionmakers. In addition, these methods and norms partially level the regulatory playing field between interests with many economic resources and those with fewer.

Of course, this basic message runs counter to the most influential form of conventional wisdom on the subject. According to the public choice account, administrative agencies are dominated by Congress, or organized interest groups, or both. Legislators control agencies well enough to ensure that legislatively important constituencies see their regulatory interests advanced, and moreover such groups do pretty well on their own in soliciting favorable regulation from agencies. Furthermore, because the regulatory advantages that favored groups realize are outweighed by the regulatory costs borne by the rest of society, regulation on this view often undermines social welfare. Regulatory government is not merely unsuccessful; it is often harmful.

The public choice account of regulation is idea rich, but evidence poor. It is easy to state, difficult to disprove, and resonates with deep-rooted and indeed often well-founded negative visions of politicians and politics. But its empirical record, charitably tabulated, does not vindicate its deregulatory policy prescriptions. Some regulation has undermined social welfare; much important regulation has not. Empirical studies go both ways. On top of that, close consideration of the administrative process rules through which agencies actually regulate disappoints the public choice theory's process expectations. If that is not enough, the theory does not bear close conceptual scrutiny either, especially with respect to its treatment of interest-group mobilization and of the relationship between Congress and agencies. The influence of the public choice theory owes not to its irresistible power, but rather to the absence of any compelling alternative.

The argument of the preceding chapters notwithstanding, however, the alternative picture of regulatory government presented in them is not offered as some kind of "just so" story according to which heroic, public-spirited regulators inevitably prevail over rent-seeking interest groups and thereby ensure that administrative regulation advances social welfare. The aim, rather, has been to identify conditions under which socially beneficial regulation might be expected, and to illustrate where those conditions have held, even on very high-stakes occasions and over the opposition of powerful interest groups and legislators. Sometimes those conditions hold. Sometimes they do not. Sometimes whether they hold may be hard to tell.

The truth is that regulation is too complex and too variant for quick measurement or pithy generalization. Thus the danger of simple models that reduce agency performance to one or a few axioms. As seductive as such models have proven to be, they mask a legally complicated regulatory state. More damaging, perhaps, they petrify low expectations about the performance of regulatory government, and in turn powerfully influence negative interpretations of regulatory reality. Fresh analysis, however, generates a more sanguine, if qualified, outlook. Good regulatory government is no more impossible than it is inevitable.

Notes

1. 5 U.S.C. §551(a)(1)(A)–(D) (defining "agency").

2. See, just for example, Michael E. Levine & Jennifer L. Forrence, Regulatory Capture, Public Interest, and the Public Agenda: Toward a Synthesis, 6 J.L., Econ. & Org. 167, 185 (1990).

3. See generally Fred S. McChesney, Money for Nothing: Politicians, Rent Extraction, and Political Extortion (1997); Frank J. Sorauf, Inside Campaign Finance: Myths and Realities (1992); M. Margaret Conway & Joanne Connor Green, Political Action Committees and the Political Process in the 1990s, in Interest Group Politics 155 (Allan J. Cigler & Burdett A. Loomis eds., 4th ed. 1995); Frank Sorauf, Adaptation and Innovation in Political Action Committees, in Interest Group Politics, above, at 175.

4. The idea of an exchange relationship between suppliers and demanders of regulation is a distinctive feature of the public choice account of regulation. See, for example, Levine & Forrence, Regulatory Capture, at 169; Sam Peltzman, Toward a More General Theory of Regulation, 19 J.L. & Econ. 211, 212 (1976); Richard A. Posner, Theories of Economic Regulation, 5 Bell. J. Econ. & Mgmt. Sci. 335, 344, 346 n. 27 (1974); George J. Stigler, The Theory of Economic Regulation, 2 Bell J. Econ. & Mgmt. Sci. 3, 4, 11–12 (1971).

5. See generally Jeffrey S. Banks, Agency Budgets, Cost Information, and Auditing, 33 Am. J. Pol. Sci. 670 (1989); Kathleen Bawn, Political Control Versus Expertise: Congressional Choice About Administrative Procedures, 89 Am. Pol. Sci. Rev. 62, 62 (1995); Arthur Lupia & Mathew D. McCubbins, Learning from Oversight: Fire Alarms and Police Patrols Reconstructed, 10 J.L. Econ. & Org. 96 (1994); Mathew D. McCubbins & Thomas Schwartz, Congressional Oversight Overlooked: Police Patrols Versus Fire Alarms, in Congress: Structure and Policy 426 (Mathew D. McCubbins & Terry Sullivan eds., 1987); McNollgast, Administrative Procedures as Instruments of Political Control, 3 J.L. Econ. & Org. 243, 248–51 (1987).

6. For one classic statement, see William A. Niskanen, Bureaucracy and Representative Government (1971). For a general examination, see, for example, The Budget Maximizing Bureaucrat: Appraisals and Evidence (Andrea Blais & Stephane Dion eds., 1991).

7. See generally Theodore J. Lowi, The End of Liberalism: The Second Republic of the United States (2d ed. 1979). For important earlier presentations, see Douglass Cater, Power in Washington (1964); J. Leiper Freeman, The Political Process: Executive Bureau-Legislative Committee Relations (rev. ed. 1965); and Ernest S. Griffith, The Impasse of Democracy: A Study of the Modern Government in Action (1939). For a more modern treatment, see, for example, James Q. Wilson, The Politics of Regulation, in The Politics of Regulation 357 (James Q. Wilson ed., 1980). Contributors to the informational capture brand of capture theory include, for example, Marver Bernstein, Regulating Business Through Independent Commission (1969), Gabriel Kolko, Railroads and Regulation, 1877–1916 (1965), and, as developed more recently, Clayton P. Gillette & James E. Krier, Risks, Courts, and Agencies, 138 U. Pa. L. Rev. 1027 (1990).

8. See generally Jeffrey M. Berry, Subgovernments, Issue Networks, and Political Conflict, in Remaking American Politics 239 (Richard A. Harris & Sidney M. Milkis eds., 1989); William P. Browne, Organized Interests and Their Issue Niches: A Search for Pluralism in a Policy Domain, 52 J. Pol. 477 (1990).

9. This is not to say, however, that the account requires that Congress is motivated to delegate only to satisfy powerful constituencies' demands. Congress delegates lawmaking power to administrative agencies who have the time, attention, personnel, and, critically, the scientific and technical resources to address regulatory problems in a way that Congress, given the scarcity of its own institutional resources, cannot. The trouble is that once Congress has delegated regulatory power to agencies, it runs the risk that agencies may pursue their own agendas at the possible expense of Congress's own preferences. David Epstein and Sharyn O'Halloran have generalized this observation by presenting a "transaction costs" approach to delegation. According to their formulation, Congress will either delegate, or directly legislate, depending on the relative costs "of making policy internally," given "the inefficiencies of the committee system," and the costs of delegating, given "congress's principal-agent problems of oversight and control." See David Epstein & Sharyn O'Halloran, Delegating Powers: A Transaction Cost Politics Approach to Policy Making Under Separate Powers 7–9 (1999); David Epstein & Sharyn O'Halloran, Administrative Procedures, Information, and Agency Discretion, 38 Am. J. Pol. Sci. 697 (1994); David Epstein & Sharyn O'Halloran, Divided Government and the Design of Administrative Procedures: A Formal Model and Empirical Test, 58 J. Pol. 373 (1996); David Epstein & Sharyn O'Halloran, A Theory of Strategic Oversight: Congress, Lobbyists, and the Bureaucracy, 11 J.L. Econ. & Org. 227 (1995).

10. On the constellation of interest groups in Washington, D.C., see generally Kay Lehman Schlozman & John T. Tierney, Organized Interests in American De-

mocracy (1986). For a review of the literature addressing the question of small groups' advantages over large groups, see William C. Mitchell & Michael C. Munger, Economic Models of Interest Groups: An Introductory Survey, 35 Am. J. Pol. Sci. 512 (1991). For original sources, see, for example, Sam Peltzman, General Theory of Regulation; Richard A. Posner, Theories of Economic Regulation; George J. Stigler, The Theory of Economic Regulation.

11. See, for example, Richard A. Posner, Theories of Economic Regulation at 345; George J. Stigler, Free Riders and Collective Action: An Appendix to Theories of Economic Regulation, 5 Bell J. Econ. & Mgmt. Sci. 359, 360–62 (1974).

12. See, for example, Richard A. Posner, The Social Costs of Monopoly and Regulation, 83 J. Pol. Econ. 807 (1975); Stigler, The Theory of Economic Regulation. For more general treatments, see, for example, James M. Buchanan et al., Toward a Theory of the Rent-Seeking Society (1980); Gordon Tullock, Rent Seeking (1993).

13. See, for example, Stigler, The Theory of Economic Regulation; Stigler, Can Regulatory Agencies Protect The Consumer?, in The Citizen and the State: Essays on Regulation (1975).

14. As Posner observes: "The economic theory [of regulation] insists that regulation be explained as the outcome of the forces of demand and supply." Richard A. Posner, Theories of Regulation. For similar observations, see, for example, Dennis C. Mueller, Public Choice II (1989); Michael E. Levine & Jennifer L. Forrence, Regulatory Capture; Sam Peltzman, Toward a More General Theory of Regulation, 19 J.L. & Econ. 211 (1976). George J. Stigler, Supplementary Notes on Economic Theories of Regulation, in The Citizen and the State: Essays on Regulation 138 (1975).

15. Stigler's is the seminal work, cited above, with important contributions (as well as some important criticisms) by Posner, including Richard A. Posner, Taxation by Regulation, 2 Bell J. Econ. & Mgmt. Sci. 22 (1971); Richard A. Posner, Theories of Regulation, above; Richard A. Posner, The Social Costs of Monopoly and Regulation, 83 J. Pol. Econ. 807 (1975), and a formal generalization and qualification by Peltzman. The foundational work was laid earlier, however, largely by Mancur Olson, James Buchanan, and Anthony Downs. See generally James M. Buchanan & Gordon Tullock, The Calculus of Consent (1962); James M. Buchanan, The Politics of Bureaucracy (1965); Anthony Downs, An Economic Theory of Democracy (1957); and Mancur Olson, The Logic of Collective Action: Public Goods and the Theory of Groups (1965); as well as William A. Niskanen Jr., Bureaucracy and Representative Government (1971). As developed in the text below, much of public choice theory is based on Olson's theory of collective action, as others have observed, including, for example, Daniel A. Farber & Philip P.

Frickey, Law & Public Choice: A Critical Introduction 23 (1991); Jack Hirshleifer, Comment on Peltzman, 19 J.L. & Econ. 241, 241 n.2 (1976); Michael E. Levine & Jennifer L. Forrence, Regulatory Capture at 169; Richard A. Posner, Theories of Economic Regulation at 343 n.18; Terry M. Moe, Toward a Broader View of Interest Groups, 43 J. Pol. 531 (1981). For a precursor, see Marver H. Bernstein, Regulating Business by Independent Commission (1955).

16. See George J. Stigler, The Theory of Economic Regulation at 4–6.

17. See George J. Stigler, The Theory of Economic Regulation at 6, where Stigler explains: "Crudely put, the butter producers wish to suppress margarine and encourage the production of bread." For an illuminating treatment of Stigler's example, see Geoffrey P. Miller, Public Choice at the Dawn of the Special Interest State: The Story of Butter and Margarine, 77 Cal. L. Rev. 83 (1989).

18. In Stigler's words:

> A consumer chooses between rail and air travel, for example, by voting with his pocketbook: he patronizes on a given day that mode of transportation he prefers. A similar form of economic voting occurs with decisions on where to work or where to invest one's capital. The market accumulates these economic votes, predicts their future course, and invests accordingly. If the public is asked to make a decision between two transportation media comparable to the individual's decision on how to travel—say, whether airlines or railroads should receive a federal subsidy—the decision must be abided by everyone, travelers and non-travelers, travelers this year and travelers next year.

George J. Stigler, The Theory of Economic Regulation, at 101.

19. Id.

20. In Stigler's words:

> The voter's expenditure to learn the merits of individual policy proposals and to express his preferences . . . are determined by expected costs and returns, just as they are in the private marketplace. The costs of comprehensive information are higher in the political arena because information must be sought on many issues of little or no direct concern to the individual, and accordingly he will know little about most matters before the legislature.

Id. at 11. Thus: "The channels of political decision-making can thus be described as gross or filtered or noisy. If everyone has a negligible preference for policy A over B, the preference will not be discovered or acted upon." Id. at 12.

21. Id.

22. Stigler, The Economic Theory of Regulation, at 4, 10–11, 17. See as well Stigler, Can Regulatory Agencies Protect the Consumer? at 181.

23. See, for example, Posner, Theories of Economic Regulation, at 337–39 and Stigler, The Theory of Economic Regulation, at 17.

24. Thus Stigler writes:

> So many economists, for example, have denounced the ICC for its pro-railroad policies that this has become a cliche of the literature. This criticism seems to me exactly as appropriate as a criticism of the Great Atlantic and Pacific Tea Company for selling groceries, or as a criticism of a politician for currying popular support. . . . Until the basic logic of political life is developed, reformers will be ill-equipped to use the state for their reforms.

Stigler, The Theory of Economic Regulation, at 17–18. Or similarly: "I shall assume, what I believe to be true, that usually the regulators are honest and conscientious. . . . Our concern is with the logic and basic forces of regulation, and they . . . transcend fluctuations in personnel and events." Stigler, Can Regulatory Agencies Protect the Consumer? at 181. Posner concurs in The Federal Trade Commission, at 82–87.

25. George J. Stigler, Old and New Theories of Economic Regulation, in The Citizen and the State: Essays on Regulation, 137, 140 (1975).

26. One might object that assigning such administrative-process expectations to the public choice theory creates a straw theory. According to this objection, the public choice theory need not predict that the administrative process appears to facilitate rent-seeking, but rather that it in fact facilitates rent-seeking while appearing open and neutral on the surface. On this view, rent-seekers and rent-suppliers would prefer to operate through open processes that though open, nevertheless somehow thoroughly disguise their activities.

One problem with this objection, however, is that it contemplates a distinction between the surface and actual features of the administrative process without providing any way of identifying one or the other. Moreover, the claim in the text above is not that the public choice theory predicts that the administrative process will facilitate rent-seeking through procedural rules that always blatantly trumpet the malign consequences of regulatory decisionmaking. Rather, the argument is, more modestly, that the public choice theory predicts process rules that are recognizably biased in favor of narrow interest groups—rules that a disinterested critic would, upon careful inspection, suspect to work in favor of the well organized.

This does mean that process rules that seem easily accessible to broad-based groups will count against the public choice theory. Although a public choice theorist could always respond that the apparent openness of procedural rules simply proves how effective rent-seeking groups are at concealing their regulatory gains, such a response threatens to render the public choice theory implausible or nonfalsifiable: Any regulatory decisionmaking procedure, no matter how welcoming to the diffuse interests that the theory holds are sacrificed in the regulatory process, counts as evidence in favor of the public-choice conclusion. Perhaps for this reason, Stigler and Posner in fact do not argue that regulatory decisionmaking process will always appear to accommodate many interests and perspectives but rather that administrative processes will be ascertainably well suited to supply regulatory rents. After all, the choice of administrative process rules rarely presents attention-getting political issues, even among most scholars, let alone most voters. Thus, there is no reason why interest groups would not seek process rules that perceptibly favor them. Moreover, according to the main claim of the public choice theory, that diffuse interests cannot effectively mobilize against narrow interests, there is no reason to think that special interest groups will face any great resistance to securing process rules that benefit them. That is, by hypothesis there is no one to put up a (procedural) fight.

Finally, the claim that public choice theory need not predict administrative process rules that perceptibly favor narrow interest groups misses the central point that, in an important sense, substantive regulatory outcomes are a function of process rules, a point developed at length below.

CHAPTER THREE
IS REGULATORY CAPTURE INEVITABLE?

1. Mancur Olson, The Logic of Collective Action (1965).

2. In addition to Olson, see generally Russell Hardin, Collective Action (1982); Elinor Ostrom, Governing the Commons (1990); Todd Sandler, Collective Action: Theory and Applications (1992); Joe Stevens, The Economics of Collective Choice (1993); Gerald Marwell & Pamela Oliver, The Critical Mass in Collective Action (1993); Mark Irving Lichbach, The Cooperator's Dilemma (1996).

3. Olson, The Logic of Collective Action, at 8. It is worth emphasizing that Olson does not at all identify groups with organizations. In fact, his central point is that groups usually lack organizational structure. They will, in other words, fail to organize so as to provide group goods. Thus Olson sometimes distinguishes between "groups" and "mobilized" groups, see, for example, id. at 134, only the latter of which have organizational apparatus.

4. More specifically, a "public good" or "group good" (used often, and here, interchangeably) is defined as a good characterized by jointness of supply and nonexcludability. A good is characterized by "jointness of supply" if one person's

enjoyment of that good does not reduce the amount of it available to anyone else. A good characterized by perfect jointness of supply is considered a "pure public good." But jointness admits of degrees. A good characterized by partial jointness of supply is one susceptible to "crowding." See generally Hardin, Collective Action, at 41 & n.8. A group is characterized by "nonexcludability" if, once it is supplied, it is infeasible to exclude others from enjoying that good. See generally Olson, The Logic of Collective Action, at 14 & n.21.

5. Thus can the collective action problem be understood as a generalized prisoner's dilemma, as Russell Hardin explains. See Hardin, Collective Action 25–28 (1982).

6. Olson, The Logic of Collective Action, at 50.

7. Id.

8. It is worth emphasizing here that Olson's argument in this connection speaks only to the level of suboptimality, not to either the absolute level of the good provided or to the amount consumed. All else equal, the bigger the group, the more a collective good is enjoyed; the smaller the group, the less a collective good is enjoyed. This speaks to the consumption of the collective good. As for the production of a collective good, in contrast, this is not affected by group size, again, keeping everything else (including the opportunity to bargain) equal. How much of a collective good will be produced depends entirely on whether any member in a given group deems it in her private interest to produce some amount of it. And that decision is not itself affected by the size of the group or the fraction of the total good going to that individual (notwithstanding Olson's occasional misleading emphasis on the fraction of the group good going to the individual who makes an investment, see id). Thus, while consumption increases and production remains constant as a group grows in size, holding everything else but size constant, the suboptimality is greater.

9. Id. at 28, 35.

10. Id. at 50, 134. Of course, sanctions and selective inducements are really two sides of the same coin, one negative and one positive.

11. See id. at 50 (defining "intermediate groups" and explaining that "group coordination or organization" makes possible the provision of some amount of the group good).

In his influential revisionist analysis of the collective action problem, Russell Hardin employs a different term, the "k group," which Hardin defines as a subgroup of any group consisting of those members who stand to benefit from providing the collective good themselves, without the benefit of contributions from anyone else in the entire group. In Hardin's words: "Let us use k to designate the size of any subgroup that just barely stands to benefit from providing the good, even without cooperation from other members of the whole group." Hardin, Collective Action, at 41 (citing Schelling for use of the term). In these terms, a k group may be of varying size (unless the group is homogenous, in which case k is equal to the number of members in the group). Where k is very large, the group is latent, in Olson's language. Where k instead has only one member, then the group in question is, in Olson's terms, a privileged group. The notion of a k group is helpful because it draws attention to the fact that the greatest determinant of the amount of the public good produced is not the size of the entire group, but rather the size of the subgroup of those members for whom providing the public good is worth their own while.

But however groups are labeled, the critical point remains the same: Given the logic of collective action, public goods will often be underproduced. They will be produced at suboptimal levels in the event that at least one of a given group's members just happens to find it in her private interest to provide some amount of the good. Group goods will be produced at suboptimal levels also when members of "intermediate groups" or small "k groups" happen to find it in their private interests to agree among themselves to produce some amount of the group good. And group goods will not be produced at all for large groups whose members are homogenous in the sense that none has a sufficient private incentive to produce any amount of the good—"latent groups" or "large k groups."

12. See, for example, Hardin, Collective Action.

13. Consider, for instance, the repeal of a certain tax provision, which would benefit all the members of some taxpaying group. If one member decided to invest in achieving the repeal, because the benefits of the repeal to that member were worth the cost, then the optimal amount of repeal (from the group's point of view) *would* be accomplished.

14. See Olson, The Logic of Collective Action, at 48, 50–51.

15. Olson says that his conclusions do not require public goods characterized by jointness, see Olson, The Logic of Collective Action, 14 n.21, but in fact some of his conclusions require public goods *not* characterized by jointness.

16. See, for example, Chamberlin, Provision of Collective Goods as a Function of Group Size, 68 Am. Pol. Sci. Rev. 707 (1974). As Hardin observes:

> One must conclude, in part, that whether larger groups are less likely to succeed than smaller ones is not entirely a logical matter, but rather that it is also in part an empirical question of what conditions correlate with size, and especially a question of whether the class of collective goods of interest includes many pure public goods.

Hardin, Collective Action, at 128.

Jointness also makes possible the superoptimal provision of public goods—a possibility seemingly overlooked in the literature on collective action. That is, where a good is rather (even if not perfectly) joint, and where more than one group member finds it in her own interest to provide some of the good, that good may be overproduced, unless those members somehow find a way to bargain over how much of the good each of them provides. But the very same obstacles that thwart bargaining among potentially intermediate groups in general will thwart such bargaining in these circumstances as well. Thus, it is entirely possible that more of the good, a superoptimal amount, will be produced than would be if there were bargaining among those who have an uncommonly (relative to the rest of the group's members) high demand for the good. Whether the superoptimal supply of public goods is a common problem raises an empirical question to which there is no immediately obvious answer.

To generalize, the nature of any particular collective-action problem ultimately depends crucially not only on whether the group in question is homogenous or instead heterogeneous with respect to demand of the good, but also on both the properties of the group good in question and the factual circumstances in which group members find themselves. Nor do these factors exhaust the complications. See, for example, Jon Elster, Nuts and Bolts for the Social Sciences 126–31 (1990 ed.), distinguishing among different species of collective-action problems depending on the marginal costs and benefits of cooperation, and Hardin, Collective Action, at 67–89, explaining different types of complicating membership "asymmetries," including but not limited to "asymmetry of demand."

17. Moreover, any bargain struck would then need to be enforced through some system of sanctions.

18. Olson, The Logic of Collective Action, at 132.

19. Here Olson relies on the conclusions of a couple of classics by E. E. Schattschneider and V. O. Key. See E. E. Schattschneider, Politics, Pressures and the Tariff (1935); E. E. Schattschneider, The Semi-Sovereign People (1960); V. O. Key, Politics, Parties, and Pressure Groups (1964 ed.).

20. In Olson's words:

> The high degree of organization of business interests, and the power of these business interests, must be due in large part to the fact that the business community is divided into a series of (generally oligopolistic) "industries," each of which contains only a fairly small number of firms.

Id. at 143. And: "[I]ndustries will normally be small enough to organize voluntarily to provide themselves with an active lobby." Id. And: "[T]he business interests of the country normally are congregated in oligopoly-sized groups or industries."

Id. And: "The multitude of workers, consumers, white-collar workers, farmers, and so on are organized only in special circumstances, but business interests are organized as a general rule."

21. Id. at 132. Olson's argument here raises the question of how those supplying the selective inducements can get away with charging an excessive price for them—that is, a price large enough to cover not only the costs of the inducements but also the additional overhead costs of lobbying and other political activities. For example, if members of Common Cause contribute to that group's lobbying activities simply because it buys them a magazine, why would not some other, comparable magazine be supplied to that group's membership, not tied to any lobbying activities, at a lower price? Olson anticipates this problem, arguing that often organizations enjoy a certain amount of monopolistic power, and can thus use rents to fund lobbying and similar activities. This response does not solve the problem, however, for it begs the question why groups would have monopolistic power with respect to the selective inducements they provide, a possibility that seems far-fetched in many cases.

22. Id. at 133.

23. For other criticisms of the "by-product theory," see Hardin, Collective Action, at 33–34.

24. See generally Schlozman & Tierney, Organized Interests in American Democracy; John P. Heinz et al., The Hollow Core: Private Interests in National Policy Making (1993).

25. See generally Russell Hardin, Collective Action, and in particular at 101–2.

26. See, for example, Olson, The Logic of Collective Action, at 159–65.

27. Hardin, Collective Action, at 90, 98.

28. Hardin, Collective Action, at 105.

29. Id. at 35.

30. For an illuminating exploration of this possibility, see R. Douglas Arnold, The Logic of Congressional Action (1990). For a similar analysis, see John Mark Hansen, Gaining Access: Congress and the Farm Lobby, 1919–1981 (1991). See also Steven P. Croley, Imperfect Information and the Electoral Connection, 47 Pol. Res. Q. 509 (1994).

31. See Hardin, Collective Action, at 107.

32. See, for example, Hardin, Collective Action, at 174–87. See also Ostrom, Governing the Commons. See generally, Lars Udehn, Twenty-five Years with The Logic of Collective Action, 36 Acta Sociologica 239 (1993); Eric Posner, The Regulation of Groups: The Influence of Legal and Nonlegal Sanctions on Collective

Action, 63 U. Chi. L. Rev. 133, 139–40 (1996). See also V. Kerry Smith, A Theoretical Analysis of the "Green Lobby," 79 Am. Pol. Sci. Rev. 133 (1985).

33. For representative treatments, see, for example, Robert Barro, The Control of Politicians: An Economic Model, 14 Public Choice 19 (1973); Joseph Kalt & Mark Zupan, The Apparent Ideological Behavior of Legislators: Testing for Principal-Agency Slack in Political Institutions, 33 J.L. & Econ. 103 (1990).

34. As Stigler puts it:

> If the representative could confidently await reelection whenever he voted against an economic policy that injured the society, he would assuredly do so. Unfortunately virtue does not always command so high a price. If the representative denies ten large industries their special subsidies of money or governmental power, they will dedicate themselves to the election of a more complaisant successor: the stakes are that important.

Stigler, The Theory of Economic Regulation, at 11. Richard Posner puts the point more gently: "Willingness to pay [for favorable regulation] is also important in the democratic . . . political system, since legislators are elected in campaigns in which the amount of money expended on behalf of a candidate exerts great influence on the outcome." Posner, Theories of Regulation, at 347.

35. See generally Jeffrey M. Berry, Lobbying for the People: The Political Behavior of Public Interest Groups 8–10 (1997); Hardin, Collective Action, at 101–8; Schlozman & Tierney, Organized Interests, at 30–34; Stephen Miller, Special Interest Groups in American Politics 113–33 (1983); Cass R. Sunstein, After the Rights Revolution: Reconceiving the Regulatory State 3 (1990); Terry M. Moe, Toward a Broader View of Interest Groups, 43 J. Pol. 531, 536 (1981); Cass R. Sunstein, Participation, Public Law, and Venue Reform, 49 U. Chi. L. Rev. 976, 987 (1982). On the difficulty the existence of such groups poses for the public choice theory, see, for example, Harold H. Bruff, Legislative Formality, Administrative Rationality, 63 Tex. L. Rev. 207, 244 (1984); Herbert Hovenkamp, Legislation, Well-Being, and Public Choice, 57 U. Chi. L. Rev. 63, 99–100 (1990); Edward L. Rubin, Beyond Public Choice: Comprehensive Rationality in the Writing and Reading of Statutes, 66 N.Y.U. L. Rev. 1, 12 (1991).

36. Many scholars see such groups as fairly representative of broad citizen interest. See, for example, Berry, Lobbying for the People, at 3; Miller, Special Interest Groups, at 118; Jeffrey M. Berry, Citizen Groups and the Changing Nature of Interest Group Politics, 528 Annals Am. Acad. Pol. & Soc. Sci. 30, 31 (1993). See also Lawrence S. Rothenberg, Linking Citizens to Government: Interest Group Politics at Common Cause 36–37 (1992).

37. Stigler, Can Regulatory Agencies Protect the Consumer? at 186–87. Similarly, Ralph Winter writes:

> Much has been made of the consumer's inability to affect his market destinies and his lack of product information. Yet surely these criticisms are even more cogent where government is involved. A product which does not satisfy consumers is far more likely to disappear than a government ruling. When the ICC prohibits new truckers from entering the market, consumers rarely know of the ruling—much less why it was made—and, of course, can do nothing to change it.

Ralph K. Winter, Jr., Economic Regulation vs. Competition: Ralph Nader and Creeping Capitalism, 82 Yale L.J. 890, 894 (1973).

38. Stigler, Can Regulatory Agencies Protect the Consumer? at 187.

39. See, for example, id. at 187, where Stigler writes: "[The consumer] is the victim without recourse of our political system which is inaccessible to groups that may be large but whose members as individuals have only small stakes in a controversy." Or see Richard Posner, The Federal Trade Commission, 37 U. Chi. L. Rev. 47, 82 (1969): "[I]n bidding for the favor of members of Congress, consumers are at a disadvantage in comparison with trade associations, labor unions, and other more familiar pressure groups. Consumers form too large, diffuse, and heterogeneous a group to organize effectively for the presentation of demands to their representatives. It is hardly surprising that so much of our economic legislation is protectionist in character" (citing Olson). See as well, Peltzman, General Theory of Regulation, at 212–13.

40. Arguably, they would have less, as business-oriented groups would better understand, and likely be more influenced by, collective action's logic. To the extent that ideological and moral motivations account for collective action, consumers and environmental groups should have an advantage over economic interests. To the extent that political entrepreneurship accounts for collective actions, the same should hold. Thus, the participation of broad-based groups in regulatory decisionmaking may be easier to explain than that of special interest groups. In this light, the existence of special interest groups rather than of public interest groups may be anomalous, notwithstanding that the public choice theory—by focusing on group size rather than the catalyst for group action—holds just the opposite.

41. Stigler, Free Riders and Collective Action, at 359. See also id. at 363.

42. Stigler, Free Riders and Collective Action, at 360.

43. See Stigler, Free Riders and Collective Action at 360–61. See as well Posner, Theories of Economic Regulation, at 345 ("[I]n the regulatory sphere, the fewer

the prospective beneficiaries of a regulation, the easier it will be for them to coordinate their efforts to obtain the regulation.").

44. Stigler, Free Riders and Collective Action, at 359–60.

45. See Stigler, Free Riders and Collective Action, at 360 & n.5 (noting that the small-numbers solution is the same as Olson's special-interest explanation).

46. Moreover, only in rather unusual circumstances would a group member contemplating contribution to a step good believe that her contribution is necessary to produce the good. Put differently, while Stigler is formally correct that, at least for some kinds of goods, the "probability that the collective action is undertaken" will be reduced by a member's decision not to contribute, in most empirical circumstances that probability is likely to be a very small one, and thus to have little influence on the member's decision.

47. Stigler, Free Riders and Collective Action, at 360.

48. Id.

49. At times, Stigler seems to recognize this, although most of his language suggests otherwise. See, for example, Stigler, Free Riders and Collective Action, at 360: "There is no critical number of individuals for which [the logic of collective action] fails—or holds."

50. Finally, even if in some specific set of empirical circumstances group size might be related to a group's ability to generate a collective good, one would need to know where the small-size effect would trigger collective action and where it would not. How small, in other words, does a small group have to be? Thus, Posner writes: "[T]he economic theory has not been refined to the point where it enables us to predict specific industries in which regulation will be found. That is because the theory does not tell us what (under various conditions) is the number of members of a coalition that maximizes the likelihood of regulation." Posner, Theories of Economic Regulation, at 347. Stigler might respond by saying that the small-size effect is sufficient to motivate collective action whenever groups are no larger than the size of existing trade associations. But trade associations are sometimes very big. So "small" turns out to be pretty big, and we should see group action for any group whose members do not exceed those of existing trade associations. Indeed, according to Stigler: "Many, many industries fulfill in good measure the small number condition." Stigler, Free Riders and Collective Action, at 362. In fact, Stigler further argues that the "small number solution has a wider scope than a literal count of numbers would suggest," id., once one considers that some group members may benefit disproportionately from the provision of the good. Those members may take it upon them to provide the good, seeing themselves "as members of a small number industry." Id.

Not surprisingly, given such qualifications, an empirical test calls into question Stigler's argument concerning group size and the effects of the presence of group members who would benefit more from the group good than other members. Regressing interest-group resources to characteristics of various industry groups' memberships, Stigler himself finds that "both staff and budget of the [interest group] are well related to the size of the covered industry, but not to concentration ratios, which our foregoing discussion would lead us to expect." Id. at 364. Furthermore: "There is, indeed, some hint of a negative correlation of [interest-group] resources and [membership] concentration ratios." Id. at 364–65.

51. See, for example, George J. Stigler, Supplementary Notes on Economic Theories of Regulation, in The Citizen and the State: Essays on Regulation 138 (1975); see also Posner, Theories of Economic Regulation, at 347; Posner, Taxation by Regulation, at 32.

52. On related questions, see, for example, Arthur T. Denzau & Michael C. Munger, Legislators and Interest Groups: How Unorganized Interests Get Represented, 80 Am. Pol. Sci. Rev. 89 (1986). The public choice theory sometimes seems to overlook the multiplying or leveraging effect of political action. Posner, for example, argues that "it is not clear why a cohesive group of customers would not be equally effective in exacting concessions from a private cartel" as they would influencing a regulator seeking to protect the cartel. See Posner, Theories of Economic Regulation, at 345 n.25. One answer is that the regulator has a vastly greater repertoire of commands and sanctions that can be used to shape the cartel's behavior. A consumer group is thus likely to enjoy greater gains from influencing regulators than from trying to buy off cartel firms. As Hardin explains:

> [W]hen the action a group undertakes is political, the benefits may enormously outweigh the costs, even when the benefits are discounted by the probability of failure. If environmentalists had to bribe industrialists not to pollute, as suggested in Coase's analysis, moral incentives would produce minuscule bribes and less effect. But they merely have to get Congress and an administrative agency to coerce industrialists into bearing the billions of dollars for cleaning up. . . . The small part of the population that contributes $2 million a year to Sierra Club political activity may well imagine that they seldom spend money so well.

Hardin, Collective Action, at 121.

53. Stigler, Free Riders and Collective Actions, at 362.

54. Id. at 362–63. See also Posner, Theories of Economic Regulation, at 346 (making asymmetry argument).

55. Posner fully recognizes this. See Posner, Theories of Economic Regulation, at 349. In the same vein, Tollison too writes: "A basic principle as well as a basic conundrum underlies the demand for legislation. The principle is that groups who can organize for less than one dollar in order to obtain one dollar of benefits from legislation will be the effective demanders of laws. The conundrum is that economists have little idea of how successful, cost-effective interest groups are formed. That is, how do groups overcome free rider problems and organize for collective action so as to be able to seek one dollar for less than one dollar? The plain truth is that economists know very little about the dynamics of group formation and action." Robert D. Tollison, Public Choice and Legislation, 74 Va. L. Rev. 339, 339 (1988).

56. See, for example, Stigler, Supplementary Notes on Economic Theories of Regulation, at 138; Posner, Theories of Economic Regulation, at 345.

57. For some of the seminal works, see, for example, Gary C. Jacobson, The Politics of Congressional Elections (3d ed. 1992); Morris P. Fiorina, The Case of the Vanishing Marginals: The Bureaucracy Did It, in Congress: Structure and Policy (McCubbins & Sullivan eds., 1987); Gary C. Jacobson, The Effects of Campaign Spending in Congressional Elections, 72 Am. Pol. Sci. Rev. 469 (1978); Gary C. Jacobson, The Effects of Campaign Spending in House Elections: New Evidence for Old Arguments, 34 Am. J. Pol. Sci. 334 (1990); David R. Mayhew, Congressional Elections: The Case of the Vanishing Marginals, 6 Polity 295, 297–304 (1974).

58. See, for example, Steven P. Croley, Imperfect Information and the Electoral Connection, 47 Pol. Res. Q. 509, 514–18 (1994).

59. See, for example, Terry Moe, An Assessment of the Positive Theory of "Congressional Dominance," 12 Leg. Stud. Q. 475 (1987); John T. Woolley, Conflict Among Regulators and the Hypothesis of Congressional Dominance, 55 J. Pol. 92 (1993).

60. See generally Harold Lasswell & Abraham Kaplan, Power and Society (1950). Moreover, as Steven Kelman observes, it is not clear that those seeking power are likely to be overrepresented among politicians, as compared with careers in finance, journalism, and industry. See Steven Kelman, "Public Choice" and Public Spirit, 87 Pub. Int. 80, 91 (1987). For an excellent recent treatment of the subtleties surrounding legislator behavior, which explores the extent to which legislators participate in lawmaking at all, see generally Richard L. Hall, Participation in Congress (1996).

61. See, for example, Gary C. Jacobson, The Effects of Campaign Spending in Congressional Elections, 72 Am. Pol. Sci. Rev. 469 (1978); Gary C. Jacobson,

The Effects of Campaign Spending in House Elections: New Evidence for Old Arguments, 34 Am. J. Pol. Sci. 334 (1990).

62. See generally Keith T. Poole & Howard Rosenthal, Congress: A Political-Economic History of Roll Call Voting (1997); Joseph P. Kalt & Mark A. Zupan, The Apparent Ideological Behavior of Legislators: Testing for Principal-Agent Slack in Political Institutions, 33 J.L. & Econ. 103 (1990); James B. Kau & Paul H. Rubin, Self-Interest, Ideology, and Logrolling in Congressional Voting, 22 J.L. & Econ. 365 (1979); Keith T. Poole & Howard Rosenthal, A Spatial Model for Legislative Roll Call Analysis, 79 Am. J. Pol. Sci. 357 (1985).

63. What is more, this richer image of legislative behavior finds support in the logic of the public choice theory itself. After all, the public choice theory repeatedly observes that the state is a regulation monopolist. Given that the state has a monopoly on regulation, it will behave like a monopolist; economic principles govern political behavior. Taking this premise seriously implies that the state will supply groups with the regulations they demand, but will charge an excessive price for them. More specifically, legislators will demand more political resources than what a "competitive" return would bring. But this means in turn that legislators will have extra resources above those minimally necessary to secure their positions, resources they can expend pursuing their independent goals, even goals that may conflict with the goals of those who demand regulation. Monopolistic pricing, in other words, should give legislators room to pursue goals other than reelection. With their monopolistic rents, they may seek to advance the interests of political underdogs, general interests, or any other goal. In this light too, then, the public choice theory's postulates generate no crisp expectations about legislator behavior.

64. See generally R. Douglas Arnold, The Logic of Congressional Action (1990).

65. See generally Kathleen Bawn, Political Control Versus Expertise: Congressional Choices About Administrative Procedures, 89 Am. Pol. Sci. Rev. 62 (1995).

66. See, for example, Susan Rose-Ackerman, Rethinking the Progressive Agenda: The Reform of the American Regulatory State 36–37 (1992); Cass Sunstein, After the Rights Revolution: Reconceiving the Regulatory State 212–14 (1975); Mathew D. McCubbins et al., Positive and Normative Models of Procedural Rights: An Integrative Approach to Administrative Procedures, 6 J.L. Econ. & Org. 307, 315–18 (1990).

67. See, for example, Posner, Theories of Economic Regulation, at 338.

68. For public choice reincarnations of the transmission belt model, see, for example, Posner, Theories of Regulation, at 350. Although the transmission belt model itself was never developed as much as posited, recent work by Mathew McCubbins, Roger Noll, and Barry Weingast can be understood as a sophisticated reincarnation of that old model.

69. See Posner, Theories of Economic Regulation, at 339 & n.12.

70. For example, compare Matthew D. McCubbins, Roger G. Noll, and Barry R. Weingast, Administrative Procedures as Instruments of Political Control, 3 J.L. Econ. & Org. 243 (1987), with Jerry L. Mashaw, Prodelegation: Why Administrators Should Make Political Decisions, 1 J.L. Econ. & Org. 81 (1985).

71. 5 U.S.C. §§551 et seq.

CHAPTER FOUR
ALTERNATIVE VISIONS OF REGULATORY GOVERNMENT

1. See generally Gary S. Becker, A Theory of Competition Among Pressure Groups for Political Influence, 98 Q. J. Econ. 371 (1983).

2. William C. Mitchell & Michael C. Munger, Economic Models of Interest Groups: An Introductory Survey, 35 Am. J. Pol. Sci. 512, 531–32. See also Becker, Competition Among Pressure Groups, at 371–72 (citing Bentley and Truman).

3. Becker's conclusions depend on several simplifying assumptions, however, including that groups are interested only in their members' incomes, that those members will somehow overcome collective-action problems in response to policies that threaten their incomes, and that public decisionmakers have no independent agenda of their own but rather respond mechanically to the demands of competing groups. Such assumptions lead Mitchell and Munger to conclude:

> Unless some stronger argument in favor of Becker's position [that interest groups maximize members' incomes and that they face no internal organizational inefficiencies] can be marshaled, it may be destined for the same status as Coase's theorem in price theory: more useful as a benchmark under extreme behavioral sand informational assumptions than as a description of reality.

Id. at 534.

4. See, for example, William N. Eskridge, Jr., Politics Without Romance: Implication of Public Choice Theory for Statutory Interpretation, 74 Va. L. Rev. 275, 298–99, 303–9 (1988); Jonathan Macey, Promoting Public-Regarding Legislation Through Statutory Interpretation, 86 Colum. L. Rev. 223, 228, 252; Jerry Mashaw, Public Law, at 874–75; John S. Wiley, Jr., A Capture Theory of Antitrust Federalism, 99 Harv. L. Rev. 713, 743–44 (1986).

5. See Stewart, American Administrative Law, at 1723–47 (explaining that rise of interest-representation model led to calls for more permissive standing doctrines).

6. Jack M. Beerman, Interest Group Politics and Judicial Behavior: Macey's Public Choice, 67 Notre Dame L. Rev. 183, 189 (1991).

7. Edward L. Rubin, Beyond Public Choice: Comprehensive Rationality in the Writing and Reading of Statutes, 66 N.Y.U. L. Rev. 1, 12 (1991).

8. See, for example, Harold H. Bruff, Legislative Formality, Administrative Rationality, 63 Tex. L. Rev. 207, 244 (1984); Herbert Hovenkamp, Legislation, Well-Being, and Public Choice, 57 U. Chi. L. Rev. 63, 102–3 (1990); Daniel Farber & Philip Frickey, The Jurisprudence of Public Choice, 65 Tex. L. Rev. 873, 892 (1987).

9. As Hardin points out:

> Anyone trying to explain political activity may then be led to think that morality is relatively important as compared with self-interest. But . . . this conclusion about the role of moral choice in the politics of the mass may be based on undue consideration of activity, when the more pervasive phenomenon may be explainable inactivity.

Hardin, Collective Action, at 124. See also id. at 11.

10. See William P. Browne, Organized Interests and Their Issue Niches: A Search for Pluralism in a Policy Domain, 52 J. Pol. 477 (1990).

11. On the possible meanings of the concept, see generally Virginia Held, The Public Interest and Individual Interests (1970); Glendon Schubert, The Public Interest (1960); Clarke E. Cochran, Political Science and "The Public Interest," 36 J. Pol. 327 (1974); Norton Long, Conceptual Notes on the Public Interest for Public Administration and Policy Analysts, 22 Admin. & Soc. 170 (1990); Barry M. Mitnick, A Typology of Conceptions of the Public Interest, 8 Admin. & Soc. 5 (1976). According to contemporary public interest theorists themselves, advancing "the public interest" is tantamount to advancing social welfare, that is, ameliorating the consequences of market failures. See, for example, Levine & Forrence, Regulatory Capture, Public Interest, at 168, where they write: "[W]e can see regulation as the necessary exercise of collective power through government in order to cure 'market failures,' to protect the public from such evils as monopoly behavior, 'destructive' competition, the abuse of private economic power, or the effects of externalities. Something like this account, explicitly or implicitly, underpins virtually all public-interest accounts of regulation."

12. Levine & Forrence, Regulatory Capture, Public Interest, at 176.

13. Id. at 176–77, 179.

14. Id. at 186.

15. Id. at 194 (emphasis added).

16. Id.

17. Id. at 194–95.

18. See Michael E. Levine, Revisionism Revised? Airline Deregulation and the Public Interest, 44 L. & Contemp. Probs. 179, 189–94 (1981); Levine & Forrence, Regulatory Capture, Public Interest, at 187, 192, 195.

19. 49 U.S.C. §1551.

20. See generally Anthony E. Brown, The Politics of Airline Deregulation (1987).

21. Levine, Airline Regulation and the Public Interest, at 191. See also Martha Derthick & Paul J. Quirk, The Politics of Deregulation 16 (1985), noting that deregulation of airlines, as well as of trucking and telecommunications, is hard to explain according to conventional accounts of regulation given that "the policy shift toward deregulation was unambiguous, and at least at the outset the dominant industry interests were overwhelmingly opposed to this shift."

22. See, for example, Levine, Airline Deregulation and the Public Interest, at 180; Levine & Forrence, Regulatory Capture, Public Interest, at 192.

23. Levine, Airline Deregulation and the Public Interest, at 180. As Derthick & Quirk recount, the deregulation of trucking and telecommunications presented "corporate and union opposition to reform as formidable as any that American society has to offer," AT&T and the Teamsters, Derthick & Quirk, The Politics of Deregulation, at 17.

24. Levine, Airline Deregulation and the Public Interest, at 195.

25. Representative accounts include Cass R. Sunstein, After the Rights Revolution, Reconceiving the Regulatory State 12 (1990); Robert B. Reich, Public Administration and Public Deliberation: An Interpretive Essay, 94 Yale L.J. 1617 (1985); Mark Seidenfeld, A Civic Republican Justification for the Bureaucratic State, 105 Harv. L. Rev. 1511 (1992); Ian Ayres & John Braithwaite, Responsive Regulation: Transcending the Deregulation Debate 16–18, 54–100 (1992). Others have used different terms to label this constellation of theories. For example, Steven Kelman uses the term "cooperationalist" to refer largely to what others mean by "republican" or "civic republican," Steven Kelman, Adversary and Cooperationalist Institutions for Conflict Resolution in Public Policymaking, 11 J. Pol. Anal. & Mgmt. 178 (1992), while Gerald Frug uses the term "administrative democracy," Gerald Frug, Administrative Democracy, in Handbook of Regulation and Administrative Law (1994), and Ayres and Braithwaite sometimes use the term "regulatory communitarianism" to capture the same basic image, Ayres & Braithwaite, at 92.

26. See, for example, Seidenfeld, A Civic Republican Justification, at 1514; Sunstein, Reconceiving the Regulatory State, at 12; Reich, Public Deliberation, at 1625.

27. On the theory's descriptive component, see, for example, Steven Kelman, "Public Choice" and Public Spirit, 87 Pub. Int. 80, 81 (1987); Reich, Public Deliberation, at 1625.

28. See, for example, Reich, Public Deliberation, at 1637; Sunstein, Four Lessons, at 282. Not that the civic republican theory idealizes administrators, however. It acknowledges that agencies may be unduly influenced by some voices.

29. Seidenfield, A Civic Republican Justification, at 1554. Seidenfeld explains:

> Administrative agencies—the so-called fourth branch of government—may be the only institutions capable of fulfilling the civic republican ideal of deliberative decisionmaking. . . . Administrative agencies . . . fall between the extremes of the politically over-responsive Congress and the over-insulated courts. Agencies are therefore prime candidates to institute a civic republican model of policymaking.

Id. at 1541–42.

30. See Sunstein, Four Lessons, at 282–84; Reich, Public Deliberation, at 1638–39. In a similar vein, see as well Cass R. Sunstein, Interest Groups in American Law, 38 Stan. L. Rev. 29, 59–68 (1985).

31. See Sunstein, Four Lessons, at 293–95.

32. See Kelman, Adversary and Cooperationalist Institutions for Conflict Resolution in Public Policymaking, 11 J. Pol. Anal. & Mgmt. 178, 200–203 (1992), at 200–203.

33. Kelman, Adversary and Cooperationalist Institutions for Conflict Resolution in Public Policymaking, 11 J. Pol. Anal. & Mgmt. 178, 200–203 (1992), at 199.

34. Id. at 180, 195.

35. See Reich, Public Deliberation, at 1635–40; Frug, Administrative Democracy, at 529–31.

36. See, for example, Sunstein, Reconceiving the Regulatory State, at 12.

37. In Ayres and Braithwaite's formulation, for example:

> Although liberal theory finds special appeal in market institutions, republican theory finds special appeal in socializing institutions. Socializing institutions seek civic virtue by changing the deliberative habits of citizens. Our analysis of a republican tripartite regulatory culture is an example of institutional design focused on a socializing institution. The regulatory culture advocated seeks to modify the deliberative habits and behavioral dispositions of actors, not just to tinker with payoffs of actors whose psychology is untouched.

Ayres & Braithwaite, Responsive Regulation, at 93.

38. Kelman, Public Choice, at 86 (original emphasis).

39. Id.

40. See Reich, Public Deliberation, at 1632–37; Frug, Administrative Democracy, at 529–30.

41. Reich, Public Deliberation, at 1632.

42. Id. at 1634 (quoting a citizen of Tacoma: "These issues are very complex and the public is not sophisticated enough to make these decisions. This is not to say that EPA doesn't have an obligation to inform the public, but information is one thing—defaulting its legal mandate is another"); id. at n.73 (quoting another Tacoma citizen: "At this point in time is Asarco in violation of any clear requirements? Why is EPA spending taxpayers' money for this process if Asarco is not violating any laws?"); id. (explaining agency's efforts were met with hostility in the local press).

43. Id. at 1634.

44. See Bruce A. Ackerman & William T. Hassler, Clean Coal/Dirty Air (1981).

45. See, for example, William Funk, When Smoke Gets in Your Eyes: Regulatory Negotiation and the Public Interest—EPA's Woodstove Standards, 18 Envt'l. L. 55 (1987).

46. As Wesley Magat, Alan Krupnick, and Winston Harrington, for example, explain:

> Most of the literature on regulation addresses what Fiorina labels "regulatory origin," as opposed to the "regulatory process." Theories of regulatory origin attempt to explain why agencies make specific decisions such as to regulate (or deregulate) some industries or economic activities but not others or to promulgate and enforce specific regulations that harm some groups while benefitting others. . . . In contrast, theories of the regulatory process seek to explain how regulatory agencies make decisions, in other words, what factors determine or explain their decisions.

Wesley A. Magat, Alan J. Krupnick, & Winston Harrington, Rules in the Making: A Statistical Analysis of Regulatory Agency Behavior 47–48 (1986) (citation omitted). So, too, Levine & Forrence observe that many theories of regulation "do not explicitly consider the relationships among actors in the governmental process nor the mechanisms by which the regulators are made to conform to the desires of organized subgroups." Levine & Forrence, Regulatory Capture, at 170. See also Mathew D. McCubbins, Roger G. Noll, & Barry R. Weingast, Administrative Procedures as Instruments of Political Control, 3 J.L. Econ. & Org. 243, 245 (1987). There are a few partial exceptions to this generalization, such as Mathew D. McCubbins, The Legislative Design of Regulatory Structure, 29 Am. J.

Pol. Sci. 165 (1985); McNollgast, Administrative Procedures; McNollgast, Structure and Process, Politics and Policy: Administrative Arrangements and the Political Control of Agencies, 75 Va. L. Rev. 431 (1989); McNollgast, Slack, Public Interest, and Structure-Induced Policy, 6 J.L., Econ & Org. 307 (1990).

47. As John Ferejohn & Charles Shipan write: "[W]e see agency policy-making as the ordinary or routine decision-making practice throughout modern government. Relatively few governmental decisions are directly mandated by legislative acts. For the most part, statutes serve as constraints on what bureaucrats can do rather than as detailed directives. . . . [I]t seems likely that a model of administrative action that puts agency actions at the front is more relevant for explaining government action most of the time." John Ferejohn & Charles Shipan, Congressional Influence on Bureaucracy, 6 J.L. Econ. & Org. 1, 3 (1990).

48. See, for example, Keith Krehbiel, Information and Legislative Organization (1991).

49. See, for example, Terry M. Moe, The Politics of Bureaucratic Structure, in Can the Government Govern? 268 (John E. Chubb & Paul E. Peterson eds., 1991); Terry M. Moe, The New Economics of Organization, 28 Amer. J. Pol. Sci. 739 (1984).

50. See, for example, Herbert A. Simon, Administrative Behavior, A Study of Decision-Making Processes in Administrative Organization (3rd ed. 1976).

CHAPTER FIVE
OPENING THE BLACK BOX: REGULATORY
DECISIONMAKING IN LEGAL CONTEXT

1. 5 U.S.C. §553.

2. 5 U.S.C. §551(4).

3. See, for example, United States v. Florida East Coast Ry. Co., 410 U.S. 224 (1973) (establishing that mere appearance of words "hearing" and "record" in agency's statute does not necessarily trigger formal rulemaking under §§553(c), 556–57, nor are those exact words required to trigger same).

4. 5 U.S.C. §553(c).

5. 5 U.S.C. §§556–57.

6. 5 U.S.C. §556(d).

7. Illustrative cases include, among many others, U.S. v. Nova Scotia Food Products Corp., 568 F.2d 240 (2d Cir. 1977); Portland Cement Ass'n v. Ruckelshaus, 486 F.2d 375 (D.C. Cir. 1973), cert. den., 417 U.S. 921 (1974).

8. See, for example, Kooritzky v. Reich, 17 F.3d 1509 (D.C. Cir. 1994); American Medical Ass'n v. U.S., 887 F.2d 760 (7th Cir. 1989); NRDC v. Thomas, 838

F.2d 1224, 1242 (D.C. Cir. 1988); Weyerhauser Co. v. Costle, 590 F.2d 1011 (D.C. Cir. 1978).

9. 15 U.S.C. §§2601–29.

10. 42 U.S.C. §§4321–47.

11. 5 U.S.C. §§601–12.

12. 44 U.S.C. §§3501–2.

13. 5 U.S.C. §§581 et seq.

14. William J. Clinton, White House Memorandum for Heads of Departments and Agencies, Subject: Regulatory Reinvention Initiative 3 (March 4, 1995). See also Vice President Al Gore, National Performance Review Accompanying Report: "Improving Regulatory Systems" 30 (1993) (promoting greater agency use of "consensus-based rulemaking").

15. Enthusiasm for negotiated rulemaking is best exemplified by Philip Harter, Negotiating Regulations: A Cure for Malaise, 71 Geo. L.J. 1 (1982).

16. For example, compare Kenneth Culp Davis, Administrative Law Treatise, §6.15, at 283 (Supp. 1970) (describing rulemaking as "one of the greatest inventions of modern government"), with Thomas O. McGarity, Some Thoughts on "Deossifying" The Rulemaking Process, 41 Duke L.J. 1385 (1992).

17. 5 U.S.C. §§554, 556–57.

18. 5 U.S.C. §554(d).

19. 5 U.S.C. §551(6).

20. 5 U.S.C. §554(a).

21. Attorney General's Comm. on Administrative Procedure, Final Report 35 (1941).

22. For a helpful overview that considers particular types of informal orders, see, for example, Robert A. Anthony, Interpretive Rules, Policy Statements, Guidances, Manuals, and the Like—Should Federal Agencies Use Them to Bind the Public? 41 Duke L.J. 1311 (1992); Gardner, The Procedures by Which Informal Action is Taken, 24 Admin. L. Rev. 155 (1972); Paul R. Verkuil, A Study of Informal Adjudication Procedures, 43 U. Chi. L. Rev. 739 (1976); Peter L. Strauss, The Rulemaking Continuum, 41 Duke L.J. 1463 (1992).

23. 401 U.S. 402 (1971).

24. 5 U.S.C. §553(b)(3)(A).

25. See generally 5 U.S.C. §553.

26. See generally Elizabeth M. Magill, Agency Choice of Policymaking Form, 71 U. Chi. L. Rev. 1383 (2004).

27. See, for example, Vermont Yankee Nuclear Power Corp. v. Natural Resources Defense Council, Inc., 435 U.S. 519 (1978).

28. 42 U.S.C. §§4321–47.

29. 5 U.S.C. §552.

30. Federal Records Act, 44 U.S.C. §1501; Presidential Records Act, 44 U.S.C. §2204.

31. 5 U.S.C. §552(b).

32. 5 U.S.C. §552(b).

33. 5 U.S.C. App. §§1 et seq.

34. On the regulatory policy significance of advisory-committee decisions, see Sheila Jasanoff, The Fifth Branch: Science Advisers as Policymakers (1990). See as well Kay Lehman Schlozman & John T. Tierney, Organized Interests and American Democracy 334 (1986), noting many observers' view "that advisory committees have much more than a consultative role—that they play an important role in policy initiation and determination" (citations omitted), and Steven Croley & William Funk, The Federal Advisory Committee Act And Good Government, 14 Yale J. on Reg. 451 (1997).

35. 5 U.S.C. App. §§5, 7, 9, 14.

36. See generally Steven Croley, Practical Guidance on the Applicability of the Federal Advisory Committee Act, 10 Admin. L.J. 111 (1996).

37. See, for just one example, Alfred A. Marcus, Promise and Performance: Choosing and Implementing an Environmental Policy (1980).

38. See, for example, Posner, The Federal Trade Commission, at 82–87 (suggesting that career motivations of administrators may compromise the integrity of their regulatory decisions). For background and complications, see, for example, Edna Earle Vass Johnson, "Agency Capture": The "Revolving Door" Between Regulated Industries and Their Regulating Agencies, 18 U. Rich. L. Rev. 95 (1983), and Beth Nolan, Public Interest, Private Income: Conflicts and Control Limits on the Outside Income of Government Officials, 87 Nw. U. L. Rev. 57 (1992).

39. For example, see Steven Kelman, Occupational Safety and Health Administration, in The Politics of Regulation 236, 250 (James Q. Wilson ed., 1980) (finding that the best explanation of OSHA's actions was the "pro-protection values of agency officials, derived from the ideology of the safety and health professional and the organizational mission of OSHA").

40. Here again the argument finds empirical support. See William T. Gormley, A Test of the Revolving Door Hypothesis at the FCC, 23 Am. J. Pol. Sci. 665, 676 (1979) (finding that political party affiliation is more predictive of agency decisionmaking than is previous employment with a regulated firm).

41. See Paul J. Quirk, Industry Influence in Federal Regulatory Agencies 176–77 (1981).

42. See Ronald N. Johnson & Gary D. Libecap, Agency Growth, Salaries and the Protected Bureaucrat, 27 Econ. Inquiry 431, 434 (1989).

43. See generally the Lobbying Disclosure Act, 2 U.S.C. §1601, and the Ethics in Government Act, 5 U.S.C. App. §10.

44. See, for example, Steven Croley, White House Review of Agency Rulemaking: An Empirical Investigation, 708 U. Chi. L. Rev. 821 (2003); Erik D. Olson, The Quiet Shift of Power: Office of Management & Budget Supervision of Environmental Protection Agency Rulemaking Under Executive Order 12,291, 4 Va. J. Nat. Resources L. 1 (1984); Richard H. Pildes & Cass R. Sunstein, Reinventing the Regulatory State, 62 U. Chi. L. Rev. 1 (1995).

45. Most importantly, Exec. Order No. 12,866, 58 Fed. Reg. 51735 (September 30, 1993); Exec. Order No. 12,498, 50 Fed. Reg. 1036 (January 4, 1985); Exec. Order No. 12,291, 46 Fed. Reg. 13, 193 (February 17, 1981).

46. For an explanation, see, for example, Cynthia R. Farina, The Consent of the Governed: Against Simple Rules for a Complex World, 72 Chi.-Kent L. Rev. 987 (1997).

47. See generally Elena Kagan, Presidential Administration, 114 Harv. L. Rev. 2245 (2001).

48. 5 U.S.C. §706(2)(A)–(D).

49. See, for example, Citizens to Preserve Overton Park, Inc. v. Volpe, 401 U.S. 402 (1971).

50. See, for example, Motor Vehicle Manufacturers Ass'n. v. State Farm Mut. Automobile Ins. Co., 463 U.S. 29 (1983).

51. For an illustration, see International Ladies' Garment Workers' Union v. Donovan, 722 F.2d 795 (D.C. Cir. 1983).

52. See, for example, Susan Rose-Ackerman, Rethinking the Progressive Agenda, The Reform of the Regulatory State 36 (1992); William N. Eskridge, Jr., Politics Without Romance: Implications of Public Choice Theory for Statutory Interpretation, 74 Va. L. Rev. 275, 309–14 (1988); Jonathan R. Macey, Promoting Public-Regarding Legislation Through Statutory Interpretation: An Interest Group Model, 86 Colum. L. Rev. 223, 227 (1986); Jerry L. Mashaw, Constitutional Deregulation: Notes Toward a Public, Public Law, 54 Tul. L. Rev. 849, 874–75 (1980); Cass R. Sunstein, Interest Groups in American Public Law, 38 Stan. L. Rev. 29, 74 (1985); Cass R. Sunstein, Interpreting Statutes in the Regulatory State, 103 Harv. L. Rev. 405, 462–502 (1989); Cass R. Sunstein, Naked Preferences and the Constitution, 84 Colum. L. Rev. 1689, 1695–97 (1984); and John Shepard Wiley, Jr., A Capture Theory of Antitrust Federalism, 99 Harv. L. Rev. 713, 739–88 (1986).

CHAPTER SIX
REGULATORY GOVERNMENT AS ADMINISTRATIVE GOVERNMENT

1. See generally Steve P. Croley & M. Elizabeth Magill, A Guide to Federal Agency Activity (forthcoming).

2. The numbers here and in the text that follows are based on data supplied to the author by the Regulatory Information Services Center (RISC) of the U.S. General Services Administration (GSA). A more detailed quantification of rulemaking and other agency activities is found in Croley & Magill, A Guide to Agency Activity.

3. 5 U.S.C. §553(a)(2).

4. Id.

5. 5 U.S.C. §553(b)(3)(A) & §553(d)(2).

6. 5 U.S.C. §552(a)(1)(D).

7. These numbers too are based on data supplied to the author by the RISC. See generally Croley & Magill, A Guide to Agency Activity.

8. Data supplied by RISC.

9. See 5 U.S.C. §552(a).

10. 5 U.S.C. §§801 et seq.

11. 5 U.S.C. §801.

12. See www.gao.gov/fedrules.

13. 5 U.S.C. §801.

14. In fact, the GAO makes publically available its opinions on whether an agency document satisfies the definition of a "rule" for CRA purposes, which the GAO is frequently prompted to provide at the request of members of Congress frustrated by an agency's determination that its work-product is not a rule. See www.gao.gov/fedrules.

15. 5 U.S.C. §551(4).

16. 5 U.S.C. §804(3).

17. The GAO's database is searchable at www.gao.gov/fedrules.html.

18. The OIRA's database is available at www.whitehouse.gov/omb.library/OMBRCYTD-2004.html.

19. Executive Order 12866, codified at 58 Fed. Reg., October 4, 1993.

20. These rankings too are based on data supplied to the author by the RISC.

21. The figures here are derived from manual counts of formal adjudication, based on agency-specific data contained in annual agency reports. More detailed information is presented in Croley & Magill, A Guide to Agency Activity.

22. 5 U.S.C. §§554, 556–57.

23. See John H. Frye III, Survey of Non-ALJ Hearing Programs in the Federal Government, 44 Admin. L. Rev. 261 (1992); Raymond Limon, Acting Deputy Assistant Director, Office of Administrative Law Judges, The Federal Administra-

tive Judiciary Then and Now—A Decade of Change 1992–2002 (2002). The difference between Frye's and Limon's numbers is attributable to the creation by Congress of new cases to be adjudicated informally. See generally Michael Asimow, The Spreading Umbrella: Extending the APA's Adjudication Provisions to All Evidentiary Hearings Required By Statute, 56 Admin. L. Rev. 1003 (2005).

24. See Limon, A Decade of Change, at appendix C.

25. See, for example, Robert A. Anthony, Interpretive Rules, Policy Statements, Guidances, Manuals, and the Like—Should Federal Agencies Use Them to Bind the Public?, 41 Duke L.J. 1311 (1992), and the Report by The Administrative Conference of the United States, Rep. 92-2, 1 C.F.R. §305.92-2 (1992).

26. House Rep. 106 1009, Committee on Government Reform, together with Minority and Additional Views, Non-Binding Legal Effect of Agency Guidance Documents, 106th Cong., 2d Sess. (October 26, 2000).

27. Id. at 1–2, 8–9.

28. See Erica Seuiguer & John Smith, Perception and Process at the Food and Drug Administration: Obligations and Trade-Offs in Rules and Guidances, 60 Food & Drug L.J. 17 (2005) (calculating slightly more than twice as many guidances as rules by the FDA during 2001–3).

29. See, for example, General Electric Co. v. EPA, 290 F.3d 377 (D.C. Cir. 2002); Appalachian Power Co. v. EPA, 208 F.3d 1015 (D.C. Cir. 2000); Chamber of Commerce v. Dept. of Labor, 174 F.3d 206 (D.C. Cir. 1999).

30. Office of Management and Budget, Proposed Bulletin for Good Guidance Practices (November 23, 2005).

31. The numbers here and in the text that follows are based on data from the Executive Office of United States Attorneys and from the Administrative Office of the U.S. Courts. Agency litigation data are presented in more detail in Croley & Magill, A Guide to Agency Activity.

32. These statistics too come from the Administrative Office of the U.S. Courts, Federal Court Management Statistics, available at www.uscourts.gov/.

33. Id.

34. Id.

35. U.S. Office of Personnel Management, Federal Civilian Workforce Statistics, available at www.opm.gov/feddata/html/2005.

36. Id.

37. Id.

38. The counts in parentheses here come from the Congressional Record Daily Digest, Resumes of Congressional Activity, and the U.S. Senate web page, prepared by Senate Daily Digest, Office of the Secretary of the Senate, available at www.senate.gov.

39. This number too comes from the Congressional Record Daily Digest, Resumes of Congressional Activity, and, separately and consistently, from the U.S. Senate web page, prepared by Senate Daily Digest, Office of the Secretary of the Senate.

CHAPTER SEVEN
PARTICIPATION IN ADMINISTRATIVE DECISIONMAKING

1. 5 U.S.C. 553(c) (emphasis added).

2. 5 U.S.C. 553(e).

3. As the court in National Petroleum Refiners' Ass'n v. FTC, 482 F.2d 672, at 683 (D.C. Cir. 1973) observed: "Utilizing rule-making procedures opens up the process of agency policy innovation to a broad range of criticism, advice and data." See generally Jeffrey S. Lubbers, A Guide to Federal Agency Rulemaking 155 (3d ed. 1998).

4. 5 U.S.C. 557(c)(1)–(3).

5. 5 U.S.C. 556(d).

6. For example, see Barry B. Boyer, Funding Public Participation in Agency Proceedings: The Federal Trade Commission Experience, 70 Geo. L.J. 51 (1981); Susan B. Flohr, Comment, Funding Public Participation in Agency Proceedings, 27 Am. U. L. Rev. 981 (1978). The Magnuson-Moss Act specifically authorized the FTC to "provide compensation for reasonable attorneys fees, expert witness fees, and other costs of participating" in its adjudications, for a time. 15 U.S.C. § 557a(h)(1) (repealed 1994).

7. See, for example, Mark Green & Ralph Nader, Economic Regulation vs. Competition: Uncle Sam the Monopoly Man, 82 Yale L.J. 871 (1973).

8. See, for example, Stephen Miller, Special Interest Groups in American Politics, 113–18 (1983).

9. Id. Gardner explicitly relied on Olson when explaining the need for Common Cause.

10. The label "public interest group" suggests that a group so labeled is entitled to some special consideration or deference. Consequently, many interest groups characterize themselves as public interest groups, or at least claim that their goals advance the public interest, which raises the question how to distinguish "public" interest groups from selfish, "special" interest groups. Although the distinction is sometimes a difficult one, political scientists have long made it. For example, in *The Semisovereign People*, Schattschneider wrote:

> Is it possible to distinguish between the "interests" of the members of the National Association of Manufacturers and the members of the American League to Abolish Capital Punishment? The facts in the two cases are not

identical. First, *the members of the ALACP obviously do not expect to be hanged*. The membership of the ALACP is not restricted to persons under indictment for murder or in jeopardy of the extreme penalty. *Anybody* can join ALACP. Its members oppose capital punishments although they are not personally likely to benefit by the policy they advocate. The inference is therefore that the interest of the ALACP is not adverse, exclusive or special. It is not like the interest of the Petroleum Institute in depletion allowances.

Schattschneider, The Semisovereign People, at 26 (original emphases). Schattschneider is surely right that the interests represented by the ALACP are qualitatively different from the interests represented by the Petroleum Institute. The difficult question is how in principle to separate them. As Jeffrey Berry persuasively argues, the fact that the ALACP's members will not directly benefit from the policy they advocate should not be dispositive: If death-row inmates were to join the ALACP, Berry argues, it would be wrong to conclude that their membership would divest the ALACP of its status as a public interest group. Building on Schattschneider's distinction, Berry defines public interest groups as "groups that seek some collective good, the achievement of which will not selectively and materially benefit the membership or activists of the organization." Berry, Lobbying for the People, at 7. Others have defined public interest groups similarly.

But this alternative definition may be too broad, depending on just what counts as a "benefit" and just what counts as "some collective good." After all, a group like the Petroleum Institute might reasonably claim that it seeks a common good that will not benefit its membership selectively. (The public at large benefits from a healthy oil industry, etc.) Again, interest groups routinely frame their goals as furthering the public interest, contending precisely that their goals will not selectively benefit their members. To distinguish public interest groups from other interest groups who claim that their goals will benefit others outside of their membership, then, it is necessary to refine Berry's definition. If the material benefits that a group's members enjoy as a result of their participation can fully account for that participation, then that group's claims that others also benefit are suspect. Group members may be in it only for themselves. Only when benefits flowing to group members cannot fully account for their continued participation can claims about others' interests be taken seriously. Thus, a "public interest group" may be defined as a group (1) in which membership is voluntary, (2) that seeks some collective good the benefits of which extend to individuals outside of its membership, (3) where the material benefits accruing to its membership cannot explain the existence and maintenance of the group. Whether such groups represent broad interests well or accurately is a separate question.

11. See, for example, Stewart, American Administrative Law, at 1763–64; J. Berry, Lobbying for the People 3 (1977); Jeffrey M. Berry, Citizen Groups and the Changing Nature of Interest Group Politics (1993); Cass R. Sunstein, Participation, Public Law, and Venue Reform, 49 U. Chi. L. Rev. 976, 987; Jack L. Walker, The Origins and Maintenance of Interest Groups in American, 77 Am. Pol. Sci. Rev. 390, 397–400 (1983); Allan J. Cigler & Burdett A. Loomis, Interest Group Politics, chap. 1 (2d ed. 1986); David Vogel, Fluctuating Fortunes: The Political Power of Business in America 112 (1989).

12. Staff of Senate Committee on Governmental Affairs, 95th Cong., 1st Sess., Study on Federal Regulation, Vol. 3: Public Participation in Regulatory Agency Proceedings (1977).

13. Id. at 13.

14. Id.

15. Id. at 14.

16. Id. at 14–15.

17. Id.

18. Cary Coglianese, Challenging the Rules: Litigation and Bargaining in the Administrative Process (1995).

19. Scott R. Furlong, Interest Group Influence on Regulatory Policy, Ph.D. diss., School of Public Affairs, American University (1992). See also his interesting follow-up work, Scott R. Furlong, Interest Group Influence on Rulemaking, 29 Admin. & Soc. 325 (1997).

20. Id. at 131.

21. Id. at 183 & table 28.

22. Jason Webb Yackee & Susan Webb Yackee, A Bias Toward Business? Assessing Participant Influence in the Notice and Comment Rulemaking Process (forthcoming in J. of Politics).

23. Susan Webb Yackee, Juggling Preferences: Assessing Inter-Institutional Attention to and Influence on Government Regulations (forthcoming in British J. In. of Pol. Sci.).

24. Susan Webb Yackee, Sweet Talking the Fourth Branch: Assessing the Influence of Interest Group Comments on Federal Agency Rulemaking, 26 J. Pub. Admin. Res. & Theory 103 (2006).

25. Marissa Martino Golden, Interest Groups in the Rule-Making Process: Who Participates? Whose Voices Get Heard?, 8 J. Pub. Admin. Res. & Theory 245 (1998).

26. Magat, Krupnick, & Harrington, Rules in the Making (1986).

27. William F. West, Formal Procedures, Informal Processes, Accountability, and Responsiveness in Bureaucratic Policy Making: An Institutional Policy Analysis, 64 Pub. Admin. Rev. 66 (2004).

28. See Schlozman & Tierney, Organized Interests, at 333–34.

29. See Croley & Funk, The Federal Advisory Committee Act, at appendix A.

30. Id.

31. See Steven Croley, Theories of Regulation: Incorporating the Administrative Process, 98 Colum. L. Rev. 1, 135–39 (1998).

32. See Croley, White House Review of Agency Rulemaking, at 860–63. For an alternative view based on Survey Methodology, see Lisa S. Bressman & Michael P. Vandenberg, Inside the Administrative State: A Critical Look at the Practice of Presidential Control, 105 Mich. L. Rev. 47 (2006).

CHAPTER EIGHT
THE ADMINISTRATIVE-PROCESS APPROACH EXPANDED:
A MORE DEVELOPED PICTURE

1. For an illustration, see, for example, Peter Schuck quoting William Ruckleshaus, former administrator of EPA: "I can remember in particular one major decision that I was faced with. . . . I remember the first hearing that was held on that matter in which a single piece of testimony from a public interest lawyer had more impact on my thinking than any of the testimony that occurred during those lengthy three-week hearings. . . . That is only one example and many more could be cited." Peter Schuck, Public Interest Groups and the Policy Process, 37 Pub. Admin. Rev. 132, 138 (1977).

2. See especially McNollgast, Administrative Procedures as Instruments of Political control, 3 J.L. Econ. & Org. 243 (1987), as well as McNollgast, Structure and Process, Politics and Policy: Administrative Arrangements and the Political Control of Agencies, 75 Va. L. Rev. 431 (1989), and McNollgast, Positive and Normative Models of Procedural Rights: An Integrative Approach to Administrative Procedures, 6 J.L. Econ & Org. 307 (1990).

3. McNollgast, Administrative Procedures as Instruments of Control, at 246.

4. See McNollgast, Administrative Procedures as Instruments of Control, at 273–74. Because McNollgast do not commit themselves to any particular position with respect to legislative motivations, their argument does not imply that regulation serves mainly the interests of rent-seeking interest groups. A Congress composed entirely of legislators motivated by the public interest would be compatible with McNollgast's vision, although McNollgast at times contemplate that legislators are motivated by reelection goals rather than a "search for the 'public interest.' " McNollgast, An Integrative Approach, at 310 and 315. But while McNollgast do not need to public choice theory, the public choice theory's legislative dominance claim needs McNollgast.

5. See McNollgast, Administrative Procedures as Instruments of Control, at 253–55, 259–60, 273. It should be noted that McNollgast's argument that Con-

gress exercises ex ante control over agencies is not limited to their claims about administrative procedure. They also argue that Congress's "structural" choices concerning the scope of agency power and the level of agency resources constitute independent constraints on agency regulators. See McNollgast, Structure and Process, at 432, 440–44. While the argument in the text that follows challenges McNollgast's procedural claims, their observations about structure seem unobjectionable: Undoubtedly Congress enjoys ex ante control over agencies in the sense that Congress establishes the range of their possible decisions. The question remains, how much Congress influences agency decisionmaking within that broad range, and whether administrative procedure promotes or curtails that influence.

6. For illustrative cases enforcing these requirements, see, for example, Weyerhauser Co. v. Costle, 590 F.2d 1011, 1030–31 (D.C. Cir. 1978) and Portland Cement Ass'n v. Ruckelshaus, 486 F.2d 375, 400 (D.C. Cir. 1973).

7. 5 U.S.C. §553(c)(i).

8. 5 U.S.C. §553(e).

9. Posner, for example, writes:

> The terminal character of many judicial appointments, the general jurisdiction of most courts, the procedural characteristics of the judicial process, and the freedom of judges from close annual supervision by appropriations committees, all operate to make the courts freer from the interest group pressures operating through the legislative process, and more disposed to decide issues of policy on grounds of efficiency, than any other institution of government, specifically the administrative agency, where these features are absent or attenuated.

Posner, Theories of Economic Regulation, at 351. But the case is not quite so clear. Agencies are of course subject to supervision by legislative appropriations committees, but how "close" such supervision is not really known. More importantly, agency decisionmakers, ALJs in particular, are almost certainly not subject to the kinds of interest group pressures operating through the legislative process either. ALJs enjoy significant independence, their tenure too is, for practical purposes, often permanent, and their procedures resemble judicial processes. What is more, agency decisions, unlike almost all legislative decisions, are subject to judicial review as well.

10. 5 U.S.C. §554(d).

11. Id. For illustrations, see, for example, Richardson v. Perales, 402 U.S. 389, 402 (1971); Demenech v. Secretary of HHS, 913 F.2d 882, 884 (11th Cir. 1990); Cellular Mobile Sys. of Pa., Inc. v. FCC, 782 F.2d 182, 198 (D.C. Cir. 1985).

12. 5 U.S.C. §557(c).

13. 5 U.S.C. §706(2)(E).

14. This aspect of judicial review of agency adjudication is well established. See, for example, American Smelting and Refining Co. v. Federal Power Comm'n, 494 F.2d 925, 945 (D.C. Cir. 1974); Marco Sales Co. v. FTC, 453 F.2d 1, 7 (2d Cir. 1971); Greater Boston Television Corp. v. FCC, 444 F.2d 841, 850 (D.C. Cir. 1970).

15. Ditto. See, for example, International Brotherhood of Teamsters v. NLRB, 587 F.2d 1176, 1178, 1181 (D.C. Cir. 1978); Alabama Ass'n of Ins. Agents v. Board of Governors of the Fed. Reserve, 533 F.2d 224, 248 (5th Cir. 1976), *vacated in part*, 558 F.2d 729 (5th Cir. 1977); ITT Continental Baking Co. v. FTC, 532 F.2d 207, 219–20 (2d Cir. 1976).

16. See, for instance, Action for Children's Television v. FCC, 564 F.2d 458 (D.C. Cir. 1977); Pillsbury Co. v. FTC, 354 F.2d 952 (5th. Cir. 1956). See, as well, House Comm. on Standards of Official Conduct, 98th Cong., Ethics Manual for Members and Employees of the U.S. House of Representatives 69 (1984) (explaining prohibitions on ex parte communications in formal agency proceedings) and Morton Rosenberg & Jack H. Maskell, Congressional Intervention in the Administrative Process: Legal and Ethical Considerations (Cong. Res. Serv. No. 90-440A, 1990). For an example of judicial unease with respect to congressional pressures on specific agency decisions even outside of the formal adjudication context, see Koniag, Inc. v. Andrus, 580 F.2d 601, 610 (D.C. Cir. 1978), which set aside the secretary of interior's determination on the grounds that a letter from a Congress member "compromised the appearance of the Secretary's impartiality."

17. Federal Advisory Committee Act, §5(b)(2)–(3), §§9–10; 41 C.F.R. §101-6.1007(b)(2)(iii).

18. For more background, see, for example, Cary Coglianese, Assessing Consensus: The Promise and Performance of Negotiated Rulemaking, 46 Duke L.J. 1255, 1276 (1997).

19. 5 U.S.C. §552(a).

20. For relevant evidence supporting this claim, see, for example, Schlozman & Tierney, Organized Interests and American Democracy, at 348, table 13.1, reporting that 82 percent of surveyed citizen groups, and 19 percent of surveyed corporate groups, indicate that the FOIA has made it easier for them to operate effectively within the bureaucracy, and that 48 percent of citizen groups and 23 percent of corporate groups say the same thing about the Sunshine Act.

21. Which it did. See, for example, H.R. Rep. No. 91–765 (1969), reprinted in 1969 U.S.C.C.A.N. 2767, on the legislative history of NEPA.

22. For empirical challenges to additional rejections of the McNollgast thesis, see Steven J. Balla, Administrative Procedures and Political Control of the Bureau-

cracy, 92 Am. Pol. Sci. Rev. 663 (1998); David C. Nixon, Robert M. Howard, & Jeff R. DeWhitt, With Friends Like These: Rule-Making Comment Submissions to the Securities and Exchange Commission, 12 J. Pub. Admin. Res. & Theory 59 (2002); William F. West, Formal Procedures, Informal Process, Accountability, and Responsiveness in Bureaucratic Policy Making: An Institutional Policy Analysis, 64 Pub. Admin. Rev. 66 (2004). For more conceptual challenges, see a series of excellent articles by David Spence, including David B. Spence, Administrative Law and Agency Policymaking: Rethinking the Positive Theory of Political Control, 14 Yale J. Reg. 407 (1997); David B. Spence, Agency Direction and the Dynamics of Procedural Reform, 59 Pub. Admin. Rev. 425 (1999); and David B. Spence Managing Delegation Ex Ante: Using Law to Steer Administrative Agencies, 28 J. Legal Stud. 413 (1999).

23. Pub. L. No. 94-409, §6, 90 Stat. 1247 (1976) (codified at 5 U.S.C. §554(d) (prohibiting ex parte communications)).

24. See generally William H. Allen, The Durability of the Administrative Procedure Act, 72 Va. L. Rev. 235, 236–40 (1986).

25. See Immigration and Naturalization Serv. v. Chadha, 462 U.S. 919, 958–59 (1983).

26. 5 U.S.C. §706(2)(D).

27. 5 U.S.C. §706(2)(A).

28. Model State Admin. Proc. Act, §3–201.

29. Id. at §3–203 to –204.

30. See, for example, State v. Broom, 439 So. 2d 357 (La. 1983); Opinion of the Justices, 431 A.2d 783, 786 (N.H. 1981).

31. On the history, see, for example, Walter Gellhorn, The Administrative Procedure Act: The Beginnings, 72 Va. L. Rev. 219 (1986) and especially George B. Shepherd, Fierce Compromise: The Administrative Procedure Act Emerges from New Deal Politics, 90 Nw. U. L. Rev. 1557, 1560–61 (1996).

32. Pub. L. No. 104–121, tit. II, 110 Stat. 847, 857–74 (codified at 5 U.S.C. §601 and other scattered sections of Titles 5 & 15 U.S.C.).

33. 5 U.S.C. §601.

34. H.R. Res. 168, 104th Cong. (1995). See generally John Copeland Nagle, Corrections Day, 43 UCLA L. Rev. 1267 (1996).

INTRODUCTION TO PART 3
PUBLIC INTERESTED REGULATION

1. See, for example, Office of Management and Budget Office of Information and Regulatory Affairs, Progress in Regulatory Reform: 2004 Report to Congress on the Costs and Benefits of Federal Regulations and Unfunded Mandates on

State, Local, and Tribal Entities (2004); Office of Management & Budget, 2000 Report to Congress on the Costs and Benefits of Federal Regulations (2000); Office of Management and Budget, Office of Information and Regulatory Affairs, Informing Regulatory Decisions: 2003 Report to Congress on the Costs and Benefits of Federal Regulations and Unfunded Mandates on State, Local, and Tribal Entities (2003); Office of Management & Budget, 1998 Report to Congress on the Costs and Benefits of Federal Regulations (1999).

Chapter Nine
The Environmental Protection Agency's Ozone and Particulate Matter Rules

1. For contemporaneous accounts emphasizing the significance of the EPA's initiative, see, for example, Dan Balz & Joby Warrick, President May Endorse Tougher Clean Air Rules; Backing EPA Would Upset Some Political Allies, Wash. Post, June 25, 1997, at A1; John H. Cushman, Jr., Administration Issues Its Proposal for Tightening of Air Standards, N.Y. Times, November 28, 1996, at A1; Joby Warrick & John E. Yong, Stricter Air Quality Rules May Test Hill's New Veto: Several GOP Chairmen Critical of EPA Move, Wash. Post, November 28, 1996, at A1; Joby Warrick, White House Taking a Hands-On Role in Writing New Clean Air Standards, Wash. Post, May 22, 1997, at A10.

2. National Ambient Air Quality Standards for Particulate Matter, 62 Fed. Reg. 38,652 (1997) (codified at 40 C.F.R. pt. 50); National Ambient Air Quality Standards for Ozone, 62 Fed. Reg. 38,856 (1997) (codified at 40 C.F.R. pt. 50).

3. 40 C.F.R. pt. 50.

4. 42 U.S.C. §§7408–9.

5. Id. at §7409(d)(1).

6. 58 Fed. Reg. 13,008 (1993); 52 Fed. Reg. 24,854 (1987).

7. National Ambient Air Quality Standards for Particulate Matter, 61 Fed. Reg. 65,637 (1996) (proposed December 13, 1996); National Ambient Air Quality Standards for Ozone, 61 Fed. Reg. 65,715 (1996) (proposed December 13, 1996).

8. Proposed PM NAAQS, 61 Fed. Reg. at 65,639–49; Proposed Ozone NAAQS, 51 Fed. Reg. at 65,719–26.

9. 61 Fed. Reg. 29,719 (June 12, 1996).

10. Proposed Ozone NAAQS, 61 Fed. Reg., at 65,719, 65,727–30. According to the Congressional Research Service, the prior ozone standard of 0.12 ppm measured over a one-hour period was approximately equivalent to an eight-hour standard of 0.09 ppm. CRS Issue Brief for Congress, James E. McCarthy, Clean Air Act Issues in the 105th Congress (March 3, 1999), at 4. Adjusting for changes

in measurement methodologies, in other words, the proposed standard did not contemplate a 33 percent reduction in maximum ozone levels, as focusing only on the change from 0.12 ppm to 0.08 ppm would mistakenly suggest.

11. Proposed PM NAAQS, 61 Fed. Reg., at 65,654–62.

12. Proposed PM NAAQS, 61 Fed. Reg., at 65, 664–65; Proposed Ozone NAAQS, 61 Fed. Reg., at 65,716, 65,733.

13. American Lung Ass'n v. Browner, 884 F. Supp. 345, 346 (D. Ariz. 1994).

14. Id.

15. Proposed PM NAAQS, 61 Fed. Reg., at 65,668; Proposed Ozone NAAQS, 61 Fed. Reg., at 65,736–37.

16. Id.

17. 42 U.S.C. §7410(a), (c).

18. Id. at §7410(a)(1).

19. See PM NAAQS, 62 Red. Reg., at 38,653.

20. See id. at 38,655–63 (noting that the agency repeatedly relied on CASAC expertise, particularly CASAC evaluation of scientific literature, when explaining the agency's rationale for its final particulate matter rule); Ozone NAAQS, Fed. Reg. 62, at 38,859–78 (noting the same for the final ozone rule); see also Review of EPA's Proposed Ozone and Particulate Matter NAAQS Revisions, Part 1: Hearings to Review EPA Proposed New National Ambient Air Quality Standards (NAAQS) for Ozone and Particulate Matter (PM) Under the Clean Air Act Before the Subcomm. on Health and Env't and Subcomm. on Oversight and Investigations of the House Comm. on Commerce, 105th Cong. 161–65 (1997) (prepared statement of Mary D. Nichols, Assistant Administrator, Office of Air and Radiation, EPA).

21. See House NAAQS Hearings, at 263.

22. For contemporary accounts, see, for example, Scott Allen, Plan to Curb Ozone Draws Pros, Cons at EPA Hearing, Boston Globe, January 15, 1997, at B2 (discussing the broad coalition of industries opposed to the EPA's proposals); Balz & Warrick, Tougher Clean Air Rules (explaining that major corporations and industry trade groups spent millions of dollars generating opposition to proposed rules); John H. Cushman, Jr., Top EPA Official Not Backing Down on Air Standards, N.Y. Times, June 1, 1997, at 1 (noting that the National Association of Manufacturers, representing electric companies, oil and coal producers, automakers, and other major industries, led lobbying effort against the EPA).

23. See, for example, John H. Cushman, Jr., Canada Says U. S. Falls Short with Proposal to Bolster Air Quality, N.Y. Times, March 18, 1997, at A17 (stating that major industry groups filed voluminous comments deriding EPA's proposals and

the science on which they were based); Warrick, Hands-On Role (noting that EPA proposals have been the target of endless attacks by industry since first unveiled).

24. See, for example, John H. Cushman, Jr., D'Amato Vows to Fight for EPA's Tightened Air Standards, N.Y. Times, June 25, 1997, at A13 (noting support for the EPA by Republican governors of New Jersey and Massachusetts, as well as by two Republican senators from Maine); Cushman, Top EPA Official (stating that Republican governor William Weld of Massachusetts supported the EPA); George E. Pataki, Editorial, Holding Our Breath, N.Y. Times, June 13, 1997, at A25 (supporting the EPA proposals).

25. See, for example, Balz & Warrick, Tougher Clean Air Rules (quoting Detroit's Democratic mayor Dennis Archer, who led the U. S. Conference of Mayors in opposition to EPA, as saying the proposed rules go "too far, too fast"); Cushman, Top EPA Official (explaining that Congressman John Dingell, Democrat of Michigan, ranking member of the Commerce Committee, which oversees the Clean Air Act, led the effort among House Democrats against the rules); Warrick, Hands-On Role (noting that many Democratic governors and mayors opposed the EPA proposals).

26. See, for example, Katherine Bouma, Groups Tell Congress to Clean Air: Many in Congress Oppose Tighter EPA Rules for Air Pollution That Could Save Thousands of Lives, Orlando Sent., June 12, 1997, at A10 (noting widespread and bipartisan congressional opposition to EPA's proposed rules).

27. Subcomm. on Energy and Env't of House Comm. on Science, 105th Cong., Report on Science Behind the U. S. EPA's Proposed Revisions to the Primary National Ambient Air Quality Standards for Ozone and Particulate Matter: Hearing Summaries, Findings, and Recommendations (Comm. Print 1997) (quoting Science Comm. chairman F. James Sensenbrenner, Jr.).

28. See, for example, Cindy Skrzycki, GOP's Best Shot at Curbing EPA: A Democrat Named Dingell, Wash. Post, July 18, 1997, at G1 (stating that Representative John D. Dingell led dozens of House Democrats in writing the president to oppose rules and sharply criticizing Browner at the oversight hearings); see also Noelle Knox, Dingell Leads Fight to Delay Stringent New Clean Air Rules, Detroit News, July 30, 1997, at B3.

29. Including, for example, Science Behind the Environmental Protection Agency's (EPA's) Proposed Revisions to the National Ambient Air Quality Standards for Ozone and Particulate Matter, Parts I–III: Hearings to Examine the Scientific Basis for EPA Proposed New National Ambient Air Quality Standards (NAAQS) for Ozone and Particulate Matter (PM) Before the Subcomm. on Energy and Env't of the House Comm. on Science, 105th Cong. (1997).

30. See, for example, Proposed NAAQS Hearings, at 33–58.

31. House Joint Hearings, May 15, 1997, at 258.

32. Id. at 289, 299.

33. Id. at 298.

34. Id. at 305.

35. Id. at 285.

36. Id. at 312.

37. Id. at 351.

38. See, for example, Kyle Niederpruem, EPA Chief Takes Naysayers in Stride, Indianapolis Star, November 14, 1997, at C1 (referring to a *Forbes* magazine cover story on Browner characterizing her as a "mission creep").

39. See PM NAAQS, 62 Fed. Reg. at 38,708–9 (responding to a request for recusal).

40. Proposed NAAQS Hearings, at 3–4.

41. House Joint Hearings at 302.

42. See, for example, Cushman, D'Amato Vows (noting that congressional opponents threatened to use the new regulatory review procedure enacted by the 104th Congress); Skrzycki, A Democrat Named Dingell (explaining that legislative reactions included proposals to kill the rules through legislation, to use the new "resolution of disapproval," and to pass a bill stalling the rules' implementation); Vicki Torres, Firms Push for Some Breathing Room, L.A. Times, October 22, 1997, at D9 (stating that House and Senate bills would impose moratoria on new rules); Congress May Override EPA's Rules, Gramm Warns, Pesticide & Toxic Chemical News, September 17, 1997, at 9 (discussing how proposed legislation in both houses would postpone standards for five years pending further study, and quoting Senator Gramm: "I have no doubt that we have the votes [to stop the EPA's rules] ").

43. See, for example, Warrick, Hands-On Role (stating that Senator John Chaffee, chair of the Environment Committee, urged the White House to seek a middle ground between the EPA and the proposed rules' opponents, to avoid a showdown with Congress).

44. See, for example, Balz & Warrick, Tougher Clean Air Rules (detailing the "fierce" internal administration struggle "that strained relations between the White House and the Environmental Protection Agency"); John McQuaid, Breaux, Landrieu Against EPA Rules: New, Stricter Regulations Unreasonable, They Say, The Times-Picayune, June 16, 1997, at A1 (noting that the president's economic advisors encouraged him to soften the proposed rules, and that the administration was "deeply split" over the proposed rules).

45. See, for example, Balz & Warrick, Hands-On Role.

46. See, for example, Cushman, D'Amato Vows ("To the dismay of environmental groups, the White House has left the environmental agency's Administrator, Carol M. Browner, to defend the proposals nearly single-handedly").

47. See Cushman, D'Amato Vows.

48. PM NAAQS, 62 Fed. Reg., at 38,871.

49. Id. at 38,668–79.

50. See, for example, H. R. Res. 1984, 105th Cong. (1997); see also Alec Zacaroli, Air Quality Standards: House Democrats Seek to Pull Legislation to Block Ozone-PM Rules from Committee, 28 Env't Rep. (BNA) 1201 (October 17, 1998); Inhofe Continues Search for Vehicle to Block New Air Rules, Inside EPA's Clean Air Rep., October 30, 1997, at 17.

51. See, for example, Dozens of Parties Sue EPA Over Air Rules; Small Business, Scientific Issues Dominate, Nat'l Env't Daily (BNA) (September 22, 1997) (noting that at least thirty-seven groups, including two states, sued the EPA over the rules).

52. See American Trucking Ass'n v. EPA, 175 F.3d 1027, 1034 (D. C. Cir. 1999).

53. See Whitman v. American Trucking Ass'n, 121 S. Ct. 903, 911–14 (2001).

54. Joint Hearings, at 308. See also id. at 349.

55. See generally the EPA's comprehensive attainment/nonattainment information at www.epa.gov/ozonedesignations.

56. See, for example, 70 Fed. Reg. 44, 470 (August 3, 2005) ("Identification of Ozone Areas for Which the 1-hour Standard Has Been Revoked").

CHAPTER TEN
THE FOOD AND DRUG ADMINISTRATION'S TOBACCO INITIATIVE

1. Regulations Restricting the Sale and Distribution of Cigarettes and Smokeless Tobacco to Protect Children and Adolescents, 61 Fed. Reg. 44,395 (August 28, 1996).

2. Regulations Restricting the Sale and Distribution of Cigarettes and Smokeless Tobacco Products to Protect Children and Adolescents, 60 Fed. Reg. 41,314 (August 11, 1995).

3. Id. at 41,362.

4. 21 U.S.C. §§201 et seq.

5. Id. at §201(g)(1)(C) & §201 (h)(3).

6. See 60 Fed. Reg. at 41,317.

7. Id. at 41,322–26.

8. See id. at 41,329–36.

9. See id. at 41,336–38.

10. See id.

11. See id. at 41,326–28.

12. See, for example, Jeff Nesmith, Restrictions on Cigarette Sales at Least 5 Years in the Making, Atlanta J. & Const., August 31, 1996, at 2A.

13. See 59 Fed. Reg. 35,738 (July 13, 1994) (announcing advisory committee public meeting on addictiveness of cigarettes). For background, see, for example, Susan H. Carchman, Should the FDA Regulate Nicotine-Containing Cigarettes? Has the Agency Established a Legal Basis and, If Not, Should Congress Grant It?, 51 Food & Drug L.J. 85, 103–10 (1996). See as well John Schwartz, FDA Panel Says Nicotine Is Addictive, Wash. Post, August 3, 1994, at A1.

14. 60 Fed. Reg. at 41,359–61, 44,569–70, table 1c.

15. 61 Fed. Reg. at 44,569.

16. See Notice of Extension of Comment Period, 60 Fed. Reg. 53,620 (1995).

17. See 61 Fed. Reg. at 44,418.

18. See 60 Fed. Reg. at 41,314, 41,346–52.

19. See 5 U.S.C. §553(d)(2).

20. 61 Fed. Reg. at 44,400–417.

21. For contemporary accounts of the interaction between the FDA and the White House, see, for example, Marlene Cimons, Legal Battle Looms over Rules to Curb Teen Smoking, L.A. Times, August 12, 1995, at A24; FDA Proposing Regulation of Tobacco Products, Chi. Trib., July 13, 1995, §1, at 10; Bob Hohler, Clinton to Instruct FDA to Rule Nicotine a Drug: New Regulations to be Aimed at Cutting Smoking by Youth, Boston Globe, August 10, 1995, at A1; Carol Jouzaitis, Alarm Bell on Teenage Smoking: Increase in Usage May Fuel FDA Bid to Regulate Tobacco, Chi. Trib., July 20, 1995, §1, at 3.

22. See President William Jefferson Clinton, Remarks During the Announcement of Food and Drug Administration Rule on Children and Tobacco (August 23, 1996), available at http://www.pub.whitehouse.gov.

23. 505 U.S. 504 (1992).

24. See, for example, Power Grab: Tobacco Lobby Launches Blitz on FDA Plan, Wilmington Star-News, January 3, 1996, at 3A; John Schwartz, Smoke, Letters, and Documentation: Tobacco Companies Swamp FDA with Final Comments on Regulation, Wash. Post, January 3, 1996, at A20.

25. See, for example, Bob Geiger, Companies Strike Back, Atlanta J. & Const., January 3, 1996, at A4 (reporting estimates of Steven Parrish, senior vice president of Philip Morris, of annual costs of the rule to tobacco industry, retailers, and advertisers).

26. See Penny Bender, Tobacco Farmers Protest Gore, FDA Regulations, The Tennessean, November 3, 1996, at 4B.

27. See Kentucky Democrat Introduces Alternative, Wilmington Star-News, September 21, 1995, at 1A.

28. Clinton Launches War on Smoking, Chi. Trib., August 10, 1995, at C1.

29. William Neikirk, Clinton Readies Tobacco Crackdown, Chi. Tribune, August 22, 1996, at 1.

30. Leslie Lloyd, FDA Told to Butt Out of Tobacco: Regulation Threat Provokes Farmers, Chattanooga Times, July 14, 1995, at A10.

31. David Daley, FDA Regulation: Delegation Sends Letter to Clinton; N. C. Lawmakers Fight Tobacco Rules, Wilmington Star-News, July 14, 1995, at 4A.

32. Paul Richter & Marlene Cimons, Clinton to Weigh Plan to Curb Teen Smoking, L.A. Times, August 4, 1995, at A14.

33. See, for example, Sheryl Stolberg, Clinton Set to OK FDA Regulation of Tobacco as a Drug, L.A. Times, August 22, 1996, at A1; Edward Walsh, FDA Can't Regulate Tobacco, Dole Says, Wash. Post, June 14, 1996, at A18.

34. 141 Cong. Rec. H.7470, 7471 (quoting the Speaker).

35. 141 Cong. Rec. H.7307, 7355 (quoting Representative Bunning).

36. Id. Kessler was first called "the National Nanny" by Delaware Governor Pete Dupont.

37. 141 Cong. Rec. H.7155 (quoting Representative Jones).

38. 141 Cong. Rec. H.7307, 7354 (quoting Representative Bunning).

39. See Marlene Cimons, Firm Adjusted Nicotine in Cigarettes, Affidavits Say, L.A. Times, March 19, 1996, at A1.

40. Regulation of Tobacco Products (Part 1): Hearings to Examine Possible Application of FDA Regulations Under the Federal Food, Drug, and Cosmetic Act to Cigarettes, Including a Proposal to Classify Nicotine in Tobacco Products as a Drug Before the Subcommittee on Health & Environment of the House Committee on Energy and Commerce, 103rd Cong. (1994). See as well Keith Glover, HEALTH: Latest FDA Tobacco Testimony Suggests Regulation Is Near, Cong. Q. Wkly. Rep., June 25, 1994.

41. See Tobacco Hearings, at 542–628, 640–767, 791, 844 (statements of William I. Campbell, president and CEO, Phillip Morris, USA; James W. Johnston, chairman and CEO, R. J. R. Reynolds Tobacco Co.; Thomas E. Sandefur, Jr., chairman and CEO, Brown & Williamson Tobacco Corp.; Andrew H. Tisch, chairman and CEO, Lorillard Tobacco Co.; Donald S. Johnston, president, American Tobacco Co.; Edward A. Horrigan, Jr., chairman and CEO, Ligget Group; Joseph Taddeo, president, U.S. Tobacco Co.; Alexander W. Spears, vice chairman and chief operating Officer, Lorillard Tobacco Co.).

42. For contemporary accounts summarizing evolving terms of proposed settlement, see, for example, Marlene Cimons, The Tobacco Settlement; Fine Print

Will Get Close FDA Inspection, L.A. Times, June 21, 1997, at A13 (summarizing the consequences of the national settlement relating to the FDA's regulatory authority); Mark Curriden, Tobacco Deal Likely This Week: Industry Says It Will Let FDA Regulate Nicotine, Dallas Morning News, June 16, 1997, at 1A (noting that the tobacco industry would agree to FDA regulation so long as congressional approval would be required for an outright ban, and so long as the FDA observed ten-year grace period before reducing nicotine levels, all in exchange for a cap on punitive damages and limits on class-action lawsuits); John Schwartz & Saundra Torry, Three-Judge Panel Appears Skeptical of FDA Attempts to Regulate Youth Smoking, Wash. Post., August 12, 1997, at A6; Maria Shao & Joann Muller, Tobacco Giant Offers Deal on Sales Curbs: Wants FDA to Halt Regulation Efforts, Boston Globe, May 16, 1996, at 1 (explaining that Philip Morris would support legislation only if the FDA is precluded from regulating tobacco); Barbara Sullivan, Philip Morris, UST Offer Plan to Curb Teen Use of Tobacco; Proposal Would Prohibit FDA Regulation, Ban "Loosies" and Vending Machine Sales, Chi. Trib., May 16, 1996, at N1 (describing "quid pro quo" and quoting tobacco executive: "If there's FDA involvement [in nicotine], the deal is not on the table").

43. See, for example, Hanoch Dagan & James J. White, Governments, Citizens, and Injurious Industries, 75 N.Y.U.L. Rev. 354, 369–70 (2000).

44. See, for example, Henry Weinstein, Cancer Society Urges Revision in Tobacco Deal, L.A. Times, July 25, 1997, at D1.

45. See 61 Fed. Reg. at 44,616–17.

46. Id. at 44,617.

47. Id.

48. Id.

49. Id. at 44,618.

50. See 60 Fed. Reg. at 41,323, 41,324–25.

51. See 61 Fed. Reg. at 44,617.

52. Id. at 44,538–39.

53. See 60 Fed. Reg. at 41,326–28.

54. See Final Rule, Jurisdictional Determination, Nicotine in Cigarettes and Smokeless Tobacco Products Is a Drug and These Products Are Nicotine Delivery Devices Under the Federal Food, Drug, and Cosmetic Act: Jurisdictional Determination, 61 Fed. Reg. 44,619 (1996).

55. Executive Summary, Annex: Nicotine in Cigarettes and Smokeless Tobacco Is a Drug and These Products Are Nicotine Delivery Devices Under the Federal Food, Drug, and Cosmetic Act, http://www.fda.goc/opacom/campaigns/tobacco/execsum.html.

56. See id. The FDA added, moreover, that courts previously deferred to the agency's prior determination not to regulate but expressly left open the possibility

that the agency might subsequently decide to regulate as new information developed. See, for example, Action on Smoking and Health v. Harris, 655 F.2d 236, 239 (D.C. Cir. 1980).

57. See Final Rule, Jurisdictional Determination.

58. 61 Fed. Reg. at 44,400.

59. 61 Fed. Reg. at 44,558.

60. See, for example, John Hoeffel, Battle Is On for Funds to Enforce FDA Tobacco Regulations, Richmond Times Dispatch, March 20, 1997, at A20; Paul Richter & Marlene Cimons, Clinton to Weigh Plan to Curb Teen Smoking, L.A. Times, August 4, 1995, at A14; Paul Dellinger, Burley Growers Protest FDA "Intrusion": Farmers Rally at Tobacco Warehouse Against Proposed Regulations, Roanoke Times & World News, November 21, 1995, at B6.

61. See, for example, S.201, The Tobacco Products Control Act of 1997, 143 Cong. Rec. S.676, 677 (introduced by Senator Ford).

62. See, for example, John Schwartz, A GOP Leader in Senate Blocks Nominee for FDA; Worry on Henney's Regulatory Views Cited, Wash. Post, October 9, 1998, at A2.

63. See Coyne Beahm, Inc. v. FDA, 966 F. Supp. 1374 (M.D.N.C. 1997), rev'd in part sub nom. Brown & Williamson Tobacco Corp. v. United States FDA, 153 F.3d 155, 167–68 (4th Cir. 1998), aff'd, 529 U.S. 120 (2000).

64. Coyne Beahm, Inc. v. FDA, 966 F. Supp. at 1389–98.

65. Brown & Williamson Tobacco Corp., 153 F.3d 155 (4th Cir. 1998).

66. 153 F.3d at 165.

67. The dissenting judge concluded that tobacco products fit "squarely within the plain terms of the FDCA," given the agency's demonstration of the pharmacological effects of nicotine, and found the panel majority's consideration of the "extrinsic effect"of congressional intent to the contrary unpersuasive. 153 F.3d at 176–82.

68. FDA v. Brown & Williamson Tobacco Corp., 529 U. S. 120, 133 (2000).

69. Id. at 161.

70. Engle v. Liggett Group, 2000 WL 33534572 (Fla. Cir. Ct. 2000). The nationally certified class was decertified in a reversal by the Florida appeals court, Engle v. Liggett Group, 853 So. 2d 434 (2003). The Florida Supreme Court, in turn, vacated the appellate court's decision, Engle v. Liggett Group, Inc., 2006 WL 1843363 (July 6, 2006), and the case is pending.

71. See generally Martha A. Derthick, Up in Smoke: From Legislation to Litigation in Tobacco Politics (2005).

72. For background, see, for example, Linda Greenhouse, Justices Reject Appeal in Tobacco Case, N.Y. Times, October 18, 2005 at A18; Myron Levin, U.S. Appeal in Tobacco Case Denied, L.A. Times, October 18, 2005, at C1; AP, $280

Billion Penalty Against Tobacco Firms Is Blocked, Wash. Post, October 18, 2005, at A18.

CHAPTER ELEVEN
THE FOREST SERVICE'S ROADLESS POLICY FOR NATIONAL FORESTS

1. Jennifer L. Sullivan, The Spirit of 76: Does President Clinton's Roadless Lands Directive Violate the Spirit of the National Forest Management Act of 1976?, 17 Alaska L. Rev. 127, 142 (2000) (quoting "Open Letter" from Mike Dombeck, chief of the United States Forest Service).

2. Wyoming v. United States Department of Agriculture, 277 F. Supp. 2d 1197, 1224 (D. Wyo. 2003).

3. Charles Wilkinson, Land Use, Science, and Spirituality: The Search for a True and Lasting Relationship with the Land, 21 Pub. Land & Res. L. Rev. 1, 9 (2000). See as well Robert L. Glicksman, Traveling in Opposite Direction: Roadless Area Management Under the Clinton and Bush Administrations, 34 Envtl. L. 1143 (2004).

4. 66 Fed. Reg. 3244 (January 12, 2001).

5. 16 U.S.C. §1598 et seq.

6. 16 U.S.C. §528 et seq.

7. National Forest Management Act, 16 U.S.C. §1613.

8. Id. at §1604.

9. Herbert Kaufman, The Forest Ranger: A Study in Administrative Behavior (1967).

10. 16 U.S.C. §1129 et seq.

11. 65 Fed. Reg. 30,276 (May 10, 2000).

12. 64 Fed. Reg. 56,306 (October 19, 1999).

13. The White House, Memorandum on Protection of Forest Roadless Areas, for the Secretary of Agriculture, October 13, 1999.

14. See, for example, Ken Rait, Clinton Must Rescue Forests from Foresters Mockery, Plan to Preserve Roadless Areas is Being Eroded by the Agency Charged with Producing It, Ventura County Star, July 26, 2000, at B7 (outlining history of roadless rule and public initiative in late 1997 and early 1998 urging administration to protect roadless areas).

15. Administration of the Forest Development Transportation System, 63 Fed. Reg. 4350 (January 28, 1998).

16. Administration of the Forest Development Transportation System: Temporary Suspension of Road Construction in Roadless Areas, 63 Fed. Reg. 4350, 4351, 4354 (January 28, 1998).

17. Statement of Mike Dombeck, Chief of Forest Service, May 9, 2000; Letter from Mike Dombeck, Chief, To: All Employees, May 9, 2000; Notice of Intent to Prepare an Environmental Impact Statement, 64 Fed. Reg. 56,306 (October 19, 1999).

18. Administration of the Forest Development Transportation System: Temporary Suspension of Road Construction and Reconstruction in Unroaded Areas, 64 Fed. Reg. 7290 (February 12, 1999). National Forest System Road Management, 65 Fed. Reg. 11,676, 11,676–77 (March 3, 2000) (characterizing its February 1999 interim rule as a "time-out").

19. National Forest System Land and Resource Management Planning, 64 Fed. Reg. 54,074 (October 5, 1999).

20. Id.

21. National Forest System Land and Resource Management Planning, 65 Fed. Reg. 67,514 (November 9, 2000).

22. Id. at 67, 529–30.

23. See, for example, Forest Service Announces Information and Comment Opportunities On Roadless Proposal, Press Release, December 1, 1999.

24. Id.

25. 65 Fed. Reg. 30,276 (May 10, 2000).

26. Glickman Proposes National Strategy to Protect Roadless Areas in National Forests, Release No. 0154.00 (May 9, 2000).

27. Statement of Mike Dombeck, Chief of Forest Service, May 9, 2000; Letter from Mike Dombeck, Chief, To: All Employees, May 9, 2000.

28. See, for example, Eric Pianin and Mike Allen, Clinton Forest Rules to Stand, Bush Leaves Opening for Logging, Mining, Drilling, Wash. Post, May 4, 2001 at A1 (noting that most of 1.6 million public comments received in the roadless initiative were supportive).

29. Mike Dombeck, USDA, Forest Service Washington Office, "An Opportunity" (December 29, 1999).

30. See, for example, Rait, Plan to Preserve Roadless Areas (noting that at the vast majority of public forums hosted by the Forest Service those in attendance supporting greater forest protection outnumbered those opposed by a four-to-one margin or greater).

31. In Idaho, A Howl Against Roadless Forests, N.Y. Times, July 5, 2000, at A10.

32. See, for example, U.S. Offers Further Delay to Forest Rules, Clinton Policy is Said to Need More Study, N.Y. Times, March 17, 2001 at A7; Bush Will Modify Ban on New Roads in Federal Lands, N.Y. Times, May 4, 2001; Bush Seeks Shift In Logging Rules, Plan to End Clinton Effort on Forest Development, N.Y. Times, July 13, 2004, at A1.

33. Special Areas; Roadless Area Conservation: Delay of Effective Date, 66 Fed. Reg. 8,899 (February 5, 2001).

34. State of Wyoming v. USDA, 277 F. Supp. 2d 1197 (D. Wyo. 2003).

35. State of Idaho v. USDA, 142 F. Supp. 2d 1248 (D. Idaho 2001).

36. Kootenai Tribe of Idaho v. Veneman, 142 F. Supp. 2d 1231 (D. Idaho 2001).

37. Id. at 1247.

38. Kootenai Tribe of Idaho v. Veneman, 313 F.3d 1094 (9th Cir. 2002).

39. 277 F. Supp. 2d at 1226.

40. Rait, Plan to Preserve Roadless Areas (noting over a dozen opinion polls showing overwhelming public support for roadless area protection, including polls in states with greater concentrations of roadless areas).

41. See, for example, Nina Mendelson, Agency Burrowing: Entrenching Policies and Personnel Before a New President Arrives, 78 N.Y.U. L. Rev. 557, 625–26 (2003).

42. See, for example, Eric Pianin, 20 in GOP Urge Bush to Back Clinton Logging Rules, Wash. Post, May 2, 2001, at A4 (noting House Republicans stating roadless rule enjoyed broad bipartisan as well as public support).

43. H.R. 4865, 107th Cong. (2002).

44. See S. 1200 (introduced by Sen. Maria Cantwell, D-Wash.); H.R. 2369 (introduced by Rep. Jay Inslee, D-Wash., and Rep. Sherwood Boehlert, R-N.Y.), 108th Cong. (2003).

45. See, for example, H.R. 979 108th Cong. (2003).

46. See, for example, Senate Democrats Say Nominees Could Lose Confirmation Battles, Wash. Post, September 6., 2001 at A2; Senators Wary of Bush Pick for Environmental Prosecutor Cantwell Grills Coal-Mining Lobbyist About Stands on Washington State Lawsuits, Superfund Cleanups, Spokane Spokesman-Review, November 7, 2001, at B8; Judiciary Committee Democrats Grill DOJ Nominee, Environment and Energy Daily, November 7, 2001, vol. 10 no. 9; Sansonetti Pledges to Uphold Environmental Laws Despite Coal Industry Ties, States News Service, November 6, 2001.

47. Hearing before the Committee on the Judiciary, United States Senate, 107th Cong. 1st Sess., November 6, 2001, at 73–75.

48. Id. at 74–75.

49. Including, for example, Oversight Hearings before the Subcommittee on Forest and Forest Health of the Committee on Resources, House of Representatives, 105th Cong., 2d Sess., February 25 and March 17, 1998; Hearing before the Subcommittee on Rural Enterprises, Business Opportunities and Special Small

Business Problems of the Committee on Small Business, House of Representatives, 106th Cong., 2d Sess., July 11, 2000.

50. Hearing before the Committee on Energy and Natural Resources, United States Senate, 108th Cong., 2d Sess., March 2, 2004, at 22.

51. 69 Fed. Reg. 42,636 (July 16, 2004).

52. Kootenai Tribe of Idaho v. United States Forest Service, 313 F.3d 1094 (9th Cir. 2002).

53. 70 Fed. Reg. 25,654 (May 5, 2005) codified at 36 C.F.R. §294 et seq.

54. 36 C.F.R. at §294.15 ("Advisory committee review").

55. USFS, Interim Directive 1920-2006-1.

56. 70 Fed. Reg. at 25,658 ("Further, the Department notes that the July 16, 2004, interim directive for the management of inventoried roadless areas (69 CFR 42648) will remain in place until January 16, 2006, and the Forest Service may renew the interim directive for an additional 18 months").

57. State of Wyoming v. United States Department of Agriculture, 414 F.3d 1207 (10th Cir. 2005).

58. See, for example, Sierra Club v. Eubanks, 335 F. Supp. 2d 1070 (E.D. Cal. 2004); Utah Environmental Congress v. Bosworth, 372 F.3d 1219, 1232 (10th Cir. 2004).

59. 70 Fed. Reg. at 25,655–56, codified at 36 C.F.R. §294.18.

CHAPTER TWELVE
SOCIALLY BENEFICIAL ADMINISTRATIVE DECISIONMAKING:
ADDITIONAL EVIDENCE

1. 68 Fed. Reg. 4580 (January 29, 2003), codified at 16 C.F.R. Part 310.

2. 60 Fed. Reg. 43842 (August 23, 1995), codified at 16 C.F.R. Part 310.

3. 15 U.S.C. §§6101 et seq.

4. See Statements of Introduced Bills and Joint Resolutions, 139 Cong. Rec. 2792, 103rd Cong., 1st Sess., March 11, 1993, estimating telemarketing industry at $400 billion annually in 1993; 68 Fed. Reg. 4,580, 4,631 (industry estimates of $274 billion for 2001).

5. See House Committee on Government Operations, H.R. Rep. No., 103rd Cong., 1st Sess.

6. 47 C.F.R. 64.1200(a)–(f).

7. 47 C.F.R. 64.1200(e).

8. 15 U.S.C. §6108.

9. 64 Fed. Reg. 66,124 (November 24, 1999).

10. 65 Fed. Reg. 10,428 (February 28, 2000).

11. 67 Fed. Reg. 4,492 (January 30, 2002).

12. 67 Fed. Reg. 15,767 (April 3, 2002).

13. 68 Fed. Reg. at 4,628 n.575; id. at 4630 n.593.

14. 68 Fed. Reg. at 4,631.

15. Id. at 4,633.

16. Id. at 4,634–35.

17. Id. at 4,638.

18. 67 Fed. Reg. 37,362 (May 29, 2002).

19. Mainstream Marketing Services, Inc. v. FTC, 283 F. Supp. 2d 1151 (D. Colo. 2003).

20. U.S. Security v. FTC, 282 F. Supp. 2d 1285 (W.D. Okla. 2003).

21. FTC. v. Mainstream Marketing Services, Inc., 345 F.3d 850 (10th Cir. 2003).

22. Mainstream Marketing Services, Inc. v. FTC, 358 F.3d 1228 (10th Cir. 2004).

23. National Federation of the Blind v. FTC, 303 F. Supp. 2d 707 (D. Maryland 2004).

24. Pub. L. No. 107–204, 116 Sta. 745 (2002).

25. 15 U.S.C. §7245.

26. Implementation of Standards of Professional Conduct for Attorneys, 67 Fed. Reg. 71,670 (December 2, 2002). The SEC released its proposal to the public on November 21, 2002, but it appeared in the *Federal Register* on December 2, 2002.

27. 67 Fed. Reg. at 71,688–89.

28. 67 Fed. Reg. at 71,699–701.

29. On the legislative history of section 307, see, for example, John C. Coffee Jr., The Latest Sarbanes-Oxley Controversy: Section 307, N.Y. L.J., November 21, 2002, at 5; John Paul Lucci, 4th and 205: How a Rush of Global Comments blocked the SEC's First Attempted Punt of Attorney-Client Privilege Under Sarbanes-Oxley, 20 Touro L. Rev. 363, 375–80 (2004).

30. See Coffee, Section 307, at 5.

31. Preliminary Report of the American Bar Association Task Force on Corporate Responsibility, July 16, 2002, at 7.

32. See Final Rule: Implementation of Standards of Professional Conduct for Attorneys, 68 Fed. Reg. 6,296–6,323. The SEC in its final rule repeatedly noted the conflict between practicing corporate attorneys and academic experts. See id.

33. 68 Fed. Reg. 6,296, codified at 17 C.F.R. Part 205.

34. 17 C.F.R. 205.2(l)–(n).

35. SEC Release Nos. 33-8186, 34-47282, available at www.sec.gov/rules/proposed/33-8186.htm.

36. See descriptions included in the SEC's *Regulatory Agendas* promulgated at 68 Fed. Reg. 74,015 (December 22, 2003); 69 Fed. Reg. 38,643 (June 28, 2004); 69 Fed. Reg. 74,259 (December 13, 2004); and 70 Fed. Reg. 28,001 (May 16, 2005).

37. Speech by SEC Commissioner: Remarks At Rocky Mountain Securities Conference, by Commissioner Paul S. Atkins, May 30, 2003, available at http://www.sec.gov/news/speech/spch053003psa.htm.

38. Id. at 4.

39. See, for example, Mary Jane Fisher, Mergers Put Heat on Congress to Take Action, Nat. Underwriter (Life & Health/Financial Services), April 20, 1998, at 1, 31.

40. See, for example, James M. Cain, Financial Institution Insurance Activities-Courts and Regulators Continue to Dominate Congress, 54 Bus. Law. 1389, 1389 (1999).

41. Ch. 106, 13 Stat. 99 (codified principally at 12 U.S.C. §§21–24 and other scattered sections of 12 U.S.C.

42. Ch. 58, 12 Stat. 665.

43. 12 U.S.C. §24.

44. Id. at §§24, 78, 377, 378.

45. Id. at §§1841–50.

46. Id. at §1843(c)(8).

47. NationsBank of North Carolina v. Variable Annuity Life Ins. Co., 513 U.S. 251, (1995).

48. O.C.C. Inter. Ltr. No. 812 [1997–1998 Transfer Binder] Fed. Banking L. Rep. (CCH) ¶ 81–260, at 90,240–42 (December 29, 1997).

49. Editorial Comment, Another Squeeze Play from the Comptroller, Nat'l Underwriter (Life & Health/Financial Services), January 19, 1998, at 40.

50. See Conditional Approval No. 262, Application by Zions First National Bank (OCC, December 11, 1997), 1997 WL 816878.

51. See, for example, Rules, Policies, and Procedures for Corporate Activities, 61 Fed. Reg. 60,341, 60,352 (1996) (codified in scattered parts of 12 C.F.R.); Legal Opinion from Julie L. Williams, Chief Counsel, to Eugene A. Ludwig, Comptroller of the Currency, Legal Authority for Revised Operating Subsidiary Regulation (November 18, 1996).

52. See Rules, Policies, and Procedures for Corporate Activities, Proposed Rule, 59 Fed. Reg. 61,033 (1994) (codified at 12 C.F.R. pt. 5).

53. See 61 Fed. Reg. at 60,351.

54. Id.

55. Id.

56. Id. at 60,351, 60,353–54.

57. Id. at 60,350, 60,353–54.

58. Id.

59. Id.

60. See, for example, Elizabeth Festa, Campbell Tells Comptroller to Back Off, Am. Banker-Bond Buyer, November 24, 1997, at 1.

61. The two years between the OCC's proposed rule and its final rule lends some support to the claim.

62. See Comptroller of the Currency Eugene Ludwig, Remarks Before the Exchequer Club on Financial Modernization and Trends in the Banking Industry, November 1996, reprinted in O.C.C. Q. J. , March 1997.

63. See Press Release, Office of the Comptroller of the Currency, OCC Approves Zions Application to Underwrite Municipal Revenue Bonds (News Release 97–110, December 11, 1997).

64. 62 Fed. Reg. 19,171 (April 18, 1997).

65. See 61 Fed. Reg. at 60,351.

66. See OCC Ruling on Revenue Bonds Gets Mixed Hill Reaction, Nat'l J.'s Congress Daily, December 12, 1997 (noting the Securities Industry Association's critical reaction to OCC approval of Zion's application to underwrite municipal revenue bonds).

67. See OCC Conditional Approval No. 262.

68. Id.

69. See Barnett Bank of Marion Co. v. Nelson, 517 U.S. 25, 34–35 (1996).

70. See, for example, Patricia A. Murphy, Is Lobbying Tug-of-War Worth the Strain?, U.S. Banker, October 1996, at 26, 26 ("Banks' singular lack of success in the 104th Congress is testimony to the power of opposing forces, especially the insurance agents. But with banks winning in the courts, their focus on Capitol Hill may start to wane"); Richard M. Whiting, The Bank Insurance Wars: Some Lessons from History, Banking Pol'y Rep., Apr. 1, 1996, at 2 (noting that "insurance agents have had their greatest success in the Congress").

71. Bank Regulator Asserts OCC Policies Are Pro-Consumer, Nat'l J.'s Congress Daily, December 4, 1997.

72. See, for example, Barbara A. Rehm, Comptroller Comes Out in Favor of Controversial Retirement CD, Am. Banker, June 30, 1994, at 2, 2; Commerce Oks Bank Reform Bill Without Amendment, Nat'l J.'s Congress Daily, June 14, 1995. House Banking Chair Leach was also highly critical. See Press Release, James A. Leach, Comment on Recent OCC Circulars about H. R. 10 (July 24, 1997); Leach Criticizes OCC Proposal on New Bank Powers, Nat'l J.'s Congress Daily, April 24, 1995.

73. See OCC Inter. Ltr. No. 649, Fed. Banking L. Rep. (CCH) ¶ 83,556.

74. See Key Insurance Groups Are Relaxing Stance on Bank Affiliations, Banking Policy Rep., November 18, 1996, at 2; Sources: Bank Insurance Language Expected by Monday, Nat'l J. 's Congress Daily, June 1, 1995.

75. See, for example, Bill McConnell, Insurance Powers Tiff Puts Reform Bill in a Vise, Again, Am. Banker, June 14, 1996, at 2; Insurance Measures Threaten Regulatory Relief Bill, Fin. Services Rep., July 5, 1995, at 6.

76. With two noteworthy exceptions: Courts invalidated the OCC's treatment of crop insurance and its decision to allow (by not objecting) a bank to underwrite and sell retirement CDs. Independent Ins. Agents of Am., Inc. v. Hawke, 211 F.3d 638, 645 (D.C. Cir. 2000) (crop insurance); American Deposit Corp. v. Schacht, 887 F. Supp. 1066, 1082 (N.D. Ill. 1995) (retirement CD).

77. See Smiley v. Citibank, 517 U.S. 735, 742 (1996); Barnett Bank of Marion County v. Nelson, 517 U.S. 25, 37 (1996); NationsBank of North Carolina v. Variable Annuity Life Ins. Co., 513 U. S. 251, 264 (1995).

78. See, for example, Fisher, Mergers Put Heat on Congress, at 31 (quoting Gary Hughes, vice president and chief counsel for securities and banking, American Council of Life Insurance: "We're really playing an end game here. Banks have won and we are trying to salvage the best environment for competition on a level playing field through functional state regulation. We're willing to give you underwriting—all we ask is functional, fair regulation."); Insurers Now Supporting Financial Services Integration, Nat'l J.'s Congress Daily, January 16, 1997 (noting that the insurance industry group has abandoned "its longstanding opposition to financial services integration" due to "recent regulations by the Office of the Comptroller of the Currency and a 1996 Supreme Court ruling, " and quoting Paul Equale, senior vice president of government affairs, Independent Insurance Agents of America: "The world is changing and as a practical issue we have to look at the next 50 years rather than the last 50. . . . Anyone who is still fighting the old wars [to preserve the insurance-banking divide] is wasting time, effort, and money").

79. 12 U.S.C. §§2901–08.

80. See Financial Services Modernization Act, 106 Pub. L. No. 102, 113 Stat. 1338 (November 12, 1999) (codified in scattered sections of 12 U.S.C.).

CHAPTER THIRTEEN
THE PUBLIC CHOICE THEORY REVISITED

1. See, for example, Cimons, Legal Battle Looms, at A24 (noting that the five largest cigarette companies and an advertising agency filed a challenging lawsuit "almost simultaneously" with the FDA's announcement of its proposed rule).

2. Skrzycki, GOP's Best Shot, at G8.

3. Cf. Commerce Oks Bank Reform Bill Without Amendment, Nat'l. J.'s Congress Daily, June 14, 1995, 1995 WL 1043455 (noting that Rep. Dingell offered, but then withdrew, an amendment to financial services reform legislation that would have made clear that state insurance commissions would maintain authority over insurance sold in the states by banks). Interestingly House Banking chair Jim Leach, a frequent critic of the OCC, characterized the OCC's approval of Zion National Bank's application to underwrite municipal bonds as "extremely credible," after the fact pointing out that it was "fully consistent' with a bill passed by the House Banking Committee, but not yet then by Congress. Mixed Hill Reaction, chap. 12, n. 66.

4. For additional support for the argument that the SEC is not crudely captured, see David C. Nixon, Robert M. Howard, & Jeff R. Dewitt, With Friends Like These: Rule-Making Comment Submissions to the Securities and Exchange Commission, 12 J. Pub. Admin. Res. & Theory 59 (2002).

5. Not surprisingly, consumer groups did not oppose the OCC's liberalizations, objecting only to certain privacy and community-development aspects of some of the financial services reform legislation.

CHAPTER FOURTEEN
THE PROMISE OF AN ADMINISTRATIVE-PROCESS ORIENTATION

1. FDA Tobacco Rule, 61 Fed. Reg. at 44,558.

2. Incidentally, the Senate Report on Public Participation found that petitions to initiate a rulemaking submitted by representatives of those outside a regulatory industry approximated or exceeded petitions submitted by regulated industries. Study on Federal Regulation, vol. 3: Public Participation in Regulatory Agency Proceedings 14–15.

3. See Review of EPA's Proposed Ozone and Particulate Matter NAAQS Revisions, Part 2: Continuation of Hearings to Review EPA Proposed New National Ambient Air Quality Standards (NAAQS) for Ozone and Particulate Matter (PM) Under the Clean Air Act Before the Subcomm. On Health and Env't. And Subcomm. On Oversight and Investigations of the House Comm. on Commerce, 105th Cong. 378–83 (1997).

4. House NAAQS Hearings, at 263.

5. Id. at 265. This is not to say, of course, that science does not have its limits. See, for example, Cary Coglianese & Gary E. Merchant, Shifting Sands: The Limits and Science in Setting Risk Standards, 152 Penn. L. Rev. 1255 (2004). However, that may be, the point is that the EPA could credibly and justifiably rebut critics who accused the agency of scientific shortcuts.

6. 70 Fed. Reg. 25,653, 25,656 (May 13, 2005).

7. Kenneth A. Shepsle, Congress Is a "They," Not an "It": Legislative Intent as Oxymoron, 12 Internat'l Rev. Law & Econ. 239 (1992).

8. See, for example, John H. Cushman, Jr., Top EPA Official Not Backing Down on Air Standards, N.Y. Times, June 1, 1997 at 1; John McQuaid, Breaux, Landrieu Against EPA Rules: New, Stricter Regulations Unreasonable, They Say, The Times-Picayune, June 16, 1997; Dan Balz & Joby Warrick, President May Endorse Tougher Clean Air Rules; Backing EPA Would Upset Some Political Allies, Wash. Post, June 25, 1997, at A1, all noting Browner's resolve.

9. See Cindy Skrzycki, GOP's Best Shot at 61, 68 (quoting Representative David McIntosh).

10. Kessler is quoted in John Schwartz, Judge Rules that FDA Can Regulate Tobacco, Wash Post, April 26, 1997, at A1.

11. See, for example, John Schwartz, Cigarettes Treated as Medical Devices: New Rules Give FDA Leeway in Regulation, Wash. Post, August 11, 1995, at A15; Shanker Vedantam & Bob Geiger, Tough Kessler Quits FDA, Durham Herald-Sun, November 26, 1996, at A1.

12. See, for example, Blow to Cigarette Makers: Judge Rules FDA Can Regulate Tobacco, Atlanta J. and Const., April 25, 1997, at A3.

13. See, for example, Forest Service Chief Quits, And Asks Bush to Hold Firm, N.Y. Times, March 28, 2001, at A19 (quoting letter from Idaho senator Larry Craig).

14. 142 F. Supp. 2d 1248.

15. 277 F. Supp. 2d 1197.

16. Ludwig's Swan-Song Speech Reassures Some Industry Critics, 25 Sec. Wk., February 23, 1998, at 1.

17. See Bill McConnell, Insurance Powers Tiff Puts Reform Bill in a Vise, Again, Am. Banker, June 14, 1996, at 2.

18. See Press Release, Representative Jim Leach, Comments on Recent OCC Circulars About H.R. 10 (July 24, 1997).

19. Comptroller of the Currency Eugene Ludwig, Remarks Before the Exchequer Club on Financial Modernization and Trends in the Banking Industry, November 1996, reprinted in O.C.C. Q.J. , March 1997. See as well, Controversial Rule Change and Financial Modernization Addressed by Comptroller of the Currency Ludwig, Bank Law. Liability, January 1997, at 3, 3–5 (quoting Ludwig concerning the Part 5 revision).

20. On Muris's reputation, especially as measured against expectations, see FTC Chairman Muris Plans to Step Down, Wash. Post, May 12, 2004, at E1 ("Muris' primary legacy will be his aggressive campaign to create a national do-

not-call list, fighting the telemarketing industry and major corporations that sell their goods and services over the phone. . . . That surprised many who had expected Muris, a Republican who as a key FTC official in the Reagan administration spoke out for limited government oversight, to lead the agency with a more hands-off approach to industry"); Chief of FTC to Resign, Bush Selects a Successor, N.Y. Times, May 12, 2004, at C1 (quoting Gene Kimmelman, senior director at Consumers Union: "[Muris] came with a strong ideological conservative bent and surprised everyone by steering a course that reflected the bipartisan tradition of the Federal Trade Commission").

21. See, for example, SEC's Chairman is Stepping Down from Split Panel, N.Y. Times, June 2, 2005, at A1.

22. Quoted in Bush Nominates G.O.P. Lawmaker to Run the SEC, N.Y. Times, June 3, 2005, at A1.

23. See John Schwartz, Smoke, Letters, and Documentation: Tobacco Companies Swamp FDA with Final Comments on Regulation, Wash. Post, January 3, 1996; John Schwartz & Saundra Torry, Three-Judge Panel Appears Skeptical of FDA Attempts to Regulate Youth Smoking, Wash. Post, August 12, 1997 at A6.

24. See House NAAQS Hearings, at 177–78, 188–91 (testimony of Sally Katzen, administrator, Office of Information and Regulatory Affairs, OMB).

25. See, for example, Dan Balz & Joby Warrick, President May Enforce Tougher Clean Air Rules: Backing May Upset Some Political Allies, Wash. Post, June 25, 1997 at A1, noting that Gore needed the support of Democratic mayors in his bid to win nomination, not the backing of environmental groups.

26. See, for example, John H. Cushman, Top EPA Official Not Backing Down on Air Standards, N.Y. Times, June 1, 1997.

27. Quoted in Balz & Warrick, Tougher Clean Air Rules.

28. See Helen Thomas, Clinton Asks FDA to Regulate Tobacco, UPI, August 10, 1995. See as well Carol Jouzaitis, Alarm Bell on Teenage Smoking: Increase May Fuel FDA Bid to Regulate Tobacco, Chi. Trib., July 20, 2995, §1 at 3; Clinton Launches War on Smoking, Chi. Trib., August 10, 1995, at C1 (observing that the president's decision to support the FDA's initiative "was fraught with political consequences because Clinton can ill afford to alienate Southerners heading into the 1996 elections" and quoting Clinton: "[Keeping cigarettes away from children] is more important than any political consequences"); Shankar Vedantam, FDA Rules to Heavily Filter Tobacco Sales, Marketing: Industry Vows to Beat Back Regulations, The Times-Picayune, August 24, 1996, at A1.

29. John Schwartz, Cigarettes Treated as Medical Devices: New Rules Give FDA Leeway in Regulation, Wash. Post, August 11, 1996, at A15.

30. President William Jefferson Clinton, Remarks During the Announcement of Food and Drug Administration Rule on Children and Tobacco.

31. See, for example, Banking on the Fed, Wash. Times, May 12, 1998, at A20; White House, OCC Working on Bank Reform "Principles," Nat'l. Journal's Congress Daily, June 18, 1996.

32. 529 U.S. at 161.

33. Mainstream Marketing Services, Inc. v. FTC, 358 F.3d 1228, 1237 (10th Cir. 2004).

CHAPTER FIFTEEN
REGULATORY RENTS, REGULATORY FAILURES, AND OTHER OBJECTIONS

1. Stigler, Old and New Theories of Economic Regulation, at 140.

2. See Robert D. Tollison, Regulation and Interest Groups, in Regulation, Economic Theory and History 73 (Jack High, ed. 1991).

3. For another example, Daniel Carpenter writes that "Stigler's argument is a powerful one and has usefully aided a generation of regulation scholars," although the argument is not one Carpenter finds persuasive. See Daniel P. Carpenter, Protection Without Capture: Product Approval by a Politically Responsive, Learning Regulatory, 98 Am. Pol. Sci. Rev. 613 (2004). Lawrence Rothenberg similarly observes that "[t]he view that producer dominance is the modal description of regulatory politics remains perhaps the primary means of conceptualizing them for popular commentators and scholars alike." Lawrence S. Rothenberg, Regulation, Organizations, and Politics: Motor Freight Policy at the Interstate Commerce Commission 4 (1994).

4. Stigler, for a provocative example, writes near the beginning of the consumers' movement:

> We are now going through a new period of salvation by public reform, similar in scale . . . to the muckraking period preceding World War I. Then we had Upton Sinclair . . . now we have Ralph Nader and his graduate and prep school students. . . . [Their reforms] will not amount to much because there is no durable, effective political basis to support or direct the efforts of professional . . . reformers. Mr. Nader must flit from automobiles to drugs to local property assessment, cognizant that the public's interests and sympathies are not forever capturable by his vendetta against the Corvair. . . . It is of regulation that the consumer must beware.

Stigler, The Citizen and the State, at 187.

5. See, for example, Daniel C. Esty, Toward Optimal Environmental Governance, 74 N.Y.U. L. Rev. 1495, 1557 (1999) (describing the danger of special-interest manipulation of regulatory issues as "much more severe in the environmental realm than in other fields of regulation"); John Cronin & Robert F. Kennedy,

The River Keepers 179 (1997) (arguing that environmental regulation is not immune from capture).

6. A classic example is provided by Ackerman & Hassler's Clean Coal/Dirty Air.

7. See Carpenter, Protection without Capture.

8. Posner, Theories of Economic Regulation, at 336–37, 350.

9. See Peltzman, Toward a More General Theory of Regulation, at 238.

10. See Stigler, The Theory of Economic Regulation, at 5.

11. Stigler, The Citizen and the State, at 181–82.

12. Id. at 185.

13. Not that every early study supported the public choice theory, however. Peltzman's study of the effects of the 1962 drug amendments, which required FDA premarketing approval of all drug effectiveness claims by manufacturers in the interest of reducing wasteful expenditures by consumers responding to exaggerated claims, concluded that the benefits forgone on effective new drugs introduced later in the market outweighed the wastes avoided of ineffective drug use, but not in any way that advanced drug producers' or suppliers' interests. The regulation required by the amendments proved wasteful, according to Peltzman, but was not demanded by any economic interest. See Sam Peltzman, An Evaluation of Consumer Protection Legislation: The 1962 Drug Amendments, 81 J. Pol. Econ. 1049 (1973). Similarly, Peltzman's examination of the CAB's policies concludes that Stigler's predictions, as formalized by Peltzman himself, find support from CAB policies up to 1968, but no support from CAB policies from 1968 to 1975, during which time the agency increasingly relied on cost-based fare structures. See Peltzman, A More General Theory of Regulation, at 238. And Posner's examination of regulatory treatments of international telecommunications and cable television finds the former inconclusively supportive of the proposition that regulation is often obtained to deliver subsidies to politically powerful customer groups. See Posner, Taxation by Regulation, at 29–33.

14. See Samuel Huntington, The Marasmus of the ICC: The Commission, the Railroads, and the Public Interest, 61 Yale L.J. 467 (1952).

15. See Lawrence Rothenberg's excellent Regulation, Organizations, and Politics: Motor Freight Policy at the Interstate Commerce Commission (1994).

16. This observation motivates Levine & Forrence's public interest theory, considered above in chapter 4. It should be mentioned that the earliest empirical studies of the effects of regulation that supported and were supported by the public choice theory were mainly studies of utilities regulation. Public choice theorists subsequently extended the scope of the theory to other regulatory programs. But given deregulation here too, especially for electric utilities, it is not clear that utility regulation provides strong support for the theory, either.

17. See Tollison, Regulation and Interest Groups.

18. See H. P. Marvel, Factory Regulation: A Reinterpretation of Early English Experience, 20 J.L. & Econ. 379 (1977).

19. See W. F. Shughart II & Robert D. Tollison, Corporate Chartering: An Exploration in the Economics of Legal Change, 23 Econ. Inquiry 585 (1981).

20. See Tollison, Regulation and Interest Groups (collecting examples).

21. Id.

22. See generally Paul J. Quirk, Industry Influence in Federal Regulatory Agencies (1981).

23. Although somewhat outside of the scope of this study, an important and incisive body of work on state and local government also seriously challenges the public choice theory's reliability. See generally Paul Teske, Regulation in the States (2004), and Brian J. Gerber & Paul Teske, Regulatory Policymaking in the American States: A Review of Theories and Evidence, 53 Pol. Res. Q. 849 (2000).

24. See Mark Kelman, On Democracy-Bashing: A Skeptical Look at the Theoretical and "Empirical" Practice of the Public Choice Movement, 74 Va. L. Rev. 199 (1988).

25. John Chubb provides one well-known example. John E. Chubb, Interest Groups and the Bureaucracy: The Politics of Energy (1985).

26. See, for example, Daniel A. Farber & Philip P. Frickey, The Jurisprudence of Public Choice, 65 Tex. L. Rev. 873, 895–900 (1987) (reviewing empirical studies that shed light on the "economic theory of legislation" and concluding that strong versions of the theory simply do not square with the evidence); Herbert Hovenkamp, Legislation, Well-Being, and Public Choice, 57 U. Chi. L. Rev. 63, 99 (1990) ("Much of the public choice literature is filled with anecdotal evidence of great legislative failures, such as the Smoot-Hawley Tariff. But such failures are no different, and probably no more frequent, than the economic market's Edsels. . . . One thing Chicago School economics has taught us is that anecdotal evidence of bad decisions by firms or even entire markets does not establish that the market is working badly enough to warrant regulatory correction"); Mashaw, Administrative Process, at 280 ("the empirical record of [the public choice theory of regulation] is one that should induce the utmost caution in its practitioners").

27. William C. Mitchell & Michael C. Munger, Economic Models of Interest Groups at 522.

28. Parts of Susan Yackee's important work, considered in chapter 7, provide the only empirical evidence supporting the claim that agencies are more responsive to interest group comments for rules generating fewer than two hundred comments.

29. Moreover, Yackee & Yackee's work rejects empirically the hypothesis that groups are able to influence agencies because they provide higher-quality informa-

tion. See Yackee & Yackee, A Bias Toward Business: Assessing Participant Influence in the Notice and Comment Rulemaking Process.

30. See, for example, John M. Mendeloff, The Dilemma of Toxic Substance Regulation: How Overregulation Causes Underregulation at OSHA (1988); Cass R. Sunstein, Paradoxes of the Regulatory State, 57 U. Chi. L. Rev. 407 (1990).

31. 31 U.S.C. §1105.

32. Office of Management and Budget, Office of Information and Regulatory Affairs, Informing Regulatory Decisions: 2003 Report to Congress on the Costs and Benefits of Federal Regulations and Unfunded Mandates on State, Local, and Tribal Entities (2003).

33. Another recent comprehensive report, OIRA's Progress in Regulatory Reform: 2004 Report to Congress on the Costs and Benefits of Federal Regulations and Unfunded Mandates on State, Local, and Tribal Entities (2004), tallies aggregate annual benefits from major rules issued between 1993 and 2003 to range from $63 to $169 billion, with annual costs ranging from $35 to $40 billion. OIRA's draft 2006 report calculates total annual benefits of $94 to $449 billion and total annual costs of $37 to $44 billion for major rules from 1995 to 2005. OMB, OIRA, Draft 2006 Report to Congress on the Costs and Benefits of Federal Regulations.

34. See, just for example, Jerry L. Mashaw, Prodelegation: Why Administrators Should Make Political Decisions, 1 J.L. Econ. & Org. 81 (1985).

Conclusion
The Regulatory State and Social Welfare

1. H.R. 6324, 76th Cong. (1939).

2. President Franklin D. Roosevelt, Veto Message, reprinted in 86 Cong. Rec. 13,942–43 (1940). For a classic and contemporaneous rationale see James M. Landis, The Administrative Process (1938).

Index

Ackerman, Bruce, 68

adjudications: by administrative law judges (ALJs), 86, 108, 110, 145–46; EPA's quasi-formal enforcement, 111; formal, 86–87, 108, 110–11, 146; informal, 87–89, 111–12; intra-agency appeals, 146; limited opportunities for participation in, 120–21; volume of agency, 108, 110–11. *See also* litigation; rules; substantive rulemaking

administrative decisioners: decisionmaking and job security of, 139; executive oversight and competing loyalties of, 139–40

administrative decisionmaking: Administrative Procedure Act governing, 4, 50, 81–92; administrative process theory on agency autonomy for, 73–76; administrative process theory on social welfare considerations of, 74, 75–76; choice of procedure for, 89–92; civic republicanism on, 64–68; by decisionmakers with job security, 139; environment of, 96–101; failures of, 51–52; information as the currency of, 135–38; judicial review leveraging effect on participation in, 140–42; judicial scrutiny of legislative versus, 141; legislative decisionmaking versus, 134–39; litigation role in, 89; "McNollgast" hypothesis on, 143–50, 154, 245, 337–38n.4; public choice market analogy of, 19–22; public choice theory on agency favoritism and, 27, 28–29, 247; public choice theory procedural predictions on, 23–25. *See also* administrative procedures; legislative decisionmaking; regulatory agencies; regulatory decisionmaking

administrative law judges (ALJs), 86, 108, 110, 145–46

administrative neutrality claim, 74, 259–60

Administrative Office of the U.S. Courts, 113

Administrative Procedure Act (APA): as agencies' decisionmaking template, 81; binding agencies to their administrative record, 276–77; on cause of action by any party adversely affected, 122; demonstrated in regulatory case studies, 258–67; described, 4; designed purpose of, 50; on facilitating regulatory participation, 118; on *Federal Register* publishing rule documents, 103; formal adjudication under, 86–87, 110; informal agency action under, 87–89; judicial review vindicating principles of, 100; "McNollgast" hypothesis on, 143–50, 154, 245, 337–38n.4; pressures leading to passage of, 148–49; "rule" and "order" as defined by, 87, 105; rule of procedure under, 204–5; section 553 of, 81–84, 88, 90, 118, 119, 144–45, 204–5, 242, 259; section 553(e) of, 126; section 554 of, 86, 88, 110, 145; section 556 of, 86, 88, 110; section 557 of, 86, 88, 110; separation-of-powers requirement of, 145; substantive rulemaking under the, 81–86. *See also* legislation; regulatory decisionmaking processes

administrative procedures: APA binding agencies to their own record, 276–77; debate over congressional adoption of, 151–52; demonstrated in regulatory cases, 258–67; as insulating Congress from interest groups, 152–53; McNollgast hypothesis on function of, 143–50, 154, 245, 337–38n.4; regulatory agency empowerment through, 266–67. *See also* administrative decisionmaking; regulatory decisionmaking processes

administrative process: comparing public choice theory and, 79; generalizations